# Unknown Conflicts of the Second World War

*Unknown Conflicts of the Second World War: Forgotten Fronts* is a collection of chapters dealing with various overlooked aspects of the Second World War. The aim is to give greater depth and context to the war by introducing new stories about regions of the world and elements of the war rarely considered.

These chapters represent new discussions on previously undeveloped narratives that help to expand our understanding of the interconnectedness of the war. It also provides an expanded view of the war as a mosaic of overlapping conflicts rather than a two-sided affair between massive alliance structures. The Second World War saw revolutions, civil wars, social upheaval, subversion, and major geopolitical policy shifts that do not fit neatly into the Allied vs. Axis 1939–1945 paradigm. This aim is to connect the unseen dots from around the globe that influenced the big turning points we think we know well but have really only a superficial understanding of and in so doing shed new light on the scope and influence of the war.

**Chris Murray** serves as Associate Editor of *Defence Report*. He is currently pursuing his PhD in Defence Studies at King's College London. Chris holds an MA in War Studies from the Royal Military College of Canada as well as a BA in Anthropology and an HBA in History from Lakehead University.

# Routledge Studies in Second World War History

The Second World War remains today the most seismic political event of the past hundred years, an unimaginable upheaval that impacted upon every country on earth and is fully ingrained in the consciousness of the world's citizens. Traditional narratives of the conflict are entrenched to such a degree that new research takes on an ever important role in helping us make sense of World War II. Aiming to bring to light the results of new archival research and exploring notions of memory, propaganda, genocide, empire and culture, Routledge Studies in Second World War History sheds new light on the events and legacy of global war.

## Recent titles in this series

### German-occupied Europe in the Second World War
*Edited by Raffael Scheck, Fabien Théofilakis, and Julia Torrie*

### British Exploitation of German Science and Technology, 1943–1949
*Charlie Hall*

### Unknown Conflicts of the Second World War
Forgotten Fronts
*Edited by Chris Murray*

### A New Nationalist Europe Under Hitler
Concepts of Europe and Transnational Networks in the National Socialist Sphere of Influence, 1933–1945
*Edited by Johannes Dafinger and Dieter Pohl*

### The Swedish Jews and the Holocaust
*Pontus Rudberg*

www.routledge.com/Routledge-Studies-in-Second-World-War-History/book-series/WWII

# Unknown Conflicts of the Second World War

Forgotten Fronts

**Edited by Chris Murray**

Routledge
Taylor & Francis Group

LONDON AND NEW YORK

First published 2019
by Routledge

2 Park Square, Milton Park, Abingdon, Oxfordshire OX14 4RN
52 Vanderbilt Avenue, New York, NY 10017

*Routledge is an imprint of the Taylor & Francis Group, an informa business*

First issued in paperback 2020

*British Library Cataloguing-in-Publication Data*
A catalogue record for this book is available from the British Library

*Library of Congress Cataloging-in-Publication Data*
Names: Murray, Chris, 1981 October 7 – editor.
Title: Unknown conflicts of the Second World War : forgotten fronts /
    Chris Murray [editor].
Description: Abingdon, Oxon ; New York, NY : Routledge, 2019. |
    Series: Routledge studies in Second World War history | Includes
    bibliographical references and index.
Identifiers: LCCN 2018042272 | ISBN 9781138612945
    (hardback : alk. paper) | ISBN 9780429464881 (ebook)
Subjects: LCSH: World War, 1939–1945. | History, Modern–20th century.
Classification: LCC D744 .U64 2019 | DDC 940.54–dc23
LC record available at https://lccn.loc.gov/2018042272

ISBN: 978-1-138-61294-5 (hbk)
ISBN: 978-0-367-66257-8 (pbk)

Typeset in Garamond
by Apex CoVantage, LLC

# Contents

# Contributors

**Disu Oluyemisi Abayomi** holds an MA in History from the University of Ibadan, Nigeria. He currently works with the National Youth Service Corps (NYSC), Nigeria. An avid researcher, he recently presented a paper titled: "Vacancies Versus Employability: Nigerian Youths Tip-Toeing in the Midst of Poverty" at an International Conference in Honour of Professor Akanmu G. Adebayo.

**James Bowden** is a historian who holds an MA in History from American Military University, United States. He has written exclusively on the Middle East for several years. Publications have included chapters for a forthcoming volume on the foreign policies of Saudi Arabia and Kuwait. Mr Bowden, a proactive researcher, frequently searches various archives and other venues to bring fresh, challenging ideas regarding the Middle East to reader's attention.

**Federico Ciavattone** is an independent researcher associated with Italian Society for Military History and American Society for Military History. He is a specialist in modern military history, modern italian history, modern European history, and gender history. His latest work was, "Gli Specialisti. I Reparti Arditi ufficiali e la Squadra X nella lotta antipartigiana 1944–45 ['Specialists'. The Brave Officials Unit and the X Squad in the anti-partisan warfare 1944–45]", Fidenza, Mattioli 1885, 2014. He is currently preparing two works – a history of the Axis Special Forces Counterinsurgency 1939–45 and a history of the Campaign of Italy from the fascist point of view 1943–45.

**Oliver Coates** currently serves as college supervisor in history at Peterhouse, Cambridge, UK. His research interests are in West African history, with particular emphasis on the Second World War, and also in South Asian history focusing on Africa/ India relations.

**Yaacov Falkov** is an Israeli historian, a visiting research fellow at Oxford University and the US Holocaust Memorial Museum, as well as a visiting lecturer in WWII history and in guerrilla warfare history and theory at Tel Aviv University and Herzliya Interdisciplinary Center. He is regarded by the Oxford History Faculty as an unrivalled expert on Soviet and Jewish anti-Nazi resistance in the Russian borderlands. His new book on the Soviet anti-Nazi guerrilla's intelligence activity, considered by the leading historians in Israel and abroad to have made a major contribution to the WWII Eastern Front historiography, will be co-published by the Yad Vashem and the Hebrew University of Jerusalem. His current projects deal with the transnational dimension of the European anti-Nazi Resistance and the Soviet intelligence and guerrilla reporting about the Holocaust.

**Robert A. Farnan** is lecturer in Social Science and Development at Chiang Mai University, Thailand and received a PhD in War Studies from King's College London in 2016. He has conducted extensive ethnographic research along the Sino-Burmese and Thai-Burmese border. His ongoing research in Critical Security Studies and International Political Sociology explores the intersection of security and development, with particular focus on the technopolitics of infrastructure, resource extraction, and urban climate change resilience in Burma and Thailand. He is currently working on a Thailand Research Fund project entitled *Infrastructure Assemblages and the Asian Highway: Public Controversy and Practices of Transparency in the Mae Sot-Myawaddy Special Economic Zone.*

**Pedro Iacobelli** holds an MA and a PhD degree from The Australian National University and currently works as assistant professor at the Pontificia Universidad Católica de Chile. He has done research in Japan and the United States as well. His research deals with the connections and circulations of people, capital and goods between Asia and Latin America. Among his most recent publications is *Postwar Migration to South America from Japan and the Ryukyu Islands* (Bloomsbury Academics, 2017)

**Robert Loeffel** is an Adjunct Lecturer at the School of Humanities & Languages at the University of New South Wales in Sydney, Australia. His research has focused on social control in Nazi Germany and subversion and collaboration (and the fear of it) in Australia during World War II. He has published in various journals including *Contemporary European History, Australian Journal of Politics and History* and *German History.* Books include *Family Punishment in Nazi Germany Sippenhaft, Terror and Myth* (2012) which evaluated the threat of family punishment as a means of terror in Nazi Germany, and *The Fifth Column in World War II: Suspected Subversives in the Pacific War and Australia* (2015) which focused on the fifth column threat in Australia.

**Chris Murray** serves as Associate Editor of Defence Report London, UK. He is currently pursuing his PhD in Defence Studies at King's College London. His studies focus on the history of irregular warfare, guerrilla movements, revolution, occupation, insurgency, and counter-insurgency operations. His regions of focus are the Caucasus, Eastern Europe, and the Balkans. Chris holds an MA in war studies from the Royal Military College of Canada as well as a BA in Anthropology and an HBa in History from Lakehead University. Chris has formally served as a maritime surface and sub-surface (MARS) officer in the Royal Canadian Navy (RCN). He has also worked in the Canadian House of Commons serving as a defence and foreign policy advisor to the offices of Members of Parliament.

**Henry Oinas-Kukkonen** (PhD) is a Senior Lecturer in History and has a title of docent (Privatdozent) in the History of International Relations and Information Networks at the University of Oulu, Finland. He has worked on history of the US Occupation of Japan, US-Finnish relations and on American plans to resettle Finnish World War II refugees into Alaska. His current research interests also include the history of information and communication technology, innovation and social web. Oinas-Kukkonen is the Head of Interrelating Distance and Interaction (IDI) research community and the Principal Investigator of the Trans-Atlantic Impacts (TAI) research group at the University of Oulu, and a Principal Investigator of the Oulu Advanced Research on Software and Information Systems (OASIS) research group. Oinas-Kukkonen is a research fellow of the Finnish Historical Society and a member of the board of the Historical Association of Northern Finland. He has been a member of the International Association for Development of the Information Society (IADIS) WWW/Internet Committee since 2004.

**Raheem Oluwafunminiyi** is currently a doctoral candidate in the Department of History and International Studies, University of Ilorin, Nigeria. His research interests are in the area of African Spirituality, Yoruba Islam, Nigeria History (Political and Democratisation) and Latin American History with special focus on Venezuela's *Bolivarianism*. His recent publication (co-authored) is titled "Controlling the Boundaries of Morality: The History and Powers of Ayelala Deity" and was published in *Yoruba Studies Review* (Special Issue).

**Katherine Rossy** is a PhD candidate in modern European history at Queen Mary University of London, UK. She is also the recipient of the Canadian government's Joseph-Armand Bombardier Canada Doctoral scholarship. Rossy's doctoral thesis examines French, British, and United Nations search efforts for kidnapped and Germanised children in post-WWII Germany between 1945 and 1949. Her research interests include war and military occupation, refugee humanitarianism, and children and childhood.

**Lu Xun** graduated from Peking University, Lund University and Chinese University of Hong Kong. He received his PhD in Modern Chinese History in 2009, and is enrolled as a research fellow at the Chinese Academy of Social Sciences. He has published on issues relating to China's diplomatic history and Sino-American relations as well as the national identity in peer reviewed journals. His recent publications include Butterfly and Dragonfly: from the Civil War to the Cold War, 1944-1950 (Beijing: Shehui kexue wenxian chubanshe, 2015).

# 1 Introduction

## Forgotten fronts

*Chris Murray*

The Second World War is a conflict of such massive complexity that we struggle to grasp the magnitude of the war. As a result, often it gets boiled down to simplistic retellings of two massive forces battling: good and evil, Axis and Allied. In popular culture, we see it in video games and movies where the story is of the Soviets, the Brits, the Americans, the Japanese, or the Nazis. The complexity and ambiguity of the war is too taxing to grapple with for these mediums. The sheer loss of life reaches numbers that are incomprehensible and abstract. The ugly truth of the brutality displayed by participants on all sides makes it difficult to glean lessons from the war. It also leaves a series of unpalatable and unsettlingly open-ended questions. The simplification is therefore a coping mechanism as well as an effort to make sense of the insensible.

There are only rare exceptions where these mediums reach out to the ugly uncertainty and ambiguity of the war with its largely open-ended close. In historical literature on the subject, there is a great deal more nuance. However, even then, there is a struggle with the same need to simplify in order to tackle the subject. Distinct approaches to doing so are generally identifiable in literature of this kind. The first is the abstract general retellings of the entire war that very much conform to the model already mentioned where a global war between the Axis of Nazis, Japanese, and only sometimes Italians face off against the Allies. The Allies are generally portrayed as two-track with the Soviets on one side and the Western powers, an amalgam of mostly American and British, on the other side. Some of these works limit themselves to one of a few fronts that are presented as representing the entire war. The Eastern Front and Western Front (both in Europe), the Mediterranean (sometimes given its due treatment and sometimes presented as a lead up to the invasion of France), and finally the War in the Pacific – which is dominated by US island hopping against Japan with only brief mention of the British in Singapore – are presented as if they are the war in its entirety.

Alternatively, there is literature that fixates on the humanity of the war, the experiences of those who actually lived through the hell. Historians, such as the popular Max Hastings, retell individual experiences that are engrossing and incredibly important to furthering our understanding but in doing so can sometimes lose the forest for the sake of the trees – in some cases, so much so that we can almost be forgiven for forgetting exactly what war is being written about. This is not to take away from incredibly poignant stories that do much to create a deeper understanding of the swirling chaos that very much deserves the moniker 'the fog of war' where in it is hard to reach beyond one's own immediate reality to grasp at the larger forces at work.

Finally, there are those narratives with narrow focus on a singular dimension of the war. These attempt to retell the story of the siege of one place, a battle for another, or the diplomacy of one relationship. They are efforts to break down the war into small pieces in search for depth over range. These are perhaps the most important in their ability to further an understanding of not only these events but also the factors influencing them. They are also the most closely related to the chapters that follow. The problem associated with these works is in striving to understand with some level of depth the nuance of a particular aspect of the war, and the greater context of those larger forces at work can be obscured.

It is a very rare thing to see these micro-level studies stitched into the mosaic of the larger war effort. Context being key, a great deal can be illuminated through the juxtaposition of the micro-level study and the larger events of the war. The appreciation of the larger context and the way these two levels interact and influence one another requires a great deal more appreciation than it is often given. Likewise, viewing these various micro-level studies collected together provides new perspectives by highlighting their unseen interconnected nature. In a sense, the book that follows illuminates the hidden ways that small, far-off events are connected to both one another and the larger war and remind us of the countless unseen factors that influence the course of every element of the war.

The great powers engaged in this war for the world's future had their view cast in many directions simultaneously and as a result seemingly divorced components of the war intruded upon one another, weighing heavily in considerations. Beyond this, there is the reality that the Second World War was not simply a single war but many overlapping wars as well. The British historian Anthony Beevor got close to the mark when he remarked:

> The Second World War should be viewed as a conglomeration of conflicts with traditional state to state warfare between great powers but also, beyond this there is an element of international civil war.[1]

The Second World War was very much a mosaic of overlapping conflicts, civil wars, and revolutions, which coalesced at the outbreak of the Second World War. When viewed in this way, the Second World War becomes as much the meeting point of several smaller conflicts as it is the conventionally viewed conflict of two great alliances. That is not to dismiss the conventional view; it is correct, but it is not the whole story. There is a symbiotic relationship underneath the narrative wherein this larger overarching conflict was the catalyst for many of these smaller conflicts as well as being rooted in some pre-existing ones. There remain huge blind spots, even within these widely published narratives, that have yet to have their due treatment. The studies of the Second World War, especially with regards to these lesser-studied elements, are critical fields of academic inquiry. This is not simply history for history's sake. Much of what occurred within the Second World War is directly transferable to contemporary conflicts and can serve to inform approaches to modern geopolitical crisis.

What we find is when we collect these various retellings of local 'micro-level' narratives focused on far-off events is the way these various, largely disconnected conflicts exerted themselves on the larger war to influence one another. Great things can have small beginnings, and likewise small things can have large and unforeseen far-off effects. In the coming chapters, several far-off and sometimes forgotten, or even unknown, elements of the Second World War will be discussed. In these disconnected retellings, common themes will begin to emerge. The first of these is that the timeline of the war itself is simplistic. Small conflicts that persisted after the close of the First World War, as well as new ones which occurred in the lead up to the Second World War, highlight that there was not a single definitive start date and the outbreak of global hostilities was the culmination of long-brewing trouble.

The following chapter concerning British recruitment in Nigeria is indicative of a larger colonial aspect to the Second World War that is largely ignored in favour of larger theatres. In Nigeria, and much of Africa, we see that British colonial forces had been on alert for 5 years prior to the outbreak of the war because of Italian encroachment in East Africa. This meant that, for Africans at least, the timeline of the Second World War looks very different. Likewise, when reading the coming chapter of China, we will see from the Chinese perspective the nature and timeline of the war is very much skewed by local realities.

We also come to see another theme emerge, the chaos of events. This refers to multiple facets of the war, the timeline itself already mentioned. The war also released social chaos, even on the home-front of stable countries like the UK. The coming chapter on the UK home-front will show how the war sowed the seeds of distrust and stoked fears of a 'fifth column' emerging of enemy-aligned dissidents seeking to erode British resolve from the inside. These fears were largely reflective of pre-war tensions in British society (fear of subversion, political conservatisms interest in fascism and communism) but also an indication of how the war was imagined to be (use of subversion) rather than the reality. This example of the power of hysteria in a modern society at war is likewise a manifestation of chaos as a force unto itself in the Second World War.

Beyond this, the reality for most corners of the war were often distantly removed from the overarching conflict and held little concern for the Axis and the Allies. The Second World War released festering tensions and with it distorted conventional social orders. Multiple local forces that were independent third party actors would emerge fighting their own war for their own reasons in their particular corner of this global chaos. Broken, as these societies became, life on the ground for local forces and civilians alike held little concern for the Axis and Allies. For individuals, questions of oscillating allegiances, collaboration, accommodation, and resistance were fluid and ever changing. For most, the necessity of this fluidity was a matter of survival.

This is a phenomenon that becomes readily apparent in our chapter dealing with the realities of war in the Indian Ocean and life along its rim. This largely overlooked theatre of war held considerable Naval dimensions for the Axis and Allies. A version of the Battle of the Atlantic played out here that was brutal and complex where all the great powers of the war crossed paths. However, this also brought massive social upheaval to the region. The economic opportunities for locals brought by the war opened the way for Indian sailors to work in areas previously unavailable. This brought with it labour movements and sailor strikes that held considerable implications to the larger war effort. There were also ethnic tensions, which emerged as a result of this competition. The most striking aspect of the war in the Indian Ocean might be the colonial element. The existence of two simultaneous French governments, Free France and Vichy, presented an added element of chaos to daily life for the inhabitants of these colonies and brought forward the reality that the whims of the far-off war held immediate impacts for them.

This can likewise be seen in our examination of northern Burma. The Kachin region and the Kachin indigenous groups' involvement in Allied clandestine warfare in this tough jungle environment is not a well-known part of the Burmese narrative. Nonetheless, these activities held considerable impact on the larger war in terms of logistical implications, lessons in guerrilla warfare, and highlighting competition among US and British operations. This also brought with it the common theme of social upheaval, which dramatically altered the social landscape of Burma through the elevation of the Kachin indigenous groups. This narrative challenges dominant discourses pertaining to the colonial understandings of the Second World War.

In the coming chapter concerning wartime collaboration in rural North China, the shades of grey that are found between collaboration and accommodation are explored. The theme of the local being caught in the middle and being 'two-faced' in an effort to simply survive highlights the complexity and uncertainty of the Second World War at the local level. Simultaneously, this highlights the various localized conflicts that occurred in concert with the larger war wherein various local forces pursued their own agendas. What emerges is this huge underlying element of civil war and revolution, which was set loose by the war.

In the coming chapter on Yugoslavia, we will see how broken, deeply divided societies were disintegrated in the face of occupation. In cases such as these, the onset of war brought with it revolutionary forces. Unconcerned with the greater war, factions inside Yugoslavia viewed the chaos as an opportunity to topple the old Serb dominated order and purse civil wars and revolutions. The weak Yugoslav government faced a fractured society with deep class, religious, and ethnic divisions over which it held little influence. Without the strength to act as a centre of gravity to rally the Yugoslav people to their cause, the flight of the Yugoslav government into exile left a void that was filled by fractious groups seeking social upheaval as a means to their own ends. Likewise, this situation was taken by some among the great powers as an opportunity to advance their own ambitions. Militarily, the use of these revolutionary forces was seen as advantageous to the greater war effort, regardless of the long-term political desirability. Alternatively, they were viewed as attractive for this very same political consideration, their ability to assist in redrawing the political landscape of the post-war world.

Completely broken or fractured societies often found themselves hostage to the currents of larger events and lost to forces of chaos beyond their reasoning. This was the case for even great powers such as Italy and France. Often enough, peoples found themselves drawn into larger issues, fighting both for Axis and Allies. In the Italian case, after its capitulation to the Allies, their forces, scattered around the world, found themselves in impossible situations, resulting in essentially two parallel Italian forces, one fighting with the Allies and the other remaining with the Axis. Sometimes this was due to the ideological dimension, but more often it was not by choice but because of local conditions and rooted in survival.

In our chapter on Baltic partisans, we will learn how these societies caught between two great powers, both intent on domination, left little room for the local population to exist – never mind fight for their liberation. Soviet efforts in the Baltic states ran into distrust and anti-Soviet sentiments that were as dangerous to communist partisans as were the Axis forces. The ambiguous nature of their standing in society and challenges to limited effective action highlights the local complexities that operated on the ground in the neighbourhoods of these great powers' massive battles. It also serves as a reminder of the limitations of these great powers to be everywhere and do everything. Lack of Soviet support of not only Baltic partisans but partisans in general is highlighted as rooted in the very considerable limitations of the Soviet state that was quite literally fighting for survival, the same as these small corners of the world. This reinforces the earlier message of a view cast in every direction with chaos serving as the presiding force in all things during the Second World War.

As the case of Italy demonstrates, this 'caught in the middle' phenomenon was not limited to individuals, and states were no less immune to the chaos of events. The coming chapter concerning Japanese diplomacy in South America will underscore how even neutral countries were sucked into the swirling chaos, often for the smallest of reasons but with both perceived as well as very real implications. The positions these nations took, even in the nature of their neutrality, held the potential for military response, trade sanctions, and other damaging measures. Likewise, for the great powers fighting the war, even tacit recognition of the 'rightness' of their cause by neutral powers had significant impacts on morale. They also held potentially useful strategic possibilities. Beyond this, the propaganda war was very real, and the attitudes of neutral countries were a critical part of this front.

This hints at a further theme that will emerge throughout the following chapters. That is, how these far-off, perceivably unconnected subjects actually tie into and influence one another in subtle but nonetheless significant ways. Theses far-off peripheral *forgotten fronts* influenced events far away, which held massive impacts for the course of the war.

In our chapters on Yugoslavia and Finland, we will witness how conflicts that, on the ground, felt incredibly localized and disconnected from the larger war held considerable influence over greater Allied relations. This is a view of the war from unique third party perspectives where whole societies found themselves stuck between two opposing forces they were largely disconnected from as they simply tried to weather the storm and survive, both the war and, as often, the peace that followed – a peace that often left societies completely overturned. For Finland, the situation was one of survival against the Soviet aggressor that suddenly changed sides, casting Finland's fight for survival in unenviable light. In the case of Yugoslavia, it brought the West and the Soviets head to head in Trieste, and the resulting peace negotiations cemented the Cold War.

The Second World War, even when a nuanced approach is taken, is often viewed as finite, ending in 1945. Through this lens, iconic images, such as the 'Little Boy' and 'Fat Man' atomic bombs detonating over Hiroshima and Nagasaki; Japanese delegates signing the Instrument of Surrender aboard the 'Mighty Mo' USS *Missouri* in the presence of General Douglas MacArthur; or the Soviet flag waving over the Reichstag, present a definite close to events. The reality, however, is something quite different. In the case of the Soviet flag over the Reichstag, one can almost see the Cold War emerging on the horizon, which would soon draw both a psychological as well as physical line through Germany that would persist for decades to come.

The truth of things is that the Second World War was not simply devilishly complex and ambiguous; it was unsettlingly open-ended. These are events that do not have a finite beginning or end; their colours bleed over the lines. At the close of the war, several conflicts continued or emerged fresh. The Greek Civil War; the Chinese Civil War; the Indonesian National Revolution; and the independence of India, which was followed by the Indo-Pakistan War, are but some examples. These events largely fed the creation of and shaped the emerging Cold War and the geopolitical realities that persist to this day, which likewise find their roots in the ashes of the First World War and the end of the great European empires.

Although these events feel long past, the reality is they are deeply connected to the present day. In places like the Balkans, the Middle East, or China, these ghosts still walk among us, shaping the world in which we exist. Even in Europe, the effects are far from distant and settled. In our final chapter, the Nazi program of kidnapping racially acceptable children, most of whom were never recovered, will be discussed. This serves to remind us that people of this

conflict and their children still carry with them the unseen scars of this fright-
ful bloodletting. The same holds true for the modern geopolitical landscape
across which these events still echo. It, too, still carries the scars of the Second
World War, some still fresh and festering while others are old and faded. In
understanding these forgotten fronts, we learn not only how interconnected
this Second World War was but gain insight into the far-reaching and often
unseen impacts it held for not just the 'big' parts of the war but the far-off
places usually not thought of in considering the Second World War narrative.

## Note

1 "Q&A with Antony Beevor: 21 June 2012," *CSPAN Video Library*. Last accessed
30 November 2012. www.c-spanvideo.org/program/Beev.

# 2 Fighting for Britain

## Examining British recruitment strategies in Nigeria

*Disu Oluyemisi Abayomi and*
*Raheem Oluwafunminiyi*

### Introduction

By far the most widespread war in human history with more than 100 million people, from more than 30 different countries, serving in military units and with over 73 million dead, the Second World War brought in its wake a conflagration which eventually altered the socio-political alignments, arrangements and structures of past centuries and the world generally. Britain, a major participant of the war, was not left out in this global confrontation. To fully carry out its war effort, and in dire need of soldiers and manpower, Britain looked to its Empire – spread across the continents of Africa and Asia – to prepare them for the war. Her colonies in West Africa particularly became a very important source of both manpower and raw materials, supplying well over 300,000 soldiers and laborers for military service in the East and North African campaigns and, after 1943, in Asia. With over 121,650[1] Nigerians demobilized after the Second World War, Nigeria and Nigerian soldiers became the center of human and material resources, a number which surpassed any military mobilization in all of the British colonies. This paper examines the series of recruitment strategies used by Britain in preparation for the Second World War. It highlights the intense efforts used to inform, sensitize, campaign and attract Africans through radio, the print media, demonstration marches and, sometimes, intimidation into voluntary enlistment. It categorically identifies three major modes or forms of recruitments: awareness and different forms of advertisement; propaganda and recruitment agents via traditional rulers and other government-related agencies; and conscription. The chapter shall also examine the roles Nigerian soldiers played in the different theaters of war, which contributed to Britain's victory in the Second World War. It concludes that in spite of these somewhat enticing strategies to lure Nigerians into joining the colonial armed forces through the enactment of the Compulsory National Service Regulations of 1940, a significant number were not receptive to the scheme, a situation which spurred an untoward plan of action that included forceful conscription to compel colonial peoples to join the war effort.

### The Second World War: a synopsis

The outbreak of the Second World War was caused by Germany's national resentment over the crushing and humiliating terms of the Treaty of Versailles.[2]

Although at the initial stage a European war, it later expanded to include several other areas across the world (Africa inclusive) through military recruitment and material mobilization, among others, for the war. The war which began in 1939 as a European conflict had by its close in 1945 assumed a global dimension involving a vast majority of the world's population and including all of the great powers, eventually forming two opposing military alliances: the Allied and Axis Powers. It was the most widespread war in human history with more than 100 million people serving in military units. In a state of total war, the major participants placed entire economic, industrial and scientific capabilities at the service of the war efforts, erasing the distinction between civilian and military resources. Marked by mass deaths of civilians, including the Holocaust and the only use of nuclear weapons in warfare in Hiroshima and Nagasaki in Japan, the Second World War resulted in the death of between 50 million to 73 million people, making it the deadliest conflict in human history by far.[3]

The Second Italo-Abyssinian War, a brief colonial war (October 1935–May 1936) fought between the armed forces of the Kingdom of Italy and those of the Ethiopian Empire (Abyssinia), formed a significant basis for the Second World War. The war resulted in the Italian military occupation of Ethiopia and its annexation into the newly created colony of Italian East Africa (Africa Orientale Italiana or AOI). In addition, it exposed the weakness of the League of Nations as an organization set up to maintain peace and order and also forestall another outbreak of war. Both Italy and Ethiopia were members of the League of Nations, yet the latter remained indolent when it appeared Italy had clearly violated the League's own Article X.[4]

Meanwhile, the two great powers of Western Europe, Britain and France, were prepared to swallow their pride and allow Germany to become a great power once more, but they would rather go to war than see Europe groaning under German hegemony. Hitler, however, did not help the cause of peace, as he was busy pursuing his expansionist plans. In violation of the Treaty of Versailles, Germany annexed Austria in 1938 and Czechoslovakia the following year. France and Britain failed to react apart from the verbal denunciation of Germany. Having gone that far without any opposition, Hitler was quite confident that he could go further. Hence, on 1 September 1939, barely six months after the annexation of Czechoslovakia, Germany invaded Poland. For Britain and France, Hitler's action was simply a provocation, resulting in the declaration of war on Germany days after. By this declaration, the Second World War had begun.[5]

## Britain's preparation for the war in Nigeria

Although open conflict did not break out until September 1939, most perceptive Europeans saw it coming. As a result, the British government had started making contingency plans in anticipation of a protracted war. As early as July 1939, the British had made secret plans to restrict imports and exports in Nigeria in the event of war. The restriction of imports would conserve foreign exchange in order to secure the supply of essential imports. In addition, import control, it was believed, could be used to help restrain purchases to specific points of supply in parts of the colony to garner foreign exchange, to contribute to a few areas of economic warfare and to place heavy pressures on a certain country abroad basically for the overall trade interests of the United Kingdom.[6]

The Second World War was a period of both continuity and change. Nigerians had been experiencing a prolonged economic crisis due to the worldwide depression in commodity prices and credit markets. The crisis continued throughout the war, but it took different forms as colonial officials restructured the economy to meet the economic and security priorities necessitated by the conflict.[7] Indeed, as had happened in 1914, the outbreak of war in 1939 was not an unexpected development. This was because, as far back as 1935, Nigeria soldiers were put on alert to prepare them for action in East Africa following the attack on Abyssinia by Benito Mussolini, the Fascist ruler of Italy.[8] Mussolini, a close friend of Hitler, did not hide his expansionist ambitions before the former unveiled his own expansionist plans. To provide for the new contingency, the colonial army was recognized.

In Nigeria, Governor Sir Bernard Bourdillon was on tour and out of radio contact on a boat in the maze of waterways that formed the Niger-Delta. To alert him that war was imminent and he was needed back in Lagos, the Chief Secretary had a message dropped to his boat by aircraft.[9] By 3 September, governors and administrators in colonial capitals from Khartoum to Lagos and from Kampala to Maseru were informed that war had been declared on Germany. British historian David Killingray observed that in each colony, local military or police forces were put on the footing, German commercial enterprises sequestrated and enemy nationals were either detained or placed under restriction, while discussions began on the future economic and social consequences of belligerence. In Nigeria, the Defense Regulations tightened government control over publications and communications.[10] Notwithstanding the above economic measures and preparations, the British government, as well as the colonial government in Nigeria, still needed more hands on the battlefield. It was this scenario that formed the basis and needs for recruitment in the entire West African colony, Nigeria inclusive.

During the Second World War, the West African colonies became important to Britain's war effort as a source of manpower and raw materials.[11] From 1940 onward, West Africa supplied over 300,000 soldiers and laborers for military service in the East African campaign, North Africa, and, after 1943, in Asia. Freetown was a major naval base for Southern Atlantic operations while Takoradi and Kano provided the strategic link in the vital air supply route to the Middle East. After the fall of Britain's territories in the Far East to the Japanese in early 1942, West Africa became a major source of tropical raw materials.[12] Throughout the war, the colonial armed forces in British West Africa were rapidly expanded, and a large volume of labor was directed into various kinds of war-work. In mid-1939, the Royal West African Frontier Force numbered about 8,000 and was a little more than a lightly armed gendarmerie; by the end of the war, the force increased to 200,000 men who had served in the armed forces, many of them as pioneer labors.[13]

It is quite difficult to assess the number of Nigerians involved in direct war-work, in building airfields, dock installations and military accommodation, because civil and military labor often overlapped. In Freetown, for example, port labor was conscripted into the West African Auxiliary Corps and placed under military law, while in Nigeria labor was conscripted for the tin mines and for dam building.[14] It is worthy to note that government wartime policies also redirected labor from civil infrastructural development to wartime needs. There are instances in Nigeria were teachers, electric workers, tailors and other trade professionals from the Public Works Department, for example, were mobilized for the war.[15] This is because the British saw the war as one that needed professionals and men with technical skills to execute.

The Second World War had a far-reaching, though uneven, impact on the entire world. Like other colonial territories, Africa was drawn into the conflict as the appendage of the belligerents. African contributions to the war efforts of Britain and France have been documented in several studies.[16] In the specific case of Nigeria, the mobilization of raw materials and of manpower, as well as the impact of the war on Nigerian economy and society, has been analyzed by various scholars.[17] Yet, there is the necessity to discuss the need for Nigerian soldiers who were mobilized for the prosecution of the Second World War and the mode of recruitment in Nigeria.

## The need for African/Nigerian soldiers

The need for Nigerian/African soldiers by Britain during the Second World War was imperative if the war was to be decisively won. This was because of the performance of African soldiers in different theaters of war, just like in the First World War, and was outstanding in terms of discipline and courage. In East Africa, for example, the Nigerian troops and their Gold Coast counterparts played a leading role in safeguarding the whole region and in the defeat of the Italians.[18] The report of the General Officer in charge of East Africa, Cunningham, is apt in describing the Nigerian soldiers and their courage:

> The Nigerian soldiers led the pursuit of the Italians and despite being unaccustomed to cold and damp, fought their way from hot, dusty to wet and cold highland of Abyssinia, where they maintained their cheerfulness and courage, in spite of strange conditions and strenuous climbing operations made necessary by the terrain.[19]

Britain, desperately short of metropolitan troops at the time, could never have won the campaign in East Africa without the reserve troops she was able to call upon from her British West African colonies. No less remarkable was the contribution made by the West African soldiers in Burma. Their conditions were even stranger than in Ethiopia. While popular fiction has visions of Africans living in the jungle, none of the West Africa soldiers had ever experienced anything like the jungle of Burma.[20]

It was against this background that Britain looked towards her different colonies in Africa for recruitment, particularly West Africa, which supplied about 50 percent of the total recruits in Africa while Nigerian recruits were the highest in the whole of the continent. Britain at this time required recruits with the simplicity of character who, in a short time, would transfer loyalty from their local chief to a white officer. This may well have been the case, as Mazrui suggests, for Ugandan recruits where men drawn from acephalous society were more able to make the transfer of loyalty to a body like that of an army.[21] The idea of martial qualities became an established convention among most European army officers serving in Africa, and ideas about martial hierarchies persisted well after the Second World War in both East and West Africa. What this clearly meant was that certain groups of people were not wanted as soldiers. The best men were sourced from societies untouched by modern ideas of government or commerce and non-literates that would provide a clean slate upon which could be written new military codes and discipline.[22] As noted by Killingray, "The blacker their face, the huskier their voice, the thicker their neck, the darker their skin and the more remote parts of Africa they come from, the better soldier they made."[23] In peacetime, Africans who had been in contact with modern ideas and methods were invariably rejected by the military, except when a small number of clerks and storekeepers were needed.

The result of such an ethnically based pattern of recruitment throughout the colonial period was that, at independence, a high percentage of recruits still came from the traditional areas.[24] This was the case in most colonies, irrespective of the European power that had controlled them. For example, in 1960, three years after Ghana's independence, the vast majority of the country's soldiers continued to come from the north.[25] The case was not different in Nigeria, following the country's first coup in 1966, where the military appeared in the ratio 50:25:25 for the North, East and Western regions, respectively. In addition, when the mid-West was created, northern Nigeria retained her ratio while others lost theirs. The above formed the basis and ingredients for potential rivalry and conflict within the armed forces in these countries in post-independence Africa.

Recruits for the colonial armies were also medically examined, and only those of certain height (ideally 5ft 8in), physique and standard of health were accepted. Although when recruits were readily available, the medical standards were high; however, when recruits were more difficult to secure or needed in large numbers, as at certain time during both wars, the medical standards were reduced or altogether jettisoned. In the Second World War, malnourished men were enlisted and then built up in three months on the military diet. The age of recruitment was of little consideration; physical appearance was the usual guide, and the minimum age of 18 for recruits, laid down in 1942, was rarely observed.[26] For instance, Isaac Fadoyebo was barely

16 when he joined the army at Abeokuta in 1942.[27] Mohammed, known as African Banana, was also 16 when he was pressed into joining the British military service in northern Nigeria against his will. He claimed he had deliberately concealed his identity from the recruiting officer.[28] Asante, who joined the army in the Gold Coast in 1942 at 17, noted that he was accepted because of his tall height. Similarly, 13-year-old John E.A. Mandambwe was enlisted in Nyasaland in 1939, having been deemed suitable for the army because he was tall enough to reach the line carved in a doorpost.[29]

Meanwhile, when the war broke out in 1939, the various colonial powers involved did not hesitate to look towards their colonies for men and material resources. Britain was not an exception.[30] Nigeria, as part of the British West African colony, was requested to supply able-bodied men. As in the First World War, this task devolved on the Nigerian regiment of the West African Frontier Force. Following this, a general mobilization was ordered with a series of propaganda to whip up anti-German sentiment among the people. For instance, in 1941, the Governor of Nigeria told the Conference of Chiefs, Northern Nigerian Provinces,[31] that God would not allow an infidel like Hitler, who believes in no God save himself, to enslave the whole world.[32] The anti-German propaganda made such a considerable impact on northern Nigeria that their chiefs told the people that the alternative to victory was defeat and enslavement by Germans. This encouraged groups and the native authority to contribute to various war funds such as Win the War Fund, War Purposes Fund, Nigerian War Relief Fund and Nigeria Troops Comfort Fund, among others.[33]

However, in September 1939, Britain's African Colonial Forces (ACF) were small and inadequately equipped for a modern war and only deemed necessary for use in Africa. With the outbreak of war in September 1939, the military situation altered this peculiar situation. In 1940, this drastically changed in Africa, with Italy's declaration of war in May followed by the collapse of France in June and the creation of The Vichy regime in July. Italy launched attacks against the British in Egypt and from her recently extended East Africa Empire against the Anglo-Egyptian Sudan, British Somaliland and Kenya. At the same time, the British colonies in West Africa found themselves placed under increasing threat as the substantial French colonial forces, previously allies, now came under administrative control loyal to the Vichy.[34]

In a bid to stem these problems, the ACFs were expanded rapidly with recruitment drives for African soldiers. Recruiters increasingly employed all means at the disposal of the colonial state, continuing with the traditional means of persuasion, through the field administration and chiefs and, later, making use of radio broadcast, films and other propaganda materials to persuade men to enlist.[35] Since not all recruitment was voluntary, it implied that conscription was part of the recruitment drive, especially in Southern Nigeria where people were forcefully conscripted into the army. The expansion was said to be rapid. For example, the King's African Rifles in 1939 had only 7 battalions, which had grown to 28 battalions by 1942 and 43 battalions by 1945, with a range of specialist corps.

Nevertheless, most of the earlier requirements for recruitment into the army were abandoned during the Second World War recruitment process, especially between 1942 and 1945. This was contrary to the norms in the previous war, as noted earlier when recruitment was targeted at selected ethnic groups (Northern Nigeria in particular) whom the British described as warlike.[36] The areas considered as recruitment centers because of their nature and lack of exposure to modernization and sheer strength had to compete with other regions formerly considered as non-recruitable centers. This was because the Second World War was a modern war that needed to be fought with non-literate combatants and literate, skilled, science-oriented and intellectual minds as well. This made the colonial officials turn to the southern part of the country for recruits, professionals from the civil service, public works department and other tradesmen, in mobilizing for the war. The age factor was another barrier in the process of recruitments which the British violated during the Second World War recruitment drive. Teenagers were massively recruited for the war across Africa, West Africa and most importantly Nigeria. Examples of these and case studies shall be identified and examined in subsequent sections.

## Recruitment strategies in Nigeria

Using the Compulsory National Service Regulations of 1940, certain classes of persons such as blacksmiths, bricklayers, carpenters, tailors and those with certain educational qualifications were required to register for possible enlistment.[37] As stated earlier, this was imperative because, in a war of this nature, professionals and skilled men were needed to successfully take active part in the war. Great efforts were, however, made during the Second World War to inform, sensitize, campaign and attract qualified Nigerians into voluntary enlistment through both advertisements on radio and the print media and demonstration marches by those already in the service to advertise the glorious life awaiting anyone who cared to enlist.[38] Recruitment tours were also undertaken to various parts of the country where traditional rulers were requested to encourage their subjects to enlist.[39] Efforts were further made to display the glorious life awaiting anyone who cared to enlist, such that aside from earning regular salaries, regular food, clothing, pride associated with military life, and good and regular health, many were assured of being cared for after army life. Apparently, this was done via posters showing good-looking and smartly dressed soldiers, most of whom were given short breaks to visit their country home after training to attract friends into enlisting. Despite these efforts, many people were not convinced to enlist on a voluntary basis. As a result, propaganda and outright conscription were resorted to in order to get the required number of men to participate in the war, especially in Asia.[40]

There were three major modes or forms of recruitments: first, through awareness and different forms of advertisement, leading to voluntary enlistment; second, through propaganda and recruitment agents, i.e. traditional rulers and other government-related agencies; and third, through outright conscription. Although a number of studies on the Second World War have deliberately avoided mentioning these forms of recruitments in their works or denied there was a reason for conscription, a comment, nevertheless, appears indifferent. When the British government was faced with the dilemma of how to raise sufficient men from 1939–1945, "[they] resorted to a variety of practices, that ranged from outright conscription to methods that forced men to enter the army or provide their labor for wartime service."[41]

Meanwhile, Nigerian chiefs, particularly those of northern extraction, played a significant role in this other method mentioned by Killingray. They served as wartime recruiters, forcefully compelling their subjects to enlist to save their kingdom and generation from Hitler's whims. The process, however, caused animosity and often undermined their (chiefs) authority, thereby incurring popular displeasure. Salifu Moshi recalled that in late 1941, as an unemployed laborer, he was collected by truck by the chief's people and later found himself in the army camp. Wendell was, however, quick to state that the chiefs did not enjoy forceful conscription of their people but had no other choice than to do so because they were under pressure to provide their quota, thereby forcing their men to enlist.[42] In Borgu, northern Nigeria, the District Officer complained that one District Head (of Yeshikera) "has mixed up recruiting with the compulsory registration of adult males and that he proposes to adopt press-gang methods."[43]

At the beginning of the recruitment in 1939, the British hoped that the traditional recruiting grounds (northern Nigeria) would provide sufficient men with suitable martial character to form the backbone of the necessary force. These soldiers were intended to be supplemented by others, less overtly suitable for a recruit, to make up the rest of the force. In Nigeria, as it was in most African countries, chiefs would assist in the process, as they had done in the past, and the entire effort could pass with minimum fuss.

A certain number of recruits were required as combatants while literate men were also needed for the newly created specialist corps, which included engineers, nurses, signals and transporters, but the majority of men were needed as uniform military labor to undertake all those unsung and unglamorous activities associated with welfare such as construction, handling supplies, garrison and guard duties. As the war proceeded, the distinction between combatants and non-combatants became blurred, and men who had been recruited to the labor corps often found themselves trained in arms and playing a direct role in the fighting. By late 1945, more than 500,000 Africans had been through the ranks.[44] It is against this backdrop that the British wartime recruitment activities occurred in Nigeria in preparation for the Second World War.

Although there are many reasons why men enlisted such as voluntary enlistment or conscription, employment and opportunism pulled most men into the ranks. In as much as the war did increase the number of wage labor opportunities, it was an erratic process. At times, job openings abruptly disappeared, for instance, the government closed down contract and minefields at the opening of the war so the army would appear to be the easy way out for the youth who wished to pursue freedom and a good life. According to different accounts on the Second World War recruitment pattern, many youths saw the army as the only opportunity to exhibit their youthful exuberance, get a regular wage, wear good clothes, eat healthy food, have good healthcare and enjoy the prestige of working with the crown forces.[45]

Marshall Kebby, who lived in Lagos, was a victim of the above. He left college in 1942, only to find out that government had frozen all clerical posts and that the commercial firms would not employ anybody. He stated thus when asked his reason for joining the army:

> because I didn't want to waste my time, I simply went up to Enugu to join the army that's all. There was no idealism whatsoever. I just wanted a job. I just wanted a military career. I had no idea of what the place (war) was about, no idea whatsoever. I just joined.[46]

Meanwhile, some others joined because the army reasonably paid well, especially for literate men, clerks and skilled artisans.

Isaac Fadoyebo's case was similar to the above. His case was that of voluntary enlistment than conscription. In early 1942, at the age of 16, he thought he would not be able to get a suitable job in Nigeria. Many years later he wrote: "I simply saw military service as a good job. Without consulting my parents and caring less about the consequences, I took a plunge into the unknown by getting myself enlisted in the army at Abeokuta."[47]

Fadoyebo got what he wanted from the army; he was trained as a military nurse orderly, with regular pay, clothes, food and good medical care such that he became the envy of his age grade when he returned home for a break after training for three weeks. As in the case of Fadoyebo, so was it with many other Africans who served in the Second World War. They were volunteers eager for the paid job, yearning for adventure, or perhaps wanting to wear a uniform to impress young women. Other men found their way into the army by means that were not of their choosing.[48]

The case of James Adewale was, however, different as he was conscripted into the army. He stated that despite being a tailor in Nigeria, he gave up his job to set out for Britain in 1943:

> I was recruited compulsorily in a place called operation pool and was sent off to London. It was clear that the alternative of going to war was prison; I was put on a ship in London heading for Normandy with war materials. On our way, we ran into enemy mines and our ship was blown-up, fortunately, I was one of the lucky survivors of that incident.[49]

Ibrahim Funtua was another case in point. Ibrahim, according to R. Trevor Kerslake, had accompanied his father on a pilgrimage to Mecca in 1930. His father died, and Ibrahim returned home many years later, having wandered in

Arabia and the Middle East not only as an orphan but also without inheritance. Dispossessed and rootless, he voluntarily joined the Nigerian Regiment in 1938.[50]

The influence of family and friends also helped to push young men into the army. This was the case with Hama Kim. In 1940, he was just a 13-year-old boy living in Kano with his uncle, a soldier in the Northern Nigeria Regiment. The glamor of soldier life was all around him, but he was rejected as being too young when he first tried to enlist. His enthusiasm was, however, rewarded as he was enlisted under the wing of the Regimental Sergeant Major and within a year had been accepted as an army band boy. Nevertheless, Kim did not join the band but stayed in Kano with the RSM and, somehow, contrived to mix with the other recruits in the barracks where he was eventually signed-up.[51] Hama Kim, Killingray observed, went on to serve throughout the war and many years later, after independence, became a major in the Nigerian army.

Adamu Sokoto was a Hausa-speaking farmer from Sokoto, northern Nigeria. He became attached to the army as a *barraki* boy,[52] employed by several soldiers to wash their clothes and perform other menial tasks. When he was old enough, he enlisted in 1943 into the 6th Battalion, Northern Nigeria Regiment and served the British in the Second World War.[53] Also in Tivland, central Nigeria, many enlisted for various reasons: some to avoid being conscripted for the tin mines and others because of economic hardship. Killingray stated that although Aond'Akaa's micro-study of Gboko suggests that young men mainly joined for adventure, he provided other reasons why individuals joined. For instance, Igbado Tyober was influenced by the First World War veterans who told of how they had killed white men with their own hands. Ujih Anuala left school to go and "see things for ourselves," while Yongu Jongur Kuji, often involved in fights, was told by people that "if I was so strong why was I afraid to go and join my mates in the army? To disprove their allegation, I left and enlisted."[54] Yaro Nevkaa joined up because he was awed by seeing a recruiting team of soldiers in full military regalia.

From the Tivland examples mentioned above, it is obvious that almost all the strategies or modes of recruitment were used in the pattern of enlistment, which included voluntary, social/societal influence, employment and opportunism, economic reasons, military pride and conscription. In addition to all the recruitment strategies mentioned above, traditional rulers, subject to the colonial authorities, often played a crucial role in wartime recruitment by encouraging men to enlist.

## Conclusion

In the event of these different modes of recruitment and forceful conscription into the war effort, what roles did Nigerian soldiers play in the different theaters of war *vis-à-vis* their contributions to the victory of Britain in the war? It must be stated here that Nigerian soldiers were the largest population recruited in the West African region. As stated earlier, these soldiers served in different capacities ranging from carriers, signalmen, carpenters, artillery-men, clerks, nurses, drivers, mechanics and suppliers. Few Africans (Nigerians inclusive), whether the small number of regular soldiers or the new recruits, had seen or had any idea about the destructive power of modern weapons such as tanks, armored cars, heavy artillery or military aircraft.[55]

Nigerian soldiers, according to Olomola, saw active service in various theaters of the war. Three thousand of them (men of the 1st West Africa Brigade) served in Italian East Africa from July 1940 to August 1941 and participated in the capture of Mogadishu, the capital city of Italian Somaliland, Marda and Babile Passes, Harrar and Abalti in Ethiopia.[56] Also, 16,500 Nigerian pioneer unit-men served in Egypt, Palestine, Libya, Morocco, Sicily and Naples from November 1943 to late 1947. About 60,000 Nigerians of the 81st and 82nd West African Divisions served in Burma from July 1943 to the end of the war in 1945 and contributed immensely to the victory of Allied Powers in Northern Burma, the Kaladan and the Arakan valleys. They were the visitors of Dodan, Myohaung, Letmauk, Apaukwa, Gwa and Sandoway.[57] This is contrary to the popular belief that Nigerian soldiers were merely onlookers in the war.[58]

During the Second World War, the British colonial authority, through the series of strategies identified above, recruited more than 121,650 Nigerian soldiers, as opposed to 13,980 in the First World War.[59] Also, the need for African soldiers was inevitable and necessitated by the volume and nature of the war. The mode of recruitment was highly controversial, nonetheless, in all the colonies; most enlisted men were classified as volunteers – overwhelmingly so in Uganda, less so in Kenya and Tanganyika, and comprising, perhaps, 70 percent of the troops in Nigeria and the Gold Coast.

Economics forced some men into the ranks; sometimes there was the desire to earn a better wage, but hardship and poverty also acted as powerful stimuli. The colonial authorities also relied to some extent upon chiefs to act as recruiting agents.[60] There is some silence on how the chiefs got their recruits, with Killingray, for instance, stating that many enlisted because they were asked to do so by their chiefs or monarchs. There were, however, cases cited earlier in the study on how chiefs, in the name of recruitment, sent their subjects to certain places and were from such places enlisted without prior knowledge. In fact, chiefs were pressured to meet a specific quota of recruitment allocated to them in their area of jurisdiction. This was most common in the northern part of Nigeria regarded by the British as a traditional recruitment center. The pressure to the European demands forced the chiefs into keying into the call for conscription; as a result, some of them (the chiefs) had their authorities questioned by their subjects.

Irrespective of the modes and patterns or areas of recruitment, African soldiers and those of Nigerian origin, in particular, demonstrated a high sense of responsibility to duty, strength, character and confidence to the colonial army and in the successful prosecution of the Second World War. Their performance was so brilliant that both the Japanese army and British commanders commended it alike. Gbor quoted a captured diary as follows:

The enemy soldiers are not from Britain but from Africa. Because of their belief, they are not afraid to die, even if their comrades have fallen, they keep on advancing as if nothing had happen. They had excellent physique and were very brave, so fighting against these soldiers is somewhat troublesome.[61]

Incidentally, Britain, in her hours of need, took more than 60,000 Nigerians to the distant jungle of Burma against the conquering Japanese. Documents have shown that many of the Nigerian soldiers fought in the battlefields of Burma and other places in Asia and East Africa, with many handed different medals for their exemplary performance and discipline.[62]

## Notes

1 While some scholars such as Killingray and Gbor put this figure at 121,650, others such as Olomola say it was 121,652. See David Killingray, *Fighting for Britain: African Soldiers in The Second World War* (Suffolk: James Currey, 2012); John W. T. Gbor, ed., *Military History: Nigeria from the Pre-Colonial Era to the Present* (Longman: Lagos, 2004); Ishola Olomola, "The Demobilization of Nigerian Troops, 1946–1950: Problem and Consequences," *ODU: A Journal of West Africa Studies*, no. 13 (1976); National Archives Ibadan (NAI)/ComCol, 1/2807/s.7/Vol.II/245.

2 Chris Harman, *A People's History of the World* (London: Bookmarks, 1999), 520.

3 Donald Sommerville, *The Complete Illustrated History of World War Two* (Leicester: Lorenz Books, 2008).

4 Arthur James Barker, *The Rape of Ethiopia, 1936* (New York: Ballantine Books, 1971), 131–2.

5 Alan John P. Taylor, *The Origins of the Second World War* (New York: Simon & Schuster Paperbacks, 1961).

6 National Archives of Nigeria, Ibadan (NAI), Chief Secretary's Office (CSO) 18/19 "Import and Export Restrictions, 1939": Secret: Import Restrictions in Emergency, 27 July 1939. See also Ayodeji Olukoju, "'Buy British, Sell Foreign': External Trade Control Policies In Nigeria during World War II and Its Aftermath, 1939–1950," *International Journal of African Historical Studies* 35 (2002).

7 Judith Byfield, "Feeding the Troops: Abeokuta (Nigeria) and World War II," *African Economic History*, no. 35 (2007): 1.

8 Chinedu N. Uba, *Colonial Army and Society in Northern Nigeria* (Kaduna: National Defence Academy, 1998). See also Austin Hubert W. Haywood and Frederick Arthur S Clarke, *The History of the West African Frontier Force* (Aldershot: Gale & Polden, 1964), 188.

9 Cited in David Killingray, "The Colonial Army in the Gold Coast: Official Policy and Local Response, 1890–1947" (PhD Dissertation, London: University of London, 1982).

10 Killingray, *Fighting for Britain*, 11.

11 Kwei Quartey, How West Africa helped win World War II, *Huffington Post*, 6 August 2012.

12 See, for instance, Michael Crowder, "The 1939–45 War and West Africa," in *History of West Africa*, ed. J. F. A. Ajayi and Michael Crowder, Vol. 2 (London: Longman, 1974); Gabriel O. Olusanya, *The Second World War and Politics in Nigeria, 1939–1953* (London: Evans Brothers, 1973). Olusanya's work is mostly concerned with political events.

13 Sam C. Ukpabi, "The Changing Role of the Military in Nigeria, 1900–1970," *Africa Spectrum* 11, no. 1 (1976): 5.

14 William Freund, "Labour Migration to the Northern Nigerian Tin Mines, 1903–1945," *Journal of African History* 22, no. 1 (1981). This is as quoted by Killingray in his "Military and Labour Recruitment in the Gold Coast during the Second World War," *Journal of African History* 23, no. 1 (1982): 83–95.

15  NAI, Comcol 1/2807. A returnee wrote to the commissioner of the colony that he was a tailor before he joined up with the army. After the demobilization, he requested the commissioner of the colony to supply him a sewing machine so he can return to his former job.
16  David Killingray and Richard Rathbone, eds., *Africa and the Second World War* (Basingstoke: Macmillan, 1986).
17  See Byfield, Feeding the Troops; Toyin Falola, "Cassava Starch for Export in Nigeria during the Second World War," *African Economic History* (1989): 73–98; Toyin Falola, "'Salt Is Gold': The Management of Salt Scarcity in Nigeria during World War II," *Canadian Journal of African Studies* 24, no. 3 (1992): 412–36; O. N. Njoku, "Contribution to War Efforts," in *Britain and Nigeria: Exploitation or Development?*, ed. Toyin Falola (London: Zed Books, 1987), 164–85.
18  Gbor, *Military History*, 145.
19  Crowder, "The 1939–45 War," 605.
20  Ibid., 605.
21  Ali A. Mazrui, *Soldiers and Kinsmen in Uganda: The Making of a Military Ethnocracy* (California: Sage Publications, 1975), 35.
22  Killingray, *Fighting for Britain*, 42.
23  Ibid, quoted G. H. Cree, who served with KAR, 1931–1945.
24  The traditional recruitment centers/areas were majorly from the northern part of each of the African countries.
25  Martin Staniland, "The 'Military Participation' of Ghanaian Ethnic Groups," *Research Review* 8, no. 2 (1971): 29.
26  Killingray, *Fighting for Britain*, 43.
27  Isaac Fadoyebo, *A Stroke of Unbelievable Luck* (Madison, WI: African Studies Program, University of Wisconsin-Madison,1999).
28  Robin Forestier-Walker and Oliver Owen, "Africa's Forgotten Wartime Heroes," *BBC News*, August 14, 2009. www.news.bbc.co.uk/2/hi/africa/8201717.stm.
29  See Killingray's, *Fighting for Britain*; Mario Kolk, *Can You Tell Me Why I Went to War? A Story of a Young King's African Riffle, Reverend John E.A. Mandambwe* (Zomba: Kachere, 2008).
30  Sam C. Upkabi, British Military Establishments in Nigeria, 1900–1960," in *Foundations of Nigerian Federalism: 1900–1960*, ed. Jonah Isawa Elaigwu and Godfrey N. Uzoigwe (Abuja: National Council on Inter-Governmental Relations, 1996), 60–86.
31  These Provinces provided the bulk of Nigerian soldiers during World War II.
32  SNP 17/4 No. 33029, Conference of Chiefs, Northern Provinces, 1941. See also Uba, *Colonial Army and Society*.
33  Uba, *Colonial Army and Society*, 325.
34  Anthony Clayton, *France, Soldiers and Africa* (London: Brassey's Defence Publishers, 1988), 128.
35  Killingray, *Fighting for Britain*, 36.
36  Uba, *Colonial Army and Society*; Haywood and Clarke, *West African Frontier Force*, 188.
37  NAI/COS/Chief Secretary, Lagos to Secretary, Northern Provinces, 10 March 1942.
38  Fadoyebo, *A Stroke of Unbelievable Luck*, 48.
39  National Archives Kaduna (NAK) 30463/Vol. 2. Recruitment of Soldiers, The letter by Chief Commander Northern Provinces to the Governor dated 27 November 1940. Cited in Uba, *Colonial Army and Society*.
40  Crowder, "The 1939–45 War," 605.
41  Killingray, *Fighting for Britain*, 45.
42  Killingray, *Fighting for Britain*, quoting Wendell P. Holbrook, *War and Tradition in the Gold Coast: 1939–1945*, (n.d).
43  Crowder, The 1939–1945 War, quoting NAK/BORGDIST/DOB/624, 'Recruiting' D.O. Borgu to Resident Ilorin, 18 April 1941.
44  Killingray, *Fighting for Britain*, 36.
45  Crowder, The 1939–1945 War; Killingray, *Fighting for Britain*; Fadoyebo, *A Stroke of Unbelievable Luck*.

46 BBC Africa Service. Marshall Kebby, interviewed by Elizabeth Obadina, Lagos, Nigeria, 1989. Cited in Killingray, *Fighting for Britain*.
47 Fadoyebo, *A Stroke of Unbelievable Luck*, 17.
48 Killingray, *Fighting for Britain*, 35.
49 BBC Africa Service, letter, James Adewale to Martin Plaut, 2 August 1989. Cited in Killingray, *Fighting for Britain*.
50 Killingray, *Fighting for Britain*, quoted R. Trevor Kerslake, *Time and the Hour: Nigeria, East Africa and the Second World War* (London: Radcliffe Press, 1997).
51 Ronald W. Graham, "There Was a Soldier: The Life of Hama Kim M.M., Marburg." *Africana Marburgensia* 10 (1985): 14.
52 Barraki Boy is a term for someone who lives in the Barracks.
53 Killingray, *Fighting for Britain*, 57.
54 Akaatenger John Aond'Akaa, "Military Recruitment and Its Impact on the Tiv, 1914–1970: The Case of Gboko," *B.A History Project*, University of Jos, 1971, 25–7.
55 Killingray, *Fighting for Britain*, 145.
56 Ishola Olomola, "Nigeria's Involvement in The Second World War, 1939–1946," (Unpublished M.Phil. Thesis, University of Ife, Ile-Ife, Nigeria, 1972), 57.
57 Olomola, "The Demobilization of Nigerian Troops," 41.
58 Toyin Falola and Matthew M. Heaton, *A History of Nigeria* (New York: Cambridge University Press, 2008), 258.
59 James S. Coleman, *Nigeria: Background to Nationalism* (Berkeley: University of California Press, 1958), 250–5; NAI/Comcol 1/2807/S.7, Vol. 2, 245.
60 Killingray, *Fighting for Britain*, 75.
61 Crowder, "The 1939–45 War," 605. Also, Olusanya, *The Second World War*.
62 They include but are not limited to the following: Johnson Ola, Jimson Oredipe, Umaru Yola, Mokwugo Okoye, Anthony Bankole, Raufu Atanda, Alfred Olu-odulaja, Moses Sampson, Emmanuel Laose, Achibong Bassey Duke, Abasi Dawodu, Felix Okoro, Alao Deji, Daniel Adebowale Adeniran, Aderibgbe Adeoye, Tiamiyu Ajao, Musa sheriff, Usman Katsina, Gabriel Kolawole, Amos Orenuga, Isaac Fadoyebo, Sergeant Adeyinka Oyekan (later Pharmacist and Oba of Lagos), Samuel Odugade Odulana (the 40th Olubadan of Ibadanland), Oba Adeyinka Adeyemo (39th Olubadan of Ibadanland), Pa Akinyemi Thomson, Usman Katsina, Dauda Kafancha, J.A Ariyo, Dauda Kafanchan and several others.

## Bibliography

Aond'Akaa, Akaatenger John. "Military Recruitment and Its Impact on the Tiv, 1914–1970: The Case of Gboko." *BA History Project*. University of Jos, 1971.
Barker, Arthur James. *The Rape of Ethiopia, 1936*. New York: Ballantine Books, 1971.
Byfield, Judith. "Feeding the Troops: Abeokuta (Nigeria) and World War II." *African Economic History*, no. 35 (2007).
Clayton, Anthony. *France, Soldiers and Africa*. London: Brassey's Defence Publishers, 1988.
Coleman, James S. *Nigeria: Background to Nationalism*. Berkeley: University of California Press, 1958.
Crowder, Michael. "The 1939–45 War and West Africa." In *History of West Africa*, ed. J. F. A. Ajayi and Michael Crowder, Vol. 2. London: Longman, 1974.
Fadoyebo, Isaac. *A Stroke of Unbelievable Luck*. Madison, WI: University of Wisconsin-Madison, African Studies Program, 1999.
Falola, Toyin. "Cassava Starch for Export in Nigeria during the Second World War." *African Economic History* no. 18 (1989).
Falola, Toyin. "'Salt Is Gold': The Management of Salt Scarcity in Nigeria during World War II." *Canadian Journal of African Studies* 24, no. 3 (1992).

Falola, Toyin, and Matthew M. Heaton. *A History of Nigeria*. New York: Cambridge University Press, 2008.

Freund, William. "Labour Migration to the Northern Nigerian Tin Mines, 1903–1945." *Journal of African History* 22, no. 1 (1981).

Gbor, John W. T., ed. *Military History: Nigeria from the Pre-Colonial Era to the Present*. Longman: Lagos, 2004.

Graham, Ronald W. "There Was a Soldier: The Life of Hama Kim M.M., Marburg." *Africana Marburgensia* 10 (1985).

Harman, Chris. *A People's History of the World*. London: Bookmarks, 1999.

Haywood, Austin H. W., and Frederick A. S. Clarke. *The History of the West African Frontier Force*. Aldershot: Gale & Polden, 1964.

Kerslake, R. Trevor. *Time and the Hour: Nigeria, East Africa and the Second World War*. London: Radcliffe Press, 1997.

Killingray, David. "The Colonial Army in the Gold Coast: Official Policy and Local Response, 1890–1947." PhD Dissertation, University of London, London, 1982.

Killingray, David. *Fighting for Britain: African Soldiers in the Second World War*. Suffolk: James Currey, 2012.

Killingray, David. "Military and Labour Recruitment in the Gold Coast during the Second World War." *Journal of African History* 23, no. 1 (1982).

Killingray, David, and Richard Rathbone, eds. *Africa and the Second World War*. Basingstoke: Macmillan, 1986.

Kolk, Mario. *Can You Tell Me Why I Went to War? A Story of a Young King's African Riffle, Reverend John E.A. Mandambwe*. Zomba: Kachere, 2008.

Mazrui, Ali A. *Soldiers and Kinsmen in Uganda: The Making of a Military Ethnocracy*. California: Sage Publications, 1975.

Njoku, Onwuka N. "Contribution to War Efforts." In *Britain and Nigeria: Exploitation or Development?*, ed. Toyin Falola. London: Zed Books, 1987.

Olomola, Ishola. "The Demobilization of Nigerian Troops, 1946–1950: Problem and Consequences." *ODU: A Journal of West Africa Studies*, no. 13 (1976).

Olomola, Ishola. "Nigeria's Involvement in the Second World War, 1939–1946." Unpublished M.Phil. Thesis, University of Ife, Ile-Ife, Nigeria, 1972, p. 57.

Olukoju, Ayodeji. "'Buy British, Sell Foreign': External Trade Control Policies in Nigeria during World War II and Its Aftermath, 1939–1950." *International Journal of African Historical Studies* 35 (2002).

Olusanya, Gabriel O. *The Second World War and Politics in Nigeria, 1939–1953*. London: Evans Brothers, 1973.

Quartey, Kwei. "How West Africa Helped win World War II." *Huffington Post*, 6 August 2012.

Sommerville, Donald. *The Complete Illustrated History of World War Two*. Leicester: Lorenz Books, 2008.

Staniland, Martin. "The 'Military Participation' of Ghanaian Ethnic Groups." *Research Review* 8, no. 2 (1971).

Taylor, Alan J. P. *The Origins of the Second World War*. New York: Simon & Schuster Paperbacks, 1961.

Uba, Chinedu N. *Colonial Army and Society in Northern Nigeria*. Kaduna: Baraka Press, 1998.

Ukpabi, Sam C. "The Changing Role of the Military in Nigeria, 1900–1970." *Africa Spectrum* 11, no. 1 (1976).

Upkabi, Sam C. "British Military Establishments in Nigeria, 1900–1960." In *Foundations of Nigerian Federalism: 1900–1960*, ed. John Isawa Elaigwu and Godfrey N. Uzoigwe. Abuja: National Council on Inter-Governmental Relations, 1996.

# 3 The Empire of Japan and the Southern Cone's neutrality after Pearl Harbor

*Pedro Iacobelli*[1]

In January 24, 1942, the Representative of the Secretary of State and Undersecretary of State for the Americas Sumner Welles (1937–1943) sent from Rio de Janeiro a telegram to President Roosevelt stating the U.S. strategic objectives in the Third Meeting of Consultation of Ministers of Foreign Affairs in the following terms:

> In the last conversation which I had with you the night before I left for Rio, we agreed that the two main objectives at the Conference from the stand point of our Government should be the breaking of political, commercial, and financial relations between the Axis Powers and the American Republics which had not yet taken such actions, and likewise the making of every effort to prevent the breakdown of the unity of the Hemisphere for the creation of which your own Administrations is solely responsible.[2]

Convened at the request of the Chilean Foreign Minister Juan Bautista Rossetti Colombino, in connection with the Japanese attack on the United States in December 1941, the meeting took place in the city of Rio de Janeiro from the 15th to the 28th of January 1942.[3] It brought to the fore the political differences pertaining to neutrality amongst the American republics during World War II[4] and provided a venue for political negotiations and disputes that mixed local interests against pro-U.S. hemispheric objectives.

Most state members backed the position held by the U.S. as uttered above by Welles, which was represented in Brazil by a large team. In short, the U.S. interpreted the "solidarity clause" – a concept which originated in previous meetings – as an obligation to all American republics to do no less than break diplomatic relations with the Empire of Japan, the Kingdom of Italy and the German Reich. However, a minority group, without forming a bloc or sharing a common agenda, and nominally composed of Peru, Brazil, Paraguay, Chile and Argentina, did not follow the American lead at first.[5] The two latter countries, furthermore, without abandoning their neutrality, forced a change in the wording of the meeting's Final Act. Instead of conveying a mandate to cease diplomatic relations with the Axis Powers, the language was moderated to state:

> The American Republics, in accordance with the procedures established by their own laws and in conformity with the position and circumstances obtaining in each country in the existing continental conflict, recommend the breaking of their diplomatic relations with Japan, Germany and Italy.[6]

The discussion on neutrality and the meaning of "continental solidarity" was the crux of the matter and ended up putting the fractious Chilean and Argentine positions in a corner.

During the war, the Axis Powers engaged in a diplomatic approach to secure a foothold in South America and profit from the skeptical anti-Pan American groups. This chapter, based on reading Japan's mainstream newspapers that covered the meeting in Rio De Janeiro – such as *Asahi Shimbun*, *Yomiuri Shimbun* and the English language paper *The Japan Times & Advertiser* – and the edited collection of Japanese diplomatic sources *Nihon Gaikō Bunsho: Taiheiyō Sensō*, advances the argument that for the Empire of Japan, Chilean-Argentine neutrality had great value because the Southern Cone's pro-neutrality position emerged as a dissident voice against Washington's dictates and thus served as propaganda for the Japanese government through several media outlets. Chile's and Argentina's position was closely followed in Tokyo throughout the meeting in Rio de Janeiro, and the final outcome – a rejection of severe diplomatic relations with the Axis Powers – was seen as their own diplomatic achievement. The first part of this study contextualizes the position of Japan and the U.S. in South America, and the second part discusses Japan's interest at the meeting in Rio de Janeiro and the strategy taken by its diplomatic corps.

## Japan, the U.S., Chile and Argentina towards the meeting in Rio de Janeiro

Throughout the history of modern Japan, the need for natural resources and space was used to justify expansion and conquest. In the late nineteenth century and the first decades of the twentieth century, the Empire of Japan sought to expand its markets and provide land to its migrants in East Asia as well as across the Pacific Ocean. Japan's early interaction with Latin American republics concluded with a series of commerce and friendship treaties that opened the region to Japanese investments. Diplomatic missions followed, first in Mexico (1891) and Brazil (1897) and later in Chile (1902), Peru (1909) and Argentina (1918).[7] State-led emigration to South America had begun earlier; from 1908, its East-West flow strengthened. The series of anti-Japanese migration laws passed in the U.S. in the early twentieth century forced those Japanese people willing to emigrate across the Pacific to choose a destination southwards of Mexico. Brazil and Peru were the most important destinations for these pre-World War II migrants.[8] At the same time, Japanese interest in South American markets grew, and Japan quickly recovered from the Great Depression in the mid-1930s. Indeed, the Japanese government sought to diversify its export markets, targeting South America as a means of overcoming the economic crisis.[9] This trend was further reinforced during the early years of World War II, as the Government of Japan saw an opportunity in the European War to fill the commercial void left by England and Germany.[10] For example, Chile's trade with Japan amounted to five percent of the Chilean total trade by 1940, which was more than the Chilean trade with all South American countries combined at the time.[11]

The growing Japanese presence in the "hemisphere" did not go unnoticed by the U.S., which by the mid-1930s had openly confronted Japan's expansion in Asia.[12] The government in Washington subsidized the creation and strengthening of a Pan-American community. The meetings by Foreign Affairs Ministers shaped the institutional scope of the Pan-American system. Conferences in Buenos Aires in 1936, Lima in 1938 and in Panama City after the outbreak of the War in 1939, and also in La Habana after the fall of France in 1940, served as a negotiating venue to advance a continental agenda that sought to unite the region in terms of military defense, economic assistance and political integration.[13]

Chile and Argentina, on the contrary, enjoyed good economic and political relations with the U.S. as well as with the Axis Powers. The meeting in Rio de Janeiro found both Southern Cone countries with unusual internal political situations. Chile's President Pedro Aguirre Cerda had passed away in November 1941, and thus the country was in the midst of a presidential campaign. Most of the country's population favored neutrality (even a pro-Allied one) as they widely believed that taking sides (and thus severing relations with friendly nations) would only harm national interests. Furthermore, severing relations with the Axis could put Chile in an uneasy position as the country was incapable of (militarily) defending its own shores.[14] In Argentina, democratic institutions were constantly under pressure, as a series of civil-military governments had governed the country since the early 1930s. As Luis A. Romero points out, Argentina's presidents were elected through fraud and corruption, a phenomenon that went hand in hand with a hike in nationalist populism.[15] Vice-President Ramón S. Castillo (1940–1943), a nationalist and diehard uriburista, assumed the head of the government when President Roberto M. Ortiz (a more moderate political leader) stepped down from power due to illness.[16]

The meeting in Rio de Janeiro was yet another opportunity to expand the U.S's influence on the continent, not only economically and militarily but especially politically. Indeed, the team led by Sumner Welles expected that, due to the fascist attack on American shores, the foreign ministers would show unanimous support to Washington's cause at the meeting.[17] While Castillo's government took a similar position to Chile's after the Japanese

attack on Pearl Harbor, that is, condemning the attack and supporting the
U.S. – furnishing the Allies' war efforts with their raw materials and production and controlling all Axis' subversive activities in their countries, among
other measures – neither Chile nor Argentina wanted to fully embrace a bel-
ligerent side in the War, either because they trusted the benefits of neutrality
for the country (as in Chile) or there was a manifest distrust of the U.S.
regional political agenda (as in Argentina).[18] As Argentine Foreign Minister
Enrique Ruiz Guiñazú put it before the meeting in Rio, for the "American
republics' solidarity does not imply an automatic response and much less a
military alliance".[19]

The Government of Japan, regardless of the U.S. hemispheric plans, sought
to strengthen its position in South America. The Gaimushō (Ministry of Foreign Affairs) held the opinion that in Latin America a strong anti-U.S.
sentiment existed. Thus, there was room for advancing their position, especially in Argentina. As Matsushita points out, for the Government of Japan
the Argentine anti-U.S. stance was important because Argentina was believed
to lead a group of Pan-American skeptic countries. Argentina was – for the
Japanese – the standard bearer of the idea of "South America for the South
American republics".[20] This scenario provided room for the Japanese to
strengthen its political and economic position in the region, which in turn
required being backed by Japan's soft power.[21]

In the 1930s and with renewed strength from December 1940, the Government of Japan pushed for an active presence in global media outlets. As
Tomoko Akami points out, the news agency Dōmei was established – under
the Gaimushō's umbrella – in regions beyond Japan's military sphere of influence. Dōmei was defined as an institution for the dissemination of Japanese
propaganda abroad and was a weapon to counterattack "news propaganda"
spread by the Allies' news agency such as Reuters, the Associated Press and
United Press.[22] The Government of Japan opened Dōmei offices in Mexico,
Brazil and Argentina and thus reflected Japan's interest in the region.[23]

During the weeks that followed the Japanese attack on Pearl Harbor, Japanese officials, in response to Anglo-American propaganda, confirmed several
times that they had no intention of aggrandizement in South America. For
instance, on December 19th, Tōgō Shigenori informed the Ministers of Foreign Affairs in Brazil, Argentina, Chile and Peru that Japan's intentions were
to erase the Anglo-American influence in Asia, securing the existence and
prosperity of Japan at the same time as achieving prosperity in East Asia and
contributing to world peace. Tōgō stressed, "Japan has no evil plans against
the South American countries".[24] A month later, at the time of the meeting
in Rio de Janeiro, Tōgō repeated once again that Japan sought to maintain
friendly relations with the neutral countries (that is, the "big four powers of
South America: Argentina, Brazil, Chile and Peru"), this time also noting that
no country in the Americas had an obligation to support the U.S. war efforts.
Moreover, in the same message, Tōgō discouraged the acceptance of the
American demand to break diplomatic relations with Japan, for "severing

diplomatic relations is a dangerous step that will introduce the country into the War".[25]

## The "neutral front" in South America

Japan's diplomatic corps in Latin America experienced the most intense weeks of the war before and after the Third Meeting of Consultation of Ministers of Foreign Affairs in Rio de Janeiro, Brazil. After the attack on Pearl Harbor, several American republics, one after the another, broke diplomatic relations with Japan (and the Axis Powers), expelling Japan's diplomats and officials and taking abusive measures against the local Japanese population such as confiscation of their assets, freezing their bank accounts, internment and deportation.[26] Before the meeting in Rio had begun, of the 21 republics, Colombia, Mexico and Venezuela had broken diplomatic relations with the Axis, and 9 other countries had declared war against them. So, the stance of those nine undecided countries was the crux of the matter in the meeting.[27] For the Japanese authorities, the neutrality of countries such as Chile and Argentina had great importance – as Tōgō revealed to the Japanese Minister Yamagata Kiyoshi – because Japan aimed to protect its naval supremacy (*seikaiken*) in the South Pacific, a region where the Japanese navy wanted to expand its control.[28] Together with the military-strategic goal, Tōgō stressed the great importance of recovering trade with the countries in the Pacific coast.[29] In January 1942, the Government of Japan hoped that through the neutral nations, Japan could obtain products of strategic value for the military such as tin and copper. But above these considerations, the Government of Japan sought through its diplomatic body to respond to the enormous pressure over the neutral republics imposed by the U.S.

Japan saw the meeting in Rio de Janeiro as a battlefield for diplomatic influence and relevance. The Japanese diplomatic corps in the Americas, in particular in Brazil, Argentina and Chile, had the mission to maintain these countries as neutral. As Tōgō mentioned to Ishii Taro, the Japanese ambassador in Brazil, "the Pacifist bloc may disappear due to the activities of neighboring countries and the strength of the U.S. involvement in the meeting".[30] For Japan, the diplomatic battle was portrayed as the continuation of their anti-imperialist battle against the U.S. by other means. Along this line, and as we shall see later, the Japanese diplomats used various strategies and tactics to give the impression (specially to the Chilean side) that a severance of diplomatic relations implied a Japanese attack on southeast Pacific shores.[31]

The Japanese press – controlled by the regime – reported the details of the Meeting of Foreign Ministers from Brazil.[32] For the Japanese media, the meeting also served as a thermometer of U.S. influence in the Americas: depending on the number of countries that remained neutral after the meeting, the Japanese could assess Washington's real influence in the region. At the same time, the constant U.S. pressure on the weaker American republics was seen as a trait of the bickering Colossus. Therefore, anti-U.S. Japanese propaganda could use either outcome for their purposes. Indeed, the Japanese press could fan propaganda in either scenario: a total American victory in the meeting (i.e. all countries severed diplomatic relations with the Axis) or a situation where some dissident voices kept their neutrality (i.e. against the wishes of the U.S. imperium).

To be sure, the Japanese press covered the meeting through the lens that the global conflict gave it and thus used all news-value material as propaganda. Indeed, the Dōmei agency served in various countries – e.g. Peru, Argentina, Brazil – as a channel for disseminating and gathering news for the Gaimushō and Japan's Board of Information.[33] From a reading of the Japanese newspapers at the time, we notice a rise in the publication of Latin American-related news and U.S. activities in the Americas after the Japanese attack on Hawaii. These reports covered basically two types of news: about the U.S. imperialistic presence in the continent and the heroic resistance of those smaller countries against the very same American pressures. Along this line, Chile and Argentina's position in the meeting had a much wider repercussion than their immediate regional contexts.

For example, the *Asahi Shimbun* labeled the U.S. attitude in the region as "disgraceful behavior" (*kyōtai*) for the way in which U.S. diplomats worked to secure the anti-Axis vote from the neutral nations.[34] The "disgraceful" element was, as *The Japan Times & Advertiser* pointed out, in the fact that "the U.S. may dictate the terms of the coming Pan-American [sic] Foreign Ministers' Conference" and through the Monroe Doctrine "become the front of democratic imperialism".[35] Indeed, the press in Japan spread the view that the meeting in Rio de Janeiro was all about American republics being pulled into the Anglo-American side of the war, or as it was put:

> the Pan-American Conference is being purposely mooted by President Roosevelt to use Latin America as his cannon fodder, just as he is using Chungking as a destructive element in the growth of the projected Greater East Asia Co-Prosperity Sphere. For this fact . . . Japan cannot remain indifferent to the venue of the Rio de Janeiro meeting.[36]

That is, the Japanese news outlet spread the image of a "despotic" American control of the region, minimizing the spaces of autonomy for the smaller American republics. Kawai Kazuo, a historian educated in the U.S., expressed his views on Washington's strategy in an editorial as follows:

> Gain control of all strategic points on both American continents. . . . The United States hopes to exploit the countries of Latin America [and] has nothing to offer except luxury goods for the few aristocrats in the Latin American capitals.[37]

Similarly, the spokesperson of the Board of Information, Hori Tomokazu warned that:

[T]he issue which cannot be condoned by Japan is the fact that the United States is making frantic efforts to drag the South American countries into the vortex of war, taking advantage of the prospective Pan-American Foreign Ministers' Conference on January 15. I can hardly emphasize [enough] that the so-called Pan-American policy, which is the national policy of the United States, is nothing but a venomous "doll" diplomacy [sic], although it is couched in fair terms such as the establishment of a joint formation of Central and South American countries and good neighborly relationships.[38]

Furthermore, the Japanese media put emphasis on the disagreements that emerged days before the meeting. For instance, an *Asahi Shimbun*'s reporter in Buenos Aires observed "an extremely fair attitude (*kōsei*) from Chile and Argentina, countries which oppose the American pressure and maintain their neutrality . . . they deserve lots of respect".[39] The same day, *The Japan Times & Advertiser* published, "South Americans have long been oppressed by the United States, and they seem to be glad that the little Japan has given such a beating to the United States".[40] Three days later, the editorial of the *Asahi Shimbun* (titled "Nanbei chūritsu koku no koshū [The attitude of the neutral countries in South America]") portrayed the existence of an anti-U.S. bloc in South America, for "Argentina, Brazil, Chile, a group of countries known as the ABC, stand against the U.S. and will fight for their neutrality".[41] One week later, Peru was also referred to as a member of the same group, and the Japanese press recommended strengthening the "historic" good commercial and political relations with the member-state of this bloc.[42] Indeed, the Japanese media did not waste any opportunity to discredit Washington's influence on the continent and to exaggerate the existence of opposition to the U.S.:

> Brazil, for instance, has already expressed views against it. Chile is also very cautious in deciding its attitude. Argentina, Chile and Paraguay are making secret activity to prevent the passage of such a radical proposal at the Rio de Janeiro conference. Argentina and Peru are also endeavoring to prevent such an extreme measure as the severance of diplomatic relations. In such a manner, the plan of the United States is not developing as it wishes.[43]

These reports were an expression of a double rationale behind the strategy taken by the Japanese governments. The news media served as a sound box for the Gaimushō's activities in South America, gave further (and global) coherence to the anti-U.S. narratives that underpinned the war efforts in the archipelago and created a "battlefield" for the Japanese and international audience as well as for the Japanese diplomats in the region.

The beginning of the meeting on January 15, 1942, saw the continuation of this trend in the way in which the Japanese media covered the conference. *The Japan Times & Advertiser*, for example, stated that "[i]t is characteristic of all these conferences that they invariably provide occasion for Washington's intervention, in one form or another, in internal affairs of Latin American countries", but "[o]f the treaties and conventions decided at the Pan-American conferences not a few still remain unratified. This fact must be considered as evidence of Latin American countries discountenancing the interventionist policy of Washington masked as a peaceful undertaking".[44] Similarly, the Asahi Shimbun published a column on the occasion of the inauguration of the meeting, praising the efforts displayed by Argentina and the likely defeat of the U.S. in Brazil.[45]

While all American republics condemned the Japanese attack and supported U.S. war efforts in Rio de Janeiro, the Japanese press exclusively focused on the pressure imposed by the U.S. and the resilience of those countries that were still reluctant to break diplomatic relations. This was particularly highlighted in the final discussion of the wording of the Final Act. As mentioned above, Article III of the Final Act established that "The American Republics . . . recommend the breaking of their diplomatic relations with Japan, Germany and Italy". However in an earlier draft, the wording had stated that "The American Republics . . . cannot continue with their diplomatic relations with Japan, Germany and Italy". The draft was modified due to the Chilean and Argentine rejection to a binding resolution that forced them to sever relations with until-then friendly nations.[46] This episode was widely referred to in the Japanese press because it represented a setback for U.S. interests.

While the Japanese press covered the meeting with clear propagandistic intentions, Japanese diplomats in Tokyo, Buenos Aires, Santiago and Rio de Janeiro kept working. Indeed, as Colonel General Carter W. Clarke, chief of the U.S. Special Service Branch in charge of the Axis intercepts, would assess a couple of months later, the Japanese played an important role in orchestrating the Axis powers' response to the changing scenario in the Americas. For Clarke, "it seems nevertheless that the Japanese to a remarkable degree are assuming leadership of the Axis Powers in the initiation and formulation of joint policies. This is particularly true in relations to Latin America. The impression is that the Japanese are abler men, better informed, than their German and Italian colleagues".[47] During the meeting, the Axis Powers coordinated their actions in Brazil as well as in Argentina and Chile. Certainly, as the Japanese diplomatic reports state, the meeting triggered closer collaboration among the Axis Powers in terms of circulation of intelligence and joint decision-making.[48] As a result of the meetings held by the Axis representatives in Brazil, for example, they coordinated the forms and timing of approaching neutral countries legations in Rio de Janeiro and expressed the "inherent danger" of breaking up relations.[49] For instance, threats of war were brought up by all three Axis ambassadors, almost at the same time, to the Brazilian Foreign Minister Oswaldo Arahna on January 16, 1942.[50]

The Government of Japan understood that a unanimous resolution breaking off diplomatic relations with the Axis would exclude Japan from the

American continent, at a time when the war had become more global than ever.[51] Against the backdrop of the U.S. pressure on the American republics, the Japanese incremented their activities directly with the neutral governments. In the case of Chile, pressure to break or maintain its neutrality was fierce and intense. Following Japanese sources, on January 17th, Ishii Taro, the Japanese ambassador in Brazil met members of the Chilean legation (no names are given) and communicated the "disadvantages" (*furieki*) of severing relations because Japan would consider Chile to be engaged in the war, and "the Chilean ships would be confiscated, all maritime communication halted and Japanese submarines could approach Chilean coasts".[52] The Chilean counterpart reassured Ishii that their government's intention was to avoid entering the war. On January 19th, Tōgō sent instructions to the Japanese minister in Santiago, Yamagata Kiyoshi, that he should "stop, like Argentina, all resolution on severing relations".[53] Yamagata acted swiftly and communicated similar threats to Foreign Minister Rossetti (then in Brazil) as well as to the Chilean defense minister.[54] While Japanese diplomats put pressure to try to secure the neutrality of a couple of countries, the Gaimushō kept insisting on their wish to pursue friendly relations with the neutral countries and at the same time stressing that Japan had recently defeated the American fleet in the Pacific and, thus, the U.S. was incapable of securing the defense to the whole perimeter of the continent.[55]

In the end, unlike the rest of the American republics, Chile and Argentina did not agree to break relations with the Axis Powers. Even though they supported a series of measures in favor of the Allies, Japan celebrated this outcome. The Southern Cone's attitude was highly praised in Japan and read as evidence of their affinity with the Axis' cause. On January 26, 1942, the speaker of the Board of Information gave the following analysis to the conclusion of the meeting in Rio de Janeiro:

> What the colossus of North America wanted was an interpretation of the so-called solidarity of America in such a way that a war by the United States of America was a war by all other American countries as well, even at the sacrifice of their sovereignty and independence . . . We are glad to learn that Argentina and Chile in spite of all the intimidation . . . have decided not to sever immediately their diplomatic relations with the Axis Powers . . . we shall remember their gallant fight for their independence and at the same time we have a feeling of high respect for such a show of independent decision.[56]

On January 27th, the Japanese legation in Santiago stated that they, together with the German ambassador in Santiago, agreed to praise the head of the Chilean legation in Brazil (Rossetti) for his effort to keep his position despite American pressure from Welles.[57] On January 31st, the minister Tōgō, in contact with German and Italian ambassadors, informed that the Imperial Government of Japan would seek to reward Chile and Argentina for their stance in the meeting of Rio de Janeiro.[58] Even though the Japanese diplomatic corps had to be relocated from Brazil, Peru and other Latin American countries, the conservation of their legation in Chile and Argentina was embraced as an historical event and a triumph of the Japanese diplomatic strategy.

## Conclusion

The extant literature on the neutrality of the Southern Cone has emphasized that it was tilted towards the Allied Powers. However, this scholarship has given little attention to the other end of the diplomatic line. For example, how was Chilean and Argentinian neutrality interpreted by the Axis Powers? And more importantly, how was it used by these powers? As this study shows, the strategic and propagandistic angles are also elements to assess the relevance of the neutrality of a given country during the global conflict. What was at stake was not support of the U.S. war efforts in terms of economic and military cooperation but the extent to which diplomatic support given to the Allies' cause was central in the post-Pearl Harbor discussion among American republics.

Japan, Chile and Argentina bore strategic value as points of intelligence gatherings and shelter for the Japanese interests (business and migrant communities) in the region. Also, in mainland Japan, these countries had the potentiality to be used as anti-U.S. propaganda. Therefore, the fight over the neutrality of the Southern Cone should be seen as a moment of confrontation between Japan and the U.S. The conservation of Chile and Argentina's neutrality was a Japanese war target which received attention from the Japanese Press; severance of the same diplomatic relations was still an unfulfilled American goal.

## Notes

1  This work was funded by CONICYT, FONDECYT Iniciación No. 11160011., contact e-mail: piacobel@uc.cl
2  United States Department of State, *Foreign Relations of the United States: Diplomatic Papers, 1941, Vol. VI: The American Republics* (Washington, DC: Government Printing Office, 1963), 32.
3  "The Chilean Minister of Foreign Affairs (Rossetti) to the Chairman of the Governing Board of the Pan American Union (Hull)," in United States Department of State, *Foreign Relations of the United States: Diplomatic Papers, 1941, Vol. VI: The American Republics* (Washington, DC: Government Printing Office, 1963), 119–20. Also, in Archivo General Histórico del Ministerio de Relaciones Exteriores de Chile (AMREL), Fondo Histórico, vol. 1959, 1941.
4  For a work that discusses the meaning of neutrality from a legal perspective, see Roberto Russell y Juan Gabriel Tokatlian, "Relaciones internacionales y política interna: los neutrales en la Segunda Guerra Mundial, un caso de estudio," *Foro Internacional* 41, no. 1 (2001): 63–103.
5  For the U.S. position in the Americas during World War II, see Michael J. Francis, *The Limits of Hegemony: United States Relations with Argentina and Chile during World War II* (Notre

Dame, IN: University of Notre Dame Press, 1977); Michael J. Francis, "The United States and Chile during the Second World War: The Diplomacy of Misunderstanding," *Journal of Latin American Studies* 9, no. 1 (1977): 91–113. For Chile's diplomatic history during the conflict, see Mario Barros Van Buren, *La diplomacia chilena en la Segunda Guerra Mundial* (Santiago: Empresa Editoria Arquen, 1998); Joaquín Fermandois, "Guerra y hegemonía 1939–1943. Un aspecto de las relaciones chileno-norteamericanas," *Historia* 23, no. 1 (1988): 5–51. And for Argentina's diplomatic history during the conflict, see José R. Sanchíz Muñoz, *La Argentina y la Segunda Guerra Mundial* (Buenos Aires: Grupo Editor Latinoamericano, 1992).

6 Italics mine. See *Final Act of the Third Meeting of the Ministers of Foreign Affairs of the American Republics* (Río de Janeiro: Organization of American States, 1942), 61, www.oas.org/council/MEETINGS%20OF%20CONSULTATION/Actas/Acta%203.pdf. Also, see "The American Representative (Welles) to the Secretary of State," 23 of January, 1942, in United States Department of State, *Foreign Relations of the United States Diplomatic Papers, 1942, Volume V: The American Republics* (Washington, DC: Government Printing Office, 1962), 34–5. For an analysis see Rafaelle Nocera, *Chile y la Guerra 1933–1943* (Santiago: Lom Editores, 2006), 162.

7 See Eikichi Hayashiya, "Nihon to Raten Amerika No Gaikō Kankei," in *Nihon to Raten Amerika No Kankei-Nihon No Kokuzaika Ni Okeru Raten Amerika*, ed. Hajime Mizuno (Tokyo: Instituto Iberoamericano, Universidad de Sofía, 1990), 5–8.

8 Pedro Iacobelli, *Postwar Emigration to South America from Japan and the Ryukyu Islands* (London: Bloomsbury Academics, 2017), Chapter 2.

9 Foreign Minister Hirota Kōki pushed for this move for a diversification in Japan's foreign markets in 1934. See Osamu Ishi, "Senkanki Nihon no Keizai gaikō," in *Nihon no gaikō, vol 1. Gaikōshi senzenhen*, ed. Inoue Toshi (Tokyo: Iwanami, 2013), 162–80.

10 See Nocera, *Chile y la guerra*; Hiroshi Matsushita, "Jyōyakuteiketsu Kara Dainiji Daisen (20seiki Ha Jime Kara 1945 Nen)," in *Nihon Aruzenchin Kōryūshi: Harukana Tomo to 100nen*, ed. Nihon Aruzenchin kōryūshi renshūiinkai (Tokyo: Nihon Aruzenchin kōryūshi, 1999), 28–39.

11 Dominique Hachette, "Relaciones económicas entre Chile y Japón," in *Chile y Japón un siglo de amistad*, ed. Oscar Pinochet de la Barra (Santiago: Comisión Chilena de Celebración del Centenario de las Relaciones Chile-Japón, 1997), 163–99.

12 See Edward S. Miller, *Bankrupting the Enemy: The U.S. Financial Siege of Japan before Pearl Harbor* (Annapolis: Naval Institute Press, 2007); Akira Iriye, *Japan & the Wider World* (Nueva York: Longman, 1997).

13 Galvarino Gallardo Nieto, *La Conferencia de Río de Janeiro: Enero 1942* (Santiago: Editorial Nascimiento, 1942), 59; Francis, *The Limits of Hegemony*, 21–5; Nocera, *Chile y la guerra*, 52. See also *Acta final de la reunión de consulta entre los ministros de Relaciones Exteriores de las Repúblicas americanas de conformidad con los acuerdos de Buenos Aires y de Lima* (Panamá: Organización de los Estados Americanos, 1939), 42, and *Acta final de la segunda reunión de consulta entre los ministros de Relaciones Exteriores de las Repúblicas americanas, suscrita en la ciudad de La Habana, el día treinta de julio de mil novecientos cuarenta* (La Habana: Organización of American States, 1940), 45, www.oas.org/consejo/sp/rc/Actas/Acta 2.pdfwww.oas.org/consejo/sp/rc/Actas/Acta 1.pdf.

14 Pedro Iacobelli, "La 'neutralidad' chilena en la Segunda Guerra Mundial (1939–1943): un análisis historiográfico con enfasis en la literatura sobre las relaciones Chile-Japón," *Revista de Historia y Geografía* 34 (2016): 95–108.

15 Luis Alberto Romero, *Breve historia contemporánea de la Argentina* (Buenos Aires: Fondo de Cultura Económica, 1994), 89; María Isabel Dieguez, "La neutralidad de Argentina durante la Segunda Guerra Mundial," *Estudios Internacionales* 22, no. 85 (1989): 53. Sanchís Muñoz adds that most political leaders and teh public opinión expressed pro-Allies; see José R. Sanchíz Muñoz, *Historia diplomática argentina* (Buenos Aires: Eudeba, 2010), 285.

16 Castillo and others favored the political image of Juan Manuel Rosas (1793–1877), an authoritarian leader in nineteenth-century Argentina. See Federico Finchelstein, *Fascismo,*

*liturgia e imaginario. El Mito del general Uriburu y la Argentina nacionalista* (Buenos Aires: Fondo de Cultura Económica, 2002).

17  For the discussion on Japanese fascism, see Shinichi Sugiki, "Shōwa Kyōkō to Fashizumu No Taitō," in *Kindai No Nihon v. 5: Taihei Yō Sensō*, ed. Masaomi Yui (Tokyo: Yoshikawa Kōbunkan, 1995), 29–50.

18  Sanchíz Muñoz, *La Argentina y la Segunda Guerra Mundial*, 283.

19  Cited in Enrique Ruiz Guiñazú, *La política argentina y el futuro de América* (Buenos Aires: Libreria Huemul, 1944), 79.

20  Cited in Matsushita, "Jyōyakuteiketsu Kara Dainiji Daisen . . . ," 36.

21  Barack Kushner argues that, unlike Germany, the Japanese propaganda was articulated by several State's organs. See Barak Kushner, *The Thought War: Japanese Imperial Propaganda* (Honolulu: University of Hawaii Press, 2006). "Soft power" bears a strategic value in wartime and can serve together with the "hard power." See Tomoko Akami, *Soft Power of Japan's Total War State: The Board of Information and Domei News Agency in Foreign Policy, 1934–45* (Dordrecht: Republic of Letters, 2014), 2–4.

22  "News propaganda," a term coined by Tomoko Akami, refers to real news but with propaganda value. Akami, *Soft Power*, 5.

23  Akami, *Soft Power*, 235–40.

24  "Message from the Minister of Foreign Affairs (Shigenori Togo) to the Ministers of Foreign Affairs of Argentina, Brazil, Chile and Peru," 19 December 1941 in Gaimushō, Jōhōkyoku, *Seifu Kōhyōshū : Taigai Kankei*, Tokio, 1941, 105–6. Also in "Notas intercambiadas," en AMRE, Fondo Histórico, volumen 1.959, año 1941.

25  "Statement of the Speaker of the Board of Information," 19 January 1942, in Gaimushō, Jōhōkyoku, *Seifu Kōhyōshū : Taigai Kankei*, Tokio, 1942, 4–5.

26  For the Mexican case, see Carlos Uscanga, "Confiscación y reclamos de las propiedades en México durante la II Guerra Mundial. El caso de la Mina Azul," in *Actas XV Congreso Internacional ALADAA* (Santiago, Chile: ALADAA Chile, 2016). And for the internment of Japanese nationals after Rio de Janeiro's meeting, see John Emmerson, "Japanese an Americans in Peru, 1942–1943," *Foreign Service Journal* 54 (1977): 40–7, 56; Daniel Masterson and Sayaka Funada-Classen, *The Japanese in Latin America* (Urbana and Chicago: University of Illinois Press, 2004). For Chile, Mauricio Paredes Venegas, "Nacionalismo, seguridad y presión internacional: la relegación de japoneses en Chile durante la Segunda Guerra Mundial" (PhD Thesis, Universidad de Chile, Santiago, Chile, 2012).

27  For Ruiz Guiñazú, the discussion around neutrality was the central point in the discussion, in Ruiz Guiñazú, *La política argentina y el futuro de América*, 82.

28  Communiqué n° 434, 19 December 1941, in Gaimushō, *Nihon Gaikō Bunsho: Taiheiyō Sensō*, Gaimushō hensan, 2010, 936.

29  Communiqué n° 440, 12 January 1942, Gaimushō, 943.

30  Communiqué n° 439, 8 January 1942, Gaimushō, 942.

31  See "Cable del 2 January1942," in AMRE, Fondo Histórico, volume 2049, year 1942.

32  For an American informed view on the Japanese media at the time, see Joseph C. Grew, *Ten Years in Japan* (Nueva York: Simon and Schuster, 1944).

33  See Akami, *Soft Power*, chaps. 6–7.

34  *Asahi Shimbun*, morning ed., 6 January 1942, 2.

35  *The Japan Times & Advertiser*, morning ed., 6 January 1942, 3.

36  *Japan Times*, 3.

37  *The Japan Times & Advertiser*, morning ed., 10 January 1942, 6.

38  *The Japan Times & Advertiser*, morning ed., 11 January 1942, 1.

39  *Asahi Shimbun*, evening ed., 10 December 1941, 1.

40  *The Japan Times & Advertiser*, morning ed., 10 December 1941, 3.

41  *Asahi Shimbun*, morning ed., 13 December 1941, 2.

42  *Asahi Shimbun*, morning ed., 6 January 1942, 2.

43  *The Japan Times & Advertiser*, evening ed., 12 January 1942, 1.

44  *The Japan Times & Advertiser*, morning ed., 15 January 1942, 6.

45 *Asahi Shimbun*, morning ed., 15 January 1942, 2. From a different angle, the *Yomiuri Shimbun*, in an interview with its reporter in Rio de Janeiro, deemed South America an important supplier of natural resources to the U.S. war efforts; see *Yomiuri Shimbun*, morning ed., 12 January 1942, 1.

46 For a full report on the Meeting, including each member's position, and the draft of Final Act produced by Cordell Hull, see "Third Meeting of Foreign Ministers of the American Republics, held at Rio de Janeiro, January 15–28, 1942," in United States Department Of State, *Foreign Relations of the United States Diplomatic Papers, 1942, Volume V: The American Republics*, 6–39.

47 "Magic Summary, 1 June 1942," National Archives and Registration Records, College Park, RG 457, Box 1.

48 Communiqué n° 438, 7 January 1942, in Gaimushō, 939.

49 Communiqué n° 442, 14 January 1942, Gaimushō, 946.

50 Ibid; Communiqué n° 445, 16 January 1942.

51 Communiqué n° 454, 19 January 1942, Gaimushō, 957.

52 Communiqué n° 448, 17 January 1942, Gaimushō, 952–3.

53 Communiqué n° 451, 19 January 1942, Gaimushō, 954.

54 Communiqué n° 452, 19 January 1942, Gaimushō, 955.

55 "Declaración del vocero del directorio de Información sobre los países neutrales de Sudamérica," 19 January 1942, in Gaimushō, Jōhōkyoku, *Seifu Kōhyōshū: Taigai Kankei*, 1942, 4–5. También aparece transcrita en Communiqué n° 453, 19 January 1942, Gaimushō, *Nihon Gaikō Bunsho: Taiheiyō Sensō*, 955–7.

56 "Comentario del vocero del Directorio de Información sobre la Conferencia Latinoamericana (*sic*) en Río de Janeiro," 26 January 1942, in Gaimushō, Jōhōkyoku, *Seifu Kōhyōshū : Taigai Kankei*, 1942, 157–8.

57 Communiqué n° 460, 27 January 1942, Gaimushō, *Nihon Gaikō Bunsho: Taiheiyō Sensō*, 963. This issue was taken by the Chilean press; see *El Chileno*, 2 March 1942, 7.

58 Communiqué n° 462, Communiqué 1942, Gaimushō, 967–8.

# Bibliography

Akami, Tomoko. *Soft Power of Japan's Total War State: The Board of Information and Domei News Agency in Foreign Policy, 1934–45*. Dordrecht: Republic of Letters, 2014.

Barros Van Buren, Mario. *La diplomacia chilena en la Segunda Guerra Mundial*. Santiago: Empresa Editora Arquen, 1998.

Dieguez, María Isabel. "La neutralidad de Argentina durante la Segunda Guerra Mundial." *Estudios Internacionales* 22, no. 85 (1989).

Emmerson, John. "Japanese and Americans in Peru." *Foreign Service Journal* 54 (1977).

Fermandois, Joaquín. "Guerra y Hegemonía 1939–1943. Un aspecto de las relaciones chileno – norteamericanas." *Historia* 23, no. 1 (1988): 5–51.

Finchelstein, Federico. *Fascismo, liturgia e imaginario. El Mito del general Uriburu y la Argentina nacionalista*. Buenos Aires: Fondo de Cultura Económica, 2002.

Francis, Michael J. *The Limits of Hegemony: United States Relations with Argentina and Chile during World War II*. Notre Dame: University of Notre Dame Press, 1977a.

Francis, Michael J. "The United States and Chile during the Second World War: The Diplomacy of Misunderstanding." *Journal of Latin American Studies* 9, no. 1 (1977b): 91–113.

Funada-Classen, Sayaka, and Daniel Masterson. *The Japanese in Latin America*. Urbana and Chicago: University of Illinois Press, 2004.

Gallardo Nieto, Galvarino. *La Conferencia de Río de Janeiro: Enero 1942*. Santiago: Editorial Nascimiento, 1942.

Grew, Joseph C. *Ten Years in Japan*. New York: Simon and Schuster, 1944.

Hachette, Dominique. "Relaciones económicas entre Chile y Japón." In *Chile y Japón un siglo de amistad*, ed. O. Pinochet de la Barra, 163–199. Santiago: Comisión Chilena de Celebración del Centenario de las Relaciones Chile-Japón, 1997.

Hayashiya, Eikichi. "Nihon to Raten America No Gaiko Kankei." In *Nihon to Raten Amerika No Kankei – Nihon No Kokuzaika Ni Okeru Raten Amerika*, ed. H. Mizuno. Tokio: Instituro Iberoamericano, 1990.

Iacobelli, Pedro. *Postwar Emigration to South America from Japan and the Ryukyu Islands*. London: Bloomsbury Academic, 2017.

Iriye, Akira. *Japan & the Wider World*. New York: Longman, 1997.

Ishi, Osamu. "Senkaki Nihon no Keizai gaiko." In *Nihon no gaiko, vol 1, Gaikoshi senzenhen*, ed. I. Toshi. Tokyo: Iwanami, 2013.

Kushner, Barak. *The Thought War: Japanese Imperial Propaganda*. Honolulu: University of Hawaii Press, 2006.

Miller, Edward S. *Bankrupting the Enemy: The U.S. Financial Siege of Japan before Pearl Harbor*. Annapolis: Naval Institute Press, 2007.

Nocera, Rafaelle. *Chile y la guerra 1933–1943*. Santiago: LOM editores, 2006.

Paredes Venegas, Mauricio. "Nacionalismo, seguridad y presión internacional: la relegación de japoneses en Chile durante la Segunda Guerra Mundial." Unpublished Ph.D. thesis, Universidad de Chile, Santiago, Chile, 2012.

Romero, Luis Alberto. *Breve historia contemporánea de la Argentina*. Buenos Aires: Fondo de Cultura Económica, 1994.

Ruiz Guiñazú, Enrique. *La politica argentina y el futuro de América*. Buenos Aires: Librería Huemul, 1944.

Russell, Roberto, and Juan Gabriel Tokatlian. "Relaciones internacionales y politica interna: los neutrales en la Segunda Guerra Mundial, un caso de estudio." *Foro Internacional* 41, no. 1 (2001): 63–103.

Sanchís Muñoz, José R. *Historia diplomática argentina*. Buenos Aires: Eudeba, 2010.

Sanchís Muñoz, José R. *La Argentina y la Segunda Guerra Mundial*. Buenos Aires: Grupo Editor Latinoamericano, 1992.

Sugiki, Shinichi. "Showa Kyoko to Fashizumu No Taito." In *Kindai No Nihon v. 5: Taihei Yo Senso*, ed. M. Yui. Tokyo: Yoshikawa Kobukan, 1995.

Uscanga, Carlos. "Confiscación y reclamos de las propiedades en México durante la II Guerra Mundial. El caso de la Mina Azul." In *Actas XV Congreso Internacional ALADAA*. Santiago: ALADAA Chile, 2016.

# 4 Finland's relations with the Allied war effort

*Henry Oinas-Kukkonen*

GRAY – a codename used by the American Office of Strategic Services (OSS) during World War II for Finland[1] – aptly describes the country's phases with the Allied Powers' war effort. This history is neither black nor white but rather is all the shades of grey.

While the Allies fought the Second World War, Finland was involved in three wars. In the first war in 1939–1940, Finland wished help from the Franco-British Alliance but ended up rejecting their expeditionary force. In the second war, 1941–1944, the Anglo-Soviet Alliance, along with some lesser Allies, declared war on Finland, which fought as a non-officially allied co-belligerent of Germany. Yet, Finland was the only Western republican democracy in North Eastern Europe, and its population admired the Scandinavian and Anglo-American culture and way of life. This led to unimaginable situations; for example, Jewish soldiers and German SS troops fought on the same side. In the third war, 1944–1945, Finland fought alongside the Allies against Germany. In the end, neither Helsinki nor Moscow was occupied, but Finland agreed to the entrance of an Allied Control Commission. The key to understanding the complex Finnish relations with the Allied war effort is to understand Fenno-Russo relations.

After suppressive Russification, the Grand Duchy of Finland declared independence from the Russian Empire in 1917. The Finns disarmed the Russian forces that were supported by the Finnish revolutionary Red Guards. The Finnish government's Civil Guards Defence Corps was aided by German troops, an enemy of the Allies, and it trained 2,000 Finnish volunteers. A Germanophile attitude was evident among them. The Red Guards were defeated in a bitter civil war. Finnish volunteers made an unsuccessful military expedition to Northwestern Russia, where the Allies had organised Finnish Reds as a British Royal Navy military unit known as the Murmansk Legion to assist 'White Russian' forces during the North Russia intervention in 1918–1919. A brother-in-law of the German Emperor was elected Finnish king, but after Germany's surrender in World War I, Finland adopted a republican constitution and established relations with the Allied Powers. A peace treaty between Finland and Soviet Russia was signed in Tartu (Dorpat), Estonia, in 1920. The Soviet-Finnish Non-Aggression Pact, signed in 1932, was unilaterally renounced by the Soviet Union two days before its invasion of Finland in 1939.

## The Winter War: a Franco-British crash landing

In August 1939, the Soviet Union and Germany signed the so-called Nazi-Soviet Molotov-Ribbentrop Pact.[2] A secret protocol assigned Finland within the Soviet sphere of influence. Adolf Hitler also omitted Finland from a list of states having friendly relations with Germany on 6 October 1939. Britain and France were Finland's most trusted European friends.[3] The share of Britain in the Finnish foreign trade was 44 percent in the exports and 18 percent in imports.[4] The Anglo-Franco Alliance declared war on Germany on 3 September 1939, but it did not want also war with the Soviet Union.

The First Lord of the Admiralty, Winston Churchill, wished to create a close-range Scandinavian-Baltic Sea theatre of operations to ensure British control of the Baltic Sea and the isolation of Germany from Scandinavian raw materials, including minerals such as iron ore. This would curtail Germany's capacity for war and allow time for rearmament and preparations for other theatres. The Allied naval and amphibious capabilities in the North were instructed to divert and tie down significant numbers of German troops. However, the goal was not to challenge the Soviets but rather lead them to abandon the German alliance and press northern countries, including Finland, as an integral part of the Alliance. It had earlier refused to grant naval bases and hindered formal Anglo-Soviet naval cooperation in the Baltic.[5]

On 30 November 1939, the Soviet Union attacked Finland without a declaration of war with an artillery barrage, air raids and a 450,000-strong army against 250,000 inadequately equipped Finns.[6] Soviet forces established expatriate Communist Otto Kuusinen's puppet government in the occupied town of Terijoki on 1 December 1939. On the next day, the new Democratic People's Republic of Finland signed a Treaty of Mutual Assistance and Friendship in Moscow. The Finns rejected it and fought for their nearly 22-year-old independence. The British Minister in Helsinki, Thomas Snow, called for anti-Soviet cooperation with Japan and possibly the United States and Italy. The Soviet Union was not seen to pose a strategic threat to British interests, and it would ruin relations with the United States and Australia, which endangered Japanese expansionism. Allied participation was not an entirely excluded option. The French wanted Britain to take a bold line to help Finland in the League of Nations and not to break Allied ranks. The Soviet Union was expelled as a manifest aggressor state from the organisation on 11 December 1939, and the French were enthusiastic to intervene in the Fenno-Soviet conflict. 'Poor little Finland' gained sympathy and positive media coverage,[7] and the League of Nations' sanction gave some legitimacy to the Anglo-Franco Allies' attempt to aid Finland.

Finland was in dire need of immediate arms supplies. It made an urgent request, buying 30 fighter aircraft from Britain, which promised to sell

20 Bristol Gladiator fighters. The Finns attempted to acquire weapons from other sources. Axis Italy dispatched 50 warplanes, but another Axis power, Germany, stopped their transit and held up a Finnish order for 54 howitzers from German factories. The British began to increase aid, promising some 5,000 anti-tank mines and 10,000 hand grenades, 100 machine guns, 100 anti-tank rifles, 25 howitzers and 12 Blenheim bombers, which were to be used for bombing the Murmansk railway. The longer the Soviets were tied up with the Finns, the less they could assist the Germans or threaten British interests in the Balkans and Middle East. The point was to damage Soviet interests without going to war, similar to what the Soviets did to the British.[8]

The war was not going as the Soviets had anticipated, as the Finnish staunch resistance scored a number of victories. The Red Army faced a disastrous defeat at Suomussalmi. Soviet divisions were encircled, paralysed by poor winter conditions. However, the Allies realised that winning some important defensive victories could not last against the superiority in terms of the number of Soviet troops, weaponry, material resources and reserves. The Finns had scarce military resources and diminishing manpower for Europe's most violent battles of 'the phoney war'.[9]

In February 1940, the Red Army began heavy air raids of towns, as well as a major offensive to destroy the Finnish defences. There seemed no hope without an Allied intervention. A collapse appeared so inevitable that even on the other side of the Atlantic, the US Department of Interior and congressmen made proposals and sketched plans for resettling Finnish refugees in Alaska. Aid to Finland and resettlement plans shook the principles of American isolationists, who, with their anti-British stand, were an obstacle to the Allies in their effort to get the United States to join the war. Sympathy towards Finland made it to many isolationists easier to yield from the strictest interpretation of the US Neutrality Acts.[10] This was a noteworthy unintended consequence of the Allied war effort.

From the Allied viewpoint, the longer the Fenno-Soviet war continued, the greater the trouble was for Germany and the Soviet Union and the better the situation for the Allies. The Commander-in-Chief of Finland's Defence Forces, Field Marshall C.G.E. Mannerheim, turned down the White Russian offer of aid because it would harm prospects with the Soviets and he worried that a direct Allied intervention would provoke Germany. Finland asked Sweden for a supply of official armed units. The Swedes feared that the Allied expedition would make them a prime target for a German *blitzkrieg*, so the request was turned down and the Finns pressed for a cease-fire and peace treaty with the Soviets. Stockholm was a base for Finnish and Soviet peace feelers. The Soviets abandoned their announced Democratic People's Republic of Finland and informed the British Foreign Office that any assistance sent to Finland would be a major cause of a closer Soviet-German Alliance. The Allies advised the Finns to appeal to Britain and France for military assistance and intervention. The Finns were estimated to need some 20,000 men, which would be enough support to avoid a defeat but not enough to win nor to take Leningrad. An independent office was to undertake the assistance and recruitment. If the Finns were to accept Soviet terms, it would be a turning point in Anglo-Soviet relations.[11]

A Soviet victory would give a serious blow to the Allied prestige. The Winter War could be used as a justification for Allied offensives in the northern areas. The French Embassy in London explained to the British Ally that their *démarche* in Sweden and Norway aimed to force those countries to help Finland. The entrance of Allied troops would involve them in the Allied side and deny Swedish iron ore from Germany. The change would result in Allied control of the Baltic Sea and all of Scandinavia. Churchill stressed this to be so essential for victory that the Soviet countermeasures would be left a matter for later concern.[12]

Large-scale naval and land operations in northern Europe boded well for the French, who desired to move the main battlefront away from their borders. However, their preference was an operation in the Finnish Arctic Sea port of Petsamo, but they were convinced it would not lead to Allied control of Swedish ore fields. Aid to Finland was to be combined with an intervention in Scandinavia and to be carried out with or without Swedish or Norwegian approval for troops to pass through their territory. Two divisions were to take over the Norwegian port of Narvik; march to Gällivare ore fields in Sweden; destroy the main shipment port, Luleå; and proceed to Finland. The British government gave its general approval in late December 1939. A special military delegation headed by Brigadier Christopher Ling was sent to Finland. In his radioed 'The Light of Freedom' address on 20 January 1940, Churchill lauded Finland as a heroic opponent of Soviet and Nazi totalitarianism. He thought that its free, democratic and parliamentary system inspired others to continue to fight. Churchill stated, 'Finland shows what free men can do'. Prime Minister Chamberlain reacted. First, 500 volunteers were sent to Finland, commanded by American General Kermit Roosevelt, son of former US President Theodore Roosevelt. In an Anglo-French meeting on 5 February 1940, it was concluded that a joint intervention force would be sent swiftly to Finland, who should provide an official invitation by 1 March 1940. The operations involving 50,000 Allied troops were to begin on 20 March 1940. Meanwhile, the Finnish leaders doubted the real motives of the Allied Powers. They pondered whether Finland would become a proxy in their German war and whether the troops would arrive in time or even be sufficient. Finland never sent an official appeal.[13] However, the battle for Finland gave hope and a moral boost to the Allied war effort.

Moscow gave the Finns the deadline of 1 March 1940 to answer their peace proposal, and the Allies had signified 5 March as the latest delivery date for an assistance appeal. The Finns were asking the Allies whether their intervention could be accelerated, stating that the figure of Allied troops given was too small. The British informed them that 20,000–22,000 soldiers could be sent on 15 March 1940, and they could reach Finland a month later. The French

War Department had led the Finns to anticipate a force of 200,000 men. The Finns wanted to have timely and meaningful assistance: 50,000 troops and 100 bomber aircraft by the end of March 1940. However, they would not appeal against the wills of the Swedish and Norwegian governments. On 29 February 1940, the Finnish Government was ready to enter into discussions about the details of a peace treaty in Moscow. Without British backing, Daladier contacted the Finnish government and unilaterally promised what Finland wanted if the country did not enter into Moscow peace negotiations. If the Finns did not accept peace negotiations, Sweden threatened to withdraw 8,000 volunteers fighting alongside the Finns.[14] The Finnish peace delegation left for Moscow on 7 March, and the Allies gave a final deadline, 12 March 1940, for the assistance appeal. If the Finns would capitulate, no further aid would be sent. Meanwhile, part of the French embarked troops and bombers began their transport for the operation.[15]

A Finnish appeal for assistance to the Allies was not sent by 12 March 1940; instead, a Finnish-Soviet peace treaty was signed in Moscow to end the 105-days-long Winter War. The Finns did not trust that meaningful Allied aid would arrive quickly enough. On the other hand, German *Reichsmarschall* Hermann Göring urged Finland to reach peace, even on heavy conditions, and Sweden, trying to avoid any involvement, urged it to bend at any cost. The Soviet Union prepared for war against Germany, wanted to keep the Allies out of Scandinavia and was ready for peace with Finland. When the Moscow Peace Treaty was signed, the French government fell and the troops on their way were ordered back,[16] but Great Britain avoided a second major war against the Soviet Union.

Along with signing the Moscow Peace Treaty on 12 March 1940, the succumbed Finland ceded ten percent of its land mass. This would include Karelian Isthmus, the second largest city of Viipuri (Vyborg) and the city of Käkisalmi (Priozersk), Ladoga Karelia, the Salla area, the Kalastajansaarento (Rybachi) Peninsula in the Barents Sea and several Finnish islands in the Gulf of Finland. A navy base at Hanko Peninsula, close to the capital city of Helsinki, was leased for 30 years. Bloodletting had a severe effect in Finland: almost 28,000 of some 3.7 million Finns were dead. About some 43,000 Finns were wounded, 15 percent or over 400,000 fled from their homes, and 80,000 children left as refugees abroad during 1939–1945; the Finnish economy and production were dashed due to the lost capacity.[17] Finland was left weakened, Germany's ally, the Soviet Union, now had a grip in the Eastern Baltic Sea and a better standing than earlier in the Barents Sea. This was not what the Allied Powers had been seeking. The Allied plans had fallen flat.

A new railway connection enabled Soviet potential for efficient and effective intervention in northern Finland and Scandinavia.[18] Finland was made to build a Salla railway line through the wilderness to connect the town of Kemijärvi to the Soviet border. On the Soviet side, the NKVD lead Main Administration of Corrective Labour Camps and Settlements or the Gulag government agency built their connection to meet the Finnish railways.[19] It was ominous, considering that Stalin had stated to the Soviet leadership during the war that the rest of the 150,000 members of the Finnish Civil Guards Defence Corps would be killed right away and nothing would be left but the 'bare bones' of a Finnish state.[20] According to Nikita Khrushchev, Stalin had always intended to annex Finland to the Soviet Union.[21] No wonder Finnish expectations for the future were gloomy.

The goals of the Allied Powers were crushed when Finland was crippled, stayed threatened and was not a draughts piece against the German-Soviet Pact. The Soviets stayed alongside the Germans, and they were to gain a route through northern Finland to Swedish ore fields and further to the Norwegian coast, to which Great Britain was exposed. Germany was already trying to reach the coast as well.

After the Moscow Peace Treaty, Germany invaded Denmark and Norway in April 1940. The Allied Finland expeditionary force had not been demolished; rather, it was under arms and was sent to the coast of Norway, but they arrived too late and were too small in number. The German invasion of France and the French collapse forced the Allies to evacuate Norway.[22] Germany, which had invaded five neutral nations within a month, and the hostile Soviet Union surrounded a beaten Finland. An Allied power alone, Great Britain, continued its fight.

### The Continuation War: a Soviet-British victory

After the Allies had lost Norway and were pushed out from all of Scandinavia, France fell in June 1940, most of continental Europe was conquered by the Germans and Britain fought to survive. Finland began to rely on German assistance against the Soviet threat during a 15-month-long period of Finnish-Soviet Interim Peace from 1940–1941.[23]

The Soviet Union did not help Britain, which fought against Germany practically alone with dwindling resources. Pro-British and Allied sentiments were still alive in Finland, although public opinion in the country was accusing them of inability. The Finnish and British military intelligence continued to cooperate. The British planned an Anglo-Finnish trade agreement to keep Finland on the side of the Allies and tried to encourage an idea of a Scandinavian military pact.[24]

In the summer of 1940, the Soviet Union alleged the Baltic states of having pro-Allied sympathies, and it occupied and annexed them as Soviet Republics. Finland signed a large trade agreement with the Soviet Union, but the Soviets tightened their relations with Finland and made various demands, for instance, regarding Petsamo nickel mines owned by a British-Canadian company.[25]

The Germans already had plans for Operation BARBAROSSA evolving and began to pressure Finland. They wanted to transit troops through Finnish territory to the conquered areas in northern Norway like they could pass through the Swedish territory. In exchange, they offered to sell modern weaponry to Finland in August 1940. At once, the Finns were to receive more arms than the Allied had delivered during the whole Winter War. The Finnish-German relationship improved, but the deal did not please the British. The Finns considered the troop transits a counterbalance, as the Soviets had a transit route to their new military base in Hanko. The Finns immediately accepted the German offer because they feared a new Soviet invasion. In September 1940, People's Commissar for Defence of the Soviet Union Marshall Semyon Timoshenko and Chief of Staff Kirill A. Meretskov informed Stalin and Soviet Foreign Minister Vyacheslav Molotov of considerations for a possible war against Finland and occupation of the country. In November 1940, Molotov pointed out in Berlin the Soviet aim to bring the Finnish question to a solution. Adolf Hitler rejected it on the basis that a war in the Baltic Sea Region was undesirable, and Germany needed Finnish wood and nickel. The Soviet Union postponed its actions against Finland. Both the Soviet Union and Germany doomed a Finnish-Swedish plan for a union in December 1940. However, the Germans proceeded to reveal to the Finnish leadership the secret agreement in the Molotov-Ribbentrop Pact from 1939 and their intentions for the Operation BARBAROSSA plan. Finland had already become economically dependent on Germany, and this was even more obvious after the Finnish-German trade agreement was signed in March 1941. In late March, the Finns received information that an anti-Soviet offensive would probably begin on 22 June. Despite their Allied sympathies, the Finnish President Risto Ryti and Mannerheim believed the Germans would win against the Soviet Union,[26] and the Finns believed the lost areas could be recovered with help from the Germans.[27] Finland secretly prepared for a war against the German enemy of the Allied Powers and against the Soviet ally of their German enemy. A collapse of the Soviet-German Pact had been a dream of the Allied Powers, and it was taking place.

Cooperation with the Germans seemed to guarantee that Finland was not left in the hands of the Soviets. Few Finns sympathised with Hitler or national socialism. The Germans accepted that Finland kept a political distance. Yet, 1,400 Finns volunteered for the German SS and fought as part of the Nordland Regiment of the 5th SS Wiking Division.[28] Recruitment was ended when Parliament intervened. After the Finnish-German military consultations in May 1941, German troops began to enter Finland and advance towards the Soviet border and towards the Arctic Sea port of Petsamo. The Allies were keenly interested in this strategic area during the Winter War. Now, the Finns let the British military attaché observe Germany's moves to the north. Furthermore, there was also a group of 300 British Winter War volunteers free and unharmed in the country, and they arranged the possibility to leave for Sweden. However, the Finnish-German cooperation led Britain to end all trade with Finland and to place it under a naval blockade as an enemy-occupied area.[29]

Finland did not formally ally with Germany and the Axis, and the country regarded itself as co-belligerent, but there was a *de facto* alliance. The Finns and Germans had agreed that the Finnish army would advance into Eastern Karelia and keep their positions until the war was over. A general mobilisation of the Finnish army began on 10 June 1941. When Operation BARBAROSSA began on 22 June 1941, the Germans declared that Finland was participating in the offensive. The Soviet Union started to bombard Finnish cities, and Finland declared war on the Soviet Union on 25 June 1941. The Continuation War began, and Finland wished to take back the lost territories of the Winter War and to take Eastern Karelia from the Soviet Union.[30] As long as the Finns could convince the Western Allies that their war was a separate war against the Soviet Union and they were not endangering the Allied war effort against Germany, ties with the British would not break and relations with the non-Allied United States would remain stable.

Operation BARBAROSSA made Prime Minister Churchill at once an ally with the Communist Soviet Union. The Finnish-German co-belligerency made Finland not only useless but also a potential enemy of Britain and the Allies. The Soviet Union retreated rapidly, partly due to Finland, which lost most of the sympathy it had gained among the Allies. Finnish ships in British ports and at sea were impounded by the British.[31]

Britain delivered war materiel to the Soviet Union via a route across the Arctic Sea. This was threatened by the Germans in Norway, and the Finnish-German operations in the north of Finland closed Murmansk and Archangel. The Anglo-Soviet alliance began to show its rough side. British aircraft carrier HMS *Furious* made a sneak attack and bombed Petsamo Harbour on 30 July 1941. The Germans used that Finnish port for their campaign against Murmansk, but only one Finnish ship was sunk and a number of civilians injured. Later, some of the British planes were operating over Finnish air space against the Germans. Finland broke diplomatic relations with Great Britain 'for the time being' on 1 August 1941, emphasising that British Legation was aiding Soviet Intelligence. There was also strong German pressure to cut ties.[32]

As the Germans moved in on Leningrad in September 1941, the Finns had a realistic chance to seal the siege of the city. The Germans were demanding the Finns advance the remaining 60 kilometres to meet their Army Group North and to attack the Murmansk railway. The Finnish government proclaimed to fight its own defensive war. The British Foreign Office declared instead that the Finnish invasion was an integral part of the European war. The Western Powers demanded a Finnish withdrawal from the war, as well as not to cut lend-lease aid via the Murmansk railway.[33]

At the end of November 1941, Finland reluctantly signed the Anti-Comintern Pact. The Soviet Union put more pressure on Britain to declare war on Finland. The British Foreign Office issued an ultimatum to Finland and demanded the Finns cease offensives and withdraw from the front by 5 December 1941. The Finns considered it impossible to stop offensives before reaching positions north of Lake Onega, which would secure the Finnish border. Cessation of the Finnish offensive was close, but the Finns did not believe that a few hours' delay would lead to war, so they kept this information secret. According to Churchill, a declaration of war on Finland was a 'historic mistake' for which he had to bear responsibility, but all had to be done to satisfy the Soviets. In Finland, many leaders could not believe that Britain would actually declare war, and they were shocked and bitter.[34]

On the 24th Finnish Day of Independence, 6 December 1941, the United Kingdom of Great Britain and Northern Ireland declared war on Finland. This was followed by declarations of war by Commonwealth countries including Australia, Canada, India, New Zealand and the Union of South Africa. In addition, the exiled Czechoslovak government supported the Allies and declared war on Finland. Only a day after the British declaration, the Finnish army reached its most eastern destination and halted. On the same day as the declaration, there was a major turn in another front when the Japanese attacked Pearl Harbor. On 11 December 1941, Germany declared war on the United States, which joined the Allies.[35] This made the Finnish relations with the Allied war effort even more complicated, as the both republican and parliamentary democracies were thought to have mutual sympathy and ties.

The United States had delivered crucial civilian aid to Finland when the country gained its independence. There was a Finnish minority in the United States, and 1938 had marked the 300th anniversary celebration of the first Finnish settlement in America. Finland had paid its debts to the United States and enjoyed wide sympathy and major civilian aid during the Winter War. It was even suggested that Finnish refugees be evacuated to Alaska in the worst American scenarios. Instead, Finland aided American refugees escaping Europe via Petsamo. The Finns stated to the Germans that it would be impossible to declare war against the United States.[36]

Finland listened to American views concerning the war. The Finns refused numerous German proposals to cut off the Murmansk railway and to become actively involved in the offensive against Leningrad. This clearly saved some of Finland's reputation in Washington and resulted in the two countries maintaining diplomatic relations.[37] Both of these concessions were also US objectives in relation with Finland, as well as the safeguarding of its Atlantic transport route for the Allied war effort.

The United States had a role in the Battle of the Atlantic, where convoys sailed through the Arctic Sea to the Soviet Union. These convoys were threatened due to German air and sea bases in Norway. The Finns had their role in the theatre. For example, Finnish Intelligence delivered exact information to the Germans about the route of an Allied convoy, PQ17, to Murmansk in the summer of 1942 and route PQ18 in the autumn of 1942. PQ17 was destroyed, and one-third of the PQ18 vessels sank; thereafter, convoy operations stopped for a quarter of a year.[38] It seems Finnish Signal Intelligence might have been noticed but perhaps not taken seriously enough by the Allied Powers in their war effort. However, this did not lead to an open conflict with the United States.

Despite the state of war, there were no military incidents, even between Britain and Finland during the war. A British operation aiming to occupy northern Norway and probably a part of Finland was not realised. A dramatic turning point was close when the Soviets falsely accused the Finns of using German battle gas. The Germans did not deliver battle gas to the Finns, who made a request due to Soviet readiness, capability and observed signs of Soviet gas use. Britain had 20,000 tonnes of chemical weapons in inventory by the end of 1941. From the stock, Churchill decided to deliver to the Soviet Union 1,000 tonnes of mustard gas and 1,000 tonnes of chlorine. Britain assured the Soviets that it would use its chemical arsenal for reprisal on Germany and Finland when an opportunity appeared. In May 1942, Churchill publicly threatened to retaliate against Germany by the use of gas, if necessary. Meanwhile, the Germans had already produced an arsenal of nerve gases: Tabun and Sarin. The Allies did not have these and were behind the Germans.[39] In the worst scenario, Finland could have become a grave arena of modern chemical warfare at the time. In any case, the usage of gas would have made the Allied Powers instigators of uncontrolled and disadvantaged chemical warfare during World War II.

The Finns were worried about the West sacrificing their independence to advance the Allied war effort, but it tried to save relations with the United States without upsetting the Germans.[40] Yet, the Finnish high command became increasingly pessimistic in 1942 about the German military victory, news concerning German atrocities on the Eastern Front and its own serious difficulties in feeding POWs and interned civilians, which was dependant upon German provisions. Two-thirds of the Finnish grain demand was secured by Germany.[41] On 4 June 1942, Hitler's visit to Mannerheim's birthday was an unwelcome surprise. US-Finnish relations deteriorated even further when Mannerheim made a return visit in late June 1942.[42] Furthermore, *Reichsführer* SS Chief Heinrich Himmler visited Finland the next month. He was interested in Finnish Jews,[43] whom the Germans had included in the protocol of the Wannsee Conference,[44] but Finland rejected the Nazi plan to exterminate the Jews. Even as late as in the summer of 1943, Finland managed to negotiate the return of a handful of Jewish citizens from the German-occupied countries.[45] The Finnish stand was recorded in the United States.

Americans had an objective to affect Finnish withdrawal from the war. It introduced an initiative, which Britain attempted to convince its Soviet Ally to accept: a negotiated Anglo-Soviet peace treaty with Finland. It was pointed out that the Finnish government was not pro-German and people were anti-Nazi. A peace treaty would damage the war morale of the Axis and relieve Soviet troops where more were needed.[46] Peace demands made by the Soviets meant a return to the previous Moscow Peace Treaty, which was regarded as a catastrophe by the Finns who were depending on the German import of food, artificial manure and other products. Well-equipped German troops were in the country and controlled all the import routes.[47] In any case, the American initiative revealed that among the Allied Powers essentially each had its own approach to Finland. The United States was active to promote a Finnish-Soviet peace treaty.

The US Chargé d'affaires in Helsinki, Robert M. McClintock, encouraged President Ryti to take Finland to the right side of the war on 21 January 1943. Ryti believed Germany would lose the war, but he hoped that the Soviets would be exhausted before that.[48]

In March 1943, US Ambassador in Moscow Admiral William Standley convinced the Soviets that the United States could persuade Finland to enter into a peace proposal, but they needed to know whether the Soviet government would accept the United States as an intermediary.[49] The Finns were told that the United States was only to bring the Finnish and Soviet governments into contact.[50] When the Americans heard the Soviet terms for peace, they considered those so hard that they decided not communicate them to the Finns. However, the Finnish withdrawal from the war was regarded as so important to the Allied war effort that the matter was not to be dropped.[51] According to Ambassador Standley, the harsh Soviet policy placed the United States 'in the position we wish to avoid, i.e., acting as an intermediary'.[52] On 9 April 1943, Standley was to talk with Molotov to tell him that no further steps would be taken and to make clear that the Finnish government, with regard to terms, was not sounded out.[53]

The German government became alarmed at the rumours of a Finnish withdrawal from the war and began to pressure the Finnish government.[54] The Germans knew about and were furious with the Finnish-US talks, and they demanded the Finns stop negotiations immediately. Finnish Foreign Minister Henrik Ramsey travelled to Germany and stated to Minister for Foreign Affairs Joachim von Ribbentrop on 26 March 1943 that Finland wanted to act openly in its aspirations. Ribbentrop ranted for an hour that the Finnish move would be treason and Germany would act as it wished.[55] To emphasise their view, the Germans cut necessary food supplies to Finland for a month in May 1943.[56] Finland's termination of the SS volunteer battalion could be regarded as a message of goodwill to the United States,[57] as the Finns regarded the United States as the best hope when dealing with the Soviets.

The Finnish War Cabinet decided to contact the United States in early August 1943. President Ryti believed the US would not leave Finland alone with the Soviets, especially when US-Soviet relations were believed to have worsened at the time. In September began secret discussions in Lisbon between the Finnish Chargé d'affaires in Lisbon Taavi Pohjanpalo, the Counsellor of the US Legation George F. Kennan and US Military Attaché Lt. Col. Robert Solberg, who came from the Special Operations Branch of the OSS.[58] According to President Ryti, the Americans explained their plans for post-war Europe, where Finland was placed in the 'northern group' of countries including England, Scandinavian countries and Holland, because of their development, mentality and way of thinking. These northern countries would reinforce Europe against both Bolshevism and Nazism. President Ryti wrote that for the first time, he heard an American official state that Finland must not make separate peace with Russia because it is not in the interests of the Allies. The Finns were encouraged to keep their army strong and develop relations with the United States because there would be an Allied landing in northern Norway. The greatest danger of all for both Finland and the United States would be, in Solberg's opinion, a Soviet-German rapprochement.[59]

Finnish Prime Minister Edwin Linkomies believed the American approach was simply a scam, and he was sceptical of inquiries made by the Americans. Kennan questioned whether Finland would fight against the Americans if they landed in northern Norway.[60] US Secretary of State Cordell Hull was convinced that the Finnish government would regard an American landing or even British landing as the best solution for avoiding the worst scenario in the war. The Finns were believed without doubt to have the desire to make their offer contingent on Allied entry into northern Norway. They would get a route to the outer world without remaining at the mercy of the Germans. Hull foresaw that the Finns calculated an American landing would also serve the purpose of ejecting the German troops from the country.[61] Chief of Staff to the Commander in Chief, Fleet Admiral William D. Leahy, was sure the Finns wished for Allied entry into northern Norway, but it had to be rejected. Employment of Anglo-American troops for ejecting German troops from Finland and affording insurance against Soviet entry into the country were regarded as logistically and militarily impractical tasks. At the time, the Finnish front was regarded as relatively quiet. It was concluded that the Soviet Union would be the best evaluator of military benefits to the Allied war effort brought by Finnish withdrawal from the war.[62]

In the autumn of 1943 onwards, an active opposition group formed within the Finnish parliament, which urged the beginning of peace talks with the Soviet Union.[63] It also had American contacts with the OSS in Stockholm.[64] Therefore, both the Finnish government and the opposition were collaborating with the Americans. However, the future of Finland was more in the hands of the Allied Powers than in American hands.

The Allied Powers agreed during the Tehran Conference in late November 1943 that Finland could remain a sovereign state if it accepted the Soviet peace demands. A separate peace with Finland would be possible, but the Soviets were not to demand unconditional surrender. Finland and its resources would be utilised in the Allied campaign against Germany. US President Franklin Delano Roosevelt was vaguely positive on Finland, but Churchill stated the Finns were to be punished. Britain was ready to accept hard Soviet terms for a Finnish armistice, even when the Finns regarded them as utterly impossible and a deathblow to independence. Furthermore, Finland had already turned these terms down in the secret, Swedish-mediated peace negotiations.[65] US military intelligence gathered vast evidence about Soviet hostility against the Finns, which was feared to lead to genocide. Within the Joint Strategic Survey Committee, a plan was drafted for the US Department of Interior about transporting the Finns to Alaska. Due to the peace negotiations, the proposed plan was held in abeyance and kept secret.[66] However, Finland had a highly different position in the Soviet, British and American war efforts. The Finns themselves chose rather to fight than to accept the Soviet terms, which were estimated as unbearable.

The Finnish government and High Command did not daydream about a victory. After the Soviet breakage of the siege of Leningrad in January 1944 and Germany's retreat to northern Estonia, fierce Soviet air raids, intensified Soviet partisan killing and terror raids against civilians within Finland were clear signs of exacerbation of the situation. In the media, a hard campaign was intensified by the Allied Powers to push Finland to yield. Yet, Finland was cautious about being caught between the German troops in Estonia and in northern Finland, and the Soviet demand for huge war reparations was unacceptable to the Finns. In any case, the Allied Powers condemned the Finnish stand.[67] On 13 May 1944, the Allied Powers offered a declaration to the people of Yugoslavia, Bulgaria, Romania and Finland, where Finland was declared for the first time an Axis vassal.[68]

When the landings took place in Normandy, the Red Army launched its Summer Offensive and forced the Finnish Army to retreat from the Karelian Isthmus and Eastern Karelia. There was an imminent threat of an outright Soviet victory and occupation. On 22 June 1944, the Soviets answered the Finnish peace request and demanded an unconditional surrender, which surprised the other Allied Powers. German Foreign Minister Ribbentrop made an immediate, surprise visit to Finland. The Finns pleaded for immediate assistance from Germany, which demanded a binding alliance in exchange. The future did not bode well for the Finns. On 25 June 1944, the Soviet News Agency *TASS* radioed views published in the government official newspaper *Izvestija* and declared the Finns as 'barbarians', 'cutthroats', 'mass murderers', worse-than-Germans who were pretending a lack an understanding of why they should pay so dearly and who would not be forgiven nor unpunished – the time of 'payback' was near. The phrasing referred to Finnish civilian internment camps in the occupied Soviet areas, where detainees died in high numbers of malnutrition and disease.[69] On 26 June 1944, President Ryti sent a personal agreement to Germany stating that Finland would not make a separate peace without prior German approval. This move led to breaking off Finnish-American diplomatic relations. On 3 July 1944, the Swiss government was entrusted with American interests and US assets in Finland.[70] The United States was a step closer to joining the Anglo-Soviet Alliance war effort against Finland.

On the frontlines, the Soviets and Finns fought fiercely, and the Finns lost again in Viipuri. In the battle of Tali-Ihantala, the Finns stopped the Soviet offensive. The peace discussions were reopened, but Finland still had some 500,000 troops. Land forces consisted of fourteen infantry divisions, one armoured division and six brigades and over a thousand field guns.[71] The Allied war effort needed to consider that force.

On 29 August 1944, the Soviet Union sent its conditions for accepting a Finnish delegation to peace negotiations in Moscow, but it did not demand unconditional surrender any more. The Finnish parliament accepted the Soviet demands on 2 September 1944: 113 to 43 for accepting the terms.[72]

The Soviet Union wanted to head to Berlin before the Western Allies, and a significant number of troops, could be freed from the Finnish front, where some 220,000 German troops would be isolated in northern Finland.[73] Mannerheim ordered Finnish troops to cease fighting on 4 September 1944, and Soviet firing stopped one day later. On 19 September 1944, Finland and the Soviet Union signed the Moscow Armistice Treaty.[74] The Allies, especially the Soviets, did not have to worry about fighting in the Arctic nor its Atlantic supply line near Murmansk, and a large number of Germans were stuck in the north.

The British considered Finland to belong to the Soviet sphere of influence. The case of Finland was not brought to the consideration of the European Advisory Commission but rather left to the Soviets. The Finns did not realise that and made futile appeals to the British to intervene. The British Political Representative in Helsinki, Francis Shepherd, stated to the Finns that Moscow would ensure that the year 1941 would not be repeated and times would be hard for Finland. The Finns were left to believe that the non-intervention was done for defending their independence. Historian H.P. Evans described this as 'nothing short of deception'.[75]

The Finns demobilised their troops according to the armistice treaty but hid arms for 35 battalions in case of a Soviet deception.[76] Some of the Finns who led this arms cache operation left the country and eventually joined the US Army.[77] The Finns also sold their intelligence material concerning the Soviets to the United States and Britain.[78] At the same time, the Finns carried out the armistice terms and advanced the Allied war effort.

## The Lapland War: the vanquished fights for the Allied Powers

Finland broke off diplomatic relations with Germany. In response, the Germans aimed to block the Gulf of Finland, preparing to invade Ahvenanmaa (The Åland Islands) and landing on Suursaari Island on 14 September 1944. Finland was thrown into a second war, with the first still ongoing against the Soviet-British Alliance, the second against Germany. The Germans were defeated by the Finns and had to surrender. Later, German POWs were turned over to the Soviets according to the Moscow Armistice Treaty. A German attempt of a *coup d'état* failed miserably in an anti-Nazi country. Instead, into Finland arrived the first Soviet members of an Allied Control Commission to observe the implementation of the Moscow Armistice Treaty on 22 September 1944.[79] Fighting in Suursaari benefited Finnish-Soviet relations, and the Finns were fighting for the Allied war effort.

In northern Finland, 108,885 civilians were evacuated from the way of retreating German troops, which had a long route to Finnmark in northern Norway. On their way, they resisted the advance of some 60,000 Finnish troops and scorched down 40 to 46 percent of the buildings in Lapland, severely mining the large area.[80]

Germany's northern flank was unprotected, and Baltic and German ports and coastal areas specifically became targets of the Soviets utilising Finnish ports and airfields in accordance with the Moscow Armistice. For instance, Soviet submarine S-13, operating from a Finnish port, sunk German *MV Wilhelm Gustloff* on 30 January 1945. Over 9,000 people died in the largest loss of life in a single vessel sinking in history.[81] Overall, the Finnish territory was utilised for the Allied war effort.

As a relief to the Finns, the last German troops left northern Finland on 27 April 1945. Looting Soviet troops, which, despite the armistice treaty and absence of Germans, kept hold in Suomussalmi, Kuusamo and Ivalo, Lapland, left by 25 September 1945.[82] In this case, the Soviets put aside the Moscow Armistice Treaty and Finnish protests.

Non-occupied Finland had its elections, parliament and government intact but was under the surveillance of the Allied Control Commission, consisting of Soviets and a few British, who tried to keep an eye on their new Soviet adversaries. The British curtailed the Finnish military to prevent Soviet attempts to utilise it, even though Finland did not become the main arena for internal Allied disagreements. Officially, peace between Finland and the Soviet-British Alliance went into effect when the Soviet Union finally ratified the Paris Peace Treaty on 15 September 1947.[83]

In the Winter War, the Franco-British Alliance tried to send an expeditionary force to Finland that would have made it join the Allies. The attempt failed. The Germans took the initiative, and Finland fought against the Soviet-British war effort in the Continuation War. Finally, the vanquished Finland fought for the Allied Powers in the Lapland War, but it was not regarded as one of the Allies. It was eventually put under the surveillance of the Allied Control Commission, and the Allied Powers throughout the war had diversified views, interests and actions regarding Finland – in all shades of grey.

## Notes

1 *From Hitler's Doorstep: The Wartime Intelligence Reports of Allen Dulles, 1942–1945*, ed. with Commentary by Neal H. Petersen (University Park, PA: Pennsylvania State University Press, 1996), 532.

2 Markku Ruotsila, *Churchill and Finland: A Study in Anticommunism and Geopolitics* (London and New York: Routledge, 2005), 65, 69.

3 Craig Gerrard, *The Foreign Office and Finland: Diplomatic Sideshow* (London: Routledge, 2005), 71, 83; Boris Vadimovich Sokolov, "The Soviet Policy towards the Baltic States in 1939–41," in *Northern European Overture to War, 1939–1941: From Memel to Barbarossa*, ed. Michael H. Clemmesen and Marcus S. Faulkner (Leiden and Boston: Brill, 2013), 76.

4 Jukka Nevakivi, "Finnish Perceptions of Britain's Role during the War, 1939–41," in *From War to Cold War: Anglo-Finnish Relations in the 20th Century*, ed. Juhana Aunesluoma (Helsinki: SKS Finnish Literature Society, 2006), 33.

5 Ruotsila, *Churchill and Finland*, 69–73, 107.

6 Henrik Meinander, "Finland and the Great Powers in World War II: Ideologies, Geopolitics, Diplomacy," in *Finland in World War II: History, Memory, Interpretations*, ed. Tiina Kinnunen and Ville Kivimäki (Leiden and Boston: Brill, 2012), 59; Ruotsila, *Churchill and Finland*, 65, 69.

7 Gerrard, *The Foreign Office and Finland*, 82, 84, 86, 88, 90, 92, 95, 98–9, 136; J. Lee Ready, *Forgotten Allies: The Military Contribution of the Colonies, Exiled Governments, and*

*Lesser Powers to the Allied Victory in World War II, Volume 1: The European Theater* (Jefferson, NC: McFarland Company, 2012), 347; Henrik Tala, *Talvisodan Ranskalaiset Ratkaisijat: Ranskan Apu Suomelle 1939–1940* (Helsinki: Minerva, 2014), 49–51, 56, 72–4, Ch. 4.

8  Gerrard, *The Foreign Office and Finland*, 93–7, 100, 105.

9  Gerrard, *The Foreign Office and Finland*, 101–2, 109.

10  Henry Oinas-Kukkonen, *Finalaska: Unelma suomalaisesta osavaltiosta* (Tampere: Vastapaino, 2017), 12–13, 33, 82, 86, 93–7, 175, 238 n. 69.

11  Gerrard, *The Foreign Office and Finland*, 104–8, 111–12, 116–17, 119.

12  Ruotsila, *Churchill and Finland*, 75–8, 81; Gerrard, *The Foreign Office and Finland*, 99–100, 106.

13  Ruotsila, *Churchill and Finland*, 77–8, 82, 90–5.

14  Meinander, "Finland and the Great Powers," 61.

15  Gerrard, *The Foreign Office and Finland*, 119–21, 124–7, 129; Tala, *Talvisodan Ranskalaiset Ratkaisijat*, 179–84, 190–1, 196–7, 251–4.

16  Sokolov, "The Soviet Policy," 79–81; Gerrard, *The Foreign Office and Finland*, 129; Meinander, "Finland and the Great Powers," 60, 66; Tala, *Talvisodan Ranskalaiset Ratkaisijat*, 254, 257, 272.

17  Marianne Junila, "Wars on the Home Front: Mobilization, Economy and Everyday Experiences," in *Finland in World War II: History, Memory, Interpretations*, ed. Tiina Kinnunen and Ville Kivimäki (Leiden and Boston: Brill, 2012), 217; Meinander, "Finland and the Great Powers," 60, 70, 74.

18  Gerrard, *The Foreign Office and Finland*, 129.

19  See e.g. Christopher Joyce, "The Gulag in Karelia: 1929 to 1941," in *The Economics of Forced Labor: The Soviet Gulag*, ed. Paul R. Gregory and Valery Lazarev (Stanford, CA: Hoover Institution Press, 2003), 177–8.

20  Georgi Dimitrov and Banac Ivo, *The Diary of Georgi Dimitrov, 1933–1949* (New Haven: Yale University Press, 2003), 124.

21  *Khrushchev remembers*. With an introd., commentary, and notes by Edward Crankshaw. Trans. and ed. Strobe Talbott (Boston: Little Brown & Company, 1970), 127, 128.

22  Ready, *Forgotten Allies*, 9–12.

23  Ruotsila, *Churchill and Finland*, 104.

24  Nevakivi, "Finnish Perceptions of Britain's," 34–6; Ruotsila, *Churchill and Finland*, 102.

25  Meinander, "Finland and the Great Powers," 67.

26  Sokolov, "The Soviet Policy," 87, 89; Meinander, "Finland and the Great Powers," 68–9, 71; Ruotsila, *Churchill and Finland*, 105; Nevakivi, "Finnish Perceptions of Britain's," 34–5.

27  Pekka Visuri, "The Making of the Paris Peace Treaty: Military Strategy and British Policy Towards Finland, 1944–47," in *From War to Cold War: Anglo-Finnish Relations in the 20th Century*, ed. Juhana Aunesluoma (Helsinki: SKS Finnish Literature Society, 2006), 48.

28  Mauno Jokipii, "Suomen SS-pataljoona toisessa maailmansodassa," in *Jatkosodan Pikkujättiläinen*, ed. Jari Leskinen and Antti Juutilainen (Helsinki: Werner Söderström Osakeyhtiö, 2007), 69.

29  Ruotsila, *Churchill and Finland*, 106; Nevakivi, "Finnish Perceptions of Britain's," 36–9.

30  Meinander, "Finland and the Great Powers," 71–2.

31  Ruotsila, *Churchill and Finland*, 102–3, 108.

32  Ohto Manninen, "War between Friends: Britain and Finland. 1941–44," in *From War to Cold War: Anglo-Finnish Relations in the 20th Century*, ed. Juhana Aunesluoma (Helsinki: SKS Finnish Literature Society, 2006), 42–4; Ruotsila, *Churchill and Finland*, 107; Nevakivi, "Finnish Perceptions of Britain's," 38.

33  Ville Kivimäki, "Introduction: Three Wars and Their Epitaphs: The Finnish History and Scholarship of World War II," in *Finland in World War II: History, Memory, Interpretations*, ed. Tiina Kinnunen and Ville Kivimäki (Leiden and Boston: Brill, 2012), 2; Meinander, "Finland and the Great Powers," 73; Nevakivi, "Finnish Perceptions of Britain's," 40.

34  Ruotsila, *Churchill and Finland*, 109, 111, 113–14, 118; Nevakivi, "Finnish Perceptions of Britain's," 39; Manninen, "War between Friends," 44.

35  *Treaty of Peace with Finland, Paris, 10th February, 1947.* Presented by the Secretary of State for Foreign Affairs to Parliament by Command of His Majesty (London: His Majesty's Stationery Office, 1948), 3; Meinander, "Finland and the Great Powers," 73–4; Manninen, "War between Friends," 45; Vít Smetana, *In the Shadow of Munich: British Policy Towards Czechoslovakia From the Endorsement to the Renunciation of the Munich Agreement (1938–1942)* (Prague: Charles University in Prague, Karolinum Press, 2014), 286, 287.

36  Oinas-Kukkonen, *Finalaska*, 22, 29–30, 55–6, 68, 79, 177, 186–91.

37  Meinander, "Finland and the Great Powers," 78.

38  Alf R. Jacobsen, "Scandinavia, Sigint and the Cold War," in *Secrets of Signals Intelligence during the Cold War and Beyond*, ed. Matthew M. Aid and Cees Wiebes (London and Portland, OR: Frank Cass Publishers, 2001), 240 n. 12; Manninen, "War between Friends," 45.

39  Patrick Coffey, *American Arsenal: A Century of Waging War* (Oxford and New York: Oxford University Press, 2014), 150–3; Ruotsila, *Churchill and Finland*, 124; Atso Haapanen, *Taistelukaasut: Suomen varautuminen kaasusodankäyntiin talvi-ja jatkosodassa* (Hämeenlinna: Karisto Oy, 2017), 166–7, 175, 181.

40  R. Michael Berry, *American Foreign Policy and the Finnish Exception: Ideological Preferences and Wartime Realities* (Helsinki: Suomen Historiallinen Seura, 1987), 208, 212.

41  Meinander, "Finland and the Great Powers," 74–5.

42  Henrik O. Lunde, *Finland's War of Choice: The Troubled German-Finnish Coalition in WWII* (Philadelphia, PA and Newbury: Casemate, 2011), 257–8.

43  Peter Longerich, *Wannseekonferenz. Der Weg zur 'Endlösung'* (München: Pantheon Verlag, 2016), 115, 156, 197 n. 375.

44  Besprechungsprotokoll, Besprechung über die Endlösung der Judenfrage. Berlin, Großen Wannsee, Nr. 56/58, 20.1.1942. [Stamp:] Geheime Reichssache!, 6. Deutsches Historisches Institut, Deutsche Geschichte in Dokumenten und Bildern (DGDB). Last Accessed 3 August 2018. www.ghwk.de/fileadmin/user_upload/pdf-wannsee/dokumente/protokoll-januar1942_barrierefrei.pdf.

45  Tapani Harviainen, "The Jews in Finland and World War II," *Nordisk Judaistik/Scandinavian Jewish Studies* 21, no. 1–2 (2000): 162.

46  Ruotsila, *Churchill and Finland*, 125.

47  Meinander, "Finland and the Great Powers," 75–6.

48  The Chargé in Finland (McClintock) to the Secretary of State, Telegram. Helsinki, January 21, 1943. *Foreign Relations of the United States: Diplomatic Papers* (Hereafter *FRUS*) 1943: Vol. 3. The British Commonwealth, Eastern Europe, The Far East (Washington: United States Government Printing Office, 1963), 222; Osmo Apunen and Corinna Wolff, *Pettureita ja patriootteja: Taistelu Suomen ulko-ja puolustuspolitiikan suunnasta 1938–1948* (Helsinki: Suomalaisen Kirjallisuuden Seura, 2009), 166, 168.

49  The Acting Secretary of State to the Ambassador in the Soviet Union (Standley). Washington, March 9, 1943. *FRUS* 1943: Vol. 3, 247–8; The Ambassador in the Soviet Union (Standley) to the Secretary of State. Telegram, Moscow, March 13, 1943. *FRUS* 1943: Vol. 3, 249.

50  The Secretary of State to the Chargé in Finland (McClintock). Washington, March 20, 1943. *FRUS* 1943: Vol. 3, 247–51.

51  Memorandum by the Acting Chief of the Division of European Affairs (Atherton) to Under Secretary of State Welles and the Secretary of State. Undated. but received by Mr. Welles on March 29, 1943. *FRUS* 1943: Vol. 3, 257.

52  The Ambassador in the Soviet Union (Standley) to the Secretary of State. Telegram, Moscow, April 6, 1943. *FRUS* 1943: Vol. 3, 262.

53  The Secretary of State to the Ambassador in the Soviet Union (Standley). Telegram 210, Washington, April 9, 1943. *FRUS* 1943: Vol. 3, 263.

54  The Secretary of State to the Ambassador in the Soviet Union (Standley). Telegram 212, Washington, April 9, 1943. *FRUS* 1943: Vol. 3, 263.
55  *Käymme omaa erillistä sotaamme': Risto Rytin päiväkirjat 1940–1944*, ed. Ohto Manninen and Kauko Rumpunen (Helsinki: Edita, 2006), 254.
56  Apunen and Wolff, *Pettureita ja patriootteja*, 204–5, 212.
57  Berry, *American Foreign Policy and the Finnish Exception*, 303–5.
58  *Risto Ryti. Sota-ajan Muistelmat 1939–1944*, ed. Hannu Rautkallio ([Espoo]: Kustannusosakeyhtiö Paasilinna, 2012), 306, editor's commentary on 308; Apunen and Wolff, *Pettureita ja patriootteja*, 236–7.
59  *Risto Ryti. Sota-ajan Muistelmat 1939–1944*, 307–10.
60  Edwin Linkomies, *Vaikea aika: Suomen pääministerinä sotavuosina 1943–44* (Helsinki: Otava, 1996), 264–5; Apunen and Wolff, *Pettureita ja patriootteja*, 241, 243.
61  Cordell Hull to William D. Leahy. Department of State, Washington, September 1, 1943. Enclosure B to JCS 496, 4, 5. United States National Archives, Records of the War Department General and Special Staffs, RG 165, Entry 421, Box 250.
62  William D. Leahy to Cordell Hull, September 7, 1943. Enclosure B to JCS 469/1. United States National Archives, Records of the War Department General and Special Staffs, RG 165, Entry 421, Box 250.
63  Meinander, "Finland and the Great Powers," 76.
64  Berry, *American Foreign Policy and the Finnish Exception*, 366–7.
65  Ruotsila, *Churchill and Finland*, 128; Visuri, "The Making of the Paris Peace Treaty," 49–50; Meinander, "Finland and the Great Powers," 76.
66  Oinas-Kukkonen, *Finalaska*, 171–4.
67  Anssi Vuorenmaa, "Neuvostopartisaaneja Suomen rintamilla," in *Jatkosodan Pikkujättiläinen*, ed. Jari Leskinen and Antti Juutilainen (Helsinki: Werner Söderström Osakeyhtiö, 2007), 510–19; Meinander, "Finland and the Great Powers," 78–9.
68  Juhani Suomi, *Mannerheim: Viimeinen kortti? Ylipäällikkö-presidentti* (Helsinki: Kustannusosakeyhtiö Siltala, 2013), 57.
69  Asiakirja 23. Tass-tietotoimiston julkaisemia radiouutisia Neuvostoliitosta. No. 4850. Sunnuntai, 25. kesäkuuta 1944. in *Sotasyyllisyyden asiakirjat*, ed. Hannu Rautkallio ([Espoo]: EC-kirjat, 2006), 96–8.
70  Berry, *American Foreign Policy and the Finnish Exception*, 413; Suomi, *Mannerheim*, 80–1; Lunde, *Finland's War of Choice*, 303; Ruotsila, *Churchill and Finland*, 130.
71  Visuri, "The Making of the Paris Peace Treaty," 50.
72  Lunde, *Finland's War of Choice*, 317–18.
73  Suomi, *Mannerheim*, 107; Lunde, *Finland's War of Choice*, 271.
74  Erkki Käkelä, "Aseveljeyden siteet katkeilevat," in *Jatkosodan Pikkujättiläinen*, ed. Jari Leskinen and Antti Juutilainen (Helsinki: Werner Söderström Osakeyhtiö, 2007), 1118; Suomi, *Mannerheim*, 244, 284; Ruotsila, *Churchill and Finland*, 130; Meinander, "Finland and the Great Powers," 83.
75  Helena P. Evans, "British Involvement in the Finnish Peace: The Paris Peace Treaty, 1947: A Mere Formality," in *From War to Cold War: Anglo-Finnish Relations in the 20th Century*, ed. Juhana Aunesluoma (Helsinki: SKS Finnish Literature Society, 2006), 91–2, 95, 101; Suomi, *Mannerheim*, 274–5, 287, 309.
76  Visuri, "The Making of the Paris Peace Treaty," 53.
77  Oinas-Kukkonen, *Finalaska*, 95.
78  Suomi, *Mannerheim*, 330–1.
79  Eero Elfvengren, "Lapin sota ja sen tuhot," in *Jatkosodan Pikkujättiläinen*, ed. Jari Leskinen and Antti Juutilainen (Helsinki: Werner Söderström Osakeyhtiö, 2007), 1129, 1130; Ready, *Forgotten Allies*, 352; Suomi, *Mannerheim*, 74, 147, 179, 256, 272–3; Lunde, *Finland's War of Choice*, 330–1.
80  Ready, *Forgotten Allies*, 352–3; Elfvengren, "Lapin sota ja sen tuhot," 1128, 1132, 1149.
81  Carlos Perez del Castillo, "The Wilhelm Gustloff," in *Military and Political Incidents: Security Forum 2009*, ed. Alexandre Vautravers and Nicholas Burtscher (Geneva, Switzerland: Webster University, 2010), 114, 117–18.

82  Elfvengren, "Lapin sota ja sen tuhot," 1148; Juha Pohjanen, "Venäläisongelma Koillis-Lapissa," in *Jatkosodan Pikkujättiläinen*, ed. Jari Leskinen and Antti Juutilainen (Helsinki: Werner Söderström Osakeyhtiö, 2007), 1147.
83  Ruotsila, *Churchill and Finland*, 131, 135; Visuri, "The Making of the Paris Peace Treaty," 52–5.

## Bibliography

Apunen, Osmo, and Corinna Wolff. *Pettureita ja patriootteja: Taistelu Suomen ulko-ja puolustuspolitiikan suunnasta 1938–1948*. Helsinki: Suomalaisen Kirjallisuuden Seura, 2009.

Berry, R. Michael. *American Foreign Policy and the Finnish Exception: Ideological Preferences and Wartime Realities*. Helsinki: Suomen Historiallinen Seura, 1987.

Coffey, Patrick. *American Arsenal: A Century of Waging War*. Oxford and New York: Oxford University Press, 2014.

Del Castillo, Carlos Perez. "The Wilhelm Gustloff." In *Military and Political Incidents: Security Forum 2009*, ed. Alexandre Vautravers and Nicholas Burtscher. Geneva, Switzerland: Webster University, 2010.

Deutsches Historisches Institut, Deutsche Geschichte in Dokumenten und Bildern (DGDB). Besprechungsprotokoll, Besprechung über die Endlösung der Judenfrage. Berlin, Großen Wannsee, Nr. 56/58, January 20, 1942. Last Accessed 3 August, 2018. www.ghwk.de/fileadmin/user_upload/pdf-wannsee/dokumente/protokoll-januar1942_barrierefrei.pdf.

Dimitrov, Georgi, and Banac Ivo. *The Diary of Georgi Dimitrov, 1933–1949*. New Haven: Yale University Press, 2003.

Elfvengren, Eero. "Lapin sota ja sen tuhot." In *Jatkosodan Pikkujättiläinen*, ed. Jari Leskinen and Antti Juutilainen. Helsinki: Werner Söderström Osakeyhtiö, 2007.

Evans, Helena P. "British Involvement in the Finnish Peace: The Paris Peace Treaty, 1947: A Mere Formality." In *From War to Cold War: Anglo-Finnish Relations in the 20th Century*, ed. Juhana Aunesluoma. Helsinki: SKS Finnish Literature Society, 2006.

Gerrard, Craig. *The Foreign Office and Finland: Diplomatic Sideshow*. London: Routledge, 2005.

Great Britain, Foreign Office. *Treaty of Peace with Finland: Paris, 10th February, 1947*. Presented by the Secretary of State for Foreign Affairs to Parliament by Command of His Majesty. London: His Majesty's Stationery Office, 1948.

Haapanen, Atso. *Taistelukaasut: Suomen varautuminen kaasusodankäyntiin talvi-ja jatkosodassa*. Hämeenlinna: Karisto Oy, 2017.

Harviainen, Tapani. "The Jews in Finland and World War II." *Nordisk Judaistik/Scandinavian Jewish Studies* 21, no. 1–2 (2000): 157–66.

Jacobsen, Alf R. "Scandinavia, Sigint and the Cold War." In *Secrets of Signals Intelligence during the Cold War and Beyond*, ed. Matthew M. Aid and Cees Wiebes. London and Portland, OR: Frank Cass Publishers, 2001.

Jokipii, Mauno. "Suomen SS-pataljoona toisessa maailmansodassa." In *Jatkosodan Pikkujättiläinen*, ed. Jari Leskinen and Antti Juutilainen. Helsinki: Werner Söderström Osakeyhtiö, 2007.

Joyce, Christopher. "The Gulag in Karelia: 1929 to 1941." In *The Economics of Forced Labor: The Soviet Gulag*, ed. Paul R. Gregory and Valery Lazarev. Stanford, CA: Hoover Institution Press, 2003.

Junila, Marianne. "Wars on the Home Front: Mobilization, Economy and Everyday Experiences." In *Finland in World War II: History, Memory, Interpretations*, ed. Tiina Kinnunen and Ville Kivimäki. Leiden and Boston: Brill, 2012.

Käkelä, Erkki. "Aseveljeyden siteet katkeilevat." In *Jatkosodan Pikkujättiläinen*, ed. Jari Leskinen and Antti Juutilainen. Helsinki: Werner Söderström Osakeyhtiö, 2007.

Khrushchev, Nikita S. *Khrushchev remembers*. With an introduction, commentary, and notes by Edward Crankshaw. Trans. and ed. Edward Crankshaw and Strobe Talbott. Boston: Little Brown and Company, 1970.

Kivimäki, Ville. "Introduction: Three Wars and Their Epitaphs: The Finnish History and Scholarship of World War II." In *Finland in World War II: History, Memory, Interpretations*, ed. Tiina Kinnunen and Ville Kivimäki. Leiden and Boston: Brill, 2012.

Linkomies, Edwin. *Vaikea aika: Suomen pääministerinä sotavuosina 1943–44*. Helsinki: Otava, 1996.

Longerich, Peter. *Wannseekonferenz. Der Weg zur "Endlösung"*. München: Pantheon Verlag, 2016.

Lunde, Henrik O. *Finland's War of Choice: The Troubled German-Finnish Coalition in WWII*. Philadelphia, PA and Newbury: Casemate, 2011.

Manninen, Ohto. "War between Friends: Britain and Finland, 1941–44." In *From War to Cold War: Anglo-Finnish Relations in the 20th Century*, ed. Juhana Aunesluoma. Helsinki: SKS Finnish Literature Society, 2006.

Manninen, Ohto, and Kauko Rumpunen, ed. *'Käymme omaa erillistä sotaamme': Risto Rytin päiväkirjat 1940–1944*. Helsinki: Edita, 2006.

Meinander, Henrik. "Finland and the Great Powers in World War II: Ideologies, Geopolitics, Diplomacy." In *Finland in World War II: History, Memory, Interpretations*, ed. Tiina Kinnunen and Ville Kivimäki. Leiden and Boston: Brill, 2012.

Nevakivi, Jukka. "Finnish Perceptions of Britain's Role during the War, 1939–41." In *From War to Cold War: Anglo-Finnish Relations in the 20th Century*, ed. Juhana Aunesluoma. Helsinki: SKS Finnish Literature Society, 2006.

Oinas-Kukkonen, Henry. *Finalaska: Unelma suomalaisesta osavaltiosta*. Tampere: Vastapaino, 2017.

Petersen, Neal H. ed. *From Hitler's Doorstep: The Wartime Intelligence Reports of Allen Dulles, 1942–1945*, with Commentary by Neal H. Petersen. University Park, PA: Pennsylvania State University Press, 1996.

Pohjanen, Juha. "Venäläisongelma Koillis-Lapissa." In *Jatkosodan Pikkujättiläinen*, ed. Jari Leskinen and Antti Juutilainen. Helsinki: Werner Söderström Osakeyhtiö, 2007.

Rautkallio, Hannu. ed. *Risto Ryti: Sota-ajan Muistelmat 1939–1944*. [Espoo]: Kustannusosakeyhtiö Paasilinna, 2012.

Rautkallio, Hannu. ed. *Sotasyyllisyyden asiakirjat*. [Espoo]: EC-kirjat, 2006.

Ready, J. Lee. *Forgotten Allies: The Military Contribution of the Colonies, Exiled Governments, and Lesser Powers to the Allied Victory in World War II*. Vol. 1, The European Theater. Jefferson, NC: McFarland Company, 2012.

Ruotsila, Markku. *Churchill and Finland: A Study in Anticommunism and Geopolitics*. London and New York: Routledge, 2005.

Smetana, Vít. *In the Shadow of Munich: British Policy Towards Czechoslovakia from the Endorsement to the Renunciation of the Munich Agreement (1938–1942)*. Prague: Charles University in Prague, Karolinum Press, 2014.

Sokolov, Boris Vadimovich. "The Soviet Policy towards the Baltic States in 1939–41." In *Northern European Overture to War, 1939–1941: From Memel to Barbarossa*, ed. Michael H. Clemmesen and Marcus S. Faulkner. Leiden and Boston: Brill, 2013.

Suomi, Juhani. *Mannerheim: Viimeinen kortti? Ylipäällikkö-presidentti*. Helsinki: Kustannusosakeyhtiö Siltala, 2013.

Tala, Henrik. *Talvisodan ranskalaiset ratkaisijat: Ranskan apu Suomelle 1939–1940*. Helsinki: Minerva, 2014.

United States National Archives and Record Administration (NARA), College Park, Maryland. Record Group 165. Records of the War Department General and Special Staffs.

U.S. Department of State. *Foreign Relations of the United States: Diplomatic Papers 1943, Volume III: The British Commonwealth, Eastern Europe, The Far East.* Washington: United States Government Printing Office, 1963.

Visuri, Pekka. "The Making of the Paris Peace Treaty: Military Strategy and British Policy Towards Finland, 1944–47." In *From War to Cold War: Anglo-Finnish Relations in the 20th Century*, ed. Juhana Aunesluoma. Helsinki: SKS Finnish Literature Society, 2006.

Vuorenmaa, Anssi. "Neuvostopartisaaneja Suomen rintamilla." In *Jatkosodan Pikkujättiläinen*, ed. Jari Leskinen and Antti Juutilainen. Helsinki: Werner Söderström Osakeyhtiö, 2007.

# 5    The illusion of enemy

## The fifth column scare in Britain

*Robert Loeffel*

By the end of June 1940, after their stunning successes in Norway, Belgium, Holland and France, it seemed that the Wehrmacht was unbeatable. Amongst the reports of the effectiveness of the Luftwaffe and their army, a more insidious factor was identified as having a significant role in the German success. The concept of the 'fifth column' had only recently emerged in the Spanish Civil War,[1] yet it was attributed as being the decisive element in the German success. The fifth column was believed to represent a giant network of spies and saboteurs whose jobs ranged from blowing up bridges, changing street signs and collecting intelligence to generally undermining the home front with defeatism, gossip and rumour.

The fifth column never existed as it was imagined and was a symptom of the distrust generated by defeat. In fact, it was its ill-defined nature that gave the term such impact in 1940. The very flimsiness of the evidence of its existence created the sense that it was more effective than it ever could be. It was in this atmosphere in mid-1940, with a continent apparently riddled with saboteurs and traitors, that the British people confronted the fifth column threat. More so than in other countries 'defeated' by the fifth column in 1940, Britain had ready-made grounds for fears of an internal enemy. They had a significant migrant population – over 60,000 had recently arrived from Germany and Italy – and the added fear of an active separatist terrorist organisation in the Irish Republican Army (IRA).[2] While these elements served as the basis for fifth column suspicions in the early part of the war, it was the fear of those in the upper echelons of power that defined the early British fears of the fifth column.

This chapter will argue that the real strength of the British fear of the fifth column was not in recently arrived Jewish migrants or communists but instead lay in a deep-seeded discord and suspicion of the upper echelons of society and those with right-wing sympathies.[3] The actions of a number of connected individuals in Norway, Belgium and France all seemed to confirm that the fifth column operated amongst the powerful in society and that, as a consequence, rumours linked to the subversive activities of the elite had the most carry and influence. It also will be argued that, in reality, the fifth column threat in Britain was not taken seriously after June 1940. The steps taken by the British government to tighten security, intern aliens, arrest British fascist leaders and create a nationwide militaria generated a sense of trust and cohesion on the home front. In comparison to other home fronts in 1940, the fifth column scare in both Canada and Australia reached overpowering proportions. Playing out a safe distance from the war, it resulted in riots, public hysteria, extensive rumours and fears and saturation reportage in the press.[4]

Recently, Robin Prior made a spirited defence of the harmony and resolve within the British home front, asserting that 'the solidarity of the population was no myth'.[5] However, others have identified that there is a more nuanced picture. Geoffrey Field has noted how many suspected 'reactionaries' were willing to 'adopt a British form of Petainism'.[6] It has been noted that British Home Intelligence and other sources detected a rise in class feeling in general.[7] John Costello suggested that there was a widespread sympathy for fascism in the British government and a desire for an accommodation with the Nazis after September 1939.[8] Richard Griffith built upon this work and recognised the strong support for peace with the Nazis amongst the upper strata of British society. Griffith has argued that among the members of the pro-German group 'The Link' were 11 Members of Parliament (MP) and 4 peers.[9] While many conservatives rejected fascism, some did share the anti-Semitism sentiment their social prejudice produced.[10] Griffith also has argued that support for the Germans was wider than just the upper echelons of British society, arguing that the positive reviews given to Arthur Bryant's pro-Nazi history *Unfinished Victory* are indicative of pro-Nazi views among the 'intellectual elite'.[11] Griffith identifies that the period after May 1940 was a 'watershed for many',[12] as public opinion instead shifted towards a resolute stand behind the war.

Before the German onslaught in April 1940, there were clear indications that members of the upper class were feared to be the real traitors in Britain. A May 1939 *Daily Mirror* editorial warned that those who were against an alliance with the Russians were usually made by individuals with 'brand new titles . . . obscure peers and negligible knights'; these people had enjoyed 'tea parties attended by Nazi agents and contact men. The whispering chorus'.[13] When the war began, these suspicions grew louder. Lord Londonderry, the former Minister for the Air, became the subject of rumours that he had been arrested as a German spy.[14] Books and spy films of the time echoed these suspicions. The film *Four Just Men* (released February 1940) had a traitor who was a prominent government MP, while *Sons of the Sea* (released April 1940) had a spy ring operating within a British Naval College. In March 1940, the purportedly factual *Hitler's Spy Ring* was published, describing the extent of German espionage in England and implicating an Air Marshal and an Admiral in spying activities. Early in the book, the Gestapo Chief in Britain boasted to his new recruit that they have 'people working for them who move in the highest social and political circle'.[15]

In March 1940, the Duke of Bedford was identified in the press as the leader of a 'group of fascists' responsible for a leaflet that demanded the government make peace with Nazi Germany.[16] The British domestic counter-intelligence and security agency MI5 assumed that Bedford had obtained the peace proposal directly from 'German sources'.[17] A week later, it was widely reported that Lord Redesdale was banned from taking his daughter and friend of Hitler, Unity Mitford, back to his private island off Scotland as it happened to be in a protected zone. That this action created widespread rumour was confirmed by Redesdale, who took it upon himself to write to *The Times* and reject the 'undercurrent of suspicion' that was being made against his family. He also conceded that, in seeking an accommodation with Nazi Germany, he had been 'in good company'.[18] A few weeks later, the public were reminded that Oswald Mosley, leader of the British Union of Fascists (BUF), was his son-in-law.[19]

It was at the start of the campaign in Norway in April 1940 that the fifth column became a phenomenon, and its early reportage emphasised that it members were from the political and military elite. On 13 April 1940, Carleton Greene, the British correspondent for the *Daily Telegraph*, identified the Port Commander at Narvik as well as the Commander of the Narvik area, Colonel Konrad Sundlo, as traitors.[20] An individual who was to become synonymous with the fifth column was Major Vidkun Quisling. Quisling, a failed right-wing politician and former Norwegian Defence Minister, had tried to mount a pro-German coup, commandeering a radio station and announcing he had formed a 'national government'. The Germans had no idea of his actions, and this in no way helped them in the fighting. Both Sundlo and Quisling were widely featured in British press reports and were credited with ensuring German success. The highly regarded correspondent Leland Stowe declared that the reason for the Germans' success was due to 'a few highly placed Norwegian civilians and defence officials'.[21] Despite the complete debacle of Quisling's attempted coup, the story of the fifth column grew. The focus on Quisling as the arch fifth columnist gave legitimacy to the whole idea of the influence subversion and that it was the members of society's elite who would provide the most valuable service.

On 15 April 1940, *The Times* newspaper implied the need to watch the well-placed with the subheading 'Watch for Quislings'.[22] The invention of the term "Quislings", readily adopted in many other Allied countries, was originated by the British. Considering its origin, it is not too outlandish to suggest that the Quisling label itself came to refer particularly to potential traitors in the upper class.[23] The term became more popular than the fifth column in the press in describing fears of subversive activity. Indicating the fears of the widespread presence of the fifth column amongst the elite, a few days later it was also reported that, 'Norwegians here say that it would be a mistake to think that Norwegian officers as a class are imbued with the Quisling (traitor) spirit'.[24] Such generous sentiments were not shared by all in England. Linking the new threat of the fifth column to their existing fascist enemies, the *Daily Mirror* reminded its readers that it was the Duke of Bedford, amongst other 'men of position', who had demanded that the government make peace with Nazi Germany.[25]

The events in Norway soon fostered the sentiment that those in high places posed the greatest risk as fifth columnists. At the Scottish Trade Union Congress, the British government was accused of harbouring fifth columnists 'even in its cabinet'. The recent loss of HMS *Royal Oak* and *Courageous* were cited to prove that 'there are people in high places in this country who have to be cleared out'.[26] First reported in a number of regional papers on 25 April, the *Daily Mirror* identified Mary Allen – pictured on the front page in uniform – the head of the Women's Volunteer Service (WVS), as an avowed fascist.[27] So far in the war, Ms Allen's contribution had been to give a public lecture where she warned that young British soldiers were at risk of being molested by young women.[28] The WVS, it was noted, had 630,000 women in its ranks. The following day – but buried on page 3 – the paper admitted that Allen (a known oddity) was actually in charge of her own much smaller and unofficial Women's Auxiliary Service and not the WVS.[29] Despite this correction, the following day the paper's agony aunt 'Cassandra' described her as a 'jackbooted, peak-capped, monocled slip of feminity (sic)' and declared that 'the time is long overdue to give this fifth column a quietus'.[30] In such a situation, it is expected that the public were unsure about who to suspect. A Mass Observation survey in late April 1940 found general confusion on what the fifth column actually meant. This report noted that the 'general definition of the fifth column is extremely variable and often exceedingly vague'.[31] For others, that the fifth column was a product of high society was self-evident. The Labour MP for Sedgefield John Leslie noted that, 'It was true that this latest example of Nazi aggression had been facilitated by traitors. But they were not traitors of the working class. The Quislings came from the upper and middle classes'.[32]

The experiences of their continental Allies with the fifth column gave the British the impetus to strengthen their home security. In early May, the British Chiefs of Staff Committee made clear their belief that the fifth column had been vital to German success. As far as the Committee was concerned, the absence of the discovery of any subversive activity in Britain thus far merely highlighted the fifth column's 'level of secrecy' and 'reinforce[d]' the view that it was real: 'such activities will only take place as part of a prear-ranged military plan'.[33] By the middle of May, the newly appointed British Prime Minister Winston Churchill felt that there was a need to further 'stiffen' measures already taken against possible subversion.[34] Before the next War Cabinet meeting, the Home Secretary approached MI5 for their assessment of the chances that home-grown British fascists were members of the fifth column.[35] It was after the German invasion of Western Europe on 10 May 1940 that the fifth column scare was broadened to incorporate fears of any and everyone, not just the connected. On 14 May, the British Envoy to the Netherlands, Nevile Bland, identified – in a memorandum circulated in Whitehall – the fifth column as the primary reason for the Germans' success. He related his suspicions that even the 'the paltriest kitchen maid' – linking treason particularly to females – as well as refugees from Germany and Aus-trian should be 'interned at once'.[36]

The image that the real fifth column was connected to those in government was enhanced by the uncovering of a traitor in the American Embassy. A cypher clerk at the embassy, Tyler Kent was passing decoded US secret communiques to a Russian woman working for German intelligence. On 20 May 1940, after watching Kent for a number of weeks, MI5 raided his home, discovering thousands of stolen telegrams, some between Churchill and Roosevelt. Kent was an associate of the MP for Pebbles and Nazi sympathiser Archibald Maule Ramsay.[37] It was in these circumstances that the Cabinet decided in favour of widespread detentions of the far right on 22 May as per the amended Regulation 18B (1A). The next day, British fascist leader Sir Oswald Mosley and Archibald Ramsay, were interned along with a number of their associates. All these arrests were given front-page attention across the country, and prominence was given to the four women arrested, which including Norah Dacre-Fox and Anne Brock-Griggs.[38] Adding extra spice, the articles in the *Daily Mirror*, *Birmingham Mail*, *Birmingham Daily Gazette* and *Daily Record* all featured photographs of the female fascists being taken into custody.[39] Brock-Griggs had already been identified by MI5 as the leader of the British Union Services Corps and responsible for putting the groups' 'emergency plan into action'.[40] Another arrested woman, Mrs Muriel Whinfield, was identified as the wife of Lt-Colonel E.C.L. Whinfield.[41] The arrest of members and the leadership of the BUF enhanced the fear that the fifth columnists were amongst the British establishment. In the aftermath of these arrests, Lord Devonshire stated in the House of Lords that these arrests had 'wrecked the possibility of fifth columnist aid in an east coast invasion'.[42] Indicating the public's belief on who constituted the fifth column, Home Intelligence noted that these arrests were met with 'strong approval' from the community.[43]

In the midst of these arrests and despite Bland's call that all should be suspected, popular rumour indicated that the public viewed the major fifth column threat as coming from those in the upper strata of society. On 21 May, a Home Intelligence report noted that a popular rumour amongst the public was that the French C-in-C General Gamelin had been shot as a 'fifth columnist'.[44] A few days later, it was determined that the 'great majority of rumours . . . are about the fifth column'.[45] A letter to the editor from a local headmaster in Belfast argued that suspicions of Quislings should not be of refugees but of 'people in business or professions'.[46] This view was shared in other parts of the country; the *Yorkshire Post and Leeds Intelligencer* noted that 'If there is a fifth column in this country, it will consist not of refugees but of Nazi sympathisers'.[47] Adding another dimension, another letter to the editor noted that 'women are even more dangerous in this respect than men'.[48]

However, what propelled the fifth column scare in Britain to its greatest heights was the decision of King Leopold of Belgium to surrender his forces on 28 May 1940. Newspapers varied on the same theme, linking Leopold to the new terms for treason, such as 'King Quisling'[49] and 'King of the fifth column'.[50] Absorbing this rhetoric, Home Intelligence noted a general

'increase in fifth column stories' due to his capitulation.[51] Across seven centres, criticism of Leopold was recorded; in Reading (in Southern England),
the public regarded Leopold as a 'super-Quisling'.[52] The day after Belgium's
surrender, in the North Midlands, the 'Defection of Leopold' was being 'suggested as a sign of fifth column activities in upper strata of society'.[53] Similar
sentiments were shared in Leeds, where it was noted that rumours suggested
that Leopold's actions confirmed the view that the fifth column came from
'the top and not the bottom'.[54] Such views were also expressed in the press.
The 29 May edition of *Bystander* noted that 'defeatists. They pervade the
"upper classes" in London like a stinking blight'.[55] In this context, the public
were far more concerned with harbouring suspicions against those from the
ruling clique rather than kitchen maids or refugees. J.C. Little of the Labour
Supply Board commented that 'There may be a movement here as formidable
as that which was revealed in Belgium, Holland, Denmark and Norway'.[56]

On 31 May, Home Intelligence reported on the 'great anxiety' recorded at
the news of the appointment of Lord Tredegar to command the paratrooper
regiment at Newport as his 'fascist sympathies were well-known'.[57] It also
noted that

> suspicion and distress has shifted from Leopold to "high quarters" . . .
> suspicion is beginning to attach itself to "Royalty". The Duke of Wind-
> sor is frequently mentioned and note should be taken of the persistent
> rumours about the members of the Royal Family being in Canada.[58]

The royal family was mindful of accusations of pro-German feelings. In late
June, the King's Lord Steward, the Duke of Buccleuch, was forced to resign
due to his pro-Nazi/anti-war stance.[59] Such examples indicate a particular
suspicion that the real fifth column existed in the upper classes of Britain.
Reflecting these suspicions, a Ministry of Information pamphlet from June
1940 warned:

> There is a fifth column in Britain. Anyone who thinks that there isn't,
> and that it can't happen here', has simply fallen into the trap laid by the
> fifth column itself. For the first job of the fifth column is to make people
> think that it does not exist. In other countries the most *respectable* and
> *neighbourly citizens* turned out to be fifth columnists when the time came.
> The fifth column does not only consist of foreigners.[60]

The fear that some in the British establishment harboured pro-Nazi sentiments was identified in the assessment by Colonel William Donovan, who
arrived in Britain in July 1940. Donovan, at the time an informal US emissary
to Britain but later the Director of the Office of Strategic Services (OSS),
reported to the US Secretary of the Navy Frank Knox the link between conservative party policy and the general suspicion some on the upper class posed
in terms of a fifth column threat. His report noted that 'The fear of radicalism

so prevalent among the rich and ruling classes in England and France was used as a potential argument for a more friendly and tolerant feeling towards the Nazi regime'.[61]

At this point, the authorities began to organise themselves against the potential of the subversive threat. Regional leaderships were established in the event of invasion, and the creation of the Home Guard on 14 May did much to allay public fears. On 2/3 June 1940, the Home Guard shooting of four people who failed to respond to road checkpoints indicated the seriousness with which they took their security tasks.[62] However, by the end of May, as the British Army began the Dunkirk evacuation, an inter-departmental Home Defence (Security) Executive was set up under Lord Swinton to deal exclusively with the fifth column.[63] A memorandum by the newly appointed Chief of the Imperial Staff, Sir John Dill, made clear his beliefs on the effectiveness of the fifth column. On 9 June 1940, he reported to a Chief of Staff Committee meeting that he was 'convinced that the potentialities of fifth column activities and the extent to which they have undoubtedly been developed necessitate their being regarded as an integral part of modern warfare'.[64] The seriousness of the threat is illustrated as Dill recommended that if any fifth columnists were discovered, they should simply be 'shot at once'.[65] By the end of June 1940, 27,000 enemy aliens and 1,335 British citizens identified as having fascist credentials were interned. The fifth column scare had a positive impact on the British security services. Initially, the scare generated such a flood of reports from the public that the security services found it literally impossible to deal with all of them. The official historian of British wartime intelligence concluded, 'MI5 was near to breaking down completely by the spring of 1940', which led to Churchill dismissing its chief, Sir Vernon Kell, on 11 June 1940, for 'not doing enough' to uncover the fifth column.[66]

While the authorities were inundated with reports of suspicious activities across the country, only a handful of these were substantiated or could be called genuine attempts to aid the enemy. A small number of prosecutions were carried out against individuals for a range of crimes. These mainly involved attempts to create organisations for the spreading of propaganda.[67] According to MI5's own assessment, its agents were responsible for the detention of 43 individuals, of which 30 had been members of the BUF or similar; only 13 cases involved aliens.[68] These small numbers of cases indicate that the threat of internal subversion was small and that those who were willing to try and undermine the war effort were quickly stopped.

The level of rumours and stories in British society in late May is reflected in the volume of newspaper stories. For all British dailies, the peak month for articles concerned with the fifth column was May 1940. However, even during this desperate time, the number of articles was not excessive when compared to other Allied countries. For example, in Australia, with far fewer newspapers and a smaller population, fifth column stories were double those seen in Britain at the same time and actually increased in number in June 1940. Of course, self-censorship could explain this; however, it would also account for the strength of rumours and stories on the home front. However, the number of newspaper stories indicates that the fear of the fifth column was never that serious.

By July 1940, with the Luftwaffe battling it out with the RAF above England and the threat of German invasion always present, a sober appraisal of the fifth column threat was starting to take hold. In the middle of July 1940, MI5 reported that it was 'very much inclined to doubt whether an organised fifth column existed'.[69] Such sentiments were shared by the public. Malcolm Smith has noted that *The Express*, which kept up the pressure on the fifth column after July 1940, found itself out of step as the public grew tired of the impression that Britain continued to be a hive of treason.[70] In the House of Commons, Churchill admitted that he 'always thought that it [the fifth column] was exaggerated in these islands'.[71] However, fears that fascist sympathisers among the elite in British society still existed. When Churchill told the British public that he did 'not believe there are many [traitors in Britain]',[72] the *Daily Mirror* observed that 'to do severe damage, a few only are needed in high places'.[73] Similarly, the *Birmingham Daily Gazette* felt inclined to remind its readers that 'the most serious enemies may be British citizens of perverted patriotism occupying social and political positions'.[74] At about the same time, the Ministry of Information felt the need to demand that '*all* classes in this country should be reminded of the value of civilisation'.[75] As if reinforcing the existing prejudice, by mid-August, the US assessment of the fifth column was made public. In response, the press noted that it was believed that subversion was made up of 'dissatisfied members of the ruling class, including society women'.[76]

## A fifth column comes to life

As the war continued, the fifth column no longer served the same purpose to the authorities as in 1940. Only half as many newspaper articles used the fifth column term in 1941 and 1942. This was despite the fact that, for example in Australia, the fifth column was virtually blamed for the Allies' defeat in Greece in April 1941 and was seen as a primary reason for the Japanese successes in February 1942. In Britain, MI5 noted every press report of cheating on ration cards, black market activity and so on and listed these reports as fifth column activity.[77] The cinema remained a popular venue for fifth column topics. In *Sherlock Holmes and the Voice of Terror* (released August 1942), the Nazi spy was identified as senior British official Sir Evan Barham, who had been substituted by a German lookalike while he was a POW during World War I. In *Went the Day Well* (released December 1942), a group of Germans pretending to be British soldiers occupy an English village. The fifth columnist is revealed as the village squire. In 1942, MI5 decided to test the extent of dissent by 'creating' its own fifth column network. This involved entrapping disaffected Britons with an MI5 operative posing as a 'Gestapo' officer; from 1942 until the end of the war, MI5 had effectively organised its own fifth column of Nazi sympathisers. The man used to pose as a Gestapo officer was Eric Roberts. Roberts was brought into MI5 in May 1940 and was chosen because of his knowledge of right-wing groups but also for his appeal to those of the upper classes, being a bank manager by profession.[78]

When this file was released in 2014, contemporary press reportage of this group presents it as a highly dangerous entity.[79] However, a reading of the transcripts of the taped conversations between the MI5 operative and his 'agents' reveal a very different situation. Far from being a well-organised and highly efficient spy network, the transcripts show these individuals giving faulty information, lacking basic knowledge of military equipment, distrusting and resentful of their fellow 'agents' and being highly unbalanced people. An intelligence report compiled late in the war identified the main individuals involved. These were two German migrants, Hans Kohout and Adolf Herzig, but the driving forces behind this small band of would-be traitors were actually British women. These women were identified as Nancy Brown, Eileen Cleave and Marita Perigoe. These women seemed far more pro-Nazi and zealous than their male colleagues. It is obvious from the files that these women took particular pleasure in the idea that they were helping Germany win the war. These women were all identified as once being members of the BUF, but they had all left the group as they felt it was not radical enough. They appeared merciless, being recorded while inciting their 'Gestapo' liaison to increase the activities and celebrating German bombings and the casualties they caused in England.

MI5 noted three elements that motivated the individuals in the wider group to commit treason. These were Nazi propaganda, the desire for change and anti-Semitism. Nazi propaganda, both within Britain and Germany, had a clear effect on those susceptible to its ideas and, as the report noted, influenced people who lived an 'empty hum-drum life'. The desire for change was contrasted to the 'pre-war apathy and stagnation in this country'.[80] Anti-Semitism was probably the strongest element which linked all these individuals together,[81] although a last linking factor would be their shared anti-communism beliefs. But as far as the main protagonists were concerned, their motivations varied. Nancy Brown's incentive for helping the Germans was her simply being 'fed up' with the war.[82] Marita Perigoe expressed a similar sentiment.[83] She explained that she felt that she 'want[ed] to do anything to hasten on the end [of the war] now'.[84] She also expressed regret at the numbers of Americans and Canadians in the country as an influencing factor.[85] Eileen Cleave expressed a particular dislike for Winston Churchill, explaining that she had lost a cousin at Gallipoli and she had 'never forgiven him for it'.[86] Eileen also said she preferred to be in German hands than American as she 'would get better treatment'.[87]

The motivations of the men involved can be considered rather prosaic – money being often mentioned.[88] A new potential male recruit mentioned by one of the women was only prepared to work for the country that 'pays him the best'.[89] Kohout determined that Nazi Germany was heading towards defeat and was solely determined to prepare a new network of contacts for the next conflict in 20 years. What is also striking is the dislike for each other from within the group itself. It was evident that, among these fascists, it was only the skill and money of the 'Gestapo' officer that was able to keep these disparate individuals together.[90] As most of the activities of this group happened towards the end of the war, what indicates both their zeal and their stupidity was their motivation to continue, even when it was evident the war was lost. Nancy Brown, for one, identified that gullibility was obviously a factor, noting in late 1943 that 'I thought the Germans were falling back in accordance with some plan and I still think so'.[91]

The menacing character given to the fifth column case came mainly from the 'secret' information it was said that these individuals were prepared to divulge. Intent to pass on information is evident; however, the quality of this intelligence is questionable. 'Windows' radar jamming technology and jet aircraft are two pieces of information that were in danger of going to the Germans. However, a closer examination of what these agents knew indicates that these secrets were not in so much danger. The only reference to jet aircraft in the entire file is when what is described as a 'tailless' aircraft is mentioned.[92] One section of the transcript records Eileen in a state of total confusion: 'Eileen continued to be most undecided about how many engines the bombers had and whether the fighters were fighters – and finally announced that they might not have been fighters at all'.[93]

About their fifth column 'case', MI5's own summary of this group speaks volumes. They were variously described as 'semi-lunatics' and 'pathological'; TM Shelford, from MI5's F3 counter-subversion section, assessed 'that the majority of them . . . are unbalanced mentally, [and are] unable to organise anything effective'.[94] It was also noted that they tended to 'exaggerate the pro-German tendencies of their associates', therefore making themselves and the strength of their 'movement' seem greater than it really was. It is worth speculating how much the British authorities embolden these individuals by setting up this group in the first place.

## Conclusion

The British public proved impervious to the fifth column fear of 1940. In Britain, the fifth column scare was tempered by the events in Norway, Belgium and France, which seemed to show that the real threat lay in those who had demonstrated fascist tendencies and were in positions of authority or were from the ruling classes. When these elements did not show their hand in Britain by the end of June 1940, the fifth column scare largely evaporated in the eyes of the British public. This was due to a combination of government action, organising the Home Guard, reorganising of the security services and interning selected fascists and refugees, which all contributed to allying public fears of subversion. The early identification of the elite in society as the potential fifth column – identifying specific individuals – rather than anonymous refugees or German migrants may have actually helped to more quickly dissipate these fears. Nevertheless, the authorities were keen to flesh out what fascist threat existed on the British home front. The fifth column 'created' by MI5 towards the back end of the war can be interpreted as an indication of the effectiveness of the British security services. The surprising aspect of this case was the high number of women who took part and the fact that, after 1942, the impeding defeat did not diminish their desire to support the Nazi cause.

## Notes

1   The term was picked up by the press almost immediately; see *New York Times*, 16 October 1936, 2, and in Great Britain, the *Western Morning News*, 16 October 1936, 7; *The Times*, 20 October 1936, 16.

2   See Paul McMahon, *British Spies and Irish Rebels: British Intelligence and Ireland, 1916–1945* (London: Boydell Press, 2008), 120–2.

3   In Britain, those who desired better relations with Nazi Germany were organised and connected. Established in July 1937, The Link attracted pro-Nazis and anti-Semites and was opposed to war with Germany and numbered about 4,300 members. Created in 1934, The January Club was specifically founded to attract right-wing support among the English establishment. The following year, the Anglo-German Fellowship was founded amongst conservative MPs.

4   See Larry Hannant, "Fear Sweeps the Nation: The Fifth Column Crisis," *The Beaver* 73, no. 6 (December 1993–January 1994): 25–6. Also Robert Loeffel, *The Fifth Column in World War II: Suspected Subversives in the Pacific* (Basingstoke: Palgrave, 2015).

5   Robin Prior, *When Britain Saved the West: The Story of 1940* (New Haven: Yale University Press, 2015), 261.

6   Geoffrey G. Field, *Blood, Sweat, and Toil: Remaking the British Working Class, 1939–1945* (London: Oxford University Press, 2011), 307.

7   Field, *Blood, Sweat, and Toil*, 77.

8   John Costello, *Ten Days That Saved the West* (London: Bantam, 1991).

9   Richard Griffiths, *Patriotism Perverted: Captain Ramsay, the Right Club, and British Anti-Semitism, 1939–1940* (London: Faber & Faber, 2011), 121.

10   Stuart Ball, *Portrait of a Party: The Conservative Party in Britain 1918–1945* (London: Oxford University Press, 2013), 65. Also see Simon Haxey, *Tory MP* (London: Gollancz, 1939).

11   Richard Griffiths, "The Reception of Bryant's Unfinished Victory: Insights into British Public Opinion in Early 1940," *Patterns of Prejudice* 38, no. 1 (2004): 24.

12   Richard Griffiths, "The Reception of Bryant's Unfinished Victory", 22.

13   *Daily Mirror*, 9 May 1939, 13. Similar views were expressed in the *News Chronicle*, 6 May 1939, 10.

14   *Daily Mirror*, 20 September 1939, 14. Also reported in other dailies.

15   E7, *Hitler's Spy Ring* (London: Hurst & Blackett, 1940), 6.

16   *Daily Mirror*, 1 March, 1940, 1.

17   KV-2-793-1, report 5 December 1941. *The National Archives of the UK*, "Records of the Security Service," KV, London 2018. http://discovery.nationalarchives.gov.uk/details/r/C160; Bedford had also written an article in the BUF newspaper *Action* in January 1940.

18   *The Times*, 9 March 1940, 4. Also reported in the *Birmingham Mail*, 9 March 1940, 8; *Daily Mirror*, 11 March, 1940, 10–11.

19   *Daily Mirror*, 9 May 1940, 11. While by the end of the month it was noted that the public wanted to know why she had not been interned; see Jeremy A. Addison, Paul Addison, and Paul Crang, *Listening to Britain: Home Intelligence Reports on Britain's Finest Hour* (London: Bodley Head, 2010), 60.

20   *The Mail*, 13 April 1940, 1.

21  *Chicago Daily News*, 14 April 1940, 1.

22  *The Times*, 15 April 1940, 5.

23  The fact that Quisling was part of the upper strata of society was reinforced when it was widely reported on 12 June 1940 that his OBE had been withdrawn.

24  Quoted in *The People*, 21 April 1940, 2.

25  *Daily Mirror*, 15 April 1940, 6.

26  *Evening Dispatch*, 25 April 1940, 5. Full quote in *Aberdeen Weekly Journal*, 2 May 1940, 4.

27  *Manchester Evening News*, 25 April 1940, 3; *Yorkshire Evening Post*, 25 April 1940, 5; *Evening Despatch*, 25 April 1940, 7; *Daily Mirror*, 26 April 1940, 1.

28  *Bath Chronicle and Weekly Gazette*, 13 April 1940, 17.

29  *Daily Mirror*, 26 April 1940, 1 and 27 April 1940, 3.

30  *Daily Mirror*, 27 April 1940, 6.

31  Fifth column pilot test, 29 April 1940. SxMOA1/1/5/4/19, The Keep Archive, Brighton.

32  *Hartlepool Northern Daily Mail*, 6 May 1940, 4.

33  CAB 80/10, "Chiefs of Staff Committee Report," 2 May 1940, *The National Archives of the UK*, "Records of the Cabinet Office CAB," London, 2018. http://discovery.nationalarchives.gov.uk/details/r/C9025063.

34  CAB 65/7/23, "War Cabinet Minutes," 18 May 1940.

35  They reported that British fascists were unlikely to have 'anything to do' with fifth column activities, noting that evidence pointed in the other direction, such as the recent pro-British instructions BUF leader Sir Oswald Mosley had given to the fascist press in Britain. CAB 65/7/28, "War Cabinet, Minutes," 22 May 1940.

36  Alfred Simpson, *In the Highest Degree Odious: Detention without Trial in Wartime Britain* (Oxford: Clarendon Press, 1992), 107. Using existing social prejudices, Jewish refugees became a focus of official suspicions. It was circulated that all German Jews had to have their passports stamped with a 'J'; if this appeared on any other pages besides the first page or was an irregular shape, it meant they were actually working for the Germans. It was also believed that Jews who had their passports stamped with the acronym 'WWJ' (which actually stood for 'economically valuable Jews') were Jews who had family members still in Germany who were being held hostage in exchange for the refugee working for the Gestapo. D1918, S35, "MI memorandum," 6 February 1940. *National Archives of Australia*. "Nazi activities in South Australia during World War II."

37  Kent's arrest appeared in the press by early June.

38  *Daily Mirror*, 24 May 1940, 1; *West Morning News*, 24 May 1940, 3; *Daily Record*, 24 May 1940, 5. Later, on 7 July 1940, the former Director of Naval Intelligence Admiral Sir Barry Domvile and his wife were also interned.

39  *Daily Mirror*, 24 May 1940, 9; *Birmingham Mail*, 24 May 1940, 8; *Birmingham Daily Gazette*, 24 May 1940, 1; *Daily Record*, 24 May 1940, 5.

40  KV 2, 2677 2, "Miss Cleave Note, 15 January 1940 & 25 January 1940."

41  *Daily Mirror*, 25 May 1940, 3.

42  *Daily Mirror*, 24 May 1940, 1.

43  Addison, Addison, and Crang, *Listening to Britain*, 21 May 1940, 34–5.

44  Ibid., 17.

45  Addison, Addison, and Crang, *Listening to Britain*, 29 May 1940, 29.

46  *Belfast News-Letter*, 23 May 1940, 4.

47  *Yorkshire Post and Leeds Intelligencer*, 23 May 1940, 3.

48  *Belfast News-Letter*, 21 May 1940, 4.

49  *Liverpool Echo*, 28 May 1940, 6.

50  *Daily Mirror*, 29 May 1940, 7.

51  Addison, Addison, and Crang, *Listening to Britain*, 28 May 1940, 44.

52  Ibid., 51.

53  Addison, Addison, and Crang, *Listening to Britain*, 29 May 1940, 50.

54  Addison, Addison, and Crang, *Listening to Britain*, 28 May 1940, 55.

55  *The Bystander*, 29 May 1940, 5.

56  *Liverpool Echo*, 30 May 1940, 6. Repeated same day in *Coventry Evening Telegraph*, the *Hartlepool Northern Daily Mail*, the *Express and Echo* and the *Derby Daily Telegraph*.

57  Addison, Addison, and Crang, *Listening to Britain*, 28 May 1940, 62.

58  Addison, Addison, and Crang, *Listening to Britain*, 31 May 1940, 58.

59  *Northampton Mercury*, 28 June 1940, 7. See also, Deborah Cadbury, *Princes at War: The British Royal Family's Private Battle in the Second World War* (New York: Bloomsbury, 2015), 141.

60  INF 1/251, "Pamphlet, 29 June 1940," My emphasis. *The National Archives of the UK*, "Records Created or Inherited by the Central Office of Information," INF, London, 2018. http://discovery.nationalarchives.gov.uk/details/r/C160.

61  William Donovan and Edgar Mowrer, *Fifth Column Lessons for America* (Washington, DC: American Council of Public Affairs, 1940), 1. This report was widely published in the British press in August 1940. See *Manchester Guardian*, 23 August 1940, 2.

62  Simon Mackenzie, *The Home Guard: A Military and Political History* (Oxford: Oxford University Press, 1995), 59.

63  CAB 65/7/39, "Minutes, 28 May 1940."

64  CAB 80/12, "Memoranda, 9 June 1940."

65  CAB 80/12, "Memorandum, 9 June 1940."

66  Francis Hinsley and Charles Anthony Goodall Simkins, *British Intelligence in the Second World War* (London: Cambridge University Press, 1979), 4, 32. See also McMahon, *British Spies and Irish Rebels*, 306.

67  On 4 June, it was reported that William Saxon Steer – a former BUF member – was tried for distributing 'sticky back' notices in public places advertising the existence of the NBBS (New British Broadcasting Station), a German propaganda radio station. He was given seven years. *The Times*, 4 June 1940. A month later, BUF member Rex Freeman and his mother were convicted of a similar activity; he was given five years and his mother one year; see *Manchester Guardian*, 4 July 1940, 2.

68  KV 4 227, "Report 1945," "Report on the work of MS (recruitment and operation of agents) during the Second World War."

69  Hinsley and Simkins, *British Intelligence in the Second World War*, 59.

70  Malcolm Smith, *Britain and 1940: History, Myth, and Popular Memory* (Abington: Routledge, 2000), 36.

71  House of Commons, Hansard, 364, 15 August 1940. See Hinsley and Simkins, *British Intelligence in the Second World War*, 59. By December 1940, MI5 had issued instructions that there had been 'no positive evidence' at all that the Germans were using the IRA as a fifth column; see McMahon, *British Spies and Irish Rebels*, 356.

72  Winston Churchill, 14 July, 1940, BBC Broadcast, London.

73  *Daily Mirror*, 16 July 1940, 5.

74  *Birmingham Daily Gazette*, 6 July 1940, 4.

75  INF 257, "Report, 1 July 1940." Combating FC and defeatism, Minister of Information. *The National Archives of the UK*.

76  *Daily Mirror*, 21 August 1940, 1.

77  INF 336, "Fifth Column in the Press," *The National Archives of the UK*.

78  KV 2 3874, "Correspondence with Colonel Harker," 31 May 1940, "Eric Arthur Roberts, alias Jack King: British: The Fifth Column Case."

79  *The Times*, 28 February 2014, 5. See various papers emphasised the alleged size of the group, describing it as 'numbering in the hundreds' *Daily Mail*, 28 February 2014 and 'a vast network', *Huffington Post*, 28 February 2014, 3. Dwelling on the information that was passed on, including information about the 'secret' radar jamming technology (Windows), amphibious tanks and experimental jet aircraft; see *The Mirror*, 27 February 2014, 2.

80  KV/2/3800, "undated report," "Mary Marita Margaret Perigoe, alias Brahe."

81  Hatred of Jews mentioned several times, 8 November 1944, 5, 10 October 1943, 12, a list of Jews to be killed (17 May 1943, 5/6).

82  KV2/3874, "The Fifth Column Case," 29 August 1942, 16 & 19.

83  KV2/3874, "The Fifth Column Case," 18 August 1942, 10.
84  KV2/3874, "The Fifth Column Case," 29 August 1942, 10.
85  Ibid., 18.
86  KV2/3874, "The Fifth Column Case," 18 August 1942, 15.
87  KV2/3874, "The Fifth Column Case," 29 August 1942, 25.
88  Mentions of money in the file are extensive. Pays Nancy (8 November 44, 6) mention of money (1 July 1943, 13) sabotage for money (1 July 1943, 15).
89  Eric Arthur Roberts, The Fifth Column Case, KV2/3874, 5 May 1943, 6, NAUK.
90  KV2/3874, "The Fifth Column Case," 17 November 1942, 5. Marita Perigoe was recorded as saying: 'The male population of this country is absolutely non-existent, they're no use whatsoever, you could exterminate the lot of them and find it would be a better world'.
91  KV2/3874, "The Fifth Column Case," 9 October 1943, 7.
92  KV2/3874, "The Fifth Column Case," 29 August 1942, 2 (cont'd).
93  KV2/3874, "The Fifth Column Case," 4 September 1942, 23.
94  KV/2/3800, "Shelford Report," 23 September 1944.

## Bibliography

*Aberdeen Weekly Journal*, 2 May 1940, 4.

Addison, Jeremy A., Paul Addison, and Paul Crang. *Listening to Britain: Home Intelligence Reports on Britain's Finest Hour*. London: Bodley Head, 2010.

Ball, Stuart. *Portrait of a Party: The Conservative Party in Britain 1918–1945*. London: Oxford University Press, 2013.

*Bath Chronicle and Weekly Gazette*, 13 April 1940, 17.

*Belfast News-Letter*, 21 May 1940, 4; 23 May 1940, 4.

*Birmingham Daily Gazette*, 6 July 1940, 4; 24 May 1940, 1.

*Birmingham Mail*, 9 March 1940, 8; 24 May 1940, 8.

British House of Commons, Hansard, 364, 15 August 1940. Last Accessed 26 August, 2018. https://hansard.parliament.uk/Commons/1940-08-15.

*The Bystander*, 29 May 1940, 5.

Cadbury, Deborah. *Princes at War: The British Royal Family's Private Battle in the Second World War*. New York: Bloomsbury, 2015.

*Chicago Daily News*, 14 April 1940, 1.

Churchill, Winston. *BBC Broadcast*, 14 July 1940, London.

Costello, John. *Ten Days That Saved the West*. London: Bantam, 1991.

*Daily Mail*, 28 February 2014, 2.

*Daily Mirror*, 9 May 1939, 13; 20 September 1939, 14; 1 March 1940, 1; 11 March 1940, 10–11; 15 April 1940, 6; 26 April 1940, 1; 26 April 1940, 1; 27 April 1940, 3; 9 May 1940, 11; 24 May 1940, 1; 25 May 1940, 3; 29 May 1940, 6; 16 July 1940, 5; 21 August 1940, 1.

*Daily Record*, 24 May 1940, 5.

Donovan, William and Edgar Mowrer. *Fifth Column Lessons for America*. Washington, DC: American Council of Public Affairs, 1940.

E7. *Hitler's Spy Ring*. London: Hurst & Blackett, 1940.

*Evening Dispatch*, 25 April 1940, 5.

Field, Geoffrey G. *Blood, Sweat, and Toil: Remaking the British Working Class, 1939–1945*. London: Oxford University Press, 2011.

Griffiths, Richard. *Patriotism Perverted: Captain Ramsay, the Right Club, and British Anti-Semitism, 1939–1940*. London: Faber and Faber, 2011.

Griffiths, Richard. "The Reception of Bryant's Unfinished Victory: Insights into British Public Opinion in Early 1940." *Patterns of Prejudice* 38, no. 1 (2004): 18–36.

Hannant, Larry. "Fear Sweeps the Nation: The Fifth Column Crisis." *The Beaver* 73, no. 6 (December 1993).

*Hartlepool Northern Daily Mail*, 6 May 1940, 4.

Haxey, Simon. *Tory MP*. Gollancz: London, 1939.

Hinsley, Francis & Charles Anthony Goodall Simkins. *British Intelligence in the Second World War*, Vol. 4. London: Cambridge University Press, 1979.

*Huffington Post*, 28 February 2014, 3.

The Keep Archive. Fifth Column Pilot Test, SxMOA1/1/5/4/19, 29 April 1940, Brighton, UK.

*Liverpool Echo*, 28 May 1940, 6; 30 May 1940, 6.

Loeffel, Robert. *The Fifth Column in World War II: Suspected Subversives in the Pacific*. Palgrave: Basingstoke, 2015.

MacKenzie, Simon. *The Home Guard: A Military and Political History*. Oxford: Oxford University Press, 1995.

*The Mail*, 13 April 1940, 1.

*Manchester Evening News*, 25 April 1940, 3.

*Manchester Guardian*, 4 July 1940, 2; 23 August 1940, 2.

McMahon, Paul. *British Spies and Irish Rebels: British Intelligence and Ireland, 1916–1945*. London: Boydell Press, 2008.

*The Mirror*, 27 February 2014, 2.

*National Archives of Australia*. "Nazi Activities in South Australia during World War II." D1918, S35, 6 February 1940.

*The National Archives of the UK*. "The Cabinet Papers: Records of the Cabinet Office." CAB, London, 2018. http://discovery.nationalarchives.gov.uk/SearchUI/browse/C44?v=h.

*The National Archives of the UK*. "Records Created or Inherited by the Central Office of Information." INF, London, 2018. http://discovery.nationalarchives.gov.uk/details/r/C160.

*The National Archives of the UK*. "Records of the Security Service." KV, London, 2018. http://discovery.nationalarchives.gov.uk/details/r/C160.

*News Chronicle*, 6 May 1939, 10.

*New York Times*, 16 October 1936, 2.

*Northampton Mercury*, 28 June 1940, 7.

*The People*, 21 April 1940, 2.

Prior, Robin. *When Britain Saved the West: The Story of 1940*. New Haven: Yale University Press, 2015.

Simpson, Alfred. *In the Highest Degree Odious: Detention without Trial in Wartime Britain*. Oxford: Clarendon Press, 1992.

Smith, Malcolm. *Britain and 1940: History, Myth, and Popular Memory*. Abington: Routledge, 2000.

*The Times*, 20 October 1936, 16; 9 March 1940, 4; 15 April 1940, 5; 28 February 2014, 5.

*West Morning News*, 16 October 1936, 7; 24 May 1940, 3.

*Yorkshire Evening Post*, 25 April 1940, 5.

*Yorkshire Post and Leeds Intelligencer*, 23 May 1940, 3.

# 6   The Indian Ocean

*Oliver Coates*

The Indian Ocean was a major theatre in the Second World War, serving as the lynchpin of Britain's fading imperial ambitions in Asia, while at the same time facilitating the movements of hundreds of thousands of soldiers, refugees, and sailors between Asia, Africa, and Australasia. The Ocean played a pivotal role in world merchant shipping; in 1939, the Suez canal was handling 20 vessels a day, totalling an average of 40 million tons of material, while on the Ocean rim, the Gulf produced some 20 million tons of oil and the Dutch East Indies some 10 million.[1] Yet vessels that plied the shipping lanes between Africa and Asia received only a fraction of the protection given to better-known Atlantic and Arctic convoys; only troopships were guaranteed protection. German and Japanese submariners hunted Allied vessels through some of the world's most remote bodies of water. By 1945, the *Kriegsmarine*'s U-boats had sunk 151 Allied ships in the Indian Ocean, carrying an estimated 935,000 tons of produce.[2] As U-Boat operations in the North Atlantic began to weaken during 1943, so the Indian Ocean earned the grim distinction of being the world's most dangerous ocean for Allied merchant seamen; even protected troopships were not immune: the *Khedive Ismail* was sunk by Japanese submarines in February 1944 despite being part of a five-ship convoy, claiming 1134 lives, including 996 soldiers from the East African Field Regiment.[3] Naturally, death at sea was not the preserve of European vessels and passengers, yet the much of the literature remains silent on the drowning of Indian and African merchant seamen; one clue to the wider cost of the war at sea can be gained from the fact that around 20 Indian vessels from one port in Gujarat were lost during the war.[4]

What of the war's impact on the peoples of the Indian Ocean rim? The ideological and experiential paroxysms provoked by the war have often been understood in terms of the histories of particular port cities, such as Singapore, Kuala Lumpur, and Ceylon.[5] The historiography of the Indian Ocean region has revealed rich connections in terms of centuries-old trading networks, the colonial circulation of print culture, and the modelling of a 'greater India' on the Ocean rim, yet research has yet to take full account of the exchanges of materials, ideas, and people that occurred during the war.[6] The flood of refugees from the Malay Peninsula to India; the growth of the *Azad*

*Hind* or Free India Government, declared in Singapore and attracting the support of many Tamil civilians resident in South-East Asia; and the influx of the tens of thousands of Africans from across the continent who came to India and Burma to serve in the British military all provide examples of the unique conjuncture of global peoples and ideas in the wartime Indian Ocean.[7]

This chapter will offer no comprehensive survey of these developments and instead seeks to demonstrate the degree to which significant elements of the wartime Indian Ocean have remained beyond the horizon of a growing historiography of wartime Africa and Asia. Two major areas considered here include the maritime war involving the British, Japanese, and German navies and the experience of the Francophone Indian Ocean, as characterised by three brief regional accounts of Madagascar, Reunion, and French Somaliland. Maritime trade has been a significant element of Indian Ocean historiography since the scholarship of K. N. Chaudhuri, Ashin Das Gupta, and S. Arasartnam, themselves influenced by Braudel's seminal account of the Mediterranean, but wartime shipping has largely remained absent from recent studies of the Ocean, although the work of labour historians and recent research on the Japanese Navy provide significant contexts for such a history.[8] In terms of the French Empire in the Ocean, the chapter draws on the work of Francophone military and imperial historians in order to present an account of the significance of the war in the Francophone Indian Ocean.

## Maritime traffic across the wartime Ocean

The war led to a significant expansion of supply traffic in the Ocean, with supply lines to Russia, via the Persian Gulf, as well as to India, the Malayan Peninsula, the Horn of Africa, and Australasia all passing through the region.[9] In May 1942, 171 vessels jammed Bombay Harbour, while ports such as far-off Freetown (on the Atlantic Coast of West Africa) served as the British Merchant Navy's entrance point to their Indian Ocean region.[10] The closure of the Suez Canal to shipping, following Axis bombing operations, represented a major shift in shipping patterns across the Ocean; mercantile trade and troop transports were now forced to make their way around the Cape, and stretches of the Southern Ocean, such as the Mozambique Channel, became major sites of Axis submarine operations.[11]

### Convoy operations

In June 1940, the first 'Winston's Specials' or *WS* convoys sailed around the Cape, with around one convoy a month arriving over the next three years bound for Egypt, India, and East Asia.[12] The lengthy itineraries of these convoys are illustrated by the case of convoy WS10 containing 12 troopships, which, having left Britain on 2 August 1941, continued to Freetown, Cape Town, Durban, Mombasa, Aden, Suez, Bombay, Colombo, and Singapore.[13] In addition to troopships, supply vessels plied the sea lanes of the Ocean, carrying ammunition, barley, coal, chrome ore, diesel, kerosene, military vehicles, mules, petrol, railway materials, salt, sugar, and tinned meat.[14] In October of 1940 alone, ships of the Royal Navy's East Indies Station escorted 127 merchant and troopships on their voyage north to the Red Sea. Tankers were an important part of this traffic, especially after the closure of India's fuel supply route from Burma following the Japanese invasion; 273 tankers worked the route from Iran to Karachi and Bombay carrying fuel for India.[15]

There has been no *The Cruel Sea* written for the Indian Ocean, yet its waters were as perilous for merchant shipping as those of the Atlantic. From early 1942, Hitler encouraged Admiral Oshima to use massacre orders, allowing the summary killing of Allied merchant seamen; the policy saw its grim inception in December 1943 with the massacre of survivors from the Dutch vessel *SS Tjisalak* then those of the American *SS Jean Nicolet* on 26 March the following year.[16] Axis auxiliary cruisers, or 'raiders,' were frequently disguised as merchant vessels, using bogus names and deceptive superstructure; Berlin sent nine auxiliary cruisers to the Ocean, with seven sent in 1940 alone.[17] The former Hansa Line vessel *Goldenfals* was among nine raiders converted from merchant vessels. The *Goldenfals* sank 16 vessels in the Indian Ocean between April 1940 and November 1941, including the sinking of the *King City*, which was carrying 5,000 tons of coal from Cardiff to Singapore around 180 miles north of Rodrigues.[18] Her efforts were accompanied by the activities of raiders such as the *Atlantis* and *Pinguin*, as well as warships like the diminutive *Graf Spree*.[19] Such operations predated Axis submarine activity in the Ocean; in the Bay of Bengal, a hunting group to counter raiders was formed as soon as war broke out.[20] Raiders often operated for months, taking respite in the remote southern waters of the Ocean before returning to claim further Allied ships; the *Graf Spree* alone occupied considerable naval resources before finally leaving the Indian Ocean for the Battle of the River Plate in the waters off Argentina.[21]

The historiography of wartime shipping in the Indian Ocean has too long remained largely one based on European, or more recently Japanese, military and mercantile strategies. It is beyond the scope of the current account to redress this imbalance, but we must appreciate the engagement of Indian and African peoples with the wartime Indian Ocean.[22] While are familiar with the impact of Axis submarine operations on Western merchant shipping, we know far less about its impact on local shipping on the Ocean rim. At Kachch, in Gujarat, around 20 merchant vessels were lost to Japanese submarines during the war.[23] For Indian merchant seamen, the war provided new opportunities and routes, especially since the lifting of restrictions on the use of 'lascars,' a highly discriminatory term used by the British to describe India seamen, in August 1938.[24] Indian seamen were exported across the Indian Ocean, where they could be called on to serve in preference to local labour.[25] At Calcutta in 1942, the Indian Seamen's Union allowed 2,000 Chinese strikers to be replaced with lascar seamen.

During the war, Indian seamen also took advantage of wartime to organise and assert their interests; in August 1939 and February 1940, Indian seamen went on strike for war bonuses and higher pay.[26] At Durban on 13 September 1939, 63 Indian seamen on the *SS Umvoti* refused to sail, while at Cape Town on 11 September sailors from the subcontinent mutinied on board the *SS Clan Alpine* and later on the *SS Clan Buchanan*. It is possible that the men had been influenced by organisations such as the Seamen's Union of Bombay and the Seamen's Union of Calcutta, whose leader Aftab Ali had links to leftist Krishna Menon and the British Communists.[27] Later in the war, in 1942, Durban saw a protest by the Indian crew of the *SS Jeypore*.[28] These challenges to mercantile firms notwithstanding, the war also brought changes in hiring seafarers in India that potentially mitigated against worker organisation; the social composition on board merchant vessels leaving Indian ports altered as the sheer demand for labour meant that wartime vessels were increasingly likely to be recruited from a disparate mix of seamen across ethnic, geographical, and religious backgrounds.[29] For Indian seamen, the war opened new spaces for worker organisation and protest and threw into sharp relief increasingly complex patterns of unionisation, but seamen were also used to break streaks and their lives were deemed far cheaper, with Asian and African seamen being consigned to flimsy rafts rather than sturdier lifeboats in the event of abandoning ship.[30]

### The submarine war

Abandoning ship was a not infrequent occurrence, often hundreds of miles from the nearest land; between August and November 1942 alone, 5 Japanese submarines were responsible for the sinking of 10 cargo ships, totalling 60,000 tons.[31] By the defeat of Germany in May 1945, the *Kriegsmarine* had assigned 57 submarines to operations in the Indian Ocean.[32] By the end of the war, Axis submarine patrols had sunk 151 Allied ships, totalling over 935,000 tons of materials and war supplies.[33] The Imperial Japanese Navy (IJN) represented a considerable threat to Allied shipping, particularly at the height of its power in 1941–2, when the Royal Navy's Eastern Fleet was outmatched by the Japanese; during these months, Admiral Somerville's force of 5 battleships, 2 fleet carriers, one vintage carrier, 7 cruisers, 16 destroyers, and 7 submarines could not compete with the 5 carriers and 4 modern battleships in Admiral Nagumo's fleet, which had already defeated the Americans at Pearl Harbour.[34] The submarine war was the most insidious and psychologically corrosive element of the Axis naval threat; by August 1943, the Ocean was the most perilous region for shipping worldwide: it required the sinking of only eight vessels to achieve this dubious distinction. As late as March 1944, the Axis Powers still had 14 submarines operating in the Ocean, with a vessel such has the *Troilus* being sunk in September 1944 under sail from Colombo.[35]

Axis submarines enjoyed an impressive range across the Indian Ocean, being particularly active in the Malacca Strait, the Mozambique Channel, and the southern islands of the Persian Gulf.[36] The Italian submarines were based in Massawa on the Red Sea, while their Japanese counterparts operated from Southeast Asia, and the German U-boats, already powerful in the South Atlantic, initially operated in the waters around the Cape and in the southern Ocean.[37] In the waters off South Africa, 32 U-boats and a number of Italian submarines were operating in 1942; they represented a considerable threat: 4 U-boats of the Seahound group operating between Durban and Lourenço Marques succeeded in sinking 20 ships, totalling 122,716 tons.[38] The waters off the Cape were an easy target for Axis submarines because the British had yet to devise an adequate convoy system in the region; the problem was brutally exposed when the Eisbär group sank 14 ships in waters off the Cape between 7 and 10 October 1942.[39]

The formidable Axis submarine threat belied considerable practical difficulties, especially for Germany. The Ocean was particularly challenging because it was not possible to combine naval and air power at such a remote distance from any German-occupied territories; submarines were forced to rely on supply vessels known as 'milch cows.'[40] After the Japanese advance in Asia, the kriegsmarine's *Gruppe Monsun* (Monsoon Group) operated out of Penang, using the port of Kobe in Japan as a terminal, as well as drawing on smaller bases at Batavia, Surabaya (Java), and the former Royal Naval base at Singapore.[41] Because escorted convoys only accompanied shipping (except troopships) in limited parts of the Indian Ocean, the region continued to present rich pickings for Axis submarines and raiders throughout the war. In this respect, the Indian Ocean contrasts with the earlier U-boat theatre of the South Atlantic, where, from 1943, the Reich deemed submarine operations to be uneconomical.[42]

From the re-opening of the Suez Canal, maritime traffic exponentially increased in the Red Sea and its southern approaches; this led to a concentration of German U-boat activity. The shipping lanes were particularly busy from 1943 into 1944 due to the build-up of Allied forces in India and Ceylon in preparation for the forthcoming offensive in Burma.[43] In September 1943, five U-boats arrived to take up positions in the Arabian Sea.[44] Convoys were introduced for troop shipping on routes from Durban to Mombasa, Aden, Bombay, and Colombo in 1943 and continued into the following year. These escorts continued to be inadequate, as reflected in the finding of Admiral Somerville's investigation into the loss of the *SS Khedive Ismail* in February 1944.[45] The risk was severe: when the huge international liners *Aquitania*, *Ile de France*, *Nieuw Amsterdam*, and *The Queen Mary* arrived in the Gulf of Aden to help transport Australian troops back home, they were accompanied by a sole cruiser, HMS *Devonshire*.[46] Despite these threats, by 1944 the Indian Ocean was less profitable for U-boats after the 'milch cow' supply vessels *Brake* and *Charlotte Schleimann* were sunk by the RN Eastern Fleet.[47] By early 1945, the Allied forces had achieved air superiority, and the submarine threat was greatly reduced.[48]

Submarines were not only used to attack enemy shipping; they also enjoyed wartime careers as cargo, mine-laying, and passenger vessels. Despite the residual threat from Axis vessels, the autumn of 1944 saw Ceylon's 26 submarines engaged not in hunting Axis vessels but rather laying mines on the Malacca strait and off the Thai and Burmese coasts.[49] The British used submarines such as the HMS *Tactician* in specialised transport roles for the Special Operations Executive (SOE), carrying Siamese students from England to rendezvous off the Siamese coast to help the resistance, as well playing a role in the training of a clandestine resistance movement on the Malay Peninsula.[50] Axis submarines were repeatedly used for transport and trade purposes. Enlarged type XX U-boats were produced to allow for greater volumes of cargo to be carried to Japan, as well as military technology such as V2 rocket blueprints.[51] The Japanese provided urgently needed raw materials for Berlin, including tungsten, bauxite, and natural rubber.[52] While the German/Japanese submarine trade has remained obscure until recently, one celebrity passenger is far better known: in 1943, German U-boat U-180 met Japanese submarine I-29 to the southeast of Madagascar and exchanged Subhas Chandra Bose and some military plans for two IJN personnel bound for Germany in order to observe U-boat construction.[53]

The toll of Axis submarine activity on African soldiers can be summed up in one tragedy. Japanese submarines proved fatal for the 1,134 people killed in the sinking of the *SS Khedive Ismail* in February 1944. Part of a five-ship troop convoy identified as KR8, sailing from Mombasa to Colombo, the *Ismail* was attacked by submarine I-27. Most of the victims were from the 301st Field Regiment, East African Artillery, who were being sent to join the 11th East Africa Division in Ceylon.[54] Among the vessel's 1,511 passengers were 996 officers and men of the 301st Field Regiment. The sinking occurred a short distance from the secret Port T Naval Base in the Maldives. A subsequent investigation showed that potential escorts for the convoy had been sent to accompany a massive floating dock that was being taking to Trincomalee.

### The coast as an object of fear

The sea was not only a vital transport link and strategic resource; it also became an object of terror during the war years, not only for seamen. Ironically, the principle fear of coastal communities was not from hostile shipping but rather from the aerial bombing. Aviation had a transformative effect on the wartime Ocean, leading to the bulldozing of coconut groves for airstrips and the use of specially trained elephants to haul planes back onto slippery runways; most islands in the Ocean had never seen a plane at the start of the war, and civilian aviation was the reserve of a tiny few, such as the 7% of Hajjis who arrived in Saudi Arabia by plane in 1945.[55] Japanese aerial bombing was a reality in Calcutta, Rangoon, and Ceylon, but it led to widespread civilian panic in India's coastal cities. Civilian perceptions of aerial bombing and coastal invasion remain important and largely un-researched aspects of the Ocean's maritime war; we will examine the cases of Madras, on the Coromandel Coast of Southern India and at real risk of Japanese invasion, and Bombay, far from the Japanese's reach on the Maharashtri Coast of Western India.

Japanese bombs fell over towns such as Vizag, Cocanada, and Calcutta.[56] The threat of an imminent Japanese invasion was made all the more credible by the rapid Japanese advance in Malaya and the fall of Singapore. In early 1942, at the height of the Japanese invasion scare, the 9th Frontier Force was deployed to Madras and charged with protecting the coast from Japanese landing; local military leaders were briefed to expect an imminent coastal invasion, south of Masulipatnam. In Madras itself, civilian preparations began almost immediately; the high court was moved to Coimbatore, the inspector general of police to Vellore, the board of revenue to Salem, and the secretariat to Ooty, and only a skeleton staff remained at Fort St George.[57] More dramatically, around 200,000 people fled Madras between the 8th and 14th of April of that year, while a platoon of the Malabar police shot the animals of Madras Zoo so they could not attempt their own escape effort.[58]

The fear was not restricted to the Bay of Bengal; at Bombay no Japanese bombs fell, but residents began to leave the port city in January 1942. Families were divided, as the middle-class Gujurati, Marwari, Cutchi, and Kathiawari families sent their women and children back to those areas of Western India.[59] Once their wages had been paid, mill workers began to leave. As in Madras, April marked the high-water mark of the bombing panic; around 55,000 workers, totalling 25% of the city's industrial workforce, left Bombay, an exodus necessitating the provision of 6 extra trains a day.[60] As residents fled, so house rents in Bombay became cheaper, while small towns neighbouring the metropolis, such as Baroda, were left to cope with an influx of urban migrants. Although Maharashtra was far from the threat of Japanese attack, the bombing panic was not limited to Bombay. At Jamshedpur, the location of Tata's steel plant, around 40% of the populace fled, totalling some 63,000.[61] Aerial bombing thus represented a significant dimension of the way in which coastal peoples experienced the war in the Ocean; air raid precautions were mounted as far away as Mauritius, and the indiscriminate nature of aerial bombing placed colonial subjects in a newly intimate relationship with the war.

## The Francophone Indian Ocean

The Indian Ocean was home to several staunch pro-Vichy regimes; it also hosted a major Allied amphibious operation in Madagascar, a French colony since 1895. The 1942 British invasion represented a major humiliation for the Vichy regime, as well as a detailed rehearsal for Allied amphibious warfare.[62] Despite being 10,200 km from France, Madagascar was home to an imaginative and brutal Vichy regime, which lost none of its venom through geographical distance.[63] But despite this hardship, Malagasy and Asian middlemen found ways to profit from the war economy; after the Allied 'liberation' of the island, Malagasy nationalists were the subject of rapprochements from

General Platt's conquering British forces. The transition to a Free French government disguised the Gaullists' decision to continue a pernicious regime of forced labour that originated under Vichy, a practice it continued until the empire-wide suppression of statute labour in 1946.[64] Away from *la Grande Île* on the smaller neighbouring island of Réunion, the new Free French governor struggled, from December 1942, to avoid overt antagonism of pro-Vichy councillors who remained in office and struggled to reconcile development of the island's ailing infrastructure, with calls to contribute to the Free French effort against Pétain at home in France. French Somaliland, with its main port settlement of Djibouti, partly relied upon Madagascar for food, especially following the fall of the Italian Empire, and provided a pocket-sized case of Vichy rule on the shores of the Ocean. French Somaliland's Vichyite regime presided over starvation but also over a program of legal and extra-legal terror that claimed victims from the *colons* and still more dramatically from the Somali population.

### Réunion

The war brought immediate changes to Réunion's population of 200,000; from 1938, the island's government had already begun to implement the 11th July decree *Organisation de la nation en temps de guerre*.[65] As the international situation deteriorated, local measures were put in place for press censorship, and watch posts were erected at strategic positions such as *Pointe des Galets* and *Sainte Rose*. Evacuation drills were held in May 1939 to guard against invasion and aerial bombing.[66] In the first months of the war, around 3,354 Réunionnais soldiers were mobilised, with further contingents leaving on 25 April and 5 May 1940. The conditions were appalling; of 1,014 who left from *Pointe des Galets* on 9 September 1939, 9 died and a further 147 required hospitalisation upon their arrival at Marseilles.[67] Réunion itself was poorly prepared for war. It boasted one infantry company of around 200 men, equipped with some 250 Lebel rifles and 12 Hotchkiss machine guns; there was no naval or air capacity.[68] On 26 May 1940, the governor informed the population of the island that the Wehrmacht had penetrated French territory, and by 22 July the first of the Vichy laws had arrived on the island. The law in question, requiring a stricter system of naturalisation, was unpopular with landowners on the island who preferred to employ Mauritian staff who were exempt from the Popular Front's minimum wage and working hour legislation.[69] Further laws followed, forbidding secret societies (August), although this only affected one group on the island; banning British radio broadcasts (November); and requiring the declaration of Jewish civil servants (December).[70]

The successful British operation against Madagascar led to an environment of increasing paranoia for Réunion's Vichy government. In May 1942, a state of alert was triggered after Madagascan officials identified the South African cruiser *HMS Frobischer* steaming towards Mauritius with 6,000 men; some 9,000 inhabitants of the island's capital of Saint-Denis were evacuated.[71]

Events reached a head when the Free French destroyer the *Léopard* arrived off Saint-Denis in the evening of 27 November 1942.[72] In a move that would reflect the importance of naval power for the Free French in the Indian Ocean, De Gaulle's envoy André Capagorry disembarked from the *Léopard* on the 28th and was installed as governor later that day. In a virtually bloodless revolution, the Free French naval forces took Saint-Denis with 90 riflemen; only a single round of sub-machine gun fire was aimed at a military lorry from the Lambert barracks – the passengers surrendered without further ado.[73] Pro-Vichy Governor Aubert retreat to Hellbourg in the mountains with 400 men; there was some resistance at *Point des Galets*, but shelling for the *Léopard* put an end to most Vichyite opposition.[74]

Governing a population weakened by British blockades, and without the option of removing the pro-Vichy political elite, constituted major challenges for the Free French on Réunion. In a declaration on Radio Saint-Denis, the governor informed residents that they must forget their differences and focus on the liberation of France; as Combeau has shown, by generally avoiding denunciation, the Free French managed to maintain the unity of Réunion.[75] This policy of accommodation manifested itself in Gaullist propaganda; the *Journal Officiel* ran an account of the island that moved seamlessly from the Vichy regime to the current Gaullist colony.[76] Despite their willingness to ignore the past, the Gaullists were keen to stress that the island was deeply patriotic in its support of De Gaulle's project to liberate France.[77] The *Association Bourbonnaise de France Combattante* was founded in January 1944 to defend this Gaullist mission; its 6,000 members raised more than one million francs.[78]

The economic and medical challenges facing Réunion under the Gaullists were formidable. An adult morality rate at 22.1% was matched by an infant equivalent of 145%; 33% of mortality on the island was accounted for by malaria, which, along with diseases such as TB, ran rampant. The blockades meant that hunger was a severe problem and malnutrition was widespread. The imports of rice, a key staple in the diet of the Réunionnais, fell from 30,000 tons a year to 5,600 in 1942, while maize imports totalled a mere 2,800 tons in the same year.[79] When Capagorry became governor in 1942, he found that only 40 days of rice and maize supplies were available. Fabric shortages had reduced many of the island's inhabitants to a state of near nudity; since June 1940, only 4% of Réunion's textile needs had been met. As if this was not enough, soap was critically low, and drugs supplies were in a dire state. Into this situation of penury came such vessels such as the *Léopard* to play a major role in ferrying supplies across the Indian Ocean from Madagascar and nearby Mauritius. The *Léopard* and the tug *Amiral Bouvet* visited Mauritius in December 1942, returning with 6 tons of cooking oil, 50,000 metres of fabric, and a dozen tons of flour; in January, the cargo vessel *Zambezia* carried 300 tons of flour and 14 tons of butter from Mauritius. These supply voyages had an enormous effect on the morale of islanders, with the governor earning the moniker *Papa de riz*.[80] An internal report by the governor in January 1945 showed that the war had witnessed the destruction of 70% of the cane fields on Réunion, with the years between 1942 and 1945 being accompanied by a deficit in sugar and rum production of 200,000 tons and 100,000 hectolitres, respectively.[81] Total losses were estimated at around 100 million francs, rising to 300 million after a major cyclone hit the island in April 1945, damaging the island's communications and destroying the telephone network.

The 8th and 9th of May 1945 saw a public holiday and festivities on Réunion. From 1939 to the end of the war, 8,539 soldiers from the island had been mobilised; 1,300 had volunteered to join the Free French force. Not all former combatants enjoyed a warm welcome home; in July 1944 when the British repatriated Vichy POWs to Réunion, they were accused of treason by their fellow islanders.[82]

## Madagascar

The Réunionnais POWs had been among the conscripts from the island sent to fight in Madagascar; on 18 September 1941, 160 men left Réunion for Madagascar.[83] They were heading for what was to become the Francophone Indian Ocean's major battlefield. Madagascar was controlled by Vichy from June 1940 to November 1942; the regime aspired to penetrate all levels of Malagasy society, with a youth brigade and sports competitions being organised to promote Vichy propaganda.[84] From the perspective of Whitehall, the fall of Singapore and the growing possibility of a Japanese invasion of Ceylon had combined in the Spring of 1942 into a major threat to Allied territory and shipping in the Ocean; Berlin also believed that the Japanese would follow an invasion of Ceylon with one on Madagascar.[85] The fear was not baseless; in April, Vice Admiral Nomuwa, the Japanese naval attaché to Berlin, had discussed using Japanese naval forces in the Western Indian Ocean; Japanese submarines had been active in the Mozambique Channel.[86] A successful Japanese invasion of Madagascar would leave South Africa exposed and endanger British naval power in the entire Indian Ocean; following an invasion of Ceylon, it was Durban that would be Britain's principle naval base in the Ocean.[87]

In April 1942, Allied forces began gathering in Durban, South Africa. The British were joined by Northern Rhodesian and East African battalions.[88] On 4 May, a British force of more than 2,000 men occupied landing beaches close to Diégo Suarez; simultaneously, British planes attacked ships moored in the port's bay, sinking the cruiser *Bougainville*, as well as the submarines *Beveziers*, *Monge*, and *Héros*.[89] Early that morning, British planes destroyed five Morane 406 fighters and three reconnaissance planes that were parked on the airstrip at Arrachart; another Vichy aircraft was destroyed after engaging the Allied fighters.[90] The amphibious operation against Diégo Suarez in May, named *Operation Ironclad*, was to be followed in September by an ambitious pincer movement against the Eastern and Western coasts of Madagascar, memorably named *Operation Steamline Jane*.[91] The capture of Diégo Suarez had removed a major naval port in the region, yet it was that port's final experience of active combat; on May 1942, a Japanese submarine attacked British ships moored in the harbour.[92]

After taking Diégo Suarez, the Allied forces faced months of operations in the interior. Further amphibious operations captured the ports of Majunga on 1 September and Tamatave on the 18th.[93] On 18 November, the Armistice of Ambalavao was signed between General Platt, commander of the Allied forces, and the Vichy authorities.[94] Following an agreement between the British government and the National Council of the Resistance, Madagascar was placed under Free French control on 14 December.[95] Many of the British troops invading Madagascar were Africans, [96]The loss of Madagascar provoked anger in Vichy France, in one case leading collaborationist propagandist André Chaumet to compare Churchill's alleged seduction of Madagascar to Oscar Wilde.[97]

Malagasy perceptions of their invaders varied and, as we shall see, liberation did not necessarily bring any improvement in daily living conditions. At Tananarive, the capital, the arrival of Britain's African troops attracted a positive response. The Africans were seen as 'zulus' and interacted with locals, trading products; the positive response to the 'Zulus' contrasted with local disdain for the 'Senegalese' or French African soldiers, who had earned a reputation for violence and even cannibalism.[98] The London Missionary Society's Richard Burton proposed himself to act as an intermediary between Platt and Malagasy nationalists. Although it is unclear how far missionary initiatives won the trust of nationalists, this latter group did work with the British, with figures such as Joseph Raseta, an opponent of the French colonial regime since the 1910s, and Jules Rakotomalala working with Platt.[99]

Malagasies had expressed clandestine resistance to Vichy before the Allied invasion. Some shunned the pro-Vichy *Radio Tananarive*, choosing instead to listen to the Free French *Radio Brazzaville*. Newsletters such as *Mifohaza* and *Kofehy Volamena* circulated despite official censorship of the press in September 1941.[100] Cinemas were also sites of resistance; in December 1940, spectators at one establishment in Diego Suarez applauded at a newsreel momentarily showing a British soldier.[101] Communists provided one major source of opposition; at Tamatave in 1941, police intelligence revealed the distribution of pamphlets with titles such as 'The Politics Necessary for the Malagasy,' and 'Miraisa Hina' or 'Unite!.' Some opponents of the Vichy regime advanced humanistic values, like Father François Razakandrainy, a critic of the regime, who nonetheless hoped that his petitions would receive a fair hearing from the Mareshal.[102] Conversely, some Malagasies welcomed Hitler, such as Maître Eugène Ratahina, who offered his support following June 1940 and hoped German troops would come to Madagascar; a portrait of Hitler would hang in Ratahina's study into the 1980s.[103]

Liberation committed the island to a second war effort in support of the Free French. Between 1938 and 1942, production had fallen 90% in key areas of the economy. Now, primary materials, particularly minerals and agricultural products, were to be used to stem the decline of production in metropolitan France; Madagascar was to provide products such as coffee that had previously been imported from Brazil.[104] Economic stagnation had encouraged the Vichy authorities to increase their intervention in the colony's economy through new forms of planning and interference in production. Local peasants were seen as being lazy and requiring coercion in order to work; sources regarding the extent of statutory labour on the island remain uneven, but in 1941 alone individuals from the regions of Tananarive, Diego-Suarez, Majunga, Tamatave, Fianarantosa, and Morondava performed some 716.604 days of forced labour.[105] Local *colons* pressured the government to expand statutory labour, but the courts played an important role; twice as many forced labour sentences were handed down under the legal code for Africans, or *indigénat*, in 1941 than in 1939.[106] Statutory labour continued to provoke debate into the Free French era until 1944; in October 1943, the Mutual Aid Society for French Citizens of Malagasy Descent criticised the practice.[107] The war reached deep into Malagasy, committing peasants to forced work while leading many houses to hang portraits of the Mareshal and potentially galvanising the nationalist movement.

### Côte Française de Somalis/Djibouti

The small territory of French Somaliland (Côte Française de Somalis, CFS) was based on the harbour at Djibouti. Following the Italian expansion in East Africa, the authorities had begun planning for the defence of the colony; the *Section d'Etudes*, the CFS's principle intelligence agency, had been complimented by the addition of a *Deuxième Bureau* in the colony in 1935.[108] Following the Italian conquest of neighbouring Ethiopia, CFS intelligence focused on aiding rebels in Ethiopia and Eritrea with advice, money, propaganda, and arms. In 1938, the situation intensified as Italian troops moved into the border region between Ethiopia and French Somaliland.

An initial period of Anglo-French cooperation preceded the Franco-German Armistice. The two countries agreed to a common defence strategy for French and British Somaliland; troops of the Somaliland Camel Corps and French forces were jointly responsible for an area including Djibouti, Zeylah, and Berbera.[109] Italy's entry into the war against the Allies on 10 June 1940 underlined the isolation of CFS; on the same day, General Legentilhomme, the French commander at Djibouti, was named supreme commander of Anglo-French forces in Somaliland. The French faced an unequal battle, with 40,000 Italian troops and aerial support pitted against some 9,000 Allied troops and a small air force.[110] Within days, on 22 June, the Franco-German Armistice was signed, and the Vichy government was inaugurated. Legentilhomme delayed the implementation of the Armistice provisions, notably demilitarisation; fighting continued from the 1st to 10th of July at Ali Sabieh, around the Djibouti-Addis Ababa railroad.[111] Pétain sent General Germain to the colony to enforce the armistice provisions, triggering the resignation of

Legentilhomme and the establishment of a pro-Vichy regime in CFS. In a dramatic turn of events, Legentilhomme refused to be repatriated on 2 August and instead escaped with two officers to join British and Free French forces in the Middle East.[112] CFS did not demilitarise and maintained a garrison of around 8,000 troops, now loyal to Pétain, for a further two years.

As we have seen in Madagascar, the National Revolution was no dead letter in Vichy's Indian Ocean outposts. It facilitated the construction of a police state in CFS, associated notably with the personage of Germain's successor as governor, Pierre Nouailhetas, a former colonial administrator from Indochina who was ultimately recalled to France in September 1942 and retired without a pension.[113] The Nouailhetas regime was inaugurated by a piece of metro-politan legislation, the 3rd of September 1940 law for the 'administrative internment of individuals who pose a threat of national defence and public safety,' which, as Prijac demonstrates, created a 'police state' in CFS.[114] Traditional Vichy scapegoats were invoked: the Freemasons and the Jews. Djibouti's two masonic lodges were requisitioned, closed, and had their contents sold. Little is known about the fate of Djibouti's 100–130 strong Yemini Jewry during the Vichy regime. Legal institutions were used to repress Djibouti's French population. In late 1940, a Martial Court was created in the port town and proceeded to issue 45 convictions, including 23 death sentences and 22 sentences of forced labour.[115] In this environment of legal repression, Nouailhetas exercised a special role in speeding the wheels of justice. Roger Donard was arrested on 19 August 1941, having been denounced under torture, and condemned to death for treason due to his alleged role in securing the escape of soldiers from Djibouti's garrison. Nouailhetas specifically authorised that the execution be conducted rapidly to deter others; executions were public affairs in Vichy CFS due to their perceived deterrent value.[116]

Vichy's Somali victims have largely remained absent from the history of the Second World War; recent research has uncovered details of cases that highlight the dramatic impact of Vichy on those Africans who became caught up in its struggle for survival. On 15 June 1941, 200 women and children were forcibly deported to Obock internment camp, on the northern coast of the Gulf of Tadjoura and close to the Gulf of Aden; officials reasoned that this would reduce the demand for food supplies.[117] Ultimately, it was the areas of Ali-Sabieh and Dikhil in the south of CFS that were the worst affected because of their geographical proximity to British and Free French forces and their exposure to Gaullists.[118]

On this southern frontier with Ethiopia and in relative proximity to British Somaliland, wartime Djibouti's worst atrocities were committed. The case of six illiterate Africans who were shot without trial in May 1941 by Vichy authorities to deter potential defectors has been known for some decades, but the details of these killings have remained obscure.[119] They demonstrate how Africans became directly bound up in Vichy's web of judicial and extra-judicial terror. On 10 May 1941, two women deemed to be of 'light morals' and active as mistresses for the local *Tirailleurs Sénégalais* were arrested; whilst in prison, they were overheard discussing the potential desertion of *Tirailleurs Sénégalais* to the Free French. Their jailer reported the incident to his *cercle* commander, Captain Chédeville, the most important official in that administrative *cercle* or province.[120] The women's revelations were plausible; on the 9th and 10th of May 22, soldiers had indeed fled to Ethiopia. At the behest of Chédeville, the women were shot at Ambocto on the morning of 11 May 1941; their Somali names were Gadabour Rer Nour and Tomal.[121]

In this paranoid environment, Somali messengers were immediately suspected of collaboration with the Free French. Also on the 11th, at the Guelilé outpost, a young Somali was arrested for having brought a certain Lieutenant Coutin, commander of the outpost, a letter from Commander Appert of the Free French forces. Coutin's superior was Chédeville, who soon arrived to interrogate the young messenger. The result of Chédeville's questioning is unknown, but the young Somali was tied to a telephone pole and summarily shot. Still later the same day, two young Somalis were arrested in Siyyaro outpost; the oldest boy, aged 17, reported that they were searching for a lost camel, while the younger, aged 12, said he had followed after the promise of a gift. The Vichyite partisans who arrested the boys referred the matter to the local commander, Chédeville, who claimed that both boys were trying to flee the area of Siyyaro. Although the younger boy was released, his older companion was sent to Hol-Hol because Chédeville himself declined to shoot him; the summary execution of the two women and the messenger that morning had presumably exhausted him. The elder boy never did find his camel and was instead shot at Holhol, in the Ali Sabieh region of southern CFS, on 12 May.[122]

At Dikhil, on 10 May, a messenger from Saïdgaban was summarily executed at the firing range; his name was Boeuh Dirane Awale, and he was 16 years old. June brought further bloodshed. Ismaël Hassan, aged 20, who worked as a messenger, was shot on the firing range at Gaël-Maël before an audience of district chiefs from Djibouti. Age was no guarantor of survival in this quasi-legal world; veteran Farah Ardi Moussa was accused of passing messages from the Free French to the CFS garrison; because he had fought in the Great War, he was guaranteed the right to a brief court martial trial, which nonetheless resulted in rapid execution.[123] Moussa had fought with the Somali Battalion in 1916 and was cited in the Order of Battle at Verdun, later winning military medals for his role in the war. At his execution, he protested, 'I won the military medal at Verdun, I do not believe I am dying by French bullets.'[124]

The defeat of the Italians in Africa during 1940 led to intense isolation for CFS. The British naval blockade of the coast of Somali in September of that year reduced the colony to destitution; Djibouti and its hinterland produced only charcoal, salt, and some animal products.[125] It was forced to rely on air supplies from the Middle East and later France, as well as black market trade with Yemen.[126] The British blockade paralysed the supply link between Diego Suarez and Djibouti; some vessels still succeeded in evading detection. In

June 1941, the submarine *Vengeur* and the sailboat *Hind* delivered essential supplies, with submarine supply operations, such as those using the *Héros* and the *Glorieux* in December 1941, continuing until their base in Madagascar fell to the British.[127] Not all supply voyages succeeded in evading British detection; the cruiser *Amir* was intercepted with supplies bound for the region. After May 1942, French Somaliland came to rely upon aerial supply; initially aircraft arrived from Syria until the defeat of Vichy in the Levant, then supplies had to come from mainland France.[128] In November 1940, the enormous six-engine seaplane *Ville de Sainte-Pierre* brought supplies, following by other shipments in the spring of 1941.

Malnutrition and scurvy became serious problems as food supplies dwindled. A limited number of dhows crossed the Bab al-Mandab Straits to import fruit from Yemen; for some traders such as one Nadji Mohamed, this trade was relatively lucrative.[129] Mohamed was not alone, the Yemeni population in CFS increased during the war years, by some 37.64% in the decade between 1936 and 46 to 5,260 people; at least part of this increase is likely connected to the wartime black market.[130] The smuggling route came ashore on the African side of the straits at Obock, which had no road connection with Djibouti; from June to December, the two Potez aircraft that brought about 700 tons of produce from Obock, on the north side of the Gulf of Tadjoura, to Djibouti on the southern shore were known as the 'potatoes air force.'[131]

As hunger increased during the winter of 1941/2, Somalis left Djibouti for the desert; children for often left to the Catholic Mission in the town, itself lacking adequate food supplies. Some Djibouti's *Tirailleurs* were rumoured to have had mental breakdowns, leading to such pressure at the hospital that the chief doctor committed suicide in despair.[132] With Japan's entry into the war in December 1941, the British blockade was weakened as resources were diverted. The *colons* of CFS remained generally Anglophobic, particularly after Mers el Kebir and Dakar; those groups who might be more willing to collaborate with the Free French and the British, such as traders and railway officials, lacked the ability to influence the governor. Free French propaganda was present in Djibouti in 1941; leaflets were dropped that reported Allied successes, and the newspaper *Djibouti Libre* was printed in Ethiopia.[133] But these efforts had little success, with Vichy producing the loyalist *Djibouti Française* newspaper and broadcasting over *Radio Djibouti*.[134] In spring 1941, the British briefly considered an assault on Djibouti, although these plans were soon abandoned.[135] Most of the colony's garrison remained loyal, despite the September 1940 defection of a number of Senegalese and European soldiers to Aden.[136]

After the success of the Allied Operation Torch on 8 November 1942 led to the retreat of German forces in North Africa, morale decisively shifted. Colonel Raynal, commander of the 1st Senegalese Battalion, along with around one-third of the Djibouti garrison, crossed into British Somaliland to join the Allied forces.[137] By December, the British were offering to recognise French claims to the CFS so long as the *colons* mounted no armed resistance;

the governor capitulated.[138] The colony finally joined the Allies on 1 January 1943, after Rayanal had re-entered the colony in late December on behalf of the Free French.[139] Later in the war, the Somali Battalion was recruited by soldiers who had been based in Djibouti and later fought in Western Europe.[140] By the end of the war, shipping had returned to the harbour at Djibouti, and the colony had a functioning, if irregular, electricity supply, with the promise of new trucks and railway equipment soon to arrive from the USA.[141] For the Somalis, the Free French rule was not free from abuses; in 1943, an uprising of the Kaboba tribal group in the Tadjoura regime was met with armed suppression, and sporadic unrest recurred among the Danakil near the Ethiopian border until the end of the war.[142]

**An Ocean at war**

We have offered only a partial picture of the Indian Ocean rim during the Second World War. Several significant, but relatively well known, topics have been completely omitted, such as the *Azad Hind* movement of Subhas Chandra Bose, the fall of Singapore, and the complex urban communities of the Malay Peninsula. Yet the two principle subjects addressed in this survey, the internationalism of the Ocean's maritime world during the war and the significant role of the French Indian Ocean, have often fallen outside the focus of historians. The role of the Persian Gulf, Arabia, and the Malay Peninsula have not been examined here, nor has relevant scholarship literature in German, Italian, and Japanese; these important areas merit further research.[143] Despite these caveats, we may nonetheless draw some conclusions.

   The project of 'cloning' Vichy in the Indian Ocean region represents a major challenge to our understanding of the role of non-Europeans in the Second World War. It warns us against any automatic dismissal of the Second World War as being a European war or any assumption that European ideologies were irrelevant to the lives of peoples in the Indian Ocean. In the cases of Madagascar and French Somaliland, we have seen that non-Europeans were caught up in the repression of Vichy. This point is in no way limited to the French Empire. The ideological projects of anti-Semitism affected Asians in the Malay archipelago and in Java, as well as in Vichy's colonies; German ideological influences on Japan drove Kempeitai round-ups of Jews in Java in August 1943 and of the Baghdadi Jewish community in Singapore in April 1943.[144]

   If the war brought new modes of repression to the Indian Ocean, it also brought a new intensity to patterns of mobility and exchanges in ideas, whether voluntary or otherwise. These classic themes of Indian Ocean historiography are evident at an intensified pace during the war years. The case of V Swaminatha Sarma, a Tamil journalist and author of biographies of Hitler and Mussolini, provides an illustration. Having moved to Rangoon from Madras in 1932, Sarma's family found their life turned upside down on Christmas 1941 as Japanese bombs fell on Rangoon. They were forced to engage in a perilous sea and land journey around the Bay of Bengal back to India. Racial categories played an invidious role; whites enjoyed air travel and even dedicated overland refugee routes. Despite the perils of disease and the misery of muddy mountain passes, Sarma's family eventually came to Tamu, near the Indian border.[145] One family's escape from Burma itself reveals how the war interrupted a long-standing Tamil diaspora across the Bay of Bengal. Even those favourite topics of pre-modern Ocean historiography, the monsoon, and the dhow trade have their influence on the wartime seas; the conflict led to a final recrudescence of the dhow trade in ports like Zanzibar, and the Ocean's monsoon system, a guarantor of mobility in the Ocean before steam, played a key role during the war, wreaking havoc in Bengal in 1942–3 and causing major damage on Réunion in 1945.

The Indian Ocean was a major naval theatre of the Second World War; uniquely, it marked the interaction between Japanese, German, Italian, French, and British forces. The war also stimulated new political projects among Asians and Africans, such as the Azad Hind movement. Within a few months of the end of the war, partition would shatter the Raj and lead to the birth of India and Pakistan's military influence within the Ocean. True, British naval power continued to play an important role in the region until the end of the 1960s, and the British purchase of Diego Garcia on the Chagos Islands marks a legacy of dominance that survives to this day. But the Ocean after 1945 had changed irreparably; the Bandung movement created new links between decolonising territories; the rise of Nasser's regime in Egypt led to intensified conflict over the Suez Canal; and the Malayan peninsula, along with Indochina, became submerged in a bloody war of decolonisation. The connections that forged the wartime Ocean had once again been reconfigured by the collapse of the British and French empires.

## Notes

1 Henri Labrousse, *L'océan Indien Dans La Seconde Guerre Mondiale* (Paris: Economica, 2007), 8.
2 Rotem Kowner, "When Economics, Strategy, and Racial Ideology Meet: Inter-Axis Connections in the Wartime Indian Ocean," *Journal of Global History* 12 (2017): 228–50, 243.
3 Ashley Jackson, *The British Empire and the Second World War* (London: Hambledon, 2005), 286.
4 Edward Simpson, *Muslim Society and the Western Indian Ocean: The Seafarers of Kachchh* (Abingdon: Routledge, 2006), 51.
5 Christopher A. Bayly and Timothy Norman Harper, *Forgotten Armies: Britain's Asian Empire and the War with Japan* (London: Penguin Books, 2005), 124–6, 137–55; Ashley Jackson, "Ceylon's Home Front during the Second World War," in *Home Fronts: Britain and the Empire at War, 1939–45*, ed. Sandra Dawson and Mark Crowley (Woodbridge: Boydell & Brewer, 2017), 111–29.
6 Isabel Hofmeyr, Preben Kaarsholm, and Bodil Folke Frederiksen, "Introduction: Print Cultures, Nationalisms, and Publics of the Indian Ocean," *Africa: Journal of the International African Institute* 81, no. 1 (2011): 1–22, 1–3.
7 Sugata Bose, *His Majesty's Opponent: Subhas Chandra Bose and India's Struggle against Empire* (Cambridge: Harvard University Press, 2011), 253–4; Kaushik Roy, "Axis Satellite

Armies of World War II: A Case Study of the Azad Hind Fauj, 1942–45," *The Indian Historical Review* 35, no. 1 (2008): 144–72, 151; Timothy Parsons, "Mau Mau's Army of Clerks: Colonial Military Service and the Kenya's Land Freedom Army in Kenya's National Imagination," *Journal of African History* 58, no. 2 (2017): 285–309, 292–3.

 8  Leila Fawaz C. Bayly. "Introduction: The Connected World of Empire," in *Modernity and Culture: From the Mediterranean to the Indian Ocean*, ed. Leila Fawaz C. Bayly (New York: Columbia University Press, 2012), 1–27, 5; Sebastian Prange, "Scholars and the Sea: A Historiography of the Indian Ocean," *History Compass* 6, no. 5 (2008): 1382–93, 1384–5; Michael Pearson, "Littoral Society: The Concept and the Problems," *Journal of World History* 17, no. 4 (2006): 353–73, 353.

 9  Rashid Ahmad Khan, "Strategic Role of the Indian Ocean During Second World War," *Pakistan Horizon* 35, no. 2 (1982): 39–50, 44–6.

10  Michael B. Miller, *Europe and the Maritime World* (Cambridge: Cambridge University Press, 2012), 279.

11  Jackson, *The British Empire*, 247.

12  Ibid., 272.

13  Ibid.

14  Ibid.

15  Ibid.; Labrousse, *L'Océan*, 127.

16  Kowner, "When Economics," 243.

17  Jackson, *The British Empire*, 277.

18  Ibid, 283–4.

19  Labrousse, *LOcéan*, 39, 53.

20  Jackson, *The British Empire*, 277.

21  Ibid.; Labrousse, *L'Océan*, 23.

22  Yvan Combeau, "Introduction," *Guerres mondiales et conflits contemporains* 246 (2012): 3–6, 3–5.

23  Simpson, *Muslim Societies*, 51.

24  Ravi Ahuja, "Mobility and Containment: The Voyages of South Asian Seamen, C.1900–1960," *International Review of Social History* 51 (2006): 111–41, 114.

25  Ibid., 130.

26  Gopalan Balachandran, "Making Coolies, (Un)making Workers: 'Globalizing' Labour in the Late-19th and Early 20th Centuries," *Journal of Historical Sociology* 24 (2011): 266–96, 285.

27  Jonathan Hyslop, "The Politics of Disembarkation: Empire, Shipping and Labor in the Port of Durban, 1897–1947," *International Labour and Working-Class History* 93 (2018): 176–200, 191–2.

28  Ibid., 192.

29  Ahuja, "Mobility," 134.

30  Bose, *His Majesty's*, 35.

31  Kowner, "When Economics," 241.

32  Ibid., 243.

33  Ibid.

34  Jackson, *The British Empire*, 293.

35  Ibid., 286.

36  Labrousse, *L'Océan*, 137–9.

37  Jackson, *The British Empire*, 246.

38  Ibid.

39  Ibid.

40  Ibid.

41  Kowner, "When Economics," 242.

42  Jackson, *The British Empire*, 248.

43  Labrousse, *L'Océan*, 93.

44  Jackson, *The British Empire*, 284.

45  Ibid., 286.
46  Ibid.
47  Ibid., 284.
48  Ibid., 315.
49  Ibid., 304.
50  Ibid., 313.
51  Kowner, "When Economics," 229.
52  Ibid.
53  Ibid., 241.
54  Timothy Parsons, *The African Rank-and-File: Social Implications of Colonial Military Service in the King's African Rifles, 1902–1964* (Portsmouth: Heinemann, 1999), 35; Jackson, *The British Empire*, 286.
55  Robert Blanchi, "The Hajj by Air," in *The Hajj: Pilgrimage in Islam*, ed. Shawkat M. Toorawa and Eric Tagliacozzo (Cambridge: Cambridge University Press, 2016), 131–54, 132.
56  Srinath Raghavan, *India's War: The Making of Modern South Asia 1939–1945* (London: Penguin Books, 2017), 268.
57  Ibid.
58  Indivar Kamtekar, "The Shiver of 1942," in *War and Society in Colonial India*, ed. Kaushik Roy (New Delhi: Oxford University Press, 2006), 330–57, 355, fn.71.
59  Ragahavan, *India's War*, 266.
60  Ibid.
61  Ibid., 267.
62  Eric Jennings, *Free French Africa in World War II* (Cambridge: Cambridge University Press, 2015), 242.
63  Eric Jennings, *Vichy in the Tropics: Pétain's National Revolution in Madagascar* (Stanford: Stanford University Press, 2001), 31.
64  Ibid., 75.
65  Hervé Le Joubioux, "L'île De La Réunion Dans La Seconde Guerre," *Revue historique des armées* 263 (2011): 81–92, 81.
66  Ibid., 84.
67  Ibid., 82.
68  Ibid.
69  Ibid., 83.
70  Ibid.
71  Ibid., 86.
72  Yvam Combeau, "La Réunion: Une Colonie Gaulliste En Reconstruction (1942–1945)," *Guerres mondiales et conflits contemporains* 246 (2012): 63–78, 63.
73  Ibid., 66.
74  Ashley Jackson, *War and Empire in Mauritius and the Indian Ocean* (Basingstoke: Palgrave, 2001), 55.
75  Combeau, "La Réunion," 67; Pierre-Éric Fageol, "La Révolution Nationale Et L'exaltation Impériale À La Réunion Durant La Période De Vichy (1940–1942)," *Guerres mondiales et conflits contemporains* 246 (2012): 41–62, 41–2.
76  Combeau, "La Réunion," 67.
77  Ibid., 75.
78  Le Joubioux, "L'Île," 90; Combeau, "La Réunion," 75.
79  Le Joubioux, "L'Île," 89.
80  Ibid.
81  Ibid., 91.
82  Ibid., 85.
83  Ibid.
84  Lucile Rabearimanana, "Les Malgaches Durant La Seconde Guerre Mondiale: Souffrances Et Rêves," *Guerres mondiales et conflits contemporains* 246 (2012): 7–22, 7.

85  Jackson, *The British Empire*, 341.
86  Ibid.
87  Ibid.
88  Gandar Dower, *The King's African Rifles in Madagascar* (Nairobi: GSI, East Africa Command, Date Unknown), 1.
89  Le Joubioux, "L'Île," 85.
90  Ibid.
91  Eric Jennings, "<<Angleterre Que Veux-Tu À Madagascar, Terre Française?>> La Propagande Vichyiste, L'opinion Publique Et L'attaque Anglaise Sur Madagascar En 1942," *Guerres mondiales et conflits contemporains* 246 (2012): 23–39, 23.
92  E. D. R. Harrison, "British Subversion in French East Africa, 1941–42: SOE's Todd Mission," *English Historical Review* 114, no. 456 (1999): 339–69, 360.
93  Jackson, *The British Empire*, 342; Martin Thomas, "Imperial Backwater or Strategic Outpost? The British Takeover of Vichy Madagascar, 1942," *The Historical Journal* 39, no. 4 (1996): 1049–74, 1065.
94  Rabearimanana, "Les Malgaches," 9.
95  Ibid.
96  Jennings, "Angleterre," 23.
97  Ibid., 26.
98  Rabearimanana, "Les Malgaches," 21.
99  Ibid.
100 Ibid.
101 Jennings, *Vichy*, 77.
102 Ibid., 75.
103 Rabearimanana, "Les Malgaches," 19.
104 Ibid., 8.
105 Jennings, *Vichy*, 70.
106 Ibid.
107 Rabearimanana, "Les Malgaches," 11; Jennings, *Vichy*, 75; *L'Amicale des citoyens français d'origine malgache*.
108 Virginia Thompson and Richard Adloff, *Djibouti and the Horn of Africa* (Stanford: Stanford University Press, 1968), 15.
109 Labrousse, "L'Océan," 113.
110 Thompson and Adloff, *Djibouti*, 15.
111 Ibid., 17.
112 Philippe Oberlé and Pierre Hugot, *Histoire De Djibouti: Des Origines À La République* (Paris: Préscence Africaine, 1985), 110.
113 Thompson and Adloff, *Djibouti*, 18.
114 Lukian Prijac, *Le Blocus De Djibouti: Chronique d'Une Guerre Décalée (1935–1943)* (Paris: L'Harmattan, 2015), 204.
115 Ibid., 206.
116 Ibid., 207.
117 Ibid., 208.
118 Ibid.
119 Thompson and Adloff, *Djibouti*, 18.
120 Tamba M'bayo, "Bou El Mogdad Seck, 1826–1880: Interpretation and Mediation of Colonialism in Senegal," in *African Agency and European Colonialism: Latitudes of Negotiations and Containment*, ed. Femi Kolapo and Kwabena O. Akurang-Parry (Lanham: University Press of America, 2007), 25–45, 175–81, 176, fn.20.
121 Prijac, *Le Blocus*, 208.
122 Ibid.
123 Personal correspondence with Dr Laurent Jolly, 28th July 2018.
124 'J'ai gagné la Médaille militaire à Verdun, je ne croyais pas mourir sous les balles françaises,' Prijac, *Le Blocus*, 209.

125 Thompson and Adloff, *Djibouti*, 19.
126 Labrousse, "L'Océan," 124; Liliana Mosca, "La Revue De Madagascar. Série De La Libération," *Africa: Rivista trimestrale di studi e documentazione dell'Istituto italiano per l'Africa* 61, no. 2 (2006): 287–305, 288.
127 Labrousse, "L'Océan," 115.
128 Ibid., 116.
129 Prijac, *Le Blocus*, 151.
130 Alain Rouaud, "Pour Une Histoire Des Arabes De Djibouti, 1896–1977," *Cahiers d'Études Africaines* 37, no. 146 (1997): 319–48, 328.
131 Oberlé and Hugot, *Histoire de Djibouti*, 111.
132 Thompson and Adloff, *Djibouti*, 20.
133 Oberlé and Hugot, *Histoire de Djibouti*, 110.
134 Thompson and Adloff, *Djibouti*, 19.
135 Oberlé and Hugot, *Histoire de Djibouti*, 161.
136 Ibid., 164.
137 Thompson and Adloff, *Djibouti*, 21.
138 Ibid.
139 Labrousse, "L'Océan," 116.
140 Thompson and Adloff, *Djibouti*, 21.
141 Ibid.
142 Oberlé and Hugot, *Djibouti*, 113.
143 Ashley Jackson, *Persian Gulf Command: A History of the Second World War in Iran and Iraq* (New Haven: Yale University Press, 2018).
144 Kowner, "When Economics," 246.
145 Sunil Amrith, *Crossing the Bay of Bengal: The Furies of Nature and the Fortunes of Migrants* (Cambridge: Harvard University Press, 2013), 203–4; Sunil Amrith, "Tamil Diasporas across the Bay of Bengal," *The American Historical Review* 114, no. 3 (2009): 547–72, 547.

# Bibliography

### Books

Amrith, Sunil. *Crossing the Bay of Bengal: The Furies of Nature and the Fortunes of Migrants*. Cambridge: Harvard University Press, 2013.
Bayly, Christopher Alan, and Leila Fawaz. "Introduction: The Connected World of Empire." In *Modernity and Culture: From the Mediterranean to the Indian Ocean*, ed. Leila Fawaz and C. A. Bayly, 1–27. New York: Columbia University Press, 2012.
Bayly, Christopher Alan, and Timothy Norman Harper. *Forgotten Armies: Britain's Asian Empire and the War with Japan*. London: Penguin Books, 2005.
Blanchi, Robert. "The Hajj by Air." In *The Hajj: Pilgrimage in Islam*, ed. Shawkat M. Toorawa and Eric Tagliacozzo, 131–54. Cambridge: Cambridge University Press, 2016.
Bose, Sugata. *His Majesty's Opponent: Subhas Chandra Bose and India's Struggle against Empire*. Cambridge: Harvard University Press, 2011.
Dower, Gandar. *The King's African Rifles in Madagascar*. Nairobi: GSI, East Africa Command, Date Unknown.
Jackson, Ashley. *The British Empire and the Second World War*. London: Hambledon, 2005.
Jackson, Ashley. "Ceylon's Home Front during the Second World War." In *Home Fronts: Britain and the Empire at War, 1939–45*, ed. Sandra Dawson Mark Crowley, 111–29. Woodbridge: Boydell & Brewer, 2017.
Jackson, Ashley. *Persian Gulf Command: A History of the Second World War in Iran and Iraq*. New Haven: Yale University Press, 2018.

Jackson, Ashley. *War and Empire in Mauritius and the Indian Ocean*. Palgrave: Basingstoke, 2001.

Jennings, Eric. *Free French Africa in World War II*. Cambridge: Cambridge University Press, 2015.

Jennings, Eric. *Vichy in the Tropics: Pétain's National Revolution in Madagascar*. Stanford: Stanford University Press, 2001.

Labrousse, Henri. *L'océan Indien Dans La Seconde Guerre Mondiale*. Paris: Economica, 2007.

M'bayo, Tamba, "Bou El Mogdad Seck, 1826–1880: Interpretation and Mediation of Colonialism in Senegal." In *African Agency and European Colonialism: Latitudes of Negotiations and Containment*, ed. Femi Kolapo and Kwabena Akurang-Parry, 25–45, 175–81. Lanham: University Press of America, 2007.

Miller, Michael B. *Europe and the Maritime World*. Cambridge: Cambridge University Press, 2012.

Oberlé Philippe, Pierre Hugot. *Histoire De Djibouti: Des Origines À La République*. Paris: Préscence Africaine, 1985.

Parsons, Timothy. *The African Rank-and-File: Social Implications of Colonial Military Service in the King's African Rifles, 1902–1964*. Portsmouth: Heinemann, 1999.

Prijac, Lukian. *Le Blocus De Djibouti: Chronique d'Une Guerre Décalée (1935–1943)*. Paris: L'Harmattan, 2015.

Raghavan, Srinath. *India's War: The Making of Modern South Asia 1939–1945*. London: Penguin Books, 2017.

Simpson, Edward. *Muslim Society and the Western Indian Ocean: The Seafarers of Kachchh*. Abingdon: Routledge, 2006.

Thompson, Virginia, and Richard Adloff. *Djibouti and the Horn of Africa*. Stanford: Stanford University Press, 1968.

### Journal articles

Amrith, Sunil. "Tamil Diasporas across the Bay of Bengal." *The American Historical Review* 114, no. 3 (2009): 547–72.

Ahuja, Ravi. "Mobility and Containment: The Voyages of South Asian Seamen, C.1900–1960." *International Review of Social History* 51 (2006): 111–41.

Balachandran, Gopalan. "Making Coolies, (Un)making Workers: 'Globalizing' Labour in the Late-19th and Early 20th Centuries." *Journal of Historical Sociology* 24 (2011): 266–96.

Combeau, Yvan. "Introduction." *Guerres mondiales et conflits contemporains* 246 (2012): 3–6.

Combeau, Yvam. "La Réunion: Une Colonie Gaulliste En Reconstruction (1942–1945)." *Guerres mondiales et conflits contemporains* 246 (2012): 63–78.

Fageol, Pierre-Éric. "La Révolution Nationale Et L'exaltation Impériale À La Réunion Durant La Période De Vichy (1940–1942)." *Guerres mondiales et conflits contemporains* 246 (2012): 41–62.

Harrison, E. D. R. "British Subversion in French East Africa, 1941–42: SOE's Todd Mission." *English Historical Review* 114, no. 456 (1999): 339–69.

Hofmeyr, Isabel, Preben Kaarsholm, and Bodil Folke Frederiksen. "Introduction: Print Cultures, Nationalisms, and Publics of the Indian Ocean." *Africa: Journal of the International African Institute* 81, no. 1 (2011): 1–22, 1–3.

Hyslop, Jonathan. "The Politics of Disembarkation: Empire, Shipping and Labor in the Port of Durban, 1897–1947." *International Labour and Working-Class History* 93 (2018): 176–200.

Jennings, Eric. "<<Angleterre Que Veux-Tu À Madagascar, Terre Française?>> La Propagande Vichyiste, L'opinion Publique Et L'attaque Anglaise Sur Madagascar En 1942." *Guerres mondiales et conflits contemporains* 246 (2012): 23–39.

Joubioux, Hervé Le. "L'île De La Réunion Dans La Seconde Guerre." *Revue historique des armées* 263 (2011): 81–92.

Kamtekar, Indivar. "The Shiver of 1942." In *War and Society in Colonial India*, ed. Kaushik Roy, 330–57. Delhi: Oxford University Press, 2006.

Khan, Rashid Ahmad. "Strategic Role of the Indian Ocean during Second World War." *Pakistan Horizon* 35, no. 2 (1982): 39–50, 44–6.

Kowner, Rotem. "When Economics, Strategy, and Racial Ideology Meet: Inter-Axis Connections in the Wartime Indian Ocean." *Journal of Global History* 12 (2017): 228–50.

Mosca, Liliana. "La Revue De Madagascar. Série De La Libération." *Africa: Rivista trimestrale de studi e documentazione dell'Istituto italiano per l'Africa* 61, no. 2 (2006): 287–305.

Parsons, Timothy. "Mau Mau's Army of Clerks: Colonial Military Service and the Kenya's Land Freedom Army in Kenya's National Imagination." *Journal of African History* 58, no. 2 (2017): 285–309.

Pearson, Michael. "Littoral Society: The Concept and the Problems." *Journal of World History* 17, no. 4 (2006): 353–73.

Prange, Sebastian. "Scholars and the Sea: A Historiography of the Indian Ocean." *History Compass* 6, no. 5 (2008): 1382–93.

Rabearimanana, Lucile. "Les Malgaches Durant La Seconde Guerre Mondiale: Souffrances Et Rêves." *Guerres mondiales et conflits contemporains* 246 (2012): 7–22.

Rouaud, Alain. "Pour Une Histoire Des Arabes De Djibouti, 1896–1977." *Cahiers d'Études Africaines* 37, no. 146 (1997): 319–48.

Roy, Kaushik. "Axis Satellite Armies of World War II: A Case Study of the Azad Hind Fauj, 1942–45." *The Indian Historical Review* 35, no. 1 (2008): 144–72.

Thomas, Martin. "Imperial Backwater or Strategic Outpost? The British Takeover of Vichy Madagascar, 1942." *The Historical Journal* 39, no. 4 (1996): 1049–74.

# 7 Between the Nazi Hammer and the Soviet Anvil

The untold story of the Red guerrillas in the Baltic Region, 1941–1945

*Yaacov Falkov*

Wedged between Russia, Belarus and the Baltic Sea and known by their common label 'the Baltic States', Estonia, Latvia and Lithuania proclaimed their independence in 1918, during the countdown to the end of World War I or immediately afterward. What followed was a fierce military and diplomatic struggle against Bolshevik Russia, the reestablished Polish state and the remnants of the German army that got stuck in the region. Having successfully overcome this obstacle, the three nations had quickly become recognized members of the international community and important trade partners of Western Europe. Alas, their peaceful development was cut short in brutal fashion by World War II. The Berlin-Moscow Axis, born in August 1939, paved the way for the Soviet invasion and occupation, in summer 1940, and the subsequent German invasion in the Soviet Union codenamed 'Barbarossa', in June 1941, had turned the Baltic states into a quasi-colonial administrative-territorial entity of the Third Reich called 'Reichskommissariat Ostland'.[1]

The Soviets did not accept the loss of the Baltic lands regarded by them as a historical domain of the Russian state and a significant segment of the 'security cordon' that Moscow traditionally – and with special energy during Stalin's times – was trying to create between its own 'core' territories and the alleged 'menace from the West'.[2] Thus, attempts were made by different Soviet political, military and security authorities to deploy across the German-occupied Baltic Region a combat, sabotage, intelligence and propaganda network that was aimed at disrupting the everyday activity of the German occupying and military apparatuses, providing military, political and economic information to the Red Army and the Communist Party leadership and preserving the Soviet influence on the local population.

Among the principal participants of that effort was the Moscow-located entity called Central Partisan Movement Headquarters and its three branches assigned with the task of developing guerrilla activities in Estonia, Latvia and Lithuania. Their achievements were the subject of a constant glorification campaign by the Soviet propaganda machine until the collapse of the Soviet rule on the Baltic soil in 1991 and later were praised again by different Russian publications. According to them, the Soviet partisans were widely supported by the local Estonian, Latvian and Lithuanian populace and therefore grew significantly in numbers; were able to inflict upon the enemy heavy losses in terms of military and civil manpower annihilated and infrastructures destroyed; and provided to the Red Army highly valuable assistance during the Soviet 'liberation' of the region, in the summer of 1944 through spring of 1945.[3]

On the contrary, the indigenous post-Soviet historiography of World War II shows no respect for the Red guerrillas' successes and underestimates their numerical strength. Moreover, it denies even the pro-Moscow irregulars' right for bearing the title 'partisans' by claiming that these 'Stalin's emissaries' were not spontaneous resisters to the foreign occupation, but rather tenaciously recruited, trained and equipped professional saboteurs who had no connection to the local lands and realities, spoke no local languages and were hardly supported by the local population.[4]

This chapter, based on the up-to-date Baltic historical research and the author's own long-term archival inquiry,[5] will present the historical picture different from both the Russian and the Baltic narratives. On the one hand, contrary to the claims of the Soviet and the contemporary Russian historians, it will show that the Red guerrillas deployed across the Baltic Region were much less numerous, popular, geographically spread and operationally successful – not only because of the effective German countermeasures and the antagonism of the local population caused by the painful experience of the preceding short-lived Soviet rule but also due to the relatively low importance of the Baltic Region for Moscow's war effort in 1941–1943, internal shortcomings of the entire Soviet Partisan movement and even, surprisingly, the Kremlin's suspicious attitude toward the Baltic communist leaders and constant tensions between their men in the field and the teams of different Soviet intelligence and security agencies.

On the other hand, the chapter will highlight – in contrast to the recent Baltic publications and the Western ones that adopted their point of view[6] – the ability of the Estonian, Latvian and Lithuanian communist guerrillas to assist the Soviet military, intelligence and security forces by discovering some German intentions and vital installations, describing the common political and economic situation in the Nazi-occupied Baltic territories, hosting special assignment groups at the forest camps, and compiling the lists of real and imagined 'war criminals' and 'traitors' which would serve the Soviets following the region's 'liberation' in late 1944 through early 1945.

## The lost year: summer 1941–summer 1942

The German military force, the *Wehrmacht*, started crossing the Soviet western border at 4 a.m. on 22 June 1941. Due to the invasion's strategic surprise, combined with the invaders' operational and tactical superiority, the German Army Group Center had sized vast Belarussian, Ukrainian and Russian territories; annihilated massive Red Army formations; and, by the end of that year, was attempting to encircle and occupy Moscow. The Army Group North, commanded by Field Marshal Wilhelm Ritter von Leeb, made its road to the Soviet 'Northern Capital' of Leningrad, and, despite its much slower progress, by late August completed the conquest of Estonia and thus of the entire Baltic Region.[7]

According to Berlin's blueprint titled 'Generalplan Ost', the occupied Estonian, Latvian and Lithuanian territories, alongside with the northeastern part of Poland and the western part of Belarus, became amalgamated into a quasi-colonial administrative-territorial entity called 'Reichskommissariat Ostland' and ruled by a 'Reichskommissar', or 'Imperial Commissioner', Hinrich Lohse, formally subordinated to Alfred Rosenberg, the Reich Minister for the Occupied Eastern Territories and the leading Nazi ideologist.[8] Initially, the majority of the local Baltic population, deeply traumatized by the horrors of the Soviet brief occupation – eradication of the local independent institutions, brutal changes in the region's economic and social life, and especially extensive persecution of the alleged 'class enemies' – had prized the Wehrmacht as a liberating force and warmly supported the new German order seen as a prologue to the forthcoming full independence restoration.[9] The rest – the local communists, their families and sympathizers, as well as the numerous Jewish communities – became immediately a subject to the ruthless extermination campaign waged by the massive Nazi oppression and killing apparatus – a mixture of SS, Gestapo, Security Police and Security Service units assisted by different local police forces and unaffiliated volunteers.[10]

The Soviets reacted to the sudden rapid loss of their extensive western territories by sporadic, ill-organized attempts of different Communist Party, military, intelligence and security entities to deploy behind the enemy's lines a vast array of underground, guerrilla and reconnaissance units. Those were expected to slow the Wehrmacht's advance by damaging local communications and exterminating local food stocks; to provide the Soviet political and military authorities with valuable information about the situation in the German rear; and to hinder the establishing of the occupying regime on the lost Soviet soil by annihilating key German installations, senior figures and collaborators, alongside with influencing the civil population in the manner favorable to the Kremlin. Yet these expectations proved unreal since the infant resistance forces were staffed mostly by random people – Communist Party bureaucrats, aged or underage laborers and peasants, encircled and frequently demoralized military and security personnel – the majority of whom was scarcely prepared for the difficult assignments in the German rear and roughly supplied. They were hunted fiercely by the Nazi security apparatus and its local assisters and suffered from malnutrition and extremal weather conditions in late 1941–early 1942; thus, only a minority of them managed to survive the first occupation's year.[11]

The Kremlin, which almost immediately after the beginning of 'Barbarossa' called the population to set the occupied territories ablaze, was too focused on its conventional defense effort, had run out of resources and could not make any real attempt to assist its desperate guerrillas. It was not before the successful conclusion of the Battle of Moscow, in January 1942, that Stalin was ready to consider the idea of establishing a centralized and professional guerrilla warfare command and not before late May of that year that such a command titled The Central Partisan Movement Headquarters (CPMH) had been actually created, supervised simultaneously by the Central Committee of the Soviet Communist Party and the High Command of the Soviet armed forces ('Stavka'), namely by Stalin himself.[12]

In the Baltic Region, the Soviet initial efforts to wage the 'people's war' against the Germans proved the least effective. The subtle social stratum of the communists and their sympathizers, which was not very popular prior to the Red occupation of 1940 and grew insignificantly until the German invasion,[13] had been easily wiped during the first weeks of the new German rule. The majority of the leaders and the hardcore activists of the local communist parties and their youth movement 'Komsomol' had fled with the rest of the Soviet civil, military and security authorities to the Soviet rear.[14] The remaining – members of the amateurish underground cells and militia-style formations that were haphazardly established in the war's first weeks – were almost entirely betrayed by the hostile local population or their own comrades and subsequently either captured and killed by the Germans or accepted the capturers' advice to become collaborators. This was exactly the fate of communist activists Neeme Ruus and Karl Säre, who remained in German-occupied Estonia in late August 1941, after being assigned by Moscow to build and lead the local communist resistance movement. To their superiors' disappointment, shortly afterwards they were exposed by the occupiers and their assistants and captured at different locations. Both had tried to save their lives by betraying their locally deployed comrades-in-arms but to no avail: the former was shot almost immediately, and the latter died at the Nazi Neuengamme concentration camp, after having compromised the activity of the Soviet intelligence in North Europe. Another Estonian prominent communist and underground activist, Hermann Arbon, managed to survive in the occupied territory for about nine months, but he was arrested in May 1942 and executed a month later.[15]

One of the very few party representatives lucky enough to finish the first occupation year unharmed was Imants Sudmalis, the 'Komsomol' leader of the Latvian port city Liepaja. Following his active participation in the week-long failed attempt to prevent the German conquest of the city, he went underground, spent about half a year moving between the Latvian-occupied countryside and the capital Rīga, joined the Soviet guerrillas in neighboring Belarus and finally arrived in Moscow in early July 1942.[16] Based on his firsthand experiences, Sudmalis provided a detailed report on the situation in enemy-occupied Latvia, including an unprecedented description of the genocidal character of the anti-Jewish atrocities.[17]

Rare attempts by the Communist Party Estonian, Latvian and Lithuanian Central Committees, as well as by the People's Commissariat for Internal Affairs, *Narodnyy Komissariat Vnutrennikh Del* (NKVD), newly established Fourth Directorate responsible for combat and intelligence operations in the

German-occupied territories, to dispatch to the region the so-called 'Organizational' and 'Operative' groups bore no fruits. Most of the groups' members had been caught and executed; the others had fled. The Germans concluded that these were mainly young communists who simply wanted to return home.[18] The main obstacles for their activity were not only the Germans' security efficacy and the popular antagonism but also the local topography and climate: the Soviet guerrillas admitted honestly that the absence of big forested territories – contrary to the neighboring Belarus – besides well-developed road infrastructure, plentiful precipitation throughout the year, extremely low temperatures in the fall of 1941 through the spring of 1942 and even the 'white nights' phenomenon during the Baltic summer, had undermined their operational capabilities significantly.[19]

Among those who perished while trying to infiltrate the Baltic lands during the period in question was the second secretary of the Lithuanian Communist Party, Icikas Meskupas. Upon his escape to Moscow, in June 1941, he was put in charge of organizing a 16-man-strong group of party activists for conducting covert propaganda and subversion activity and promoting local anti-Nazi resistance in occupied Lithuania. But his actual underground activity did not last long. Parachuted into the Latvian-Lithuanian border region in March 1942, Meskupas and his men were very soon tracked and killed in a skirmish with the Lithuanian police.[20] Thus, the sporadic sabotage acts – mostly derailing of trains and shootings at German and local uniformed forces, which were reported in eastern Lithuania in late 1941 and the first half of 1942 – should be attributed either to the small uncoordinated groups of the encircled but still not captured Red Army soldiers or to the Soviet special units which acted unsystematically from neighboring Belarus without being able to become permanently established on Lithuanian soil.[21]

In Latvia, too, the Gestapo successfully neutralized many Moscow high-ranking communist agents, such as Frīdrihs Alba, Boriss Vaščonoks, and Arvīds Rendenieks.[22] Otomārs Oškalns and Ieva Paldiņa, the leaders of a communist 'Operative Group', who attempted to enter Latvian northeastern part through German-occupied Russian Leningrad region in the first half of 1942, were successfully repelled by the enemy's security forces.[23] The NKVD envoys as well were not spared from failures: 29-year-old NKVD female parachutist Olga Grenenberg, who arrived in Rīga in the autumn of 1941 without having been properly prepared for surviving in a hostile environment, was captured soon by the Gestapo, spent twenty-six long months in German captivity and finally died by firing squad in August 1944.[24]

## Hard birth: summer 1942–summer 1943

The establishment of the centralized partisan command, CPMH, in late May 1942, did not lead immediately to the desired improvement of the Soviet guerrillas' organizational skills; their physical presence and influence in the enemy's rear; or their combat, sabotage and intelligence capabilities. The principal constraint was the Wehrmacht's new successful summer offensive in the southern sector of the Eastern front that captured the attention of the Soviet military and civil leadership, exhausted the resources that might have otherwise been used by the partisans and enlarged enormously the Soviet enemy-occupied territories that had to be 'set ablaze' according to Stalin's order. Besides, there was a series of other negative factors that slowed down the development of the Soviet irregular warfare: the unwillingness of the NKVD and the military intelligence to share their growing influence behind the frontline with the newly established partisan organization; the inability of the Soviet-devastated industry to supply the partisans with the equipment badly needed for promoting the anti-German irregular activity, especially light, long-range radio transmitters and long-range transport airplanes; and the severe shortage of experienced guerrilla specialists who could have been used for carrying out operations and training of new recruits in combat, sabotage, intelligence and propaganda fields.[25]

Overcoming of all those obstacles proved a very hard task even for Panteleimon Ponomarenko, a newly appointed CPMH head, who served simultaneously as the Belarussian communist leader and enjoyed very close relations with Stalin. No wonder that his primary mission – the creation of a separate guerrilla staff for each occupied Soviet republic and each Red Army highest operational command, the so-called 'front' – was not accomplished before the beginning of 1943; by this time, there were many Soviet territories in the Wehrmacht's rear, including the Belarusian and Ukrainian regions of strategic importance, that had not been 'embraced' by the activity of Ponomarenko's men. The Stalin's still-unexplained decisions to dismantle and then quickly to recreate the CPMH in March 1943 had not made Ponomarenko's life easier. They harmed the slowly evolving chains of the guerrilla command and logistics and created a permanent source of tension within the partisan movement since the recreated CPMH had lost its control over the Ukrainian republican partisan headquarters, now subordinated exclusively to Nikita Khrushchev, the Ukrainian communist leader and Ponomarenko's old political rival. The outcomes in the operational dimension were unsurprisingly bad: by spring 1943, the Soviet partisans had posed no major combat and sabotage threat to the German military and civil authorities, and their intelligence achievements were almost entirely of tactical significance.[26]

Alas, the changing strategic context, in summer 1943, had not left CPMH much time for healing its systemic wounds and improving operational performances in the field. Stalin's demand during the last stage of the Soviet strategic counter-offensive near the Russian city of Kursk, to wage a massive derailing operation titled 'Rail War' in the German rear, had compelled the guerrilla command to throw tens of thousands of fighters – no matter how professional – to the frequently suicidal assaults against the German railroads. The outcomes looked splendid on paper and became even more glorious in the Soviet postwar publications and movies dedicated to the anti-Nazi guerrilla war, yet the currently available Russian and German sources show clearly that the actual influence of 'Rail War' on the Wehrmacht's logistic and combat efforts was much less significant than was claimed by the partisans themselves and Moscow's propagandists. By the end of the 'Rail War' operation, in mid-September 1943, the enemy had already repaired most of the railroad segments damaged by the partisans, thus diminishing the strategic effect of the entire Soviet sabotage enterprise to almost nonexistent.[27]

In these circumstances, the Baltic Red partisan forces were predestined to a very hard birth. In early summer 1942, a few weeks after the CPMH establishment, the People's Defense Commissariat (Ministry) of the Soviet Union delivered to Estonian, Latvian and Lithuanian Communist Parties a few hundred fighters of Baltic origin who should have been used for the creation of the Red Army Baltic regular formations and now had to be reoriented to performing guerrilla tasks.[28] But this gesture was hardly sufficient for creating a vital irregular warfare mechanism. It seems that in an attempt to capture the Kremlin's attention and thus to get more manpower and resources for their infant underground and guerrilla activity, the Baltic communist leaders decided to enhance the 'visibility' of their combat operations in the German rear. On 12 June 1942, a Belarus-based Red Latvian partisan commander, Aleksandrs Groms, had crossed with a mixed 150-strong Latvian-Belarusian team on the Latvian border and seized control of the small border village of Šķaune but was compelled to retreat to the Belarusian forests.[29] Similarly, a few weeks later, a unit titled 'The Partisan Regiment For Soviet Latvia', which was being built in the Leningrad region for about half a year, received a sudden order to launch an attack against the German targets in the northeastern Latvian borderland but was quickly exposed, severely harmed and repulsed.[30] Another fiasco struck the Latvian communist leadership in late August 1942, when a few sabotage units dispatched to Latvia via western Belarusian forests failed to penetrate the Latvian border, and one of their radio operators fell in German captivity and compromised vital information to his interrogators.[31] Likewise, forty-eight hurriedly prepared representatives of the Estonian Communist Party Central Committee were sent to cross the frontline in mid-August 1942, suffered heavy losses in firefights with the Germans while moving over occupied Russia's Kalinin Region, and after reaching the Estonian soil were quickly liquidated by the local Home Guard ('Omakaitse') units.[32]

All this suffering was for nothing. At that exact time, the Kremlin was preoccupied with the Red Army defensive operations, especially with the preparations for the Battle of Stalingrad and its outbreak, in late August 1942, while Ponomarenko's CPMH was investing its main energy and resources in supporting the regular military effort and developing guerrilla infrastructures in the strategically important occupied regions of Russia, Belarus and Ukraine. The Baltic territories were still too far from the main fighting theaters of the Red Army and thus irrelevant in terms of resource investment. For that reason, in September 1942, many hurriedly established Latvian communist guerrilla units lacked armament, munition, food and even clothes and shoes.[33] It was not before the late autumn of 1942 that the Soviet State Defense

Committee felt ready to deal with the establishing of CPMH Baltic commands. Lithuanian and Estonian Partisan Movement Headquarters (PMHs) had arisen in November that year under the supervision of the republican communist leaders Antanas Snečkus and Nikolai Karotamm, who fled to Moscow in the wake of the German invasion in 1941.[34] The creation of Latvian guerrilla command was even further delayed – until early 1943 – and its chief, Colonel Arturs Sproǵis, was chosen for his NKVD background and previous guerrilla experience gained during the Spanish Civil War.[35]

The new headquarters were granted offices in Moscow; many months after their official proclamation, their different segments were badly understaffed or continued to exist only on paper. Especially harmful was the lack of professional manpower in departments responsible for recruitment and training of the Baltic communist guerrillas, as well as for their logistic support. For example, in 1943, when the partisan school of Ukrainian PMH had employed fifty-six permanent professional instructors and was capable of training simultaneously up to ninety-six cadets, the parallel structures of Estonian and Latvian PMHs complained about having at their disposal only a few coaches who were preparing small groups of future irregulars.[36]

Apart from the already-mentioned objective reasons, this delay in development of the Baltic PMHs might well have had a hidden political motive. Stalin had little trust in the Baltic communist leaders and their protégés within the newly established Baltic Red guerrilla. Many of them were active in their countries of origin until the Soviet annexation in 1940 and thus avoided the 'purges' that struck the foreign communists, including the prominent Balts like Jaan Anvelt, who took refuge in the 'state of peasants and farmers' during the 1920s and the 1930s. By 1942–43, these people became useful due to their alleged ability to develop the anti-Nazi resistance behind the enemy lines and were thus less suitable for immediate extermination. But this fact alone made them no more trusted by the Soviet dictator and his aides.[37] Moreover, the Kremlin should have been aware of the alarming fact that following the German military and political success in 1941, the senior Baltic 'national communists', including the guerrilla leaders, had developed sensitivity to the peculiarities of the Baltic societies, especially to the economic aspirations of the local peasantry; admitted that some mistakes had been made during the 'sovietisation' process in 1940–41; and later on even showed their readiness to cooperate with the local national resistance against the Nazis.[38]

In this regard, one of the Latvian former guerrilla commanders had guessed many decades later that Ponomarenko's leisurely reaction to the Latvian PMH repetitive requests for radio equipment, during the period between November 1942 and April 1943, might have well derived from his will to compel the Latvian guerrillas to contact their superiors in Moscow through the transmitters of their Russian and Belarusian colleagues. This arrangement had ostensibly enabled control of the entire correspondence between the Latvian communist leadership in Moscow and its forces behind the frontline and provided the Kremlin with the 'evidences' of 'nationalist inclinations' among the Latvian senior communists and guerrilla leaders. For that single reason, some of the eavesdropping targets had lost their positions during the war or shortly afterward.[39] If true, this tricky move was possibly sanctioned by Stalin himself. When, in March 1943, frustrated Snečkus, Karotamm and their colleague, the Latvian Communist Party leader Jan Kalnberzin, sent to the Soviet leader a collective complaint about the chronic severe lack of radio equipment, ordnance and transport airplanes, they got no answer and kept complaining to other less-senior instances.[40]

Whatever the reason, in late 1942–early 1943, the new Baltic Headquarters' physical presence in the occupied Baltic territories continued to be merely a wish without real outcomes. Currently, Russian 'official' historians claim that by this time there were about 2,250 Soviet guerrillas across the entire region – 200 in Latvia, 650 in Estonia and 1,400 in Lithuania. These numbers had allegedly grown threefold and even more until late 1943.[41] But the independent Russian researchers and their Baltic colleagues deny this as pure nonsense. According to their assessment, in the beginning of 1943 only a small number of the Red guerrillas in the Baltic countries – 46 in Estonia, 199 in Lithuania and 200 in Latvia – were actually subordinated to Ponomarenko's CPMH.[42] Other Soviet 'partisans' who infiltrated the Baltic lands during the discussed period or were trying to do this were representatives of different Soviet intelligence and security services and had no connection to Baltic PMHs. In Lithuania alone, between 1941 and 1943, there were more than 700 fighters that belonged to different Soviet special units. Moreover, many of those presented by Baltic PMHs as their 'active partisans' frequently performed only minor occasional tasks and did not even live in the forests. Thus, labeling them as 'active guerrillas' was a clear exaggeration that aimed at impressing the highest Soviet authorities and hiding the unpleasant truth about the true insignificant size of the communist partisan movement in the Baltic Region.[43]

In the spring of 1943, the three Baltic communist guerrilla commands had made the coordinated attempt to improve this grim picture by enhancing their presence and activity in the areas of their operational responsibility. Between March and May, the Estonian PMH managed to dispatch behind the frontline five 'organizing groups'. Those were manned by a few Estonian communists and many Estonia-born Russians and tasked with establishing contacts with whatever underground communist organizations they could find in occupied Estonia, conducting propaganda activities, forming new partisan units and reporting on Wehrmacht troops and the mood of the local population.[44] The Latvian PMH had promoted, from March onwards, the establishment of the so-called 'Latvian Partisan Brigade', on the basis of the seventy-man-strong 'Special Latvian Union of Partisan Forces' that had already been active, under the command of Vilis Samsons, in the densely forested Belarusian Osweja area, close to the Lithuanian and Latvian borders. Like in the Estonians' case, the majority of these 'Latvian' irregulars were not ethnic Latvians but Latvia-born Russians, Latgalians,[45] local Jewish Holocaust survivors and Red Army soldiers who remained in the forests after the encirclement by Wehrmacht or escaped from the German POW camps.[46] In late April, the Lithuanian Red guerrillas, led by Motiejus Šumauskas-Kazimieras and Henrikas Zimanas-Jurgis, had also based their forty-six-man-strong 'Operative Group' in Osweja forests, while gathering strength, trying to learn about the situation inside Lithuania and awaiting the opportunity to bring themselves to Lithuanian territory.[47]

And yet, multiple negative circumstances were still strong enough to lay this effort to waste. Apparently, chief among them was the CPMH persistent incapability – or probably unwillingness – to improve the poor logistic chains of Baltic PMHs. In June 1943, three months after the abovementioned unanswered complaint to Stalin, Sproģis claimed again, exasperated, that the agents prepared by his men for clandestine work in the cities of Rīga, Liepāja and Daugavpils could not be dropped into occupied Latvia since the Latvian PMH failed to obtain even a single airplane necessary for that mission.[48] The wireless communication capabilities of all three Baltic PMHs had not improved as well, as revealed by a series of their requests for urgent assistance – as helpless as previous – and pessimistic reports dated April–August 1943.[49] Apart from the transmitters, supply problems had affected the ability of Baltic PMHs to defend their field units from the harsh weather conditions that characterized the region in the extremely cold and stormy summer of 1943. The absence of substitutional supplies of clothes, footwear, medicines and weapons had diminished significantly the mobility and firepower of the communist irregulars, damaged their health and thus weakened them critically.[50]

Another significant obstacle for enhancing the Red guerrillas' activity in the Baltic Region during the period in question had been the persistent hostility of the operational environment. By the summer of 1943, there already were signs of growing discontent between the Baltic peoples and the occupying German authorities, and even a series of sporadic disobedience acts labeled by the Germans as 'Marxist' in the Latvian eastern borderlands.[51] But the general attitude of the local public toward the Soviet Union and its desire to restore control over the region was still highly negative.[52] Without 'social water' deep enough to 'swim', hide and eat in, the Red guerrilla 'fish' was easy prey for the Nazi security apparatus and its local assisters, who enjoyed full intelligence and operational superiority in the areas of the partisan activity. A report by the German Security Service (SD), dated January 1943, presents very detailed and precise knowledge about the Latvian communist partisans' deployment and activity in the Belarusian Osweja region. It appears that the Germans had learned the exact geographical coordinates of the guerrilla's forest camps, the numbers of its fighters, the names and biographies of commanders, the *modus operandi* in the eastern Latvian border areas, etc.[53] Between May and September 1943, this information was used by German counterintelligence agencies for neutralizing a series of single agents and underground cells connected with the Latvian PMH; some of them, like Ivan Bogdanov, were recruited and sent back to the forest camps as double agents.[54] In Lithuania, in July 1943, a group of the Red guerrillas that had been active near the northeastern Lithuanian city of Zarasai was liquidated in a gun battle with the local police. The only irregular captured alive was Marytė Melnikaitė, a twenty year old female 'Komsomol' member, who was trained at a sabotage school near Moscow and infiltrated into Lithuania via Belarus. She was transferred to the German police, tortured and executed five days later.[55]

To complement these 'pinpoint strikes', the German and local security forces also undertook major counterinsurgency operations that aimed at striking the Red guerrillas at their 'hotbeds' and shattering their local base of public support and supplies. The 'Winter Magic' (*Winterzauber*) operation, conducted in February–April 1943 by a joint German-Baltic-Ukrainian force under German command, resulted in almost complete depopulation of northwest Belarus and severe damage to the local guerrilla infrastructure and interruption of its activity, including in the eastern Lithuanian and Latvian borderlands.[56] Shortly afterwards, in May 1943, the Nazis had launched in the Latvian eastern areas another anti-guerrilla operation which lasted until September that year. Its outcome had been detainment and deportation of several thousand local inhabitants, including the partisans' families and sympathizers.[57]

But there was also another, very surprising, environmental component that hindered the activity of Baltic PMHs during the discussed period – the growing influx to the region of Soviet reconnaissance and sabotage units sent by different military, intelligence and security bodies, such as the civil intelligence, counterintelligence and security service: the People's Commissariat for State Security, *Narodny komissariat gosudarstvennoi bezopasnosti*, NKGB which inherited NKVD responsibilities, in 1943), as well as the military counterintelligence and security service (SMERSh), the military strategic (GRU) and operational (RU) intelligence bodies, etc. In the summer of 1943, the head of Latvian PMH Sproģis complained repeatedly to his superiors in Moscow about the complete lack of coordination between his forces and these 'newcomers' and accused the latter in competing with the 'real' Red partisans for the local sources of food, clothes and other necessary resources. The complainer's ultimate demand was immediate restoration of Latvian PMH's full control over the Soviet sabotage and intelligence activity in the area.[58]

The reaction of the relevant intelligence and security services was no less strong: not only did they dismiss completely all the accusations against them but probably tried to harm Latvian PMH's work. On one occasion, in July 1943, a special courier between the Latvian First Partisan Brigade and Latvian PMH and communist leadership in Moscow was suddenly arrested after arriving at an airfield near Leningrad and held in custody without explanations for ten days. His superiors were not informed about the event, and the sealed envelope with secret documents that he was bringing to the Latvian senior officials was illegally confiscated and opened. In his reaction to this scandalous incident, Sproģis highlighted its shattering influence on his staff's operational work:

> Since then, we do not dare to demand from the Latvian Brigade the delivering of agents' names and other sensitive information, since our envelopes are being detained and opened by strangers.[59]

These were, then, the multiple negative circumstances that in the spring and summer of 1943 prevented the three Baltic communist guerrilla headquarters from relocating their operational center from Belarus and northeastern Russia into the Baltic countries. The abovementioned mission of the five Estonian 'organizing groups' proved a failure; by the end of June of that year, all of them were apprehended or annihilated by the German and the Home Guard's anti-guerrilla raids.[60] Their Lithuanian colleagues survived the Nazi counterinsurgency measures in Osweja region but were forced to postpone their move westward until the autumn of 1943.[61] The attempt by Latvian PMH to 'export' its activity to the Latvian territory seemed a bit more successful. In May, the Latvian guerrillas in the Osweja region had split themselves in two groups. One of them, under Samsons' command, moved northward along the Latvian border, still without crossing it, and succeeded in establishing a constant contact with a few pro-Soviet resistance cells based firmly in eastern Latvia.[62] Slightly later, Sudmalis, who came back from Moscow and joined Samsons, had successfully entered Latvia, reached Rīga and launched a buildup of a tiny communist underground. Its cells operated also outside the Latvian capital, trying to centralize the local communist resistance, gathering intelligence, disseminating propaganda and organizing sporadic terror acts against the German and collaborators' installations.[63] Yet, the relocation of the 'Latvian Partisan Brigade' to Latvia was delayed for the undetermined future.

Accordingly, the operational achievements of the Baltic Red guerrillas during the discussed period had been insignificant for the overall Soviet war effort. In May–July 1943, Latvian PMH had strongly criticized the insufficiency of its forces in terms of intelligence provided to him about the enemy and the general situation in occupied Latvia. At the same time, the guerrillas admitted their inability to gather military information within the Latvian borders and to translate the limited civil data brought to their Belarusian and Russian bases from Latvia by occasional sources and couriers.[64] In mid-1943, the Belarusian partisans who had reached the Lithuanian border and succeeded in gathering some sporadic information about the situation in Lithuania reported to their superiors that:

> The lack of our propaganda, especially printed, is felt in Lithuania. The same is true about the partisan movement. There are all the necessary circumstances for its establishment, but it must be supervised by the Soviet operatives.[65]

## Frustration and limited operational efficacy: autumn 1943–autumn 1944

Following its decisive victory at Kursk, in August 1943, the Red Army raced west toward the Dnepr River, took the Ukrainian city of Kharkov and cleared the economically vital Donbass region. The Germans reacted by the rapid evacuation of all of eastern Ukraine and an attempt to rebuild their defenses using the Dnepr itself as a barrier, but the Soviets had sized bridgeheads on the Dnepr's western bank; by 6 November, the Red Army troops were already marching through the streets of the Ukrainian capital of Kiev.[66]

It was in that strategic context that the Soviet highest civil and military authorities started to show a great interest in the Baltic Region and demanded much broader and effective activity by the locally deployed Communist guerrillas. Especially accented was the intelligence gathering aimed at supporting the Red Army operational planning and actual fighting. For instance, Lithuanian PMH had received in November 1943 a very detailed list of subjects in occupied Lithuania – enemy forces' concentrations, communication infrastructures, ground defense lines, airfields, armament stockpiles, industry plants, etc. – which were of high interest for the Red Army.[67] Later on, in December 1943 to February 1944, the Baltic Red guerrillas were asked to start delivering their periodical intelligence summaries to the Red Army Baltic fronts, the Baltic fleet, the military intelligence and other military authorities.[68]

The fulfillment of these and other similar demands depended primarily on the Baltic Red guerrillas' geographical location: they had to stop their maneuvering in the forested territories outside the Baltic States, far from the main Estonian, Latvian and Lithuanian urban centers and communication infrastructures that served the German civil administration and military forces, and put permanently their boots on Baltic ground. But this was a very hard task to perform. So much so that during the winter of 1943–44, the Estonian territory, previously 'free' of significant Soviet partisans' activity, included the following: of fifteen partisan groups and units officially subordinated by then to the Estonian PMH, only three were constantly communicating with their dispatchers from the Estonian soil, while only one, commanded by 'Malsroos', was reportedly located near Tallinn.[69]

The Latvian Red guerrillas, who since May 1943 were trying to leave the Osweja area for different destinations on the Latvian soil, had achieved this goal but stepwise and after many months of devastating clandestine advance through the territory ruled by the enemy and inhabited by people who were still hostile to the Soviets. The Osweja force, hardly pressured by the Latvian communist leadership in Moscow, had crossed the border by three sub-groups heading to three different places in eastern Latvia between September and December 1943. The rest, led by Samsons and deployed in Russia, next to the Russian-Belarusian-Latvian border triangle, had not reached its final destination in the very close northeastern Latvian forests until March 1944, only a few months before the Soviet summer offensive finally swept the Germans out of the region.[70] At that same time, the Lithuanian Red guerrillas were still distrusted by the wide circles of the local Lithuanian population and completely incapable of confronting the German and Lithuanian security forces. Thus, except for a series of insignificant incursions, they had not been able to infiltrate the inner Lithuanian regions. Their principal permanent base on the Lithuanian soil became, since the late summer–autumn of 1943, the Rūdininkai (Rudniki) Forest that occupies about 40,000 hectares of the southeastern Lithuanian territories, near the Belarusian border.[71]

The lengthy relocation alone was not sufficient for increasing the Baltic Red guerrillas' operational capabilities. The second crucial effort that aimed at achieving this target was the recruiting and training of additional manpower. Unfortunately for the three Baltic PMHs, the reserves of the young ethnic Balts living in the Soviet Union and available for this task were almost completely dried by the end of 1943: some were recruited earlier; others had already made their way to the so-called Estonian, Latvian and Lithuanian Riflemen Divisions of the Red Army that came into being in early 1943 and by autumn of that year were fighting on the Russian and Belarusian soil. The problem was partly solved by the recruitment of teenagers – Baltic, Jewish, Russian and others – who were born in Estonia, Latvia and Lithuania, evacuated to the Soviet Union, and still could not be recruited to the regular army because they were under the official recruitment age of eighteen.[72]

Another part of the solution was conscription, sometimes forceful, of the local population in the Baltic eastern regions that by now hosted the Soviet guerrillas' bases. Many of these new recruits were not of Baltic origin.[73] For instance, Zimanas had adopted in late 1943 a significant number of the Jewish escapees from different ghettos – thus creating the clear Jewish majority in some guerrilla groups and even establishing 'purely Jewish' units – and at some stage was forced to hide their national identity in an attempt to prevent deterioration of the vital relationships between his partisans and the local Lithuanian population characterized by a strong anti-Jewish stance. The Soviet prisoners of war who managed to escape from the POW camps in Vilnius, Kaunas, Alytus and other places were warmly welcomed as well. As a result, until the very end of the German occupation in Lithuania, the local Lithuanians and Poles constituted no more than a third of the communist guerrillas deployed in Rūdininkai, whose total number hardly surpassed 1,000. For the occupation's last six months, there were a few communist guerrilla groups that consisted mainly of Lithuanians – not only in the eastern borderlands but also in the more inner territories such as the Kaunas, Šiauliai and Kedainiai regions. Yet, they still were the clear minority – no more than 36 percent – in the predominantly not-Lithuanian mass of the 'Lithuanian' partisans.[74]

At the end of the day, the recruitment efforts of Baltic PMHs did not pay off: despite the later attempts of the Soviet and the Russian official historiography to present the local pro-Soviet, anti-Nazi resistance as a mass phenomenon, the real numbers of the fighters recruited until the occupation's end were relatively low. The current Lithuanian research speaks about up to 5,000 Lithuanian communist guerrillas and underground fighters throughout the entire German occupation period and stresses the fact that many of these people performed only minor tasks and thus were not 'real' resisters.[75] The Latvian up-to-date assessment counts about 4,000 Soviet irregulars – not only partisans but also special combat, sabotage and reconnaissance forces – who were active in Latvia in 1941–44.[76] Finally, recent Estonian sources estimate the total Red guerrillas' number in their country as no higher than

1,400.[77] Of all those, only approximately 2,500 were actually active in the beginning of 1944 – an insignificant number if compared to the 152,000 national Baltic partisans who would resist the renewed Soviet occupation by 1947.[78]

In 1944, similarly to the preceding periods, the lack of manpower was not the only obstacle in the way of the Baltic Red guerrillas' strengthening, streamlining and further geographical spreading. The severe logistic difficulty persisted, despite the constant protests sent to the highest Soviet political and military authorities, and since January 1944 – following the sudden and, by many accounts, premature CPMH dissolution by Stalin – even worsened, when the Baltic PMHs were forced to lean on the supply chains of the Red Army relevant fronts.[79] 'Our most urgent task was the obtaining of weapons', recalled Antons Riekšņa who entered southeastern Latvia in late March 1944.[80] The harsh infighting between the Baltic Red guerrillas and their comrades-turned-rivals from the Soviet special services did not disappear, either. It had reached its nadir in May 1944, on the eve of the region's liberation, when Sproģis and Snečkus accused the NKGB 'guests' of 'anti-Soviet behavior' – a very strong accusation at that time. This ostensibly included 'stealing' of partisan agents, plundering of Latvian and Lithuanian villages and even killing of local inhabitants, among them the partisans' sympathizers.[81]

At the same time, the Nazi's highly effective counterinsurgency effort, supported by different local police units and 'self-defense' militias, kept suppressing communist resistance across the region, including the apparently effective Rīga-based underground supervised by Sudmalis that ceased to exist in February 1944.[82] In Lithuania, as early as May 1944, German intelligence possessed a very detailed database on the Zimanas communist guerrillas – the exact locations of their camps and airfield in the Rūdininkai forest, names of units and commanders, numbers of fighters and assessment of armament.[83] 'They knew everything about us, used this knowledge skillfully, and would have smashed us completely, if they had more time and resources', recalled Jewish-Lithuanian female partisan paratrooper and radio operator Nina Papirmacher.[84] Moreover, the Gestapo had effectively exploited the hostility between Moscow and the Polish government in exile to instigate a parallel 'small war' between the Red guerrillas and the Polish national underground, the Home Army (*Armia Krajowa*), thus diminishing the Snečkus men's ability to act against the Germans.[85] In Estonia, German counterinsurgency proved especially effective: its organizers had exposed the identities of the predominant majority of the Estonian partisans sent into Estonia by the Karotamm headquarters, along with their local relatives and likely friendly contacts. As a result, only twenty-five tiny Red guerrilla cells, totaling just sixty-eight fighters, managed to survive in occupied Estonia between March and September 1944. Their previously highly prioritized task of promoting covert communist activities was now all but neglected in favor of minor reconnaissance assignments.[86]

In these persistently negative circumstances, the operational achievements of the Red Baltic guerrillas were far from remarkable. The Soviet postwar and the current Russian publications had prized them while counting numerous deadly blows to German key facilities, alongside with derailing and destruction of hundreds of German trains.[87] But this seems to be a baseless exaggeration since, for many of these actions, no mention has been found in relevant contemporary German and local documentary sources. In Estonia especially, these task were impossible to fulfill since the Estonian PMH guerrillas had operated by small cells of two to five members and frequently lacked sufficient armament and explosives. In the eastern borderlands of Latvia and Lithuania, there were many registered partisan attacks on the German forces and infrastructures,[88] but the majority of them were of minor significance. The Red guerrillas clearly avoided painful skirmishes with the Germans and the local security forces – thus enabling a smooth evacuation of the Nazi occupying apparatus – and preferred instead the encounters with the rural self-defense militias and unarmed peasants. In this regard, their two most notorious actions – in the Lithuanian and Latvian Kaniūkai and Mazie Bati villages – should be mentioned. Executed in January and May 1944 respectively, both had resulted in many innocent local people being killed or injured and their homesteads plundered and destroyed.[89]

The performance of intelligence tasks by the men of Karotamm, Snečkus and Sproģis appears to have been more successful. Although their attempt to cover the region with a vast network of human sources proved highly ineffective – the intelligence department of Latvian PMH had admitted that its sources were basically educated poor peasants and clerks from the eastern Russian-speaking parts of the country with no approach to the key figures and vital entities of the German civil and military authorities[90] – observations by agents and scouts, reading of open local publications and even interrogating of captured Germans and their aides had borne some valuable fruits. For instance, Latvian PMH reported proudly in August 1944 that its reconnaissance agents were able to recognize the precise location of thirty-eight stocks of fuel, armament, food and military equipment across occupied Latvia, including eighteen stocks in the capital city of Rīga.[91] The Soviet Airforce operations, based on this information, had caused major devastation to the Latvian cities and multiple casualties among their inhabitants.[92] Another remarkable intelligence achievement has been the forewarning of the Kremlin about the initial signs of the German retreat from 'Ostland'. A regular situational intelligence report of Lithuanian PMH disseminated on 9 September 1943 included for the first time a separate chapter titled 'Evacuation of the German officials' families' and provided an unprecedented description of the civil German population's withdrawal from Lithuania and neighboring Belarus.[93] The Baltic communist guerrillas followed closely the evacuation of different German entities until the end of the German rule in the region in summer through autumn 1944.[94]

Apart from the Red Army, the Soviet intelligence and security community enjoyed the assistance of the Estonian, Latvian and Lithuanian communist guerrillas and sometimes regarded it as very helpful. Their information on the common situation in the occupied Baltic Region, especially in its major cities, as well as the rich collections of the identification documents and other papers – public transport tickets, employees records of service, house management lists, etc. – issued by the occupying and the local authorities and thoroughly gathered by the partisan operatives and agents, allowed the NKGB, the military intelligence and other services to develop their own networks of agents in the Wehrmacht's operational depth. No less important was the assistance provided by the partisans – despite the tensions described above – to the single operatives and agents of different Soviet intelligence and security services, as well as to their different 'special' groups, by giving them a temporary or permanent shelter at the forest camps; guiding them in the local operational environment; and sometimes even by 'loaning' them the partisan operatives, local assistants and intelligence sources.[95] One of this cooperation's most remarkable examples is dated late 1943–early 1944, when the Soviet intelligence officer nicknamed 'Ivan Ivanovich' effectively infiltrated the Lithuanian city of Kaunas, delivered his reports to Moscow via a partisans' radio transmitter and took refuge in a partisan camp after having been exposed by the Germans.[96]

Besides, in the last occupation months and the immediate aftermath of the German retreat from the Baltic States, the local communist guerrillas proved very helpful for the vast Soviet security and counterespionage apparatus that entered the recaptured territories together with the Red Army and sometimes even slightly beforehand. The long lists of the supposed 'German spies' and 'anti-Soviet elements' among the local population, compiled by the partisans, enabled not only the legitimate effort of neutralizing the former and present Nazi collaborators but also the new wave of Stalin's political manhunt on Baltic soil.[97]

## The final lost battles: autumn 1944–spring 1945

In September through November 1944, the Red Army successfully expelled the Germans from Estonia, Latvia and Lithuania; there was no longer any need to maintain the Baltic PMHs, and they were dissolved by the Soviet People's Commissar of Defense. The relevant officers and soldiers were delivered to the Red Army and the Soviet intelligence and security services; many other former Red guerrillas had filled the ranks of the reestablished Soviet Baltic administrative apparatus. But there was still a place on the Latvian soil that remained uncaptured by the Soviets – Courland or Kurzeme in Latvian, a small region near the Baltic Sea which comprises about 27,000 square kilometers of swamps, lakes and wooded dunes. Here the remnants of the Wehrmacht Army Group North and of the Latvian auxiliary forces had barricaded themselves, creating the so-called 'Courland Pocket', while the local ports of Liepāja and Ventspils served for evacuating German soldiers and wounded, as well as for shipping out forced laborers and prisoners needed to build up the Reich's defenses. Between October 1944 and May 1945, the

Soviets had launched six offensives that aimed at annihilating the 'Pocket' but were repulsed by its defenders, at the heavy cost of many thousands of dead, wounded and imprisoned soldiers on both sides. Thus, the Wehrmacht force remained trapped but undefeated in Courland until the Nazi Germany capitulation on 8 May 1945.[98]

In the late autumn of 1944, after having understood their inability to break through the German defenses exclusively by means of conventional warfare, the Soviets had made an attempt to wage a local insurgency behind the German lines. Supported by different Soviet military, naval, intelligence and security agencies – by this time, Latvian PMH was already dissolved – it was expected to provide them with vital military and other information from within the 'Courland Pocket', as well as to diminish the adversary's fighting potential by damaging its forces, installations, and communications. Its core consisted of a few Communist Party and Latvian PMH operatives, such as Andrejs Macpāns, who had reached Courland in late 1943 and since then had been trying – without much success – to set up the anti-Nazi resistance. The approaching of the frontline in the autumn of 1944 gave that effort a new birth. The guerrillas adopted in their ranks a growing number of the escaping Soviet POWs and enemy deserters – mostly from the Latvian auxiliary forces – while their logistic gaps were filled, at least partly, by different Soviet special assignment groups that landed in Courland. Together they were able to provide the Red Army with some valuable information – especially regarding the Wehrmacht installations and defending forces at the seaports – and managed to commit a series of sabotage acts against the German communication lines.[99]

Alas, this operational 'renaissance' came to its end in March 1945, following the wide-scaled German anti-guerrilla operation inflicted upon the Courland Red partisans – by this time, a few hundred fighters – and forced them to take refuge in the local forests until the Germans finally surrendered.[100] Amazingly, German security superiority within the 'Courland Pocket' proved decisive even during that very final stage of World War II and prevented the Soviets from assisting the hunted and besieged irregulars effectively.

## Epilogue: neither giants nor dwarfs

The features of the Baltic Red guerrillas' phenomenon have been deliberately blurred since the last shell exploded in Courland. Contrary to what the Soviet and the Russian official historiography has zealously claimed, the men and women who took part in this anti-Nazi resistance enterprise were not numerous, predominantly of Baltic origin and operationally effective enough to influence the major fighting events on the Eastern front – nor were they professional but utterly ineffective irregulars, as some of the Baltic historians present them. The currently available Soviet archival sources and uncensored testimonies of the guerrillas themselves create a different picture. The Baltic

Red guerrillas, consisting of three Estonian, Latvian and Lithuanian subgroups, had no more than a few thousand members and even less active fighters throughout the entire Nazi occupation period; were ethnically heterogeneous, with Balts constituting less than 50 percent of the manpower; predominantly very poorly fed, dressed, trained and equipped; and nearly worthless as combatants and saboteurs. Nonetheless, this ragtag force succeeded in infiltrating the occupied Baltic Region – mostly to the eastern borderlands but sometimes also to the more remote places like Courland – survived there despite severe human losses until the approaching of the Red Army; and even provided at least partially valuable intelligence and other assistance to the Soviet political, military, intelligence and security authorities.

But the most striking fact in the Baltic Red guerrillas' story is that their weaknesses derived not only, and probably not primarily, from the objective circumstances, like the minor importance of the Baltic geographical theater for the Soviet war effort, and from the negative features of the operational environment, especially the high effectiveness of the German security apparatus. It appears that their operational potential had been constantly diminished and even damaged – probably intentionally – by the leadership of the Soviet Partisan Movement and different Soviet Special Forces that were active in the occupied Baltic Region. That revelation opens the door for a much broader discussion about the tense relationships between different Soviet elites during World War II and their influence on the war outcomes.

## Notes

1  Inesis Feldmanis, *Latvija Otraja Pasaules karā (1939–1945): jauns konceptuāls skatījums* (Rīga: Latvijas Universitāte, 2015), 30–57; Anatol Lieven, *The Baltic Revolution: Estonia, Latvia, Lithuania and the Path to Independence* (New Haven, CT: Yale University Press, 1994), 183; Andrejs Plakans, *A Concise History of the Baltic States* (Cambridge: Cambridge University Press, 2011), 355–6; Geoffrey Swain, *Between Stalin and Hitler: Class War and Race War on the Dvina, 1940–46* (London and New York: RoutledgeCruzon, 2004), 3–7, 14–46.

2  Markku Jokisipilä, "Somija un Baltijas republikas Padomju Savienības un Vācijas spīles (1939–1944)," in *Latvijas Vēsturnieku komisijas raksti (LVKR)*, 15. sējums, Andris Caune, Inesis Feldmanis, Heinrihs Strods, Irēne Šneidere (Redakcijas kolēģija) (Rīga: Latvijas Universitātes Latvijas vēstures institūts, 2005), 99–126; Alfred J. Rieber, *Stalin and the Struggle for Supremacy in Europe* (Cambridge: Cambridge University Press, 2015), 201–11.

3  Aleksandr Drizul, *Bor'ba latyshskogo naroda v gody Velikoi Otechestvennoi voiny* (Rīga: Zinātne, 1970); Rudolf Lumi, *Partizanskaia voina i antifashistskoe dvizhenie v Estonii v period Velikoi Otechestvennoi voiny* (Tallinn: Institut istorii partii pri TsK KP Estonii, 1968); Motiejus Šumauskas, *V vodovorote bor'by* (Moskva: Politizdat, 1975); Vladimir Zolotariov, *Partizanskoe dvizhenie. Po opytu Velikoi Otechestvennoi voiny 1941–1945 gg* (Zhukovskii-Moskva: Kuchkovo Pole, 2001), 256–62, 272–81.

4  Feldmanis, *Latvija Otraja Pasaules karā (1939–1945)*, 62; Heinrihs Strods, "Nacionālie un padomju partizāni Baltijā 1941.-1956. gadā: kopējais un atšķirīgais," in *LVKR*, 17. sējums, Andris Caune, Heinrihs Strods, Antonijs Zunda (Redakcijas kolēģija) (Rīga: Latvijas Universitātes Latvijas vēstures institūts, 2006), 19–35.

5  Yaacov Falkov, *Meragle ha-ye'arot: pe'ilutam ha-modi'init shel ha-parţizanim ha-Sovyeţim 1941–1945* (Jerusalem: The Hebrew University Magness Press and The Yad Vashem Press, 2017).

6   Lieven, *The Baltic Revolution*, 183; Alexander Statiev, "The Soviet Union," in *Hitler's Europe Ablaze: Occupation, Resistance, and Rebellion during World War II*, ed. Philip Cook and Ben H. Shepherd (New York City, NY: Skyhorse Publishing, 2014), 206.

7   Daina Bleiere, Ilgvars Butulis, Inesis Feldmanis, Aivars Stranga, and Antonijs Zunda, *Latvija Otrajā Pasaules Karā* (Rīga: Jumava, 2008), 244–8; David R. Stone, "Operations on the Eastern Front, 1941–1945," in *The Cambridge History of the Second World War*, ed. John Ferris and Evan Mawdsley, Vol. 1 (Cambridge: Cambridge University Press, 2015), 337.

8   Feldmanis, *Latvija Otraja Pasaules karā (1939–1945)*, 54–7; Iuliia Kantor, *Pribaltika: Voina bez pravil (1939–1945)* (Sankt-Peterburg: Zhurnal 'Zvezda', 2011), 99–125; Antonijs Zunda, "Vācu nacistu okupācijas politika Latvijā padomju historiogrāfijas skatījumā," in *LVKR*, 13. sējums, Andris Caune, Inesis Feldmanis, Heinrihs Strods, Irēne Šneidere (Redakcijas kolēģija) (Rīga: Latvijas Universitātes Latvijas vēstures institūts, 2004), 202–3.

9   Bericht unseres Vertrauenmannes, Mitte August 1941, "Eindrücke aus dem Baltikum," Bundesarchiv-Militärarchiv (BA-MA), RW 5/52, UdSSR Nr. 85, S. 168–9; Swain, *Between Stalin and Hitler*, 17–46.

10  Bleiere, Butulis, Feldmanis, Stranga, and Zunda, *Latvija Otrajā Pasaules Karā*, 261–77; Kantor, *Pribaltika*, 122–5; Kārlis Kangeris, "Policijas struktūras Latvijā vācu okupacijas laikā," in *LVKR*, 16. sējums, Andris Caune, Inesis Feldmanis, Heinrihs Strods, Irēne Šneidere (Redakcijas kolēģija) (Rīga: Latvijas Universitātes Latvijas vēstures institūts, 2005), 278–318; Heinrihs Strods, "Latvijas pirmās padomju okupācijas aktīvistu vajāšanas (1941. gada 23. jūnijs – 1945. gads)," in *LVKR*, 16. sējums, 106–204.

11  Falkov, *Meragle ha-ye'arot*, 27–30; Statiev, "The Soviet Union," 191–7.

12  The State Defence Committee's Order No. 1837cc 'Instructions about the Central Partisan Movement's Headquarters and the Partisan Movement's Headquarters subordinated to the military councils of the relevant fronts', 30 May 1942, The Russian State Archive of Socio-Political History (RGASPI), f. 69, op. 1, d. 1, l. 1–5.

13  On the eve of 'incorporation' of the Baltic countries into the USSR (1940–41), there were about 1,500 registered communists in Lithuania, about 1,000 in Latvia, and only 133 in Estonia. See: Boris Sokolov, "Baltijas valstis (1939–1945) Krievijas historiogrāfijā: kontrnacionālisms," *LVKR*, 15. sējums, 93.

14  Juris Pavlovičs, "Okupācijas varu maiņa Latgalē 1941. gada vasarā," in *LVKR*, 13. sējums, 215–25; Swain, *Between Stalin and Hitler*, 48–51.

15  Pekka Erelt, "Neeme Ruus – reetur ja reedu," *Eesti Ekspress*, 5 February 2002, http://ekspress.delfi.ee/kuum/neeme-ruus-reetur-ja-reedetu?id=69015693; Erik Nørgaard, *Mordet i Kongelunden* (København: Lindhardt og Ringhof, 2017), 9–19; Pruun Katk, *Saksa fašistlik okupatsioon Eestis 1941–1944. Dokumente ja materjale* (Tallinn: Eesti Raamat, 1988), 145; Lumi, *Partizanskaia voina i antifashistskoe*, 13–14; Valdur Ohman, "EKP Keskkomitee I sekretäri Karl Säre arreteerimisest, reetlikkusest ja tema saatusest," *Tuna*, Nr. 4 (2001): 38–47.

16  Bleiere, Butulis, Feldmanis, Stranga, and Zunda, *Latvija Otrajā Pasaules Karā*, 325–6; Marģers Vestermanis, *Vēstules nākamībai. Latvijas partizāņu kustības un komunistiskās pagrīdes cīnītāju pirmsnāves atvadas* (Rīga: Liesma, 1965), 23–6.

17  'On the situation in occupied Latvia', an undated report signed by 'Sudmal' from the summer of 1942, The Lithuanian Special Archives (LYA), f. 1, ap. 1, b. 26, l. 4–8.

18  Swain, *Between Stalin and Hitler*, 73–4.

19  The Secretary of the Central Committee of the Latvian Communist Party, Ernests Ameriks, to the CPMH head, Ponomarenko, 'The report by Ieva Paldiņa, the commander of the Central Committee of the Latvian Communist Party organizational group an of the partisan regiment "For Soviet Latvia," on the Latvian partisans' activity,' 20 August 1942, RGASPI, f. 69, op. 1, d. 445, l. 29–34; The Estonian Partisan Movement Headquarters to unknown recipient, undated report from the late spring of 1944, The State Archives of Estonia (ERAF), f. 4, n. 1, s. 33, l. 6.

20  Rimantas Zizas, *Sovietiniai partizanai Lietuvoje 1941–1944 m* (Vilnius: Lietuvos istorijos instituto leidykla, 2014), 71, 73–5, 98–9.

21  Audronė Janavičienė, "Sovietiniai diversantai Lietovuje (1941–1944)," *Genocidas ir rezistencija*, no. 1 (2007): 98–121.
22  Bleiere, Butulis, Feldmanis, Stranga, and Zunda, *Latvija Otrajā Pasaules Karā*, 324.
23  Zolotariov, *Partizanskoe dvizhenie*, 34.
24  Interview with a former Latvian KGB colonel Felix Sausverd, Riga, 26 February 2006.
25  Falkov, *Meragle ha-ye'arot*, 30–4, 106–20, 156–66, 177–202.
26  Ibid., 34–6, 321–7.
27  Viacheslav Boiarski, *Partizany i armiia. Istoriia uteriannykh vozmozhnostei* (Minsk: Harvest, 2001), 224–9; Aleksandr Gogun, *Stalinskie kommandos. Ukrainskie partizanskie formirovaniia 1941–1944* (Moskva: ROSSPEN, 2012), 192–3; Sebastian Stopper, "'Die Straße ist Deutsch.' Der sowjetische Partisanenkrieg und seine militärische Effizienz," *Vierteljahrshefte für Zeitgeschichte 59* 3 (2011): 385–411.
28  Order no. 77929 signed by the acting Commissar of Defense Yefim Shchadenko, 17 July 1942, RGASPI, f. 69, op. 1, d. 445, l. 26–26ob.
29  Swain, *Between Stalin and Hitler*, 93.
30  Ibid., 94; Heinrihs Strods, *PSRS kaujinieki Latvijā (1941–1945)*, Part 1 (Rīga: Žurnāla "Latvijas Vēsture" fonds, 2006), 58–112.
31  Heinrihs Strods, *PSRS kaujinieki Latvijā (1941–1945)*, Part 2 (Rīga: Žurnāla "Latvijas Vēsture" fonds, 2007), 26–7, 83.
32  Peeter Kaasik, "Partisan Movement in Estonia from 1941–1944," in *Estonians in Russian Armed Forces in 1940–1945*, Book 12, Compiled by Leo Õispuu (Tallinn: Tallinna Raamatutrükikojas, 2016), 27.
33  Strods, *PSRS kaujinieki Latvijā (1941–1945)*, Part 2, 139.
34  Janavičienė, "Sovietiniai diversantai Lietovuje (1941–1944)," 98–121; Kaasik, "Partisan Movement in Estonia from 1941–1944," 27.
35  Strods, *PSRS kaujinieki Latvijā (1941–1945)*, Part 1, 65.
36  Unknown reporter to the Secretary of the Central Committee of the Ukrainian Communist Party Nikita Khrushchev, 27 July 1943, The Yad Vashem Archive (YVA), M-37/13, 6; Excerpt from CPMH Order no. 005, 8 January 1943, ERAF, f. 4, n. 1, s. 233, l. 10; The head of Latvian PMH intelligence department Kalnin to Sproģis, 'A report on the officers' special training for the activity in the enemy's rear,' 12 January 1944, The Latvian State Historical Archive (LVVA), 302. f., 2. apr., 33. l., 12.-13. lpp.
37  Meelis Saueauk, "Riikliku julgeoleku rahvakomissariaat (NKGB) Eestis 1944–1946," *Tuna*, Nr. 3 (2008): 36–7; Wojciech Roszkowski, *The Shadow of Yalta: A Report* (Warsaw: Warsaw Rising Museum, 2005), 55, 81.
38  The draft of 'The Final report of the Latvian PMH on the development and the outcomes of the Partisan Movement's activity in the temporarily occupied territories of the Latvian Soviet Socialist Republic,' 31 August 1944, LVVA, 302. f., 2. apr., 13. l., 238. lpp.; Swain, *Between Stalin and Hitler*, 133–4, 218–20.
39  Vilis Samsons, "Sarakste ar akadēmiķi Vili Samsonu" in Strods, *PSRS kaujinieki Latvijā (1941–1945)*, Part 2, 358.
40  A collective letter to Stalin signed by Snečkus, Karotamm and Kalnberzin, 9 March 1943, LYA, f. 1, ap. 1, b. 3, l. 2; The minutes of the meeting at Bel'cheko's office, 11 June 1943, RGASPI, f. 69, op. 1, d. 726, l. 146–7.
41  Zolotariov, *Partizanskoe dvizhenie*, 138, 165.
42  Sokolov, "Baltijas valstis (1939–1945) Krievijas historiogrāfijā," 95.
43  Janavičienė, "Sovietiniai diversantai Lietovuje (1941–1944)," 98–121.
44  Kaasik, "Partisan Movement in Estonia from 1941–1944," 28.
45  An ethnic minority in eastern Latvia. See: Plakans, *A Concise History of the Baltic States*, 32, 40.
46  Strods, *PSRS kaujinieki Latvijā (1941–1945)*, Part 1, 226; Part 2, 69–70, 154.
47  Janavičienė, "Sovietiniai diversantai Lietovuje (1941–1944)," 98–121; Rimantas Zizas, "Raudonųjų partizanų ir Pietryčių Lietuvos kaimų savisaugos ginkluoti konfliktai 1943 m.,

I dalis," in *Lietuva Antrajame pasauliniame kare*, Compiled by Arvydas Anušauskas and Česlovas Laurinavičius (Vilnius: Lietuvos gyventojų genocido ir rezistencijos tyrimo centras. Lietuvos istorijos institutas, 2007), 401–28.

48 The speech of Sprogis during the discussion at the CPMHon the Partisan Movement's condition, 11 June 1943, RGASPI, f. 69, op. 1, d. 726, l. 146–7.

49 Snečkus to the Head of CPMH Radio communication Department Ivan Artemiev, 30 April 1943, LYA, f. 1, ap. 1, b. 141, l. 45; The report by the Radio communication Department of Lithuanian PMH, 'On the radio communication capabilities of the Lithuanian Partisan Movement Headquarters,' 16 May 1943, Ibid., l. 60–1; Snečkus to Artemiev, 3 June 1943, Ibid., b. 138, l. 67–8; A radio station operator 'Butkus' to the Radio communication Department of Lithuanian PMH, undated report from August 1943, Ibid., b. 1, l. 46.

50 Strods, *PSRS kaujinieki Latvijā (1941–1945)*, Part 2, 134.

51 Swain, *Between Stalin and Hitler*, 109.

52 Strods, *PSRS kaujinieki Latvijā (1941–1945)*, Part 2, 134.

53 'Agenturmeldung über die Stärke der Partisanen und ihre Tätigkeit im Rajon Osweja in der Zeit vom 1.1. bis 22.1.43,' YVA, JM 11359.

54 An undated report of the Latvian First Partisan Brigade on the German double-agent Ivan Bogdanov, May 1943, LVVA, 302.f., 1.apr., 67.l., 4.lpp.; An undated report of the Latvian First Partisan Brigade on the German double-agent Avdeenko, September 1943, LVVA, 302. f., 1. apr., 67. l., 32.lpp.

55 Brigita Balikienė, "Diversantė MM," *Istorijos*, January 9, 2006, www.delfi.lt/gyvenimas/istorijos/diversante-mm.d?id=8459550.

56 Kārlis Kangeris, "Latviešu policijas bataljoni lielajās partizānu apkarošanas akcijās 1942. un 1943. Gadā," in *LVKR*, 13. sējums, 332–57; Natalia Kirillova and Viacheslav Selemenev, Comp., *Tragediia belorusskikh dereven' 1941–1944. Dokumenty i materialy* (Minsk-Moskva: Fond 'Istoricheskaia pamiat', 2011), 6; Swain, *Between Stalin and Hitler*, 107–8.

57 Kārlis Kangeris, "'Nodeva reiham' – Latvijas ģenerālapgabala iedzīvotāji darbos Lielvācijā," *Latvijas Zinātņu Akadēmijas Vēstis*, no. 12 (1990), 34–48; Swain, *Between Stalin and Hitler*, 122–6.

58 The speech of Sprogis' during the discussion at the CPMH on the Partisan Movement's condition, 11 June 1943, RGASPI, f. 69, op. 1, d. 726, l. 146–7; Sprogis to Ponomarenko, 30 June 1943, Ibid., d. 742, l. 1–2.; 'On the lack of coordination between the NKVD and GRU "Operative Groups" and the local partisan detachments,' a report signed by Sprogis and Kalnin and addressed to Bel'cheko, 19 August 1943, Ibid., d. 742, l. 2–2ob.

59 Sprogis to Ponomarenko, 12 August 1943, LVVA, 302. f., 1. apr., 32. l., 66. lpp.

60 Kaasik, "Partisan Movement in Estonia from 1941–1944," 28.

61 Janavičiené, "Sovietiniai diversantai Lietuvoje (1941–1944)," 98–121; Zizas, "Raudonųjų partizanų . . .," 401–28.

62 Swain, *Between Stalin and Hitler*, 123.

63 Bleiere, Butulis, Feldmanis, Stranga, and Zunda, *Latvija Otrajā Pasaules Karā*, 325–6.

64 Strods, *PSRS kaujinieki Latvijā (1941–1945)*, Part 2, 91–2, 2014–205; A letter to Sprogis signed by Belchenko and Anisimov, 20 July 1943, LVVA, 302. f., 1. apr., 29. l., 99. lpp.

65 Ponomarenko to Molotov, an undated report from the summer of 1943, NARB, f. 1450, op. 2, d. 5, l. 48; 'Shurman' to Ponomarenko, an undated report from the summer of 1943, Ibid., l. 49–50.

66 Stone, "Operations on the Eastern Front, 1941–1945," 350–1.

67 An undated CPMH order from November 1943, LYA, f. 1, ap. 1, b. 18, l. 81.

68 The intelligence department of the 1st Baltic Front Headquarters to Sprogis, 31 December 1943, LVVA, 302. f., 2. apr., 33. l., 1. lpp.; The head of the Red Army paratroopers command major-general Dosik to Karotamm, 4 February 1944, ERAF, f. 4, n. 1, s. 59, l. 37.

69 The undated map of the active Estonian PMH's radio transmitters, the winter of 1943–4, ERAF, f. 4, n. 1, s. 3, l. 13.

70  'The Report by the Latvian Partisan Movement Headquarters on the development and operational achievements of the partisan movement in the temporarily occupied territories of the Latvian Soviet Socialist Republic,' 31 August 1944, The Latvian State Historical Archive (LVVA), 302. f., 2. apr., 13. l., 270. lpp.; Swain, *Between Stalin and Hitler*, 122–3, 130–3.

71  Janavičienė, "Sovietiniai diversantai Lietuvoje (1941–1944)," 98–121; Zizas, "Raudonųjų partizanų . . .," 401–28.

72  Ibid.; Interview with a former Jewish-Lithuanian partisan Nina Papirmacher, Israel, Kiryat Yam, 6 April 2006.

73  Bleiere, Butulis, Feldmanis, Stranga, and Zunda, *Latvija Otrajā Pasaules Karā*, 333.

74  Janavičienė, "Sovietiniai diversantai Lietuvoje (1941–1944)," 98–121.

75  Ibid.

76  Strods, *PSRS kaujinieki Latvijā (1941–1945)*, Part 2, 237, 381.

77  Peeter Kaasik, "Soviet Partisan Movement in Estonia 1941–1944," *Estonica. Encyclopedia about Estonia*, Eesti Instituut, October 1, 2012, www.estonica.org/en/Soviet-partisan_movement_in_Estonia_1941-1944/

78  Heinrihs Strods, "Nacionālie un padomju partizāni . . . ," 34.

79  Falkov, *Meragle ha-ye'arot*, 166–8.

80  Antons Riekšņa, *Caur mežiem un purviem* (Rēzekne: Latgales Kultūras Izdevniecība, 2010), 124.

81  Snečkus to Sudoplatov, 16 May 1944, LYA, f. 1, ap. 1, b. 28, l. 82; Sproģis to Kalnberzin and the head of the NKGB 4th Directorate Sudoplatov, 23 May 1944, LVVA, 302. f., 2. apr., 5. l., 43. lpp.

82  Vestermanis, *Vēstules nākamībai*, 25.

83  Wehrmachtbefehlshaber Weißrutenien Abt. Ic – Az.: 3/Pa 1920/44 geh. H. Qu., den 28.5.1944, 'Bandenverzeichnis. Stand: 25.5.1944', S. 30, BA MA, RW 5/467.

84  Interview with a former Jewish-Lithuanian partisan Nina Papirmacher, Israel, Kiryat Yam, 6 April 2006.

85  'Ausw. Amt Pol 756 g v. 7.3. Abschrift,' BA-MA, RW 5/464, S. 111; Janavičienė, "Sovietiniai diversantai Lietuvoje (1941–1944)," 98–121.

86  Kaasik, "Soviet Partisan Movement in Estonia 1941–1944," 29.

87  Panteleimon Ponomarenko, *Vsenarodnaia bor'ba v tylu nemetsko-fashistskikh zakhvatchikov 1941–1944* (Moskva: Nauka, 1986), 276; Alfreds Raškevics, "Za Sovetskuiu Latviiu," in *Sovetskie partizany: Iz istorii partizanskogo dvizheniia v gody Velikoi Otechestvennoi voiny*, ed V. Bystrov and Z. Politov (Moskva: Gospolitizdat, 1961), 590–630; Zolotariov, *Partizanskoe dvizhenie*, 186, 272–81.

88  Anlage 1 zu W Bfh Ostland Ia Nr. 527/44 geh. v. 31.1.44, 'Bandenlage Januar 1944. In den Sicherungsgebieten Lettland und Litauen mit Truppenverteilung, Stichtag: 31.1.1944,' BA-MA, RW 41/51 K-1; Ibid., Anlage 1 zu W Bfh Ostland Ia Nr. 1602/44 geh. v. 31.3.1944, 'Bandenlage März 1944. In den Sicherungsgebieten Lettland und Litauen mit Truppenverteilung, Stichtag: 31.3.1944,' Ibid., RW 41/51 K-2.

89  *Case of Kononov vs. Latvia (Application no. 36376/04)*, European Court of Human Rights, Grand Chamber, Strasbourg, May 17, 2010, https://hudoc.echr.coe.int/eng#{%22appno%22:[%2236376/04%22],%22itemid%22: [%22001-98669%22]}; 'Informacja o śledztwie dotyczącym zbrodni popełnionej w Koniuchach', Komunikat, 30 June 2018, Institut Pamięci Narodowej, https://ipn.gov.pl/pl/dla-mediow/komunikaty/9980,Informacja-o-sledztwie-dotyczacym-zbrodni-popelnionej-w-Koniuchach.html; Swain, *Between Stalin and Hitler*, 140, 247–8; Andrius Tumavičius, 'Kaniūkų kaimo tragedija', Lietuvos gyventojų genocido ir rezistencijos tyrimo centras (February 2014), http://genocid.lt/UserFiles/File/Atmintinos_datos/2014/02/201402_kaniuku.pdf.

90  'The Report by Latvian Partisan Movement Headquarters on the development and operational achievements of the partisan movement in the temporarily occupied territories of the Latvian Soviet Socialist Republic', 31 August 1944, LVVA, 302. f., 2. apr., 13. l.,

232–79. lpp.; Felix Sausverd, a retired colonel of the Latvian KGB, approved this by claiming that the Latvian communist guerrilla intelligence had failed to infiltrate the Nazi occupying apparatus: Interview with Felix Sausverd, a former Latvian KGB colonel, Rīga, 26 February 2006.

91  'The Report by Latvian Partisan Movement Headquarters on the development and operational achievements of the partisan movement in the temporarily occupied territories of the Latvian Soviet Socialist Republic,' 31 August 1944, LVVA, 302. f., 2. apr., 13. l., 262. lpp.

92  Strods, *PSRS kaujinieki Latvijā (1941–1945)*, Part 2, 10.

93  'A concluding informational report of the Lithuanian Partisan Movement Headquarters from 9 September 1943 based on the materials provided by the partisans on 7–9 September 1943,' signed by the assistant to the intelligence chief of the Lithuanian PMH Gladutis, 9 September 1943, LYA, f. 1, ap. 1, b. 26. l. 72.

94  'Intelligence reports of the Lithuanian Partisan Movement Headquarters,' Baranauskas to Anisimov, 10 October 1943, LYA, f. 1, ap. 1, b. 22. l. 111; 'Intelligence Digest No. 12', Baranauskas to CPMH, 16 October 1943, Ibid., l. 113; 'Intelligence report' by Yurison, 18 October 1943, ERAF, f. 4, n. 1, s. 51, l. 5; 'Intelligence report' by Yurison, 22 October 1943; Ibid., l. 8–9; 'Intelligence report' by 'Kadriorg', undated document from October 1943, Ibid., l. 11; 'Intelligence report' by Vial'tsev, 20 December 1943, Ibid., l. 24; 'The Report by the Latvian Partisan Movement Headquarters on the development and operational achievements of the partisan movement in the temporarily occupied territories of the Latvian Soviet Socialist Republic', 31 August 1944, LVVA, 302. f., 2. apr., 13. l., 262. lpp.

95  The intelligence department's head of the 2nd Baltic Front, lieutenant-colonel Romanov, to Snečkus, 7 February 1944, LYA, f. 1, ap. 1, b. 28, l. 10; The deputy head of the Intelligence Directorate of the Red Army General Headquarters brigadier-general Nikolai Sherstniov to Sproģis, 28 March 1944, LVVA, 302. f., 2. apr., 33. l., 94. lpp.; Sproģis and Kalnin to Romanov, 8 January 1944, Ibid., 2. lpp.; A report by Aleksandrs Groms, the head of the intelligence department of the Latvian First Partisan Brigade, to unknown recipient, 15 March 1944, Ibid., 1. apr., 161. l., 140. lpp.

96  Interview with Nina Papirmacher, Israel, Kiryat Yam, 6 April 2006; Baranauskas to the commander of the Lithuanian NKGB 'Operative Group' Aleksandras Gudaitis-Guzevičius, LYA, f. 1, ap. 1, b. 28, l. 25.

97  Strods, *PSRS kaujinieki Latvijā (1941–1945)*, Part 2, 327.

98  Vincent Hunt, *Blood in the Forest: The End of the Second World War in the Courland Pocket* (Warwick: Helion & Company, 2017), 21–2.

99  Bleiere, Butulis, Feldmanis, Stranga, and Zunda, *Latvija Otrajā Pasaules Karā*, 331–3; Drizul, *Bor'ba latyshskogo naroda*, 855–6, 861–2; Vilis Samsons, *Kurzemes meži šalg . . . Partizāņu un izlūku cīņa kara pēdējā gada Kurzemē 1944–1945* (Rīga: Liesma, 1974), 15–17, 57–118; Macpāns to the Headquarters of the Latvian Communist Party, 13 June 1944, LVVA, 302. f., 4. apr., 12. l. 115. lpp.

100 Samsons, *Kurzemes meži šalg*, 175–6, 503, 529–42; Strods, *PSRS kaujinieki Latvijā (1941–1945)*, Part 1, 176–86.

# 8 Indigenous resistance as irregular warfare

## The role of Kachin forces in SOE and OSS covert operations during the Burma campaign

*Robert A. Farnan*

## Introduction

In March 1943, the Kachin people of northern Burma did not need to be told that war was about to descend on their mountainous homeland. By March of that year, they would witness its build-up first hand, as a reported convoy of fifty-eight Japanese vehicles began their approach to the town of Sumprabum from the south. Simultaneously, across the Mali Hka River to the east – in an area west of the Nmai Hka River known as 'the Triangle' – the Japanese were amassing a sizeable force with the express aim of ousting the British from Burma. By the time the news of this offensive reached the military commander of the Northern Kachin Levies (NKL), Australian Colonel Ralph Gamble, the Japanese 18th Division had circumvented the main arterial road, advancing through the dense jungle to outflank his position on the right.

For the local Kachin, as Japanese atrocities mounted, it was hardly a question of whether they would resist the invader. Even though resources were scarce, and despite the fact that they would initially neither be fed nor armed, Kachin mobilisation was swift, as able-bodied men and women swelled the early ranks of the Levies' various platoons. As a portend of the unique combat environment, strategic autonomy, organisational adaptability and tactical learning that would characterise, inhibit but also bolster their struggle, local Kachin people undertook in great numbers the arduous task of feeding and defending their communities for themselves. They did this by digging for root vegetables, for instance, as well as by ambushing Japanese patrols, often with the most rudimentary of weapons.[1] Despite the hardships faced by the Levies, morale remained high as it was believed the Japanese could be held off until reinforcements from India were brought into Fort Hertz.[2]

This high morale would prove to be misplaced in the coming days. Gradually, optimism gave way to panic as the IV Corps, stationed in India, declared that it would no longer be able to reinforce the Levies at Fort Hertz. Instead, it put forth a clever, even daring, plan to evacuate the remaining Allied forces out of Burma over the icy Chaukan Pass. This perilous route, skirting the north-western precipices of the great Himalayan range separating Burma from India, reaches close to ten thousand feet. The difficulty of this crossing is attested to by the fact that, by 1942, only five Europeans had successfully traversed the Chaukan, and none had done so in the preceding fifty years.[3] With no such evacuation option of their own, the Kachin held firm in their jungle hideouts, haranguing and sniping at the Japanese as they advanced northwards to the west of the main road connecting Sumprabum to the last allied stronghold in Burma, Fort Hertz.

However, without reinforcements and despite inflicting considerable casualties, the Kachin Levies were unable to hold off the advance of the well-supplied Japanese forces. By 18th March, Suprabum had fallen, and Colonel Gamble was forced to withdraw his headquarters to La Awn Ga village, fifteen miles further north.[4] The following week, having endured persistent Kachin ambushes and with their supply lines stretched, the Japanese advance finally came to a halt at Sumprabum. This gave the Levies a respite from fighting and the much-needed time and opportunity required to reconstitute itself. Foreshadowing the strategic significance this small town in northern Burma would have on the subsequent Allied war effort in mainland Asia, Fort Hertz, in what would become a Kachin state, emerged as a crucial staging post for aerial resupply and troop reinforcement, as two Gurkha companies were flown in to help consolidate Levie defensive positions. With ground forces now supported in the air by the introduction of United States Army Air Forces (USAAF) fighter aircraft from Assam, subsequent Japanese offensives were halted at the Hpuncha Hka River. This would be the furthest north the Japanese would reach during the war in Burma,[5] but it was only the beginning of the involvement of the indigenous Kachin peoples in the war.

The principle question animating this chapter unpacks the significance of these events by asking: what role did the oft-overlooked indigenous forces, particularly the Northern Kachin Levies and Kachin Rangers, play in Special Operation Executive (SOE) and Office of Strategic Services (OSS) covert operations during the Second World War? It tackles this question by chronologically assessing the pre-conflict formation of the SOE's 'left-behind' scheme in Burma under the auspices of the Oriental Mission; the subsequent development of the India Mission in the period following the British retreat in 1942; and the SOE DILWYN and OSS KNOTHEAD operations respectively. In doing so, it is able to identify and illuminate across these periods not only the key role played by indigenous forces in this arena of war but also, relatedly, three specific and critical ways in which the allied relationship with these indigenous groups rendered the campaign in northern Burma unique.

These three interrelated factors are as follows. The first is the extent to which the campaign's unique combat environment, particularly its harsh terrain and lack of transport infrastructure, necessitated the adoption of covert special operations that focused not only on the standard activities of sabotage and intelligence gathering but also (especially) on the development of supply logistics and 'soft' infrastructure. The former is understood here as aerial resupply and the latter as the recruitment and training of indigenous forces. The importance of supply logistics and 'soft' infrastructure to the Burma campaign has, like the Kachin forces with which they were intertwined, been overlooked in histories of the SOE (and indeed OSS) in favour of the more overt and conventional special operations activities of sabotage and intelligence gathering.

The second factor is the strategic autonomy that would come to characterise operations in this region. Because of the relative dearth of allied manpower and materials in northern Burma, a consequence of the prioritisation by the British War Office of the European theatre, SOE officers and their indigenous allies were generally left more or less to their own devices and were thus able to foster a degree of autonomy and independence that was unheard of in other theatres of war.

The third factor, interconnected with those above, refers to the way in which the Allied-indigenous relationship fostered organisational adaptability and tactical learning, again an aspect of the Second World War in this region that has often been overlooked. As I will show, this is exemplified by the acknowledged necessity of recruiting either Burmese or Anglo-Burmese personnel who knew how to traverse the hostile environment and could go undercover and also by the gradual adoption of long-range aerial penetration as a means by which to overcome and learn from the mistakes of earlier overland infiltration attempts.

This analysis has implications for military history scholarship, which has hitherto downplayed the role of Kachin groups in the Burma campaign and in doing so has therefore overlooked these important nuances that contribute to our understanding of how the war in this region unfolded. This renders northern Burma, I would argue, another 'forgotten front'. The chapter proceeds as follows. First, in the remainder of the introductory section, I contextualise the role of the Kachin in this operational arena, with a brief background of the geopolitical significance of the war here in what would become Kachin state and of the colonial administration of Burma. I then discuss the state of knowledge on special operations during the Burma campaign before chronologically assessing the institutional trajectory of both the SOE and OSS. As intimated above, I assess their formation during the embryonic stages of conflict through to their subsequent maturation as offensive, force-multiplying, covert organisations following their early infiltration operations – DILWYN and KNOTHEAD – behind Japanese lines in 1943.

## The Kachin and the geopolitical significance of northern Burma

Approximately the same size as Afghanistan and the U.S. state of Texas, Burma is the second largest country in Southeast Asia after Indonesia. As the westernmost country on the mainland, it stretches 2,052 kilometres from its northern reaches near the border of India and China, southward down the Bay of Bengal, skirting Thailand's boundary along the Isthmus of Kra.[6] Situated along the mainstream of two of Southeast Asia's great rivers, the Salween and the Irrawaddy, the country's physical environment is also divided into three distinct zones; coastal, central plain and upland mountains. It is the latter that also forms the country's political borders with neighbouring China, India, Laos and Thailand. It is these jungle-covered upland mountain regions that are of principle concern to us as the places inhabited largely by the country's ethnic minority groups such as the Kachin. A horseshoe-shaped ring of mountains surrounds the Burman-dominated central plain and has historically acted as a kind of internal physical constraint on state expansion into the hills. Apart from the Shan, the indigenous peoples of this upland region did not organise themselves into centralised, rice-cultivating paddy states, nor for that matter adopt the country's Hindu-Buddhist cosmology of the lowland state peoples.

The remoteness of some of these areas from central authority extends from pre-colonial times through to the annexation of the country into British India and up to the Japanese occupation. To this day, there are regions of northern Burma, such as in Kachin country, that are effectively beyond the reach and control of the country's central government. Additionally, this is a harsh landscape and difficult terrain, with nearly impenetrable jungle combined with climatic extremes posed by Burma's seasonal monsoon. Despite the geopolitical significance of the country more broadly, sandwiched between China and India, Burma's north was unsurprisingly one of the most complex and challenging theatres of the Second World War.

## The Kachin and the colonial administration of Burma

On the eve of the Japanese invasion, Burma exhibited all the signs of a classic colonial economy. Since the British 'pacification' of Burma after the third Anglo-Burmese war in the late nineteenth century, the British imposed control over upland ethnic areas and transformed the politico-economic structures that once upheld pre-colonial society.[7] Economically, the country was gradually integrated into the globalised economic system, dominated by the British, that primarily focused on resource extraction and the exportation of raw materials, which hindered the development of home-grown industries and inculcated a dependency on the importation of foreign manufactured goods. The political ramifications and social divisions that accompanied the British occupation were also not evenly distributed but rather affected different ethnic groups and regions in different ways. The exacerbation of these social divisions by British colonial policy are most starkly evident in the institutionalisation of 'lowland' and 'upland' areas under the administrative banners of 'Burma Proper' and the 'Frontier Areas'.[8] The former was under a direct system of rule, in which the pre-colonial, patronage system of hereditary *myothugyi* or chiefs were replaced by a rational, hierarchical model of bureaucratic state control that aimed to integrate land and labour (and indeed property rights) into the global capitalist system.

In contrast, the upland 'Frontier Areas', of which the traditional Kachin homeland is part and which constitutes approximately 40–45% of Burma's land area, was governed through indirect rule.[9] This system relied upon a series of treaties between the British government and local authorities, such as the Shan *sawbwas* or Kachin *duwas* – 'feudal' elites that were subsequently afforded significant autonomy when compared to lowland social groups. This was reflected in the sparse physical infrastructure and relative under-development of the frontier areas compared to 'Burma Proper'. Ultimately, these colonial governing structures fostered the economic division of labour based on ethnicity and race in what John S. Furnivall termed the 'plural society'.[10] Exemplified, he argued, by segregated communities, the 'plural society' contributed to the marginalisation of Burma's indigenous population, par-ticularly the Burman section of society. For these lowland peoples, a lack of communications and the problem of trust was further hindered by the British policy of favouring 'hill tribe peoples', such as the Kachin, in the state bureau-cracy, especially the police force and military. This early-ethnicised division of labour goes some way towards explaining why the Kachin would later be favoured for recruitment by SOE/OSS over Burmans.

## The SOE and OSS in the Burma campaign

It is necessary to briefly discuss the academic literature surrounding SOE's involvement in the Burma campaign and the relative dearth of debate around the role played by the Kachin. Although contemporary scholarship on the Second World War in Asia is beginning to reassess the military impact of the SOE and OSS during the Burma campaign, relatively little attention has been given to the role of indigenous forces such as the Kachin in these operations. If covert operations specifically, and irregular warfare operations more gener-ally, have been neglected from historical accounts of the Burma campaign, the guerrilla forces that were recruited alongside SOE and OSS officers have been doubly marginalised and, in some cases, expunged from the historical record. This is understandable – yet nevertheless unsatisfactory – for two reasons, first because of the orthodox disposition of military history towards conventional warfare, irregular warfare practitioners and the roles they play are often down-played if not entirely forgotten. Second, because official histories, such as the one written by Major General Kirby,[11] excluded SOE's role in the first Burma campaign, they also ignored the sizeable contribution made by indigenous Kachin forces in the retention of an Allied foothold in northern Burma.

This eurocentrism is indicative of a great deal of scholarship on special operations in Burma. The European experience has come to over-determine the literature on SOE when compared to the OSS. This can be attributed in part to the relative disparity in scale and the sheer numerical difference in operational sites between the former and the latter; at the onset of hostilities in Burma in 1942, the operational scope of the SOE far exceeded that of the OSS. Nevertheless, although greater attention is being paid to irregular forces, the majority of this work makes short change of the Asian war, let alone Burma. Neville Wylie (2005) and Richard Duckett (2018) in their own respective works have highlighted this problem, with the latter noting that the 2006 edited volume *Special Operations Executive: A New Instrument of War* features only one non-European study.[12] Conceived in terms of phases, the historiography of the SOE – and to a similar extent the OSS – is said by Wylies to be in its third phase, in which scholarship has been derived from materials – such as SOE archives, official histories and personal memoirs – that were made publicly available during the course of the 1990s.[13]

Duckett's 2018 work, *The Special Operations Executive in Burma*, addresses a considerable gap in the literature on irregular warfare during the Burma campaign and serves, alongside the memoirs of Ian Fellowes-Gordon and Richard Dunlop, as inspiration behind this present chapter. Duckett's work is significant because it eschews fidelity to the conclusions reached by the official histories such as that of Cruickshank's, which have tended to downplay the role of Killery's Oriental Mission in the lead up to hostilities in 1941–42.[14] Instead, by choosing to highlight the important – if slightly unglamorous – aspects of covert operations (planning, recruitment, logistics), Duckett has shown that there is still considerable work to be done on SOE and OSS involvement in the Burma campaign, not least of all the role played by indigenous forces. Taking his lead, this chapter makes a concerted effort to foreground Kachin involvement, drawing wherever possible from primary sources. Crucial to this undertaking is a re-orientation of traditional military histories of the SOE and OSS in Southeast Asia, in favour of a greater exploration of supply logistics as well as recruitment and training infrastructure. This heuristic disposition allows us to appreciate the invariable inconsistencies that exist from one account of the conflict to the next.

This insight goes to the interpretive heart of re-writing forgotten military histories. Such inconsistencies do not simply relate to the correlation between strategic planning and tactical action but more essentially to what actors and actions get seen and/or heard as authoritative in the first place. While it is not my intention here to go into the dearth of postcolonial readings of the Burma campaign,[15] it is nevertheless important to recognise the explanatory purchase such a perspective has in helping us differentiate between inconsistencies in historical accounts and acts of colonial erasure. This problem can be highlighted by interrogating Cruickshank's claim that the strategically most significant action taken by the Kachin Levies was that they denied northern Burma to the Japanese and prevented them from establishing an aircraft landing strip at Fort Hertz. Undoubtedly, its loss would have been disastrous to Allied resupply efforts over 'the hump' because it would have enabled interception of such aircrafts by Japanese Zero fighters. It is in investigating how this was prevented from happening that we can shed light on the underexamined role of Kachin indigenous forces in special operations and also reimagine the centrality of (soft) infrastructure and logistics in the Burma campaign more broadly.

The Burma theatre as a whole has received considerably less attention among SOE historians than Malaya and Singapore. This propensity in the historiography is observable from the beginning periods of SOE operations under the auspices of what became known as the Oriental Mission, onwards to various 'left-behind' schemes aimed at recruiting indigenous forces in Burma's frontier areas. In part, this can be attributed to the celebrity that was attached to Freddie Spencer-Chapman, the principal figure of the SOE's Oriental Mission. A renowned mountaineer, Chapman's work organising resistance to the Japanese behind enemy lines was made famous in his account *The Jungle is Neutral* (2003 [1949]), which describes his reconnaissance operations along the spine of the Malay Peninsula.[16] It is therefore necessary at this juncture to explore more closely the trajectory of the conflict, starting with the SOE's involvement in recruiting indigenous people during the First Burma campaign.

## The pre-conflict formation of the SOE's 'left-behind' scheme and the Oriental Mission

This section looks at the period between October 1940 and December 1941, when the SOE came to recruit from the Kachin population of northern Burma under the Oriental Mission. It serves to highlight how Kachin forces, despite the limited resources afforded to them, would play a key role in both enabling the Allied retreat in 1942 and its subsequent covert offensives. It also shows how the Kachin impacted the first Burma campaign in a manner that has generally been disavowed in the literature – in terms of logistics and 'soft' infrastructure.

Burma, let alone its ethnic minorities, was not a high priority for the British imperial government in 1940. This meant that the Oriental Mission had a difficult operational outlook from the start. It was under-equipped with weaponry – such as machine guns and mortars – and had no properly streamlined command structure into which the Kachins would enter. The country's relative liminality, on the geopolitical interstices of India and China, was made glaringly apparent by the Government of India Act of 1935, which removed it from the administrative jurisdiction of British India. Henceforth, the War Office shifted responsibility for Burma's defence from India to Westminster's imperial coffers.[17] Drawing from a broader discourse of martial races[18] – and military tradition of recruitment that this entailed – the most significant development that emerged during this period was the agreement to organise 'left-behind' parties that would recruit indigenous guerrilla forces to operate behind enemy lines, tasked with holding up the Japanese advance.

And advance they would. In the twilight hours of 7–8 December 1941, the Japanese landed at Patanni and Kota Bahru in southern Thailand and eastern Malaya. This marked "the first land battle of the great Asian war"[19] and the start of their lightning advance across the Kra Peninsula into southern Burma, towards the capture of the strategic British airstrips of Tavoy and Victoria Point.[20] These were embarrassing losses, followed by the fall of the 'fortress' at Singapore in February 1942 and the rapid retreat of British Empire forces into

India.[21] The Oriental Mission's 'left-behind' scheme thus took on even greater significance. The scheme was initially established in Britain in 1940 to train soldiers to attack German troops behind the lines in the event of the occupation of Britain. In contrast to the relative administrative and geographic uniformity of the original scheme, in Burma it was divided between the 'Frontier Areas' and 'Burma Proper'. In the latter, political machinations over the administration of central Burma required the more forthright intervention of Governor Dorman-Smith; in the hilly frontier areas, the 'left-behind' scheme drew its strength from the recruitment of the Kachin, Karen and Shan people who dominated them.

The implementation of the 'left-behind' schemes in the 'Frontier Areas' moved more quickly than those in 'Burma Proper', which were still in consultation in January 1942. In contrast, by early February 1942, the Levies' scheme was already established throughout the Delta districts of the Irrawaddy to the Siamese border and further northwards into Shan and Kachin lands. In these more northerly areas, the organisation of the 'left-behind' scheme fell upon Lieutenant Colonel Stevenson of the Burma frontier force.[22] Stevenson answered directly to Governor Dorman-Smith by 'special appointment'. Because it required the cooperation of both the civilian government and military, his work in raising an indigenous fighting force was undertaken covertly, under the (false) pretences that the Oriental Mission was not recruiting indigenous people. Actually, Stevenson had an Oriental Mission code number (0.8200)[23] and had already begun organising the defence of frontier villages. Locals were being trained to fight against the Japanese and deny them food and to perform logistical sabotage, including blowing up bridges and other infrastructure. While ostensibly beyond the remit of the SOE, Stevenson and other Levie officers were in practice almost entirely recruited and trained by the SOE in the arts of sabotage.

This destruction of infrastructure was key to the Oriental Mission's role in delaying the Japanese northward advance, following their army's breakthrough at Toungoo in April 1942.[24] These actions – and the cover provided by the Kachin population for retreating British Empire forces – are seldom acknowledged in official histories yet were vital to the British retention of northern Burma. As Christopher Bayly and Tim Harper note, "the human line which held back the tide of defeat was the one scratched together by the resolute hill people of the north, the Chin and Kachins who gave the British a vital few days of grace".[25] One site of particular significance during this retreat was the Shweli Bridge between Lashio in northern Shan state and Bhamo in southern Kachin state, which was seen as a vital choke point in the defence of Myitkyina, Sumprabum and Fort Hertz. Designated for demolition in the event of Japanese advancement, the failure to destroy the bridge in May 1942, when the Japanese did indeed arrive, and subsequent disagreements over culpability point to the increasing importance placed by the allies on both infrastructure and logistics in the retention of northern Burma. And this important nuance is highlighted in the process of foregrounding the role of the Kachin.

The logistical dimension of SOE operations in 1942 and the assistance provided by the Kachin were also evident in the demolition of five key bridges north of Myitkyina. This indigenous-supported activity crucially enabled the Allies to retain their territory north of Sumprabhum. This was strategically significant because it contained Fort Hertz's airstrip, a strategic prize vital to the Burma campaign. It denied the Japanese a launching pad for fighter aircraft and enabled the installation of radar warning systems (logistically crucial in such rugged terrain). It also provided a much-needed escape route to India for fleeing civilian and military personnel in mid-1942, as well as a return channel following counter-offences in 1943. The securing of a forward operating base inside Burma also enabled the British, with their indigenous allies, to support the regional interests of the U.S. This included maintaining a supply line to Chiang Kai-Shek's nationalist forces in China, *the* signature geostrategic objective of the U.S. in what they called the China-Burma-India (CBI) Theatre. The defence of the aerial route known as 'the hump' connecting India and China was fundamental to this strategy. The logistical and infrastructural ground war in northern Burma, substantially assisted by indigenous forces, was thus fundamental to the success of the air war.

The Allied retention of northern Burma would ultimately play a decisive role in the evolution of the Kachin Levies and the eventual reoccupation of the country by Allied forces. Launched from the predominantly Shan town of Sumprabum and Fort Hertz in early 1943, infiltrations back into Japanese-occupied Burma were the earliest actions of their kind undertaken by SOE and OSS personnel. Although the sabotage of infrastructure that accompanied these actions was acknowledged in 1942, reports by the Oriental Mission of the immediate strategic significance were not fully appreciated. An especially noteworthy – yet decidedly under-appreciated – feature of these interventions was the role played by the indigenous Kachin people in helping the SOE and OSS rescue the crews of downed aircraft which were making these supply runs. Illustrated with much aplomb by former SOE operative Ian Fellowes-Gordon in *The Battle for Naw Seng's Kingdom* (1971), the downplaying of the importance of these extraction missions is indicative of the broader disavowal of the role of the Kachin in SOE and OSS operations to secure and hold northern Burma.

## India Mission and the development of logistics and soft infrastructure

This chapter turns now to examine the development of the logistics and soft infrastructure so vital to these objectives and to the on-going recruitment of the indigenous Kachin forces, as well as to the nascent strategic tensions that began to boil over into outright competition between the British and Americans in this theatre.

At the time of Britain's retreat to India, the situation in the CBI Theatre was dire. Morale was low and operational capacity severely restricted due to the government's policy of directing resources (and strategic priorities) to Europe. This began to change by August 1943, following the Quadrant Conference and the absorption of the Oriental Mission into the 'vastly expanded' auspices of the India Mission.[26] Twelve months of preparatory work by the India Mission established command and control parameters, country sections, logistical systems, training centres and more offensive operations.[27] A key task of the Burma Country Section (BCS) was the development of soft infrastructure – namely personnel training and logistical supply – of which the Kachin would play a central role. It had been noted in some quarters that the damage from Britain's catastrophic retreat from Burma, its 'Far-Eastern Dunkirk',[28] had been lessened with the help of the Kachins. Locals provided shelter and safe passage for civilian and military personnel fleeing the Japanese. They also, in many cases, offered the first point of resistance – principally in the form of sabotage and hit-and-run attacks – which saved valuable time for the allies as they consolidated northern positions.

In addition, part of this re-organisation stipulated that the staff officers of country sections should develop country-specific language proficiency and cultural knowledge. For the BCS, there was limited operational capacity in these much-needed intercultural communication skills. Only a dozen personnel with specialist knowledge of Burma had emerged in September 1942 out of the maelstrom of retreat.[29] As a result, the BCS officer corps increasingly relied upon indigenous troops who had accompanied the army to India. But of the 20,000 indigenous Burmese that were in-country during the start of hostilities with Japan, only 6,140[30] had made the arduous journey overland across the Chin Hills to Manipur or through the jungles of the Hukawng Valley, traversing the mighty Chindwin River into Assam, India. These indigenous allies, of whom a significant proportion was Kachin, were therefore in short supply and extremely valuable. As I will show shortly, the competition for indigenous Kachin recruits that began to emerge among army and SOE officers was only exacerbated by the entrance into northern Burma of the American OSS, as well as the creation at the end of 1942 of the Chindits.

It is unsurprising that of the developing 'soft' infrastructure in the BCS, the most notable was the establishment of a network of training schools. From July 1942 to May 1943, across the length and breadth of the subcontinent from Tagore in the east to Kharakvasla in the west, the India Mission provided paramilitary training and courses in jungle warfare and survival to personnel and recruits.[31] As part of this, recruits also received lessons in other dark arts of espionage including reconnaissance, intelligence gathering, enemy infiltration, and ciphers and codes in their indigenous tongues. In addition to the obvious difficulties this posed in a country where "more than 100 indigenous languages are spoken",[32] the challenge was in the lack of sufficient manpower and material resources. This included not only the basic military equipment required for staging subversive activities, such as radios, but also interpreters, trainers and recruits required for the very operations themselves. Nevertheless, despite the dearth of resources, the overriding objective of the India

Mission remained: to get behind enemy lines and determine how the BCS could be best directed towards orchestrating a guerrilla campaign throughout northern Burma against the Japanese.

Although material scarcity hindered the India Mission's ability to disrupt the Japanese war effort, the soft infrastructure gradually formed compelled the War Office to clarify the complementary role that SOE and its indigenous irregular forces would play alongside regular military forces. Rationalisation of command and control occurred near the end of 1943, providing a bedrock for the on-going success of SOE's Kachin Levies. However, there remained a logistical disparity in regards to the distribution of materials, with SOE in the 'Far East' receiving a mere 10% of available resources compared to the UK and North Africa's share, which was 68%.[33] This logistical deficit and the resultant disparity of resources for irregular forces, such as the Kachin Levies, would have important ramifications for the operational environment of northern Burma. Because of the relative dearth of manpower and materials, SOE officers and their indigenous allies were generally left to their own devices and were thus able to foster an unprecedented degree of strategic autonomy together. In addition, because these material-logistical deficits were disproportionately felt in northern Burma, it encouraged greater operational adaptability and tactical learning – and, therefore, greater necessity for coop-eration between allies, the British, the U.S., and the indigenous Kachin.

These factors – strategic autonomy as well as greater operational adaptabil-ity and tactical learning – were further fostered in the increasing competition between the SOE and the OSS, and the Kachins found themselves the middle. A companion organisation to the British SOE, the OSS shared its North Atlan-tic cousin's global remit during the Second World War. Its first section, known as Detachment 101 (Det.101), was launched in April 1942 and placed under the command of Colonel Carl Eifler. Operating under the broader purview of Lieutenant General Joseph 'Vinegar Joe' Stilwell, Det.101 was based in Nazira in Assam, India, and tasked with providing support to Chiang Kai-Shek's nationalist forces based in Yunnan. Stilwell's operational remit was beyond the British chain of command, answering directly only to those in Washington. This afforded Stilwell significant independence to push ahead with the U.S strategy of retak-ing northern Burma. Perhaps inevitably, with Det.101's entrance into northern Burma in 1942, tensions emerged between OSS and SOE over leadership. The pace with which Det.101 was inserted into the field belied an agreement reached late in 1942 subordinating American involvement under British control; by mid-1943, the U.S. had emerged as a senior partner in the war in Asia.

Eifler, under pressure from Stilwell demanding "booms from the Burma jungle", planned to insert clandestine units into the Myitkyina area by 1943.[34] Indeed, two Det.101 units were undertaking training in October 1942 even while command and control agreements were not yet reached between the two sides. The northern Det.101 operation, 'A' or 'Able' Group, departed for Fort Hertz from Nazira in December 1942, with the objective of launching attacks behind enemy lines. They were to sabotage the enemy's logistical capacity, including destroying communication and transport infrastructure such as the railway line and aerodrome at Myitkyina. Though ostensibly a shared aim, one aspect of these American activities troubled the British: the composition of A Group out of co-opted Anglo-Burmese personnel. It was deemed "absolutely essential to even the simplest of agent operations . . . that the individual . . . pass himself off as a native of the area and be accepted by the people". As Richard Dunlop, a former member of Det.101 explains, "with a few extraordinary exceptions, all agents who were to work successfully behind the Japanese lines were to be natives of Burma".[35] The (uneasy) British agreement to share personnel with the Americans was an attempt to leverage influence over what they realised was an increasingly ascendant OSS operation.

The involvement of indigenous forces affected this relationship in other ways. Det.101's A Group, under the command of Colonel Raymond Peers since December 1943, gradually decided that it was not advantageous to continue cooperating alongside Colonel Gamble's Kachin Levies.[36] They cited both the difficulties of overland penetration, particularly during the approaching monsoon and, more acutely, the potential security problem posed by Shan porters, who the Americans suspected of working as Japanese informers. With the potential for their operatives to be compromised by involvement with the British-led Kachin Levies, Eifler declared that Det.101 could not risk being subordinated under British command and must instead recruit their own Kachin forces, separate from those raised by the Levies. It thus became clear that the resolutions of September 1942 were being undermined by the OSS and that the Kachin themselves were being steadily co-opted as part of the U.S.' CBI strategy, which paid little heed to Britain's imperial interests. Indigenous forces were being used by the Americans to justify their encroachment on British operations. This underlines the importance of paying heed to the impact of indigenous personnel in this theatre of war (as well as the less 'glamorous' aspects of warfare such as logistics to which they were tied).

The lack of joint strategic direction in Southeast Asia was eventually addressed following the aforementioned Quadrant Conference, where a South East Asia Command (SEAC) was created under the control of Admiral Lord Louis Mountbatten and OSS and SOE were demarcated areas of operation. The OSS were given free reign to launch operations from their base in Nazira into Burma, while SOE's India Mission was given a similar remit from within China. Although intended to defuse the simmering tensions, the outcome highlighted the gradual reconfiguration of roles being played out by Kachin indigenous forces, as well as the principle alliances that were being fostered from mid-1943 onwards as the U.S took the lead in clandestine operations in the region.[37] These developments underscore the various ways in which, during this period, Allied relationships with indigenous groups rendered this a unique campaign in the Second World War. We have seen how the degree of strategic autonomy afforded the Allied officers in this region rendered knowledgeable indigenous allies an ever-more valuable asset, such that it would help bring OSS and SOE operatives into competition, as well as the organisational adaptability required in order to maintain some sway over such crucial indigenous recruits.

## SOE DILWYN and OSS KNOTHEAD

This section looks further at the unique alliances and evolving relationships between both organisations (SOE and OSS) and their Kachin allies through the DILWYN (British) and KNOTHEAD (American) operations, respectively. The rivalry of the SOE/OSS is fundamental to understanding the trajectory of this war effort, and we are seeing how intrinsic to this rivalry the Kachin peoples were.

Despite the growing disparity in resources, both SOE DILWYN and OSS KNOTHEAD share some common features, which can be characterised by the strategic autonomy, organisational adaptability and tactical learning fostered in the unique combat environment of northern Burma. The earlier of the two special operations, DILWYN, was set out in March 1943 from Fort Hertz with the objective of making contact with potential Kachin guerrillas in the Myitkyina area and establishing an underground railway there. This was part of BCS' broader plan to establish a network of infiltration teams throughout the mountainous hills of eastern Burma, in part of what is now Kachin state. It was led by Captain Kumjae Tawng and comprised of a group of four Kachins. They were tasked with establishing a landing zone and reception party for another Kachin operative, Major Shan Lone, who had planned to arrive with wireless transmitter equipment. However, after two initial attempts failed on the 19th and 21st of March because of navigational and mechanical difficulties, Major Lone was forced to make his way towards the DILWYN operation overland, not arriving until six months later on the 21st November.[38]

Shan Lone, by his own account, had to face an "arduous journey which can hardly be appreciated without knowing the conditions in that part of the country at that time of the year".[39] He

> had to follow narrow footpaths, overgrown with weeds and tall grasses, abounding with snakes. One can imagine untold hardships in marching during rains in the hills, with malaria, leeches, flies, mosquitoes and many jungle diseases, the leeches in particular being so numerous they dropped like hail from the trees.[40]

In part because of this overland ordeal, the use of airborne infiltration methods, still in its infancy, was stepped up; by 20th October 1943, it had been adopted as the tactic of choice for penetrating Japanese lines in this dense, rugged junglescape. Indeed, such a strategy became so readily accepted that a second DILWYN operation was launched even before the major had arrived to meet the first. The case of Shan Lone thus exemplifies the organisational adaptability and capacity for tactical learning that would come to characterise SOE and latterly OSS operations during this time, showcasing the critical ability of the SOE to learn from earlier mistakes.

What is clear from DILWYN's early experience of infiltration – and the subsequent on-the-ground issues BCS faced – is the importance of key logistical facets, particularly the establishment of lines of communication with India. As Troy Saquety elaborates, "without a long range, reliable, secure, and portable radio system, these agents could not communicate back to (India). These groups were effectively worthless if they could not establish communications".[41] The organisational adaptability that was required (alongside the strategic autonomy that was fostered) helped to establish such communication and deal with technological problems. Like many other aspects of the war in the CBI Theatre, the technological problems were of a somewhat unique character. For instance, in addition to the great distances that had to be traversed in Asia, the transmission of signals, such as through radio waves, also had to overcome atmospheric irregularities brought about by the region's volatile seasonal monsoon. This was in addition to the already trying overland conditions associated with the largely tropical jungle environment of Burma, making secure and reliable lines of communication a sizeable challenge. The OSS was more successful in overcoming these logistical challenges. They developed a lightweight portable receiver transmitter with an inbuilt power supply, which could operate over great distances, and also rapidly enlisted the Kachin population in intelligence gathering.

At around the same time that SOE's DILWYN was trying to find its feet in northern Burma, the OSS began to make their own attempts at infiltration southwards, under the banner of Operation KNOTHEAD, into the area around Myitkyina and Bhamo.[42] It soon became evident that the British and Americans had yet to formally resolve, at the operational level, the command and control conflicts that had earlier undermined cooperation at the geopolitical level. In order to prevent any conflicts over operational jurisdiction, it was agreed that the Taiping River would be used to demarcate the Kachin territory of northern Burma into two separate zones, with the OSS operating to the river's north and the SOE to its south. As Duckett notes, "this demarcation caused disgust amongst British operational personnel, who believed that they were abandoning many of their loyal Kachins to the Americans".[43] Again we note how central the indigenous Kachin fighters were to the complex and shifting Anglo-American alliance in this theatre.

Despite the treatise, a month later the OSS' Det.101 reneged on the deal and began to deploy infiltration units into SOE areas of operation. Undertaken in advance of the American offensive against the 18th Japanese division at Myitkyina, this incursion resulted in a new agreement, in which Eifler would, for 'medical reasons', relinquish his command in northern Burma to Lieutenant Colonel Peers by December. This effectively acted to quell the conflict of interest between the SOE and OSS in the CBI Theatre, paving the way for greater coordination between the two and for the activation of the aforementioned second DILWYN mission. This was to be deployed alongside OSS units – which totalled thirty-five men who were already operating behind Japanese lines. These were not intelligence gathering missions, as initially stipulated, but rather the OSS' first paramilitary operations in Burma. They were clearly acting on their own accord and independent from either British or Chinese oversight. By January, drawing on British support, the organisation grew rapidly, eventually leading to the successful recruitment of 400 Kachin guerrillas.[44]

It should be noted that the tension between the OSS and the SOE over Kachin recruits and in the field was not solely the result of competition between each organisation. It was also because of another force that was operating in an already complex arena: the Chindits. The Chindits led long-range penetration campaigns and were the target of much criticism from the start by the more conventionally minded officers in the British and Indian armed forces. Such disdain was largely due to the vast resources they demanded, creating an uneven distribution of resources. This was made starker by the perceived favouritism towards Wingate, commander of the Chindits, by both Wavell and Churchill. Moreover, by also stoking Kachin grievances against the Japanese during a period in which the British reconquest of Burma was far from assured, the Chindits could also be viewed (as they were by many at the time) to be a potentially destabilising force for the allies, undermining the secret operations of the SOE and OSS because they contributed to, rather than helped alleviate, inter-organisational competition for Kachin recruits.

Again, the operational command and control complexity of the CBI Theatre reared its head, reawakening longstanding memories of two previous instances in which the Kachin had been abandoned by colonial authorities, first following the 1942 retreat and second after the military failure and withdrawal in 1942 of the Chindits' first operation. Aware of these failings, the SOE were determined to maintain Kachin loyalty in the face of both American and internal British pressure. Nevertheless, despite these misgivings, the BCS eventually decided to cease DILWYN, flying the remaining personnel to Kolkata and effectively vacating the field to the OSS by June 1944.[45] By August 1944, with effectively free reign in Kachin territory, Stilwell and the OSS' Det.101 capitalised on the preparatory work of the SOE's India mission following their eighteen-month presence in the country. This ascendancy of the OSS was never more apparent than when, in the previous month, the British were forced largely by necessity to agree to be resupplied by air by OSS planes flying out of Nazira. Much can be made of how the Americans capitalised on the work of the British, but I have shown that it is also critical to highlight the considerable impact of the Kachin themselves in this murky theatre of war.

## Conclusion

Ultimately, this chapter's reconsideration of the covert operations undertaken by SOE and OSS during the Second World War has been done in light of the role – hitherto under-examined – played by indigenous Kachin forces in the Burma campaign. Scholarship of the SOE and OSS, which is itself sparse to begin with, has tended to ignore pre-conflict dynamics, focusing on the more overt and conventional perceived sabotage and intelligence-gathering dimensions (or lack thereof) of SOE/OSS and less on its role as a recruiter of indigenous fighters. In doing so, we have also overlooked the importance of supply logistics and 'soft' infrastructure to this 'forgotten front'.

To explore how the Kachin were significant to the Allied war effort, I have analysed the origins of the SOE's 'left-behind' scheme and the development of its Oriental and India Missions. Particular emphasis has been placed on the tensions that subsequently emerged between the SOE and OSS once the latter became more prominently involved after 1942. As I have shown, exploring the machinations, both geostrategic and quotidian, that emerged over the recruitment of Kachin guerrillas allows for a more nuanced take on alliance formation in this theatre of war, showing how the relationships gradually fostered with the local Kachin population were central to SOE/OSS rivalry and, more importantly, fundamental to the overall trajectory of the Allied war effort in Burma.

By analysing the role of indigenous Kachin forces in the CBI Theatre, I have shed light on three significant aspects by which the Allied relationship to the Kachin can be said to be mutually constitutive of the unique combat environment of which they were a part. First, I have shown how Burma's unique combat environment – difficult terrain and lack of transport infrastructure – impacted upon the institutional trajectory and tactical struggles faced by the SOE and OSS. As I have argued, these geographic factors helped to push both organisations away from a solely sabotage and intelligence-gathering remit and towards a more logistical and 'soft' infrastructure-oriented role.

Second, it is clear that both the SOE DILWYN and OSS KNOTHEAD covert operations played an invaluable part in gathering information to assist in the Allied retention of northern Burma. Yet this chapter has made clear that, partly because of the limitations placed upon it by lack of resources, priority was given to the development of aerial resupply logistics, communications and soft infrastructure, such as guerrilla training, rather than merely on demolition and reconnaissance work. The lack of Allied manpower and materials resulted in these operations being characterised by a large degree of strategic autonomy, in which SOE/OSS personnel – including indigenous Kachin – were able to act independently, generally free from the traditional operational oversight commonly found in other theatres of war.

Last, the third interconnected – though often overlooked – aspect relates to the way the Allied-indigenous relationship generated the conditions for organisational adaptability and tactical learning. As I showed, this was typified by the trial-and-error acceptance of long-range aerial penetration and also by the recruitment of Burmese and Anglo-Burmese personnel who were savvy in negotiating the local context and, therefore, able to operate covertly behind Japanese lines.

## Notes

1  Ian Fellowes-Gordon, *Amiable Assassins: The Story of the Kachin Guerrillas of North Burma* (London: Robert Hale Limited, 1957), 16.

2  Ian Fellowes-Gordon, *The Battle for Naw Seng's Kingdom: General Stilwell's North Burma Campaign and Its Aftermath* (London: Lee Cooper, 1971) 21.

3  Ibid.

4  Fellowes-Gordon, *Amiable Assassins*, 16.

5  Ibid., 16–17.

6  Donald M. Seekins, *Historical Dictionary of Burma (Myanmar)* (Oxford: Scarecrow Press, 2006), 2.

7  Sir Charles Crosthwaite, *The Pacification of Burma* (London: Frank Cass & Co. Ltd, 1912).

8  Edmund R. Leach, "The Frontiers of 'Burma'," *Comparative Studies in Society and History* 3, no. 1 (1960): 49–68.

9  Seekins, *Historical Dictionary of Burma (Myanmar)*, 18.

10  John Sydenham Furnivall, *Colonial Policy and Practice: A Comparative Study of Burma and Netherlands India* (New York: New York University Press, 1956).

11  Stanley Woodburn Kirby, *The War against Japan* (London: HMSO, 1959).

12  Mark Seaman, ed., *Special Operations Executive: A New Instrument of War* (London and New York: Routledge, 2006).

13  Richard Duckett, *The Special Operations Executive in Burma: Jungle Warfare and Intelligence Gathering in World War II* (London and New York: I.B. Tauris, 2018) 7.

14  Charles Cruikshank, *SOE in the Far East* (Oxford: Oxford University Press, 1986); Alan Ogden, *Tigers Burning Bright: SOE Heroes in the Far East* (London: Bene Factum, 2013).

15  For an exception to this, see Tarak Barkawi, *Soldiers of Empire: Indian and British Armies in World War II* (Cambridge: Cambridge University Press, 2017).

16  Christopher Bayly and Tim Harper, *Forgotten Armies: The Fall of British Asia, 1941–1945* (London: Allen Lane, 2004), 133.

17  Richard Duckett, *The Special Operations Executive in Burma: Jungle Warfare and Intelligence Gathering in World War II* (London and New York: I.B. Tauris, 2018), 38.

18  Heather Streets, *Martial Races: The Military, Race and Masculinity in British Imperial Culture, 1857–1914* (Manchester and New York: Manchester University Press, 2004).

19  Bayly and Harper, *Forgotten Armies*, 115.

20  Duckett, *The Special Operations Executive in Burma*, 42.

21  Michael D. Leigh, *The Evacuation of Civilians From Burma: Analysing the 1942 Colonial Disaster* (London: Bloomsbury, 2014); Philip Woods, *Reporting the Retreat: War Correspondents in Burma* (London: Hurst & Company, 2017).

22  Cruikshank, *SOE in the Far East*.

23  Ibid., 68–9; Duckett, *The Special Operations Executive in Burma*, 41.

24  Alan K. Lathrop, "The Employment of Chinese Nationalist Troops in the First Burma Campaign," *Journal of Southeast Asian Studies* 12, no. 2 (1981): 403–32.

25  Bayly and Harper, *Forgotten Armies*, 174.

26  The National Archive, HS 1/200, "'Notes for Mackenzie'," *Special Operations Executive: Far East: Registered Files* (1942): 1.

27  Duckett, *The Special Operations Executive in Burma*, 76–8.

28  Stephen Bates, "Elephant Man's Heroic Rescue Mission in 'Far East Dunkirk' Revealed on Film," (2010). Last Accessed 15 June 2018. www.theguardian.com/world/2010/nov/01/elephant-man-gyles-mackrell-invasion-burma.

29  The National Archive, HS 7/104, "'Reformation in India June-Dec 1942'," *Special Operations Executive: Histories and War Diaries* (1945): 1.

30  The National Archive, WO 106/2677, *War Office: Directorate of Military Operations and Military Intelligence, and Predecessors: Correspondence and Papers* (1942).

31  Duckett, *The Special Operations Executive in Burma*, 79.

32  Seekins, *Historical Dictionary of Burma (Myanmar)*, 6.

33  Duckett, *The Special Operations Executive in Burma*, 85.

34  Richard Dunlop, *Behind Japanese Lines: With the Oss in Burma* (New York: Skyhorse Publishing, 2014), 109.

35 Ibid., 219 (epub edition).
36 Ibid., 260 (epub edition).
37 Bayly and Harper, *Forgotten Armies*, 351.
38 Duckett, *The Special Operations Executive in Burma*, 105–6.
39 Ibid., 95.
40 Ibid., 106.
41 Troy Saquety, *The Oss in Burma: Jungle War Against the Japanese* (Lawrence: University Press of Kansas, 2013).
42 Dunlop, *Behind Japanese Lines: With the Oss in Burma*, 400 (epub edition).
43 Ibid., 106.
44 Ibid., 107.
45 Ibid., 108.

# Bibliography

Barkawi, Tarak. *Soldiers of Empire: Indian and British Armies in World War II*. Cambridge: Cambridge University Press, 2017.

Bates, Stephen. "Elephant Man's Heroic Rescue Mission in 'Far East Dunkirk' Revealed on Film." (2010). Last Accessed 15 June, 2018. www.theguardian.com/world/2010/nov/01/elephant-man-gyles-mackrell-invasion-burma.

Bayly, Christopher, and Tim Harper. *Forgotten Armies: Britain's Asian Empire & the War with Japan*. London: Penguin Books, 2005.

Chapman, F. Spencer. *The Jungle Is Neutral*. Singapore: Marshall Cavendish Editions, 2003.

Crosthwaite, Sir Charles. *The Pacification of Burma*. London: Frank Cass & Co. Ltd, 1912.

Cruikshank, Charles. *SOE in the Far East*. Oxford: Oxford University Press, 1986.

Duckett, Richard. *The Special Operations Executive in Burma: Jungle Warfare and Intelligence Gathering in World War II*. London and New York: I.B. Tauris, 2018.

Dunlop, Richard. *Behind Japanese Lines: With the Oss in Burma*. New York: Skyhorse Publishing, 2014.

Fellowes-Gordon, Ian. *Amiable Assassins: The Story of the Kachin Guerrillas of North Burma*. London: Robert Hale Limited, 1957.

Fellowes-Gordon, Ian. *The Battle for Naw Seng's Kingdom: General Stilwell's North Burma Campaign and Its Aftermath*. London: Lee Cooper, 1971.

Furnivall, John Sydenham. *Colonial Policy and Practice: A Comparative Study of Burma and Netherlands India*. New York: New York University Press, 1956.

Kirby, Stanley Woodburn. *The War Against Japan*. London: HMSO, 1959–1969.

Lathrop, Alan K. "The Employment of Chinese Nationalist Troops in the First Burma Campaign." *Journal of Southeast Asian Studies* 12, no. 2 (1981): 403–32.

Leach, Edmund R. "The Frontiers of 'Burma'." *Comparative Studies in Society and History* 3, no. 1 (1960): 49–68.

Leigh, Michael D. *The Evacuation of Civilians from Burma: Analysing the 1942 Colonial Disaster*. London: Bloomsbury, 2014.

The National Archives of the UK, HS 1/200. "Notes for Mackenzie." *Special Operations Executive: Far East: Registered Files* (1942): 1.

The National Archives of the UK, HS 7/104. "Reformation in India June-Dec 1942." *Special Operations Executive: Histories and War Diaries* (1945): 1.

The National Archives of the UK, WO 106/2677. "Withdrawal of forces from Burma to Assam." *War Office: Directorate of Military Operations and Military Intelligence, and Predecessors: Correspondence and Papers*, 1942 June.

Ogden, Alan. *Tigers Burning Bright: SOE Heroes in the Far East*. London: Bene Factum, 2013.

Saquety, Troy. *The Oss in Burma: Jungle War against the Japanese*. Lawrence: University Press of Kansas, 2013.

Seaman, Mark, ed. *Special Operations Executive: A New Instrument of War*. London and New York: Routledge, 2006.

Seekins, Donald M. *Historical Dictionary of Burma (Myanmar)*. Oxford: Scarecrow Press, 2006.

Streets, Heather. *Martial Races: The Military, Race and Masculinity in British Imperial Culture, 1857–1914*. Manchester and New York: Manchester University Press, 2004.

Woods, Philip. *Reporting the Retreat: War Correspondents in Burma*. London: Hurst & Company, 2017.

Wylie, Neville. "SOE: New Approaches and Perspectives." *Intelligence and National Security* 20, no. 1 (2005): 1–13.

# 9 From resistance to revolution

## Occupied Yugoslavia

*Chris Murray*

During the Second World War in a small corner of Eastern Europe, Yugoslavia came to represent a potent symbol of defiance, as well as the largest resistance force anywhere in the world. The Yugoslavs would field an entire army of volunteer guerrillas. These fighters were fierce, resilient, comparable to any Allied army and operated continuously within Axis-occupied territory throughout the war. They would harass and draw off considerable Axis forces while creating massive free territories within the Axis zone of occupation.

These resistance forces would become a considerable source of friction for the Allies. Yugoslav resistance was fractured, and two diametrically opposed forces emerged. On the one side stood the remnant of the Royal Yugoslav Forces, loyal to the Yugoslav crown; on the other emerged revolutionary communist partisans. These forces would wage a war of resistance against the occupying Axis Powers while simultaneously fighting a bloody civil war that led both sides to make temporary alliances with occupying forces and engage in fratricidal massacres.

The political dimensions of the Yugoslav case served as a major point of contention between the 'Big Three' and came to highlight the growing divide within the US-UK-USSR relationship as the end of the war approached. This resistance changed the course of the war, influenced Allied relations, and threatened to destabilize the post-war peace by bringing the Allies to the brink in South-Eastern Europe.

## Yugoslavia gains significance

The Balkans first emerged as a key strategic objective for both the Axis and the Allies very early in the war. Even before the German invasion of Poland, the region had garnered increased attention in Whitehall.[1] Both the Axis and Allies were eager to peaceably secure the region and ensure continued access to its resources, which were critical to fighting the coming war.[2] Shortly after the invasion of Poland, the British and French became deeply concerned with growing Axis political pressure and encroachment into the Balkans. Denying the Germans access to this vital asset became an immediate priority.

Allied considerations were several, including limiting the expansion of the war, protecting access to Balkan resources, but, most critically, protecting vital logistical routes through the Eastern Mediterranean. This was initially pursued through attempts to establish a neutral Balkan bloc that would prevent the Axis from gaining control of the Aegean, which from the Allied perspective threatened the stability of the port at Salonika, the Turkish Straits, and the Suez Canal.[3] For this reason, tremendous significance was placed on uniting the three great powers of the region, Turkey, Greece and Yugoslavia.[4] Yugoslavia in particular weighed heavily in Balkan considerations due to its geographical position on the potential frontline and because it held the largest military in the region.[5]

The spring of 1940 served to rapidly alter the landscape and sow chaos in Allied plans. First France was attacked, and a new government, the Churchill War Ministry, took power in Britain. Shortly afterwards, Anglo-French fears of Italy joining the Axis were realized. Before these facts could be appreciated, France was compelled to surrender, leaving the British almost entirely alone.[6] To deepen this sense of crisis, Britain's greatest fears were realized when Italy invaded Greece in late October, the lynchpin of the Eastern Mediterranean, turning the Balkans into the focal point of the entire war.[7]

Yugoslavia's position was unenviable, and Germany effectively accomplished the strategic encirclement of the country by early 1941. This placed tremendous pressure on Yugoslavia to side with the Axis, who continued to pursue a non-committal policy. As Eden describes it in his memoirs, "though already enmeshed the Yugoslavs were still wriggling to avoid committing their country to the Axis"[8] The British Government could only watch as Yugoslavia slowly drifted towards the Axis camp.[9]

When Yugoslavia's Prince Regent Paul finally bowed to Axis pressure and signed the Tripartite Pact on 27 March 1941, a spontaneous popular coup d'état in Belgrade overthrew the government almost immediately.[10] Senior Air Force officers removed Regent Prince Paul from power, and a new Royal Government was formed under the young King Peter, who was declared to have reached the age of majority.[11] The news was greeted with enthusiasm in Britain. As Churchill describes it:

> [T]he news of the revolution in Belgrade naturally gave us great satisfaction. Here at least was one tangible result of our desperate efforts to form an Allied front in the Balkans and prevent all falling piecemeal into Hitler's power.[12]

British enthusiasm was, however, premature and quickly dashed. King Peter's new government was, in principal, anti-Axis and pro-British with the intention of standing with the Allies. That said, the Yugoslavs were hedging their bets and trying to avoid provocative action since they were far from prepared to do much beyond issuing declarations.[13]

The reality was the coup held complex political dimensions that reached far beyond the Tripartite Pact and were rooted in domestic strains. As Sir Llewellyn Woodward describes it:

> [T]he coup was a protest, not merely against the signature of the Tripartite Pact, but also against the dictatorial methods of the fallen Government and its predecessors. It was not even certain that there would be a complete reversal of foreign policy.[14]

## Coup d'état and invasion

These internal difficulties were part of the Yugoslav's reluctance to move quickly and firmly in solidarity with the Allies, to whom they naturally felt allegiance. The British would be deeply disappointed to discover that, as a result, under Prince Paul the Yugoslavs had been slow in coordinating military preparations and were still only partially mobilized.[15] This lack of preparedness would hold tremendous military consequences for the Allies. On the day of the coup, Hitler issued *Führer Directive No. 25*, which ordered the immediate invasion and dismemberment of Yugoslavia.[16] The invasion came on 6 April 1941, and Axis forces overwhelmed the Yugoslav Military, which rapidly collapsed, formally surrendering on 17 April 1941.[17]

The Royal Yugoslav Military collapsed with such swiftness that many units dissolved into the heavily wooded mountains intact and without ever surrendering their arms. From here, it would not be long before they began to regroup to carry out the traditional Balkan guerrilla war.[18] In the face of brutal Axis occupation policies, these forces quickly grew into a national guerrilla war of resistance.

In the interim, the hasty collapse and surrender of Yugoslavia, along with the flight of the newly minted Royal Yugoslav Government of King Peter into exile, was a considerable setback for the Allies. The arrival of the Royal Yugoslav Government in London damaged the British view of the Yugoslavs and marked the beginning of a whole host of new problems within the fragile alliance.[19] Churchill was personally bewildered as much as disappointed by the Royal Yugoslav Government's flight, having written to the Commander-in-Chief of the Middle East on 13 April 1941:

> We do not see why the king or Government should leave the country, which is vast, mountainous and full of armed men. German tanks can no doubt move along the roads and tracks, but to conquer the Serbian Armies they must bring up infantry. There will be the chance to kill them. Surely the young King and the Ministers should play their part in this.[20]

Within weeks of Yugoslavia's surrender, the Allies were hearing news of uprisings emerging across Yugoslavia. This early resistance was local and spontaneous with little coordination. However, some more organized groups soon followed, led by former military commanders, such as General Mihailović and his Serbian Četniks.[21] News of this rebellion was received in London with equal amounts of enthusiasm and anxiety.[22] Widespread resistance that tied down Axis forces was a most welcome development both militarily and from a morale standpoint.[23] However, the rebellion was beyond the reach of the British to assist, and concern arose over its ability to survive independently so that it might play a future role within the war effort.[24] Supply in particular was a painful question, as a letter from the Royal Yugoslav Government's Prime Minister Simović to Churchill, penned in the last days of October 1941, highlights:

> My dear PM [Prime Minister], On October 29th I received the following telegram from the leader of our troops [Mihailović] in occupied Yugoslavia: '*In God's name send us help while the weather is still fine . . .*' I am sending this telegram to show you what the situation there is, and if it is possible to beg you to send help immediately.[25]

### Guerrilla war turns to civil war

The news coming out of Yugoslavia concerning the rapid expansion of the Yugoslav revolt was deeply worrisome for the Allies. In late 1941, the British had become increasingly aware of the growing divisions within the resistance between Royalist and Communist elements and were keen to stifle divisions that could turn the revolt into a civil war.[26] They, however, had little ability to reach out to the Yugoslav resistance in any meaningful way.

By this time, several large forces had emerged in Yugoslavia. The remnants of the Royal Yugoslav Military, under General Draža Mihailović and still loyal to the Serbian Yugoslav King, now in exile in London, were the first to appear. These forces were to enjoy the immediate support of the Allies, who were glad for a welcome bit of good news.

Meanwhile, the invasion of the Soviet Union added a new dimension to affairs.[27] A new resistance force of Communist Partisans entered the field in Yugoslavia, led by the Moscow-trained Josip Broz Tito, in the wake of these events. The Partisans were well organized and quickly began to not only fight the occupiers but attempt to establish their own form of local communist rule. With their revolutionary intent, resistance in Yugoslavia very quickly turned to civil war.[28]

It is, however, a misleading simplification to explain Yugoslav resistance as two-sided. There were also collaborators of various stripes, ranging from some Četnik units in temporary accommodation with the occupying powers to fully collaborative regimes like that of the Ustaše. There were both ethnic- and religious-based local militias as well, adding to the confused state of events. This was not simply a two-sided civil war, nor was it simply a war of occupation or even a revolution – it was all of these things.[29] This multi-dimensional reality meant that it would not be long before the chaos of these various resistance groups fighting amongst themselves for legitimacy and control over the future course of Yugoslavia took hold of events.

The news coming out of Yugoslavia regarding the rapid expansion of the revolt carried with it complexities that were difficult to fully appreciate. By late 1941, the British were already becoming increasingly aware of growing divisions within the Yugoslav revolt between Royalist and Communist elements. Indeed, by November 1941, the British were already hearing reports of open war between Yugoslav Partisans and Royalist Četniks.[30] By the fall of 1941, the British had become concerned enough with the situation that they had decided there was a real need to get inside of Yugoslavia to avoid the burgeoning civil war. They were concerned with ensuring the resistance remained alive and, critically, that it directed its energy towards the enemy not internal feuds.[31] It was with this impetus, the first of what would become a considerable program of British Liaison Officers (BLO), was sent into Yugoslavia.

In parallel to this emerging civil war, the Soviets had, by early September, begun pushing hard for the British to open a second front in Europe to relieve their own front. With the British looking for ways to assist the Soviets, many within Whitehall began to look to Yugoslav resistance.[32] This newfound significance Yugoslavia held for the war effort was problematic on several fronts. Militarily, the advantages were becoming clearer, but diplomatic and long-term political considerations were intervening to muddy the waters.

## Yugoslavia was deeply fractured

The reality was that the war had come at a moment of great fragility for the young Yugoslav state. Yugoslavia was a country made up of diverse ethic, political and religious forces that had little time, since its creation at the end of the First World War, to forge a new national identity. When the Second World War came to Yugoslavia, the state and government were weak. Both internal divisions and political upheaval plagued the country. The Yugoslav army was in no way immune to these issues and was, likewise, fragmented and rife with internal conflict.[33] Yugoslavia was a country unprepared for defence.[34] It was a powder keg of divisions that had been ready to explode, and invasion served as the spark.

Underlying tensions within Yugoslavia's political climate would contribute to turning occupation and resistance into civil war.[35] Fratricidal atrocities were committed in appalling numbers after Yugoslavia fell to the Axis invaders by all the various groups operating within occupied Yugoslavia. Indeed, much of the region's multi-ethnic population became both perpetrators and victims of spontaneous local massacres.[36] These upheavals created new dividing lines within Yugoslavian society that targeted forces like ethnicity, religion and class to forge a violent form of nationalism that turned neighbour against neighbour.[37]

Making matters worse, Axis occupation policies were disjointed and actively sought to exploit these tensions, leading to the bloodiest, most chaotic conditions in occupied Europe.[38] Hitler had ordered Yugoslavia 'dismembered' and approved the establishment of the Ustaše-ruled puppet state, the Independent State of Croatia (NDH).[39] The subsequent German occupation was a slapdash 'divide and rule' affair that was only successful in the short-term goal of disruption.[40] Divisions between Italian and German approaches to occupation emerged rapidly and prevented any real coordination between various Axis spheres of influence within Yugoslavia, which included Bulgaria and Hungary. Italian conflict with Ustaše added to a sense of internal Axis conflict brewing just below the surface of these competing and incoherent occupation policies.[41]

The resulting social and political upheavals set loose by these occupation programs exerted themselves upon Allied policy and were to hold considerable implications both militarily and politically. This reality meant that Axis occupation and the war of resistance were tied up in internal struggles that made Allied responses a deeply complex issue.

## Soviet pressure and Tito

The British and French had established much of the Allied policy in the Balkans early in the war – before the entry of the Soviets and shortly after the Americans. Thus upon their entry, they inherited a particular framework to Balkan and indeed Mediterranean strategy. Occupied as the Soviets and Americans were with their own priorities, both had their primary gaze focused elsewhere and were happy to allow the British to take the lead in the Mediterranean, which was logical given the circumstances and Britain's outlook.[42] For the British, the Mediterranean was a key strategic consideration because of a global naval-centric view that emphasized the region in regards to maritime supply.[43]

Although the Soviets were aware of the situation in Yugoslavia through Comintern channels, they had remained quiet on the subject of Tito's Communist Partisans, content instead to echo British support of Mihailović and the Royal Yugoslav Government.[44] Soviet policy had been born out of the desperation of the autumn of 1941. Reeling back towards Moscow in response to BARBAROSSA, Soviet interests were strictly in resistance to the Germans and not questions of ideology and revolution.[45] At this stage, the Soviets were still concerned with survival and anxious that nothing upset their alliance with Britain. What mattered was to maintain friendly relations and obtain as much material and military support as they could from their Western partners.[46]

When Churchill arrived in the Soviet Union for the Second Moscow Conference with news for Stalin that there would be no second front in Europe in 1942, the Soviet position regarding Yugoslavia shifted. The Soviets began broadcasting a pro-Partisan, anti-Mihailović propaganda campaign via Radio Free Yugoslavia that ran directly contrary to the message being broadcast by the BBC.[47] This favour towards the Partisans was likely part of a larger Soviet effort throughout Europe to incite revolution in place of the second front that the Western Allies were failing to provide. Going forward, Yugoslavia would contribute to growing tensions between the British and Soviets.

The British remained committed to their support of the Royal Yugoslav Government and their man on the ground, Mihailović. This continued support was being measured with roots in both military and political considerations. As the British Chief of the Imperial General Staff (CIGS) Alan Brooke describes it in a letter to Churchill dated 2 June 1942, Mihailović was still viewed as the best option for long-term stability. As he put it:

> [W]e are right in backing Mihailović. If we do so successfully not only will we have a certain control over the revolt but we will: (i) Continue to contain at least the present number (i.e. 30) Axis divisions in Yugoslavia (ii) build up a serious threat to the German flank when they are extended in Russia (iii) prepare the way for any operation we may eventually make in the Balkans.[48]

In addition, the argument against the Partisans was also laid out in the same letter, with Alan Brooke describing:

> Partisans or Communists, against whom Mihailović has often complained, embarrass not only the enemy but ourselves as they drive the more moderate opponents of the Axis into co-operation with any power that can restore a semblance of law and order.[49]

## Britain's difficulties with their Yugoslav allies

Despite this view, other forces were working to swing the pendulum against these arguments. Within months of the Royal Yugoslav Government's arrival in London, it became clear that the Yugoslavs were incredibly volatile. King Peter's dismissal of his Prime Minister, Gen. Simović, on 12 January 1942 helped foster a growing sense of doubt within the British government.[50] This would be worsened by the uproar it caused among Yugoslav military units stationed in Cairo, who mutinied over the decision.[51] These events pitted the Foreign Office against British Military leadership in Cairo and, after several months of difficulties, required the British to intervene to quash the mutiny.[52] In late 1942, King Peter again reorganized his government, presenting a still stronger picture of a shaky ally.[53]

The British Government was facing the growing realization that Yugoslav leadership was unreliable. King Peter expressed to the British an assessments of his ministers, which did not help to inspire confidence, writing "to save their own skins, they are capable of doing harm to their country."[54] There would be yet another Royal Yugoslav Government crisis in June 1943 that would leave Whitehall urging King Peter to shrink his government to a few key ministers and relocate to Cairo, under the impetus of being closer to Yugoslavia but also, conveniently, further from London.[55] This occurred in conjunction with a growing dissatisfaction with Mihailović, centering on a lack of anti-Axis activity and internal divisions within Yugoslav resistance forces, which were leading Whitehall to see the Yugoslavs as fence-sitters and infighters.[56]

Despite a growing awareness of Partisan anti-Axis activity, the British view of the Partisans was far from an entirely positive one. There was considerable apprehension regarding the political make-up of the Partisan forces.[57] For this reason, any suggestion concerning co-opting the Partisan movement was still being met with considerable concern by elements within the British Government. At this time, the Special Operations Executive (SOE) and Foreign Office continued to argue that in considering the long view and post-war political considerations, Britain's focus should be solely directed towards Mihailović, the Royal Yugoslav Government's official representative in the country.[58]

Despite growing, albeit tacit, support by the USSR in the way of propaganda, the Soviets were still apprehensive about the difficulties Yugoslavia was presenting to larger Allied relationships and the overall war effort. In November 1942, the Partisans captured Bihać and established the Anti-Fascist Council for the National Liberation of Yugoslavia (AVNOJ).[59] This development caused concern among the Soviets that the Partisans would begin to openly oppose the Royal Yugoslav Government in London and raise uncomfortable questions about the monarchy that could severely damage Allied relations.[60]

At almost the same moment within the highest levels of the British Government, questions were being raised about the future of British Yugoslav policy. Whitehall was certainly not keen to see revolutionary movements making waves in Britain's purported post-war sphere of interest; however, events in Yugoslavia were demanding redress.[61] In a report drafted by Eden on the subject of Mihailović dated 17 December 1942, he expressed to Churchill his concern about the challenges facing current Yugoslav policy, stating:

> It might be argued that it is our short-term interest to break with Mihailović, who is at present contributing little to the general war effort, and to transfer our support and assistance to the Partisans, who are offering active resistance to the occupying forces. On the long view, however, I believe that we should be wise to go on supporting Mihailović in order to prevent anarchy and Communist chaos after the war.[62]

At the Casablanca Conference (SYMBOL) 14–24 January 1943, the invasion of Sicily (HUSKY) had been set, and with it new priorities arose regarding diversionary action in the Balkans by Yugoslav resistance fighters.[63] British focus was set on supporting their Italian campaign and widening the Allied drive up the Mediterranean and Aegean. Thus, the Allied decision taken at SYMBOL to focus on the Mediterranean for a significant offensive action in 1943 served as a catalyst for a substantial change in Yugoslav policy.[64]

In a letter to Stalin dated 12 February 1943, Churchill described British goals as aimed at "clearing the Mediterranean, promoting an Italian collapse with the consequent effect on Greece and Yugoslavia and wearing down of the German Air Force; . . . to be closely followed by an operation in the Eastern Mediterranean".[65] As Alan Brooke described it, "what was wanted was to knock all the props from under the Germans in the defence of the Mediterranean, let them alone to bear this full burden."[66] This change would lead to re-evaluations concerning the more active, if politically undesirable, Partisans that would hold later consequences to Anglo-Soviet relations and post-war Yugoslavia.[67]

The urgent need for increased action came at a moment when relations were particularly strained between Mihailović and BLOs. This was due largely to the fact that most of Mihailović's energies were being directed towards fighting the Communists whilst the British received ULTRA intelligence confirming Partisan-control of large areas of Croatia, as well as parts of Bosnia and Montenegro.[68] The British were thus faced with, as Woodward would put it:

> [T]he alternatives of supporting a leader who, at all events at the time, was giving no help to the Allied cause or of withdrawing support from him. In the latter case, even if British support were not given to the Partisans, the result at the end of the war might be a Communist revolution or a violent civil war in Yugoslavia.[69]

At a terribly inopportune moment, a serious diplomatic row broke out between the British and the Yugoslavs in early March 1943. This was the result of a speech delivered by Mihailović in the presence of Colonel Bailey that criticized the British for advancing policies without regard to the repercussions they held for Yugoslavia, claiming the Italians were his only friends and his real enemies were the Communists.[70] As a result, the Chiefs of Staff issued the *March Directive* on 20 March 1943, ordering the SOE to establish contact with groups outside of Mihailović's area of control.[71] Whitehall's growing dissatisfaction with Royal Yugoslav Government was such that Churchill would send a letter to the Yugoslav Prime Minister, via King Peter, explaining the British Government was:

> [B]ecoming seriously disturbed at recent developments in Yugoslav affairs and are increasingly apprehensive in regard to the future unless steps are taken to effect a greater measure of unity, not only among the various elements of resistance within the country, and among the Serbs, Croats, and Slovenes, but also among Yugoslav circles abroad.[72]

The British Government was certainly aware that their long-term interests were better served by maintaining a British-dependant Yugoslav monarchy. As Lord Selborne, Minister of Economic Warfare from 1942 to 1945 and head of the SOE, once wrote to Churchill, "I should prefer . . . King Peter in Serbia to Communism."[73] There were, however, more immediate military concerns that were intervening to push British policy in a direction that would pose a later problem for Allied relations.

The British policy of fomenting revolt and embracing those willing to fight was lent greater urgency by the Third Washington Conference (TRIDENT) in May 1943. It was at TRIDENT that Churchill and Roosevelt moved the date for the cross-Channel invasion of France (OVERLORD) to the spring of 1944.[74] The British had also pushed the Americans to focus Allied operations in Italy with HUSKY. Agreement on this strategy served to reinforce the notion that British activity inside Yugoslavia must focus on tying down Axis forces as a *feint* for the Italian campaign and the Partisans were starting to be viewed in Whitehall as the stronger option in this regard.[75]

Shortly after TRIDENT, the SOE mission TYPICAL, headed by Capt. Deakin, was parachuted into Tito's Headquarters (HQ) on 28 May 1943.[76] This was the result of earlier initial contacts established with satellite Partisan commands in Croatia in conjunction with the *March Directive*.[77] Along with this mission came concerns, which proved justified, that direct contact with Tito and a BLO at his HQ would, by extension, imply *de facto* recognition and with it hold possible political repercussions.[78] This would mark a major turning point for the Allies and the beginning of a Communist post-war Yugoslavia that would put the British and Soviets at odds in the Balkans.

The immediate effect was to challenge the British government to seriously evaluate the long-term political dimensions their Yugoslav policies were creating. Eden conveyed this conflict in a letter to Churchill concerning the 'Mihailović-Partisan Dispute' on 24 June 1943, writing:

> [T]aking a long-term view there was no doubt that our interests lay in backing Mihailović and thereby enabling him to preserve Yugoslavia – or at least Serbia – from Chaos and anarchy when liberation comes . . . There has been no doubt that it is the Partisans who have been causing the Axis the most trouble and that they constitute a military organisation to be reckoned with. The recent Chiefs of Staff request, therefore, that sabotage and other operations by guerrillas and resistance groups in the Balkans should be supported and encouraged as far as possible induced us to reconsider our policy towards the Yugoslav Partisans.[79]

It was decided during this period that Brigadier-level missions would be sent in to both Tito and Mihailović's HQs as part of Britain's aim to incorporate Yugoslav resistance more directly in the larger war strategy.[80] In August at the Quebec Conference (QUADRANT), the plans for OVERLORD were further cemented, with a tentative date set for D-Day. As a result, it was decided that operations in the Balkans should be limited to supplying guerrillas, thus driving Yugoslav policy further away from direct British control.[81] Shortly thereafter, and only a week before the Brigadier mission (MACMIS) headed by

Fitzroy Maclean landed at Tito's HQ via parachute, Italian capitulation was formally announced. This had given the Partisans the opportunity to secure a considerable amount of military hardware from the surrendering Italians. It had also left the Partisans in control of several key coastal areas, which served to advance their standing with the British and place them in an excellent position to be supplied by sea from Allied bases in Italy.[82]

As Eden and his counterpart, Soviet Minister of Foreign Affairs Molotov, continued the difficult task of negotiating the troubled Anglo-Soviet relationship, Churchill was pushing both Stalin and Roosevelt for greater action in the Balkans and the Mediterranean as a whole, as an alternative means of opening a second front.[83] The relationship between the Allies was showing considerable wear in 1943 and demonstrated an urgent need to formalize the strategic details related to policy and planning. It was in this moment of Allied crisis in the fall of 1943 that the Cairo (SEXTANT) and Tehran (EUREKA) conferences approached.[84]

There was little agreement on the future course among the Allies. Churchill was continuing to labour towards establishing the foundations for a continued pursuit of a Mediterranean approach to the Allied war effort.[85] Anglo-American relations, as well as Churchill's relationship with Roosevelt, were suffering as a result of these efforts. Churchill's doubts regarding OVERLORD had left CIGS Alan Brooke concerned over what would come of negotiations at SEXTANT and EUREKA.[86] He wrote in his war diary on 8 October 1943:

> [Churchill is] endangering his relations with the President and with the Americans, and so the whole future of the Italian campaign. . . . The Americans are already desperately suspicious of him, and this will make matters far worse. . . . It should be remembered that the Americans always suspected Winston of having concealed desires to spread into the Balkans. These fears were not entirely ungrounded! They were determined that whatever happened they would not be led into the Balkans. . . . Anyhow the Balkan ghost in the cupboard made my road none the easier in leading the Americans by the hand through Italy![87]

## The case of Tito v. Mihailović

Tito and his Partisans had managed during this period to find themselves in a much stronger position than Mihailović to attract Allied support. This was rooted in several factors. Geographically, Tito's position on the coast was logistically enviable and allowed for larger support with greater ease.[88] Beyond this, however, the nature of Tito's organization in comparison to that of Mihailović's played a critical role in growing their ranks, which coupled with a very different approach to fighting the occupiers that one could argue made Tito's eventual supremacy inevitable.

Mihailović's organization was largely drawn from the military and loyal to a government that had become increasingly disconnected from Yugoslavia. On top of this, it was entirely Serbian in its make-up. Further adding to its problems, Mihailović was navigating relations with largely autonomous and regionally rooted commanders.[89] These forces were concerned entirely with weathering the storm and protecting civilians from Axis policies of reprisals.[90]

Tito, alternatively, commanded a mobile force drawn largely from the industrial working class and displaced peasants. His strategy was therefore radically different; he remained mobile with little regard for holding the territory he was fighting in. Tito even invited reprisals against civilians, judging correctly that this would generate more recruits.[91] His organization was multiethnic; committed to fighting the occupiers; and based on a new, unifying political identity.[92] Adding to this, Partisan command had existed in the form of the Communist Party, who were outlawed subversives before the war had even begun. This meant that their command was centralized, as well as ruthlessly disciplined.[93]

### Sole support for Tito

As the war began to turn in the Allies' favour, their needs in the Mediterranean evolved. The improved military situation lent urgency to reassessing Allied policy in Yugoslavia. The need to tie down Axis forces in the region as part of a *feint* to protect the Italian campaign pushed the British to take a more active interest in the Balkans – Yugoslavia in particular.[94] This need for increased activity motivated a more critical line from Britain towards Mihailović's inactivity. This, in turn, was stimulus for a more considered British study of the Partisans.[95]

Yugoslavia became a significant part of Churchill's efforts during SEXTANT and EUREKA. It was during SEXTANT that Maclean arrived in Cairo, back from his Yugoslav mission, to deliver his infamous *Blockbuster* report on his appraisal of the current situation inside the country.[96] This might have been one of the final pieces in the British case for adopting a radically new policy in Yugoslavia. In considering Maclean's report, elements of the British government, including Churchill, became convinced that, despite the political distastefulness of it all, they would need to embrace the Partisans.[97]

Elements within Whitehall had increasingly come round to the pro-Partisan argument, not unjustifiably. It should be remembered that at a time when the British were struggling to cajole Mihailović to take action against Axis rail traffic, the Partisans were not simply attacking rail traffic – they had gone so far as to seize a rail line and locomotive.[98] The Partisans had their own train. By the time Maclean had arrived in Yugoslavia, the Partisans were operating a somewhat erratic but reliable Partisan railway, a fact on which both Maclean and Deakin reported.[99] By this point, the civil war was all but won by the more aggressive Partisans, and the difference between the two groups, in the eyes of the British, was becoming as clear as night and day.

During this same period, however, events in Yugoslavia were taking on a worrying form. On 29–30 November 1943, the AVNOJ held their second session at Jajce. There they made the declarations that the Soviets had worried would come out of the Bihać sessions a year earlier. This included a prohibition on the return of King Peter until after a plebiscite at war's end. These declarations were received rather poorly in Moscow, where concerns over the implications for the current Allied negotiations occurring were seen as the paramount priority.[100] The results were not as disastrous as the Soviets had feared, but British suspicion of the Soviet Union's post-war ambitions had been roused.[101]

The Jajce declarations had come on the same day the 'Big Three' were sitting down for the first time at EUREKA: 28 November 1943–1 December 1943.[102] These meetings began to highlight that, despite the notion of the British being the Allied lead in the Mediterranean and Balkans, the Americans and Soviets were both beginning to encroach. Leading up to the conferences, the Americans had begun to make plain that they did not share the same belief in the possibilities the Mediterranean held as the British. The Americans were exerting their military and economic influence while disregarding the concerns of the British. The Americans were also taking a far harder line with the British government than they were taking with the Soviets.[103] American delegate Harry Hopkins had gone so far as to warn Churchill's physician Charles Moran that "we are preparing for a battle at Tehran. You will find us lining up with the Russians."[104]

Churchill had to fight hard on behalf of Mediterranean operations and went in knowing he was fighting an uphill battle.[105] Churchill had specifically advocated strongly in favour of maintaining support for Tito as a way to preserve influence over the greater regional concerns held by the British. In doing so, Churchill's efforts ran up against Stalin, who stated quite bluntly at a meeting of Combined Chiefs of Staff, "the figures given by the PM regarding German divisions in the Balkans were wrong."[106]

In making these efforts, Churchill was able to achieve a compromise that prevented the complete neglect of the Mediterranean campaign. This was critical in the eyes of the British because of concerns still harboured by individuals such as Churchill and CIGS Alan Brooke over the potential success of OVERLORD.[107] For Churchill, EUREKA had been a battle to protect Mediterranean operations from OVERLORD. As he put it:

> OVERLORD will continue to hamper and enfeeble the Mediterranean campaign that our affairs will deteriorate in the Balkans, and that the Aegean will remain firmly in German hands. All this is to be accepted for the sake of an operation fixed for May upon hypotheses that in all probability will not be realised at that date, and certainly not if the Mediterranean pressure is relaxed.[108]

## The Soviets and *fait accompli*

EUREKA had, in addition to these difficulties, shown that the Soviets were becoming more intransigent, far less keen to see British assistance arrive so close to the Red Army's avenue of advance.[109] As Alan Brooke describes it in his *War Diaries* on 28 November 1943:

> This would bring in the British and Americans on his left flank in an adventure westward through the Balkans. He had by then pretty definite ideas about how he wanted the Balkans ran after the war and this would entail, if possible, their total inclusion in the future Union of Soviet Republics. British and American assistance was therefore no longer desirable in the Eastern Mediterranean.[110]

After EUREKA, the British had a clear understanding that the Americans and Soviets were rivals as well as allies who were both laying the foundation for post-war influence, and their different objectives were surging forcefully to the surface.[111] Moving forward, Churchill would redouble his efforts to coax Roosevelt but found it increasingly more effective to reach out to the Soviets directly, circumventing the Americans.[112]

By December, the view of Mihailović was that he was, in Maclean's words, "anything but whole-hearted in his resistance to the Germans."[113] On 7 December 1943, the Foreign Office delivered a report that argued "the more likely prospect [is] Yugoslavia being unified after the war in the form of a Communist state closely linked to the Soviet Union."[114] Elements of the British government, including the Foreign Office with Eden among them, were becoming painfully aware of an uncomfortable truth: the Royal Yugoslav Government alone might not be able maintain a unified Yugoslavia at war's end.[115] Instead, this would require the acquiescence and assistance of the Partisans in making a peaceful transition to a unified post-war Yugoslavia.[116]

Taking the long view, the British Government was anxious to avoid chaotic post-war transitions that could destabilize the region and threaten British interests in Greece.[117] The Foreign Office, for long-term political considerations, had arguably been Mihailović's greatest defender. Nevertheless, the report was quite damning, arguing, "Mihailović is not only of no military value to the Allies but has also become a standing obstacle to any sort of Yugoslav unity either now or in the near future."[118] With these considerations in mind, the British were coming round to the notion that sooner rather than later they would have to, as Maclean put it, "reconcile our *de jeur* obligations with the *de facto* situation which existed inside the country."[119] As Oliver Harvey would write it in his diary:

> Fitzroy is sure that Tito represents the future government of Yugoslavia, whether we like it or not, a sort of peasant communism, and we should be wise to come to terms and try to guide them. This also has been more or less agreed upon.[120]

Moving forward with sole support for Tito and the abandonment of Mihailović, Whitehall was under no illusions. Mr. Stevenson, the British ambassador to the Royal Yugoslav Government, made it plain he thought the

Partisans were openly revolutionary.[121] Although Whitehall was suspicious of Soviet intentions, they had so far remained relatively quiet on the subject. Meanwhile, it was clear that the strength of the Partisans meant it was almost inevitable that they would end up in control of Yugoslavia. The British had compelling military reasons to support the Partisans against the Germans, and this contributed to a weak negotiating position with Tito. Furthering the difficulties was the Royal Yugoslav Government's stubborn refusal to abandon Mihailović and recognize the reality that the Partisans, whom they sought to discredit, had a firm hold over two-thirds of their country.[122]

## Tito and Allied troubles in the north of Italy

By the summer of 1944, the British were advancing northward through Italy, and it became critical to coordinate operations with the Partisans. Whitehall was concerned that the Germans would attempt a rapid withdrawal from the Balkans altogether and needed Partisan assistance in taking steps to cut off their retreat. The British were also starting to seriously consider the repercussions of the not-unlikely outcome of sooner rather than later joining up with the Partisans at the top of the Adriatic.[123]

At the same time, Whitehall was discussing Soviet intentions in the Balkans and policies aimed at checking Soviet advances whilst ensuring Britain's interests. On 7 June 1944, Eden issued a lengthy memorandum to the War Cabinet on the subject of 'Soviet Policy in the Balkans.'[124] In it, Eden states that he had become "disturbed by developments which seem to indicate the Soviet Government's intention to acquire a dominating influence in the Balkans."[125] Eden went on to outline the current situation faced by the British, probable future outcomes, and proposed a series of possible courses of action, at least two of which became incorporated into British strategy shortly thereafter. He argued, "we should not hesitate to make our special interests in the Eastern Mediterranean and therefore in Greece and Turkey, and indeed our interests elsewhere in the Balkans, clear to the Russians" but also warned "in any steps we take to build up our influence, we must be most careful to avoid giving the impression of a direct challenge."[126] Eden's memorandum also stated:

> In Yugoslavia, Tito, by his own efforts and our own support, will probably emerge as the governing force whether or not as the result of civil war against Serbia. The probability is that the Red Army will eventually gain contact with the Partisans and this will ensure Tito's position.[127]

Faced with this prospect, Eden argued that the British needed to cement their approach to dealing with the Soviets in the Balkans as it was clear they would soon be at odds in the region. He proposed that, given "the suggestion that we should drop our support of Tito now or at any foreseeable future date is out of the question," the British Government should "give full support . . . to all the 'Communist' elements in order to influence them in our direction and take the wind out of the Russian sails."[128] Eden argued "the advantage of giving full support to Tito would be that we should be backing a probable winner and make it less necessary for him to look to Russia for support."[129]

Privately, Whitehall was following the Tito-Šubašić negotiations closely with mounting concern.[130] Churchill expressed his growing discontent with Tito in a letter to Eden on 15 July, claiming Tito "has given nothing in return for what we have done for him and while he lies under our protection on the island of Vis is the best time to bring the consciousness of this home to him."[131] The Foreign Office was likewise becoming annoyed with Tito's handling of the ongoing Šubašić negotiations.[132] This culminated in Churchill personally meeting Tito for the first time at Naples on 12 August 1944 in what would later be called 'The Naples Conference.'[133] On the day of this meeting, Churchill had sent Tito a memorandum stating the British Government expected:

> [T]hat Marshal Tito will make a positive contribution to the unification of Yugoslavia by including in the declaration which has already agreed with the Yugoslav PM to make, not only a statement regarding his intention not to impose Communism on the country but also a statement to the effect that he will not use the armed strength of the Movement to influence the free expression of the will of the people on the future regime of the country.[134]

During these meetings, Churchill attempted to corner Tito into making a public declaration promising not to impose Communism, but Tito evaded doing so, which only served to heighten Churchill's growing suspicions.[135] These misgivings would reach their climax when, in September, Tito disappeared from the Allied base on the island of Vis. It was soon learnt that on the evening of 18 September, Tito had taken off in a Soviet aircraft and was flown to Moscow for secret negotiations with Stalin. Once there, agreements had been reached granting Soviet *de facto* recognition of Tito's government and the Red Army's limited interference and presence in Yugoslavia, which would primarily be focused on operations assisting the Partisans in securing Belgrade.[136]

The British realized that the Red Army would very soon enter Yugoslavia and that they would largely be absent from the scene.[137] In a letter to Churchill on 13 September 1944, Eden had expressed the reality of this concern as well as the limits of Britain's options in addressing the problem:

> there is a grave danger that liberation may only mean the outbreak of civil war or the bloody suppression of non-partisans in Serbia by Tito's men backed up perhaps by Russian arms. The only chance of avoiding such a situation is that control of the country should be assumed at the earliest possible moment military conditions permit by a single united Yugoslav Government fully recognised and supported by all the United Nations, in particular the Soviet Union.[138]

On 1 October, the Red Army entered Yugoslavia, and Belgrade was liberated on 20 October.[139] During the interim, the Fourth Moscow Conference (TOLSTOY) occurred between 9–18 October 1944. Churchill, CIGS Alan Brooke, and Eden met with Stalin and Molotov to establish post-war spheres of influence in Eastern Europe and Balkan Peninsula. This included the now infamous *percentage agreement*. In it, Churchill and Stalin agreed to specific levels of shared involvement in various Balkan countries, creating post-war spheres of influence that guaranteed British interests in Greece.[140]

The Tito-Šubašić agreement was finalized shortly afterwards, on 1 November in Belgrade, essentially ending the Royal Yugoslav Government and any chance of the Yugoslav Crown's return. Churchill agreed with King Peter that the agreement was not what was hoped for but in December urged the King to accept it. Both Churchill and Eden pointed out there had been a revolution in Yugoslavia and this was the only practical way of keeping the principal of monarchy alive in Yugoslavia.[141]

Shortly after the liberation of Belgrade, the Red Army moved out of Yugoslavia, leaving the Partisans and Western Allies to deal with some of the bloodiest fighting of the war as the Germans, Ustaše, Četniks and collaborators began to flee northward.[142] Concerns over the political implications of Allied forces meeting the Partisans in Northern Italy became realized. Tito had already made clear his intention of laying claim to Istria, Trieste and Venezia Giulia, whilst the British position had been that these questions must be dealt with at war's end during the peace negotiations.[143] There was immediate concern, however, that if Tito secured control of the region, he would take matters into his own hands and present the British with a *fait accompli*. Tito was likewise distrustful of British intentions and suspected they would attempt to keep him out of the region. Both sides therefore felt the need to strengthen their position by occupying the region.[144]

## The Cold War becomes clearer

It was in this mood that the British approached the Malta Conference (ARGONAUT and CRICKET) between 30 January and 2 February. It was here Churchill and Roosevelt met in preparation for the 'Big Three' meeting at Yalta (ARGONAUT and MAGNETO) set for 4–11 February. Yalta had been set to lay final plans for the defeat of Germany and to discuss post-war European policies. Dark clouds of the Soviets' making hung over the conference, and discussions would have to contend with the overwhelming military presence the Red Army held in Eastern Europe.[145]

Yalta came at a time when British relations with the Soviets were already deteriorating and their intentions in Eastern Europe were becoming clear.[146] The Soviets had gone to Yalta sure that, apart from Greece, they had a free hand in the Balkans and would face no serious opposition. The unspoken truth of the situation was that any decisions made at Yalta regarding the Balkans had to face the reality that the Red Army was there and the program of establishing Communist powers was already underway.[147] Eden would remark in his memoirs, "Stalin's attitude to small countries struck me as grim, not to say sinister."[148]

The British had gone to Yalta on the defensive and with open eyes on their limitations in the Balkans. John Colville, who was serving on Churchill's staff at the time, reports that Churchill, on the eve of leaving for Yalta, remarked that he knew the Balkans were lost to the Soviets and the only thing he would accomplish was the preservation of Greece.[149]

Yalta left the British with a feeling that their allies were more adversaries than friends.[150] Soviet expansion raised concerns that Stalin was ignoring Churchill's *percentage deal.* Moving forward, the British were convinced that if they wished to preserve Greece and what little position the Western Allies had in the Balkans, they would need to maintain what good relations remained with the Soviets. The alternative they feared would be to ignite another massive regional conflict.[151]

Churchill wrote Eden on 11 March 1945 to voice his assessment of the current situation as it concerned Yugoslavia. He expressed the feeling that "henceforward our inclination should be to back Italy against Tito."[152] He went on to say, "I have lost my relish for Yugoslavia which state must rest on the basis of the Tito-Šubašić agreements etc. On the other hand I hope we may still save Italy from the Bolshevist petulance."[153] Eden, however, urged Churchill against abandoning what was left of their influence in Yugoslavia to "leave the whole business to Tito and Moscow."[154]

Churchill continued to lament events in Yugoslavia, describing his feelings in a memo to his private office on 25 April 1945:

> In view of the way in which all our affairs are being sold down the counter in Yugoslavia and the mockery of the 50/50 agreement with Russia I really cannot write to King Peter except in the strain that it has not been within my power to alter the course of events and that I am sure that we have done all we could in the circumstances. I cannot however claim that the result is at all satisfactory.[155]

### Closing days

Meanwhile, new troubles were brewing in Venezia Giulia as the Partisans made their manoeuvre for Trieste. The Partisans had begun a major offensive on 20 March to drive the Germans out of the rest of Yugoslavia and made rapid progress towards the Italian border.[156] On 1 May, the Partisans entered Trieste just ahead of the Allies.[157] On 2 May, a New Zealand division accepted the surrender of German forces in the Trieste area and moved in, reporting the Partisans were in the process of occupying the city.[158]

From General Alexander outwards, the Chiefs of Staff, the lower levels of military command, as well as within the higher levels of the British Government, there was considerable concern over Tito's attitude. If Tito decided to resist Allied efforts to control the region and intended to defend his claim by force, General Alexander would be unable to maintain control of the region with his existing forces.[159] Harold Macmillan, who was serving as Minister Resident in the Mediterranean during this period, was alarmed that the vital question remained unaddressed of whether or not to use force if the Yugoslavs opposed Alexander's occupation of the whole of Venezia Giulia.[160]

On the same day, in response to these reports, Churchill reiterated Britain's intention to halt supply to the Partisans. This was in response to Tito clearly attempting to rush territorial claims. This was in direct contradiction to an agreement made at Yalta on 10 February between the 'Big Three' that a commission would be established to settle the line of separation in Venezia Giulia between the Allied Military Government and the Yugoslavs.[161] British concerns were validated the next day, on 3 May, when a Yugoslav communiqué issued by Tito stated that "Allied forces had entered Trieste and Gorizia without Yugoslav permission, and that their action might have 'undesirable consequences' unless a settlement were reached by mutual agreement."[162]

One week later, on 7 May, Germany surrendered, ending the war in Europe, and brought with it questions of how to proceed. The British were convinced that Tito's attempt to seize Trieste, when viewed in conjunction with the Soviet's increasingly aggressive posture, required a response. The British was becoming convinced that to let Tito have Trieste would be to give it to the Soviets, who were starting to look like a potential enemy. Soviet support of Tito's claim on Trieste was enough to cement this view.[163]

For the British, Trieste was an essential supply port, a vital outlet for much of Central Europe and the key to protecting lines of communication.[164] Tito's negotiations with General Alexander on administration of the area were to prove strained and fruitless.[165] The Yugoslavs were meanwhile carrying out executions and deportations among the Italian segment of the population, resulting in extremely tense relations between the British and American troops and the Yugoslav forces.[166] The result was that Trieste was quickly becoming a possible flash point where any misstep might prove the spark that would ignite a global conflict.[167]

As Alistair Horne notes in his official biography of Macmillan, "There was the general picture of chaos in the area, and alarm . . . that the situation was drifting dangerously close to war, under the most disadvantageous term, with the Titoist Yugoslavs."[168] Correspondence between Stalin and Churchill had become strained by this time.[169] Both London and Washington viewed the potential dangers in Trieste quite seriously – to the point that there were concerns that operations would need to be mounted against the Partisans.[170] For the British, there was the question at this stage of what could be expected from the Americans and their new President, Harry Truman.[171]

Churchill wrote to Truman on 2 June to express the growing concern over events in Trieste. He explained the news was bad and that the Yugoslavs were threatening to use force.[172] In referencing a suggestion brought forward by Lord Halifax, Churchill argued that "unless we had a satisfactory answer from

Marshal Tito within three days, our Ambassadors should tell Marshall Tito that Field Marshal Alexander was taking matters into his own hands."[173] Churchill would go on to make the case to Truman that:

> If we once let it be thought that there is no point beyond which we cannot be pushed about, there will be no future for Europe except another war more terrible than anything that the world has yet seen. But by showing a firm front in circumstances and in a locality which are favourable to us, we may reach a satisfactory and solid foundation for peace and justice.[174]

Much to Churchill's relief, Truman would prove to be a stronger character than Roosevelt had been on this front. As Macmillan wrote in his diary on 13 May, "the Americans have suddenly hardened; the President [Truman] will not be 'pushed about' any more. . . . He proposes a stiff note to Tito, amounting almost, if not quite, an ultimatum. This of course entirely alters the position."[175]

Truman expressed his view to the British that the Western powers had to decide if they would follow through and "uphold the fundamental principle of territorial settlement by orderly process against force, intimidation or blackmail."[176] For Truman, the question was not simply about taking sides between the Italians and Yugoslavs but deciding if the Allies would permit uncontrolled land grabbing tactics, which he likened to Hitler's own methods.[177] Truman held to the position that in order to prevent chaos, General Alexander must see to it that the administration for the entire region be taken on by Allied Military Government (AMG) in the interim.[178]

As a result of these decisions, Truman initiated a correspondence with Stalin and issued a series of stern warnings, making clear to the Soviets that they had found the 'red line.' The Western Allies were putting their foot down in Venezia Giulia and would have no more.[179] As Truman would put it to Stalin in a letter dated 12–23 May 1943,

> we cannot view this simply as a boundary dispute between Yugoslavia and Italy but must look upon it as a question of principle which involves the specific settlement of territorial disputes, and the foundation of a lasting peace in Europe.[180]

Within the course of the next several days, there were clear indications that Tito was going to back down. On 9 June, an agreement was signed that saw Yugoslav troops slowly begin to withdraw from the area that had been established as falling under AMG control. On 20 June, a further military agreement was signed that seemed to avert the crisis and diffuse the potential for immediate conflict.[181]

Although Tito was checked and the Soviets had not pushed the issue, the situation was far from resolved. Stalin would continue to push hard for the

Yugoslav cause with increasingly strong anti-Western rhetoric. On 21 June 1945, he would write to Churchill, arguing the deadlock was because:

> [T]he Allied Command in the Mediterranean refuse to entertain even the minimum wishes of the Yugoslavs, to whom credit is due for liberating the area from the German invaders, an area, moreover, where the Yugoslav population predominates.[182]

At Potsdam, the situation worsened as the Soviets dug in, refusing to acknowledge the lack of free elections within their sphere of influence. They hurled accusations at the British over the Varkiza Agreement concerning Greece whilst ignoring the Soviets' own reverse position concerning the Tito-Šubašić agreement.[183] The Tito-Šubašić agreement had not been carried out, and, as Eden pointed out, Tito's administration had imposed "a strictly controlled party organisation backed by political police and that the control of the press almost as strict as in Fascist countries."[184] Stalin refused to discuss Yugoslavia and questions concerning Venezia Giulia without Yugoslav delegates present. Although the British were agreeable, Truman vetoed the idea.[185]

The British had been surprised by Truman's position on this front, as had the US State Department who had drafted an even sterner brief than the Foreign Office. The result of all this was no progress was made. Memorandum and counter-memorandum circulated with the British calling for the governments of South-East Europe not to "anticipate the peace settlement by violent and unilateral actions" while the Soviets reiterated the Yugoslav's claims.[186]

Stalin is said to have remarked at Potsdam, "in politics one should be guided by the calculation of forces."[187] It would seem that this statement demonstrates clearer than anything else the approach taken by the Soviets, who held massive military advantage in Eastern Europe. Potsdam wound up with more unresolved than accomplished, and British complaints about Tito fell on deaf ears.[188] The end result for the situation concerning the Italians and Yugoslavs in Venezia Giulia, which had brought the British and Soviets so close to the edge, was what General Alexander described as "a most unhappy wrangle . . . over the future of the area which was not to be settled until nine years after the end of the war."[189]

## Notes

1 David Dilks, ed., *The Diaries of Sir Alexander Cadogan 1938–1945* (New York: G.P. Putnam's Sons, 1972), 153–72.
2 CAB 66/5/20 "Record of the Fourth Meeting of the Supreme War Council" 19 December 1939, 2, *The National Archives of the UK*. "The Cabinet Papers – Records of the Cabinet Office" CAB, London 2018. http://discovery.nationalarchives.gov.uk/SearchUI/browse/C44?v=h
3 CAB 66/4/9 "The Balkan Problem"11 December 1939; CAB 65–22–8 "Campbell to Eden" 16 March 1941; CAB 66/8/30 "Balkan Policy in the New Situation" 11 June 1940;

Winston S. Churchill, *The Second World War, Vol. 3: The Grand Alliance* (Cambridge, MA: The Riverside Press, 1949), 97–8; Heather Williams, *Parachutes, Patriots and Partisans: The Special Operations Executive and Yugoslavia, 1941–1945* (Madison: University of Wisconsin Press, 2003), 21.

4   CAB 66/8/30 "Balkan Policy in the New Situation" 11 June 1940, 3; Dilks, *Sir Alexander Cadogan*, 117–18, 163–4, 171.

5   CAB 66/4/9 War Cabinet Meeting "The Balkan Problem" 11 December 1939; Anthony Eden, *The Eden Memoirs: The Reckoning* (London: Cassell, 1965), 219; Dilks, *Sir Alexander Cadogan*, 170–2.

6   CAB 66/7/14 "Balkan Policy in the New Situation" 11 June 1940, 1; Churchill, *The Grand Alliance*, 157–8.

7   CAB 65–6–53 "Allied policy in the event of an Italian attack on Yugoslavia" 30 April 1940, 468–70; CAB 66/7/14 "Implications of Possible Italian Action in the Mediterranean" 21 April 1940.

8   Eden, *The Reckoning*, 194.

9   CAB 66/22/8 "Campbell report from Belgrade" 16 March 1941; CAB 66/22/8 "Confidential Annex" 17 March 1941; Dilks, *Sir Alexander Cadogan*, 365; Churchill, *The Grand Alliance*, 159; Victor Rothwell, *Anthony Eden: A Political Biography, 1931–1957* (Oxford, UK: Manchester University Press, 1992), 57.

10   PREM 3/510/11 Telegram "Eden to Mr. Campbell: Belgrade" 24 March 1941. *The National Archives of the UK.* "Records of the Prime Minister's Office" PREM, London 2018. http://discovery.nationalarchives.gov.uk/SearchUI/details?Uri=C233; Eden, *The Reckoning*, 227.

11   CAB 65/18/11 "Conclusions of a Meeting of the War Cabinet" 27 March 1941, 169–70; Churchill, *The Grand Alliance*, 161–73; Fitzroy Maclean. *Eastern Approaches* (London, UK: Penguin Books, 1991), 292; Ben Shepherd. *Terror in the Balkans: German Armies and Partisan Warfare* (Cambridge, MA: Harvard University Press, 2012), 75; Michael McConville, *A Small War in the Balkans: British Military Involvement in Wartime Yugoslavia 1941–1945* (Uckfield, East Sussex, UK: The Naval & Military Press Ltd., 2007), 13–15.

12   Churchill, *The Grand Alliance*, 163–73.

13   Milan Deroc, *British Special Operations Explored: Yugoslavia in Turmoil 1941–1943 and the British Response* (New York: Columbia University Press, 1988), 27.

14   Sir Llewellyn Woodward, *History of the Second World War: British Foreign Policy in the Second World War*, Vol. 1 (London: Her Majesty's Stationery Office by McCorquodale & Co., 1970), 543.

15   CAB 65/22/7 "Belgrade Telegram No. 380: Mr. Campbell to Mr. Eden, 10 March 1941" 13 March 1941, 75; CAB 65/18/11 "Conclusions of a Meeting of the War Cabinet" 27 March 1941, 169–70; CAB 65/22/12 "Conclusions Minute 2 Confidential Annex" 11 April 1941, 5; Eden, *The Reckoning*, 220, 231.

16   Churchill, *The Grand Alliance*, 164; V. Greiffenberg, "The Balkan Campaign: The Invasion of Yugoslavia," *US Army Center of Military History.* SSUSA Historical Division, 1947. Last Accessed 1 June 2018. www.history.army.mil/html/books/104/104-18/CMH_Pub_104-18.pdf, 5–6; Jozo Tomasevich, *War and Revolution in Yugoslavia, 1941–1945: The Chetniks* (Stanford: Stanford University Press, 1975), 55; De Bello, "Führer Directive No. 25," Last Accessed 29 May 2018. https://web.archive.org/web/20161011133405/ww2.debello.ca/library/410327.html

17   Maclean, *Eastern Approaches*, 292; Shepherd, *Terror in the Balkans*, 76; Deroc, *British Special Operations*, 22–4; Michael Lees, *The Rape of Serbia: The British Role in Tito's Grab for Power* (New York: Harcourt Brace Jovanovich, Publishers, 1990), 71.

18   Marcia Christoff Kurapovna, *Shadows on the Mountain: The Allies, the Resistance, and the Rivalries that Doomed WWII Yugoslavia* (Hoboken, NJ, USA: John Wiley & Sons, Inc. 2010), 51.

19   PREM 3/510/11 "Churchill to Commander-in-Chief Middle East" 13 April 1941; Williams, *Parachutes, Patriots and Partisans*, 58; FO 898/11 "Hugh Dalton: memorandum on

Propaganda," 6 Dec 1941. *The National Archives of the UK.* "Records Created or Inherited by the Foreign Office" FO, London 2018. http://discovery.nationalarchives.gov.uk/SearchUI/details?Uri=C130; Dilks, *Sir Alexander Cadogan*, 365.

20  PREM 3/510/11 "Churchill to Commander-in-Chief Middle East" 13 April 1941.

21  Stevan K. Pavlowitch, *Hitler's New Disorder: The Second World War in Yugoslavia* (New York: Columbia University Press, 2008), 57; Matteo J. Milazzo, *The Chetni Movement and the Yugoslav Resistance* (Baltimore: John Hopkins University Press, 1976), 14–23.

22  Williams, *Parachutes, Patriots and Partisans*, 44–5; Mark C. Wheeler, *Britain and the War for Yugoslavia 1940–1943* (New York: Columbia University Press, 1980), 63; Pavlowitch, *Hitler's New Disorder*, 104.

23  Churchill, *The Grand Alliance*, 168; Dilks, *Sir Alexander Cadogan*, 366–7; Williams, *Parachutes, Patriots and Partisans*, 42; Jasper Rootham, *Miss Fire: The Chronicle of a British Mission to Mihailovich* (London: Chatto & Windus, 1946), 2; Fitzroy Maclean, *The Heretic: The Life and Times of Josip Broz-Tito* (New York: Harper & Brothers, Publishers, 1957), 84–5.

24  PREM 3/409/2 "The Prospects of Subversion Summary," i; PREM 3/510/2 "Ministry of Economic Warfare to The PM: In reply to your Minute M.837/1. Of August 28th [1941], signed H.D. (Dalton)" 30 August 1941; PREM 3/510/4 "Admerality to C-in-C Mediterranean" 15 October 1941.

25  PREM 3/510/4 "Simovitch to Churchill" October 1941.

26  PREM 3/510/1 War Cabinet: Intelligence Committee (operations), Yugoslav Revolt "Extract of a Letter dated 11 December [1941] from the Minister of Economic Warfare to the PM" 14 December 1941; PREM 3/409/7 Letter: From Hugh Dalton to Churchill "Summary of fortnightly Report from Cairo" 11 December 1941.

27  PREM 3/510/4 "War Cabinet, Defence Committee (Operations): Yugoslav Revolt, Memorandum by the Secretary of State for Foreign Affairs [Anthony Eden]" 31 October 1941.

28  Deroc, *British Special Operations*, 131, 170–1.

29  David Martin, *The Web of Disinformation: Churchill's Yugoslav Blunder* (New York: Harcourt Brace Jovanovich, Publishers, 1990), xxiii.

30  PREM 3/510/1 "War Cabinet Intelligence Committee (operations): Yugoslav Revolt, Extract of a Letter dated 11 December [1941] from the Minister of Economic Warfare to the PM" 14 December 1941; PREM 3/409/7 "Hugh Dalton to Churchill: Summary of fortnightly Report from Cairo" 11 December 1941; PREM 3/510/4 "War Cabinet Defence Committee (Operations): Yugoslav Revolt, Memorandum by the Secretary of State for Foreign Affairs [Anthony Eden]," 31 October 1941.

31  PREM 3/510/1 "War Cabinet Intelligence Committee (operations): Yugoslav Revolt, Extract of a Letter dated 11 December [1941] from the Minister of Economic Warfare to the PM" 14 December 1941; PREM 3/409/7 "Hugh Dalton to Churchill: Summary of fortnightly Report from Cairo" 11 December 1941; PREM 3/510/12 "CIGS to PM" 2 June 1942.

32  PREM 3/510/1 "War Cabinet Chiefs of Staff Committee: Yugoslav Revolt" 26 February 1942; PREM 3/510/12 "CIGS to PM" 2 June 1942; Pavlowitch, *Hitler's New Disorder*, 61–2; Frederick William Dampier Deakin, *The Embattled Mountain* (London: Oxford University Press, 1971), 69.

33  Shepherd, *Terror in the Balkans*, 76.

34  Deroc, *British Special Operations*, 20–34; Woodward, *British Foreign Policy Vol. 1*, 543; Fitzroy Maclean, *Eastern Approaches*, 292.

35  Shepherd, *Terror in the Balkans*, 72–6; Williams, *Parachutes, Patriots and Partisans*, 56–7.

36  Max Bergholz, *Violence as a Generative Force: Identity, Nationalism, and Memory in a Balkan Community* (Ithaca and London: Cornell University Press, 2016), 4.

37  Ibid., 6.

38  Rootham, *Miss Fire*, 2; Williams, *Parachutes, Patriots and Partisans*, 56–7.

39  Deroc, *British Special Operations Explored*, 136.

40  Rootham, *Miss Fire*, 210.

41  Milazzo, *The Chetni Movement*, 1–10.

42  Williams, *Parachutes, Patriots and Partisans*, 182; Basil Davidson, *Partisan Picture* (Bedford, UK: Bedford Books Ltd., 1946), Ch. 1; Kurapovna, *Shadows on the Mountain*, 115.

43  CAB 66/5/20 "Record of the Fourth Meeting of the Supreme War Council" 19 December 1939; FRUS "The Conferences at Cairo and Tehran," 331, 478–80; CAB 66/5/20 "Record of the Fourth Meeting of the Supreme War Council" 19 December 1939; CAB 66/44/2 War Cabinet "Weekly resume no. 222" 2 December 1943, 5–6; CAB 66/4/9 War Cabinet "The Balkan Problem"11 December 1939; CAB 66/44/32 War Cabinet "Weekly resume no. 225" 23 December 1943, 5; PREM 3/511/3 "Churchill to Molotov" 14 April 1944; CAB 66/57/14 War Cabinet "Weekly resume no. 270" 2 November 1944, 7; Churchill, *The Grand Alliance*, 98; Churchill, *Closing the Ring*, 330–1; Eden, *Memoirs: The Reckoning*, 188–9.

44  Walter R. Roberts, *Tito, Mihailović and the Allies, 1941–1945* (New Brunswick, NJ: Rutgers University Press, 1973), 42, 58.

45  Maclean. *The Heretic*, 140–4.

46  Ibid., 140; Roberts, *Tito, Mihailović and the Allies*, 42.

47  McConville, *A Small War in the Balkans*, 46, 59–60; Martin, *The Web of Disinformation*, 161; Williams, *Parachutes, Patriots and Partisans*, 82–5.

48  PREM 3/510/12 "CIGS to PM" 2 June 1942.

49  Ibid.

50  PREM 3/510/2 "Churchill to the Yugoslav PM" 25 August 1941; PREM 3/510/2 "Ministry of Economic Warfare to The PM: In reply to your Minute M.837/1. Of August 28th [1941], signed H.D. (Dalton)" 30 August 1941; PREM 3/510/4 "Churchill to Yugoslav PM" October 1941; PREM 3/510/4 "Message sent through Admiralty: Chiefs of Staff to C-in-C Mediterranean" 7 November 1941; PREM 3/510/4 "Office of the Minister of Defence to Churchill" 23 October 1941; PREM 3/510/4 "Simovitch to Churchill" 20 (presumed) October 1941; PREM 3/510/1 "War Cabinet Chiefs of Staff Committee: Yugoslav Revolt" 26 February 1942; Dilks, *Sir Alexander Cadogan*, 428; Wheeler, *Britain and the War for Yugoslavia*, 123–5.

51  PREM 3/510/5 "King Peter to Churchill: Generally very dissatisfied with my Government" 9 December 1942; Wheeler, *Britain and the War for Yugoslavia*, 131–41.

52  Ibid.

53  PREM 3/510/5 "Anthony Eden to PM: Mihailovic" 17 December 1942; PREM 3/510/5 "King Peter to Churchill: Generally very dissatisfied with my Government" 9 December 1942.

54  PREM 3/510/5 "King Peter to Churchill: Generally very dissatisfied with my Government" 9 December 1942.

55  CAB 65/34/33 "Yugoslavia 'Conclusions'" 31 May 1943, 69–70; PREM 3/510/7 "Situation in Yugoslavia" 18 June 1943, 5; CAB 65/34/41 "Yugoslavia 'Conclusions'" 21 June 1943, 97; CAB 66/38/13 "Yugoslav Government Crisis" 22 June 1943; PREM 3/510/13 "Stevenson to Eden" 25 November 1943; PREM 3/510/13 "Memorandum by Eden: Yugoslav Government Crisis" 22 June 1943.

56  PREM 3/510/5 "Anthony Eden to PM: Mihailovic" 17 December 1942; Deakin, *The Embattled Mountain*, 153–4; McConville, *A Small War in the Balkans*, 50–4.

57  CAB 66/45/19 "The position in Yugoslavia" 10 January 1944; PREM 3/510/10 "Stevenson to FO"11 December 1943; CAB 65/40/19 "War Cabinet Minutes" 28 December 1943; CAB 66/49/34 " FO Report from Lt-Col. Hudson: Recommendations" 21 April 1944; PREM 3/511/12 "Report from Selborne for PM" 11 May 1944; Eden, *The Reckoning*, 433; Winston S. Churchill, *The Second World War, Vol. 5: Closing the Ring* (Cambridge, MA: The Riverside Press, 1949), 471; Deakin, *The Embattled Mountain*, 200.

58  Williams, *Parachutes, Patriots and Partisans*, 86–9.

59  Maclean, *The Heretic*, 159–61.

60  Roberts, *Tito, Mihailović and the Allies*, 77, 323.

61  The Office, U. S. Secretary, Office of the Combined Chiefs of Staff 1943, ed., *SEXTANT Conference November-December 1943: Papers and Minutes of Meetings SEXTANT*

and *EUREKA Conferences* (Washington, DC: Joint History Office, 2003), 463–4; FRUS "The Conferences at Cairo and Tehran," 795. FRUS "The Conferences at Cairo and Tehran," *Foreign Relations of the United States, University of Wisconsin Digital Collection.* "Foreign relations of the United States diplomatic papers" (FRUS). Last Accessed 29 May 2018. https://uwdc.library.wisc.edu/collections/FRUS/; Churchill, *Closing the Ring,* 331–2.

62 PREM 3/510/5 "Anthony Eden to PM on Mihailovic" 17 December 1942, 3.

63 FRUS "Casablanca Conference Papers," 747–9; *USSR Foreign Ministry, Commission for the Publication of Diplomatic Documents.* "Correspondence between the Chairman of the Council of Ministers of the USSR and the Presidents of the USA and the Prime Ministers of Great Britain during the Great Patriotic War of 1941–1945. Volume 1: Correspondence with Winston S. Churchill and Clement R. Attlee (July 1941–November 1945)." (Moscow: Progress Publishers, 1957), No. 104, 27 January 1943.

64 FRUS "Casablanca Conference Papers," 584, 747–51, 761, 770; USSR, *Correspondence Vol. 1,* no. 104, 92.

65 USSR, *Correspondence Vol. 1,* No. 112, 9 February 1943.

66 Alex Danchev and Daniel Todman, eds. *War Diaries 1939–1945 Field Marshal Lord Alanbrooke* (London: Weidenfeld and Nicolson, 2001), 476.

67 "The Armstrong-Bailey Recommendations" *Found in,* Martin, *The Web of Disinformation,* 315; PREM 3/510/10 "Stevenson to FO" 11 December 1943; PREM 3–511–12 / CAB 66–49–34 "FO Report from Lt-Col. Hudson: Recommendations" 21 April 1944, 1–3; HANSARD "War and the International Situation" 22 February 1944 vol 397 cc663–795. *HANSARD UK Parliament* "HANSARD 1803–2005" Last Accessed 29 May 2018. https://api.parliament.uk/historic-hansard/index.html

68 PREM 3/510/12 "CIGS to PM" 2 June 1942; PREM 3/409/5 "SOE Activities: Summary for the PM" Quarter: April to June 1943; PREM 3/510/7 "War Cabinet, Annex II: Situation in Yugoslavia: Report" 18 June 1943; Deakin, *The Embattled Mountain,* 153–4; Wheeler, *Britain and the War for Yugoslavia,* 218–20.

69 Sir Llewellyn Woodward, *History of the Second World War: British Foreign Policy in the Second World War,* Vol. 3 (London: Her Majesty's Stationery Office by McCorquodale & Co., 1971), 288.

70 Martin, *The Web of Disinformation,* 76–8.

71 PREM 3/510/6 "Sir Alexander Cadogan to Churchill" 23 March 1943; WO 202/162 "Reports on conditions and personalities in Yugoslavia. Mission reports from FUGUE, ROUGHSHOD and 2nd Kasovski and Yablanca areas" 17 March 1943, *The National Archives of the UK.* "Records created or inherited by the War Office, Armed Forces, Judge Advocate General, and related bodies" WO, London 2018. http://discovery.nationalarchives.gov.uk/browse/r/h/C259; PREM 3/510/6 "Churchill to Sir Alexander Cadogan" 27 March 1943; Williams, *Parachutes, Patriots and Partisans,* 138; Martin, *The Web of Disinformation,* 87; Deakin, *The Embattled Mountain,* 191.

72 PREM 3/510/6 "Foreign Office draft of Churchill letter to Slobodan [J]Yovanovitch" 29 March 1943.

73 PREM 3/511/12 "Report from Selborne for PM" 11 May 1944.

74 PREM 3/510/7 "Richard Casey to Admiral Cunningham: Enclosing report" 1 June 1943; FO 371/37609, "Situation in Yugoslavia: activities of General Mihailovic: Partisan movement" 1943; Williams, *Parachutes, Patriots and Partisans,* 143; CAB 65/34/33 "Conclusions" 31 May 1943; Danchev, *Alan Brooke,* 401–11.

75 PREM 3/510/7 "Richard Casey to Admiral Cunningham: Enclosing report" 1 June 1943; PREM 3/510/12 "The Situation in Yugoslavia" 2 June 1942; PREM 3/510/7 "Situation in Yugoslavia" 18 June 1943; PREM 3/510/7 "Selborne to Churchill" 18 June 1943; PREM 3/510/7 "Churchill to L.C. Hollins" 23 June 1943; PREM 3/510/13 Eden to Churchill "Yugoslavia Mihailovic Partisan Dispute" 24 June 1943; PREM 3/510/7 "Selborne to Churchill" 29 June 1943; CAB 7/14/43 "Report by the Joint Intelligence Sub-Committee" 14 July 1943; USSR, *Correspondence Vol. 1,* No. 112, 9 February 1943; Churchill, *Closing the Ring,* 332, 463; Danchev, *Alan Brooke,* 406.

76  Wheeler, *Britain and the War for Yugoslavia*, 232; Deakin, *The Embattled Mountain*, 63; David Stafford, *Camp X* (Toronto: Lester & Orpen Dennys, 1986), 181.

77  Roberts, *Tito, Mihailović and the Allies*, 116–17; William Jones, *Twelve Months with Tito's Partisans*, 1st ed. (London: Bedford Books Limited, 1946), 2.

78  PREM 3/510/13 "Eden to Churchill: Yugoslavia Mihailovic Partisan Dispute" 24 June 1943.

79  Ibid.

80  Roberts, *Tito, Mihailović and the Allies*, 116–17; Williams, *Parachutes, Patriots and Partisans*, 150; Deakin, *The Embattled Mountain*, 108.

81  William Deakin, "The Myth of an Allied Landing in the Balkans during the Second World War," in *British Policy towards Wartime Resistance in Yugoslavia and Greece*, eds. Phyllis Auty and Richard Clogg (London: The Macmillan Press, 1975), 108–9.

82  PREM 3/510/9 "Note on the Situation in Yugoslavia" 27/28 October 1943; CAB 66/43/15 "Weekly resume no. 219" 11 November 1943, 6; CAB 66/44/2 "Weekly resume no. 222" 2 December 1943, 5–6; CAB 66/44/32 "Weekly resume no. 225" 23 December 1943, 5; CAB 66/44/41 "Weekly resume no. 226," 30 December 1943, 5–6; Churchill, *Closing the Ring*, 330–1, 464; Maclean, *Eastern Approaches*, 410.

83  USSR, *Correspondence Vol. 1*, No. 112, 9 February 1943, No. 129, 111, No. 163, 137, No. 167, 145; Danchev, *Alan Brooke*, 346–8, 360–6, 406, 443.

84  Office of the Combined Chiefs of Staff, *SEXTANT Conference*, 385; FRUS "The Conferences at Cairo and Tehran," 331; McConville, *A Small War in the Balkans*, 97.

85  Office of the Combined Chiefs of Staff, *SEXTANT Conference*, 385; FRUS "The Conferences at Cairo and Tehran," 33; PREM 3/510/13 "Former Naval Person [Churchill] to President Roosevelt" 23 October 1943; Churchill, *Closing the Ring*, 331–2, 352, 367–70; Danchev, *Alan Brooke*, 346–8, 406, 443, 459, 463–5, 483; Warren F. Kimball, ed., *Churchill & Roosevelt the Complete Correspondence, Vol. 1: Alliance Emerging: Oct 1933–Nov 1943* (New Jersey: Princeton University Press, 1984), 177.

86  PREM 3/510/13 "War Cabinet to General Wilson" 23 October 1943; PREM 3/510/13 "Former Naval Person [Churchill] to President Roosevelt" 23 October 1943; Danchev, *Alan Brooke*, 459.

87  Danchev, *Alan Brooke*, 459.

88  CAB 66/43/15 War Cabinet "Weekly resume no. 219" 6; CAB 66/44/2 War Cabinet "Weekly resume no. 222" 2 December 1943, 5–6; CAB 66/44/32 War Cabinet "Weekly resume no. 225" 23 December 1943, 5; CAB 66/44/41 War Cabinet "Weekly resume no. 226," 5–6; PREM 3/510/9 Note on the Situation in Yugoslavia 27/28 October 1943, 3; Alan Brooke, *War Diaries*, 468; Churchill, *Closing the Ring*, 330–1, 464; Churchill, *The Grand Alliance*, 98; Deakin, *The Embattled Mountain*, 227; Eden, *Memoirs: The Reckoning*, 188–9; Maclean, *Eastern Approaches*, 410.

89  Roberts, *Tito, Mihailović and the Allies*, 68; Rootham, *Miss Fire*, 45.

90  Pavlowitch, *Hitler's New Disorder*, 55, 60–1; Maclean, *Eastern Approaches*, 336; Maclean, *The Heretic*, 105–7.

91  PREM 3/510/12 "CIGS to PM" 2 June 1942; *United States' Library of Congress, Federal Research Division of.* "Yugoslavia: The Resistance Movement" Last Accessed 29 May 2018. www.loc.gov/item/91040323/; Simon Trew, *Britain, Mihailović, and the Chetniks, 1941–42* (London: St. Martin's Press, 1997), 41–4; Williams, *Parachutes, Patriots and Partisans*, 60; William James Millar Mackenzie, *The Secret History of SOE: The Special Operations Executive 1940–1945* (London: St. Ermin's Press, 2000), 116–17; Maclean, *Eastern Approaches*, 313; Timothy Snyder, *Bloodlands: Europe between Hitler and Stalin* (New York: Basic Books, 2010), 233–4; Misha Glenny, *The Balkans: Nationalism, War & the Great Powers, 1804–1999* (New York: Penguin Books, 2001), 489.

92  Bergholz, *Violence as a Generative Force*, 195–6.

93  Shepherd, *Terror in the Balkans*, 95–6, 151–2; Michael Richard Daniell Foot, *SOE an Outline History of the Special Operations Executive 1940–1946* (London: The Bondy Head, 2014), 168, 183; Glenny, *The Balkans*, 489; Pavlowitch, *Hitler's New Disorder*,

56; Max Hastings, *All Hell Let Loose: The World at War 1939–45* (London: Harper Press, 2011), 465–8; Maclean, *Eastern Approaches*, 311–13; Foot, *S.O.E.*, 168.

94 David Hunt, "British Military Planning and Aims in 1944," in *British Political and Military Strategy in Central, Eastern and Southern Europe in 1944*, ed. William Deakin, Elisabeth Barker, and Jonathan Chadwick (New York: St Martin's Press, 1988), 2; Elisabeth Barker, "Problems of the Alliance," in *British Political and Military Strategy*, 42, 48–9.

95 Elisabeth Barker, "Some Factors in British Decision-Making," in *British Policy towards Wartime Resistance*, ed. Auty and Clogg, 24; S.W. Bailey, "British Policy Towards General Draža Mihailović," in *British Policy towards Wartime Resistance*, ed. Auty and Clogg, 76.

96 McConville, *A Small War in the Balkans*, 97; Maclean, *Eastern Approaches*, 390.

97 PREM 3/510/10 "FO to Washington, Repeated to Mr. Stevenson" Cairo, 7 December 1943, 2–3; CAB 66/51/4 "Soviet Policy in the Balkans" 7 June 1944, 1–2. CAB 66/51/4 "Soviet Policy in the Balkans" 7 June 1944; PREM 3/511/2 "Eden to Churchill" 28 December 1943; Maclean, *Eastern Approaches*, 390; Deakin, *The Embattled Mountain*, 181.

98 PREM 3/510/10 "Immediate for Chiefs of Staff, From Air Ministry" [presumed] 22 December 1943; Martin, *The Web of Disinformation*, 202–3; WO 201/1599; WO 202/140 "sheet 424" 19 December 1943; PREM 3/511/12 "British Ambassador to the Yugoslav Government in Cairo [Stevenson] to FO" 15 February 1944; Maclean, *Eastern Approaches*, 437; Lees, *The Rape of Serbia*, 115; Eden, *Memoirs: The Reckoning*, 431.

99 PREM 3/510/9 Note on the Situation in Yugoslavia 27/28 October 1943, 2; CAB 66/43/15 War Cabinet "Weekly resume no. 219" 6; PREM 3/409/5 "SOE Activities" Quarter: October to December 1943, 6; CAB 66/44/2 War Cabinet "Weekly resume no. 222" 5–6; CAB 65/36/34 War Cabinet: Balkans "Conclusions" 6 December 1943, 227; CAB 66/44/32 War Cabinet "Weekly resume no. 225" 5; Maclean, *Eastern Approaches*, 343; Deakin, *The Embattled Mountain*, 264.

100 Williams, *Parachutes, Patriots and Partisans*, 187; Roberts, *Tito, Mihailović and the Allies*, 177.

101 PREM 3/409/7 "From Palmer to Churchill: Communism in Resistance Movements" 10 November 194; PREM 3/510/10 "Telegram From Eden to British Ambassador to Yugoslav Government" 21 December 1943; CAB 65/45/4 "Confidential Annex" 11 January 1944, 1–2; Danchev, *Alan Brooke*, 483.

102 Williams, *Parachutes, Patriots and Partisans*, 187.

103 Lewis E. Lehrman, *Churchill, Roosevelt & Company: Studies in Character and Statecraft* (Guilford, CT: Stackpole Books, 2017), x.

104 Dilks, *Sir Alexander Cadogan*, 581–2; Max Hastings, *Finest Years: Churchill as Warlord 1940–45* (London: Harper Press, 2010), 431.

105 Office of the Combined Chiefs of Staff, *SEXTANT Conference*, 385; FRUS "The Conferences at Cairo and Tehran."

106 PREM 3/510/9 "Churchill to Eden" 28 July 1943; FRUS "The Conferences at Cairo and Tehran," 545; FRUS "Cairo Tehran / SEXTANT 1943," 547; Danchev, *Alan Brooke*, 483; Churchill, *Closing the Ring*, 370, 467; Williams, *Parachutes, Patriots and Partisans*, 187.

107 PREM 3/510/13 "War Cabinet to General Wilson" 23 October 1943; PREM 3/510/13 "Former Naval Person [Churchill] to President Roosevelt" 23 October 1943; USSR, *Correspondence Vol. 1*, No. 112, 9 February 1943, No. 129, 15 March 1943; FRUS "The Conferences at Cairo and Tehran," 478–80, 529, 537–8, 545–7; Churchill, *Closing the Ring*, 331–2, 352, 367–70; Danchev, *Alan Brooke*, 346–8, 406, 443, 459, 463–5, 483; Kimball, *Correspondence: Vol 1*, 177; Kurapovna, *Shadows on the Mountain*, 115.

108 Churchill, *Closing the Ring*, 332.

109 Office of the Combined Chiefs of Staff, *SEXTANT Conference*, 543–7; FRUS "The Conferences at Cairo and Tehran," 537–8; Danchev, *Alan Brooke*, 483; Williams, *Parachutes, Patriots and Partisans*, 187; Churchill, *Closing the Ring*, 370.

110  Danchev, *Alan Brooke*, 483–4.
111  Foot, *SOE*, xiv.
112  Hastings, *Finest Years*, 435–6.
113  Maclean, *Eastern Approaches*, 401–2.
114  PREM 3/510/10 "FO to Washington, Repeated to Mr. Stevenson" Cairo, 7 December 1943, 2–3.
115  PREM 3/511/2 "Eden to Churchill" 28 December 1943; PREM 3–512–5 "Foreign Secretary Eden to PM Churchill" 13 September 1944.
116  PREM 3/511/1–2 "War Cabinet: Eden and Churchill correspondence" early 1944; PREM 3/511/2 "Eden to Churchill at SEXTANT" 7 January 1944; PREM 3/511/7 "Churchill to Eden" 9 January 1944; PREM 3/510/10 "Eden to Churchill" 22 December 1943; PREM 3/512/5 "Foreign Secretary Eden to PM Churchill" 13 September 1944.
117  PREM 3/511/2 "Eden to Churchill" 28 December 1943; PREM 3/409/7 "Selborne to Churchill: Communism in Resistance Movements" 10 November 1943; PREM 3/510/10 "FO to Washington, Repeated to Mr. Stevenson" Cairo, 7 December 1943, 2–3.
118  PREM 3/510/10 "FO to Washington, Repeated to Mr. Stevenson" Cairo, 7 December 1943, 1–2.
119  Maclean, *Eastern Approaches*, 462.
120  John Harvey, ed., *The War Diaries of Oliver Harvey* (London: Collins, 1978), 320.
121  Woodward, *British Foreign Policy Vol. III*, 303.
122  Ibid.
123  Maclean, *The Heretic*, 231; Maclean, *Eastern Approaches*, 461.
124  CAB 66/51/4 "Soviet Policy in the Balkans" 7 June 1944.
125  Ibid.
126  Ibid.
127  Ibid.
128  Ibid.
129  Ibid.
130  Roberts, *Tito, Mihailović and the Allies*, 233.
131  Ibid., 239–40.
132  Ibid., 240.
133  Maclean, *Eastern Approaches*, 465.
134  PREM 3/512/3 "War Cabinet Memorandum: PM Churchill to Marshal Tito, Naples" 12 August 1944
135  PREM 3/512/3 "War Cabinet: Minutes of Conference at Naples" 12 August 1944; FO 371/44263 "Churchill to Eden" 31 August 1944; Williams, *Parachutes, Patriots and Partisans*, 229.
136  Winston S. Churchill, *The Second World War, Vol. 6: Triumph and Tragedy* (Cambridge, MA: The Riverside Press, 1949), 230; MacLean, *Eastern Approaches*, 497–8; Eliezer Yapou, "Yugoslavia: Between Četniks and Partisans," in *Governments in Exile, 1939–1945*, 2006. http://governmentsinexile.com/yapoucontents.html; Gaj Trifković, "'Damned Good Amateurs': Yugoslav Partisans in the Belgrade Operation 1944," *The Journal of Slavic Military Studies* 29, no. 2 (April 2016): 255; Roberts, *Tito, Mihailović and the Allies*, 263.
137  PREM 3/511/12 "Maclean: The New Yugoslavia in Relation to the Soviet Union" 18 May 1944; PREM 3/512/5 "Foreign Secretary Eden to PM Churchill" 13 September 1944.
138  PREM 3/512/5 "Foreign Secretary Eden to PM Churchill" 13 September 1944.
139  *Library of Congress*, "Yugoslavia: The Resistance Movement."
140  Martin, *The Web of Disinformation*, 195; Churchill, *Triumph and Tragedy*, 227–8; David Reynolds, *In Command of History: Churchill Fighting and Writing the Second World War* (New York: Random House, 2005), 461; Milazzo, *The Chetni Movement*, 176; Eden, *The Reckoning*, 482.
141  Woodward, *British Foreign Policy Vol. III*, 356–9.

142  *Library of Congress*, "Yugoslavia: The Resistance Movement."

143  Alistair Horne, *Macmillan 1894–1956: Volume I of the Official Biography* (London: Macmillan, 1988), 245–6; Maclean, *The Heretic*, 231.

144  Horne, *Macmillan*, 245–6; Harvey, *Diaries*, 380; Maclean, *The Heretic*, 231, 262–9.

145  Roger Hermiston, *All Behind You, Winston: Churchill's Great Coalition 1940–45* (London: Aurum Press, 2016), 344.

146  Horne, *Macmillan*, 253.

147  Woodward, *British Foreign Policy Vol. III*, 561–2; Hermiston, *All Behind You*, 327.

148  Eden, *The Reckoning*, 512.

149  John Colville, "Memoirs," in *Action This Day: Working with Churchill*, ed. Sir John Wheeler-Bennett (London: Macmillan Press, 1968), 92–3.

150  Hermiston, *All Behind You*, 345.

151  PREM 3/513/10 "Churchill: Memo to his Private Office" 25 April 1945; Lees, *The Rape of Serbia*, 334; Eden, *Memoirs: The Reckoning*, 482–3, 523.

152  PREM 3/513/6 "Churchill to Foreign Secretary" 11 March 1945.

153  Ibid.

154  Roberts, *Tito, Mihailović and the Allies*, 317; Woodward, *British Foreign Policy Vol. III*, 364–5.

155  PREM 3/513/10 "Churchill memo to his Private Office" 25 April 1945.

156  Roberts, *Tito, Mihailović and the Allies*, 319.

157  Ibid.; Maclean, *The Heretic*, 297–8.

158  Woodward, *British Foreign Policy Vol. III*, 369.

159  Horne, *Macmillan*, 270.

160  Ibid., 245–6.

161  Woodward, *British Foreign Policy Vol. III*, 367.

162  Ibid., 369.

163  Maclean, *The Heretic*, 297–8; Horne, *Macmillan*, 245–6, 256.

164  Roberts, *Tito, Mihailović and the Allies*, 315.

165  Ibid.; USSR, *Correspondence Vol. 1*, No. 467, 15 May 1945; Horne, *Macmillan*, 245–6, 256.

166  Woodward, *British Foreign Policy Vol. III*, 369.

167  Maclean, *The Heretic*, 297–8; Horne, *Macmillan*, 245–6, 256.

168  Horne, *Macmillan*, 270.

169  USSR, *Correspondence Vol. 1*, No. 450, 28 April 1945; USSR, *Correspondence Vol. 1*, No. 467, 15 May 1945.

170  Horne, *Macmillan*, 256.

171  Woodward, *British Foreign Policy Vol. III*, 370–1.

172  Ibid., 378–9.

173  Ibid.; "Churchill to Truman (No. 64) 2 June 1945" in Gregory W. Sand, ed., *Defending the West: The Truman-Churchill Correspondence, 1945–1960* (Westport, CT: Praeger, 2004).

174  "Churchill to Truman (No. 64) 2 June 1945" in Sand, *Truman-Churchill Correspondence*.

175  Horne, *Macmillan*, 259–60.

176  Woodward, *British Foreign Policy Vol. III*, 371.

177  Ibid.

178  Roberts, *Tito, Mihailović and the Allies*, 315.

179  *USSR Foreign Ministry, Commission for the Publication of Diplomatic Documents*. "Correspondence between the Chairman of the Council of Ministers of the USSR and the Presidents of the USA and the Prime Ministers of Great Britain during the Great Patriotic War of 1941–1945. Volume 2: Correspondence with Franklin D. Roosevelt and Harry S. Truman (August 1941-December 1945)." (Moscow, USSR: Progress Publishers, 1957) No. 322, 21–23 May 1945, No. 330, 23–29 May 1945, No. 334, 8 June 1945.

180  USSR, *Correspondence Vol. 2*, No. 322, 21–23 May 1945.

181  Woodward, *British Foreign Policy Vol. III*, 380.

182  USSR, *Correspondence Vol. 1*, No. 493, 21 June 1945.
183  Sir Llewellyn Woodward, *History of the Second World War: British Foreign Policy in the Second World War*, Vol. 5 (London: Her Majesty's Stationery Office by McCorquodale & Co., 1976), 489–91.
184  Ibid., 491–2.
185  Ibid.
186  Ibid., 492–3.
187  Dilks, *Sir Alexander Cadogan*, 778.
188  Ibid.
189  Roberts, *Tito, Mihailović and the Allies*, 315.

## Bibliography

Auty, Phyllis, and Richard Clogg, eds. *British Policy towards Wartime Resistance in Yugoslavia and Greece*. London: Macmillan Press, 1975.

Bergholz, Max. *Violence as a Generative Force: Identity, Nationalism, and Memory in a Balkan Community*. Ithaca and London: Cornell University Press, 2016.

Churchill, Winston S. *The Second World War, Vol. 3: The Grand Alliance*. Cambridge, MA: The Riverside Press, 1949.

Churchill, Winston S. *The Second World War, Vol. 5: Closing the Ring*. Cambridge, MA: The Riverside Press, 1949.

Churchill, Winston S. *The Second World War, Vol. 6: Triumph and Tragedy*. Cambridge, MA: The Riverside Press, 1949.

Danchev, Alex, and Daniel Todman, eds. *War Diaries 1939–1945 Field Marshal Lord Alanbrooke*. London: Weidenfeld & Nicolson, 2001.

Davidson, Basil. *Partisan Picture*. Bedford, UK: Bedford Books Ltd., 1946.

Deakin, F. W. D. *The Embattled Mountain*. London: Oxford University Press, 1971.

Deakin, William, Elisabeth Barker, and Jonathan Chadwick, eds. *British Political and Military Strategy in Central, Eastern and Southern Europe in 1944*. New York: St Martin's Press, 1988.

De Bello. "Führer Directive No. 25." Last Accessed 29 May, 2018. https://web.archive.org/web/20161011133405/ww2.debello.ca/library/410327.html.

Deroc, Milan. *British Special Operations Explored: Yugoslavia in Turmoil 1941–1943 and the British Response*. New York: Columbia University Press, 1988.

Dilks, David, ed. *The Diaries of Sir Alexander Cadogan 1938–1945*. New York: G.P. Putnam's Sons, 1972.

Eden, Anthony. *The Eden Memoirs: The Reckoning*. London: Cassell, 1965.

Foot, M. R. D. *SOE: An Outline History of the Special Operations Executive 1940–1946*. London: The Bondy Head, 2014.

*Foreign Relations of the United States, University of Wisconsin Digital Collection*. "Foreign Relations of the United States Diplomatic Papers (FRUS)." Last Accessed 29 May, 2018. https://uwdc.library.wisc.edu/collections/FRUS/.

Glenny, Misha. *The Balkans: Nationalism, War & the Great Powers, 1804–1999*. New York: Penguin Books, 2001.

Greiffenberg, V. "The Balkan Campaign: The Invasion of Yugoslavia." *US Army Center of Military History*. SSUSA Historical Division, 1947. Last Accessed 1 June, 2018. www.history.army.mil/html/books/104/104-18/CMH_Pub_104-18.pdf.

*HANSARD UK Parliament*. "HANSARD 1803–2005." Last Accessed 29 May, 2018. https://api.parliament.uk/historic-hansard/index.html.

Harvey, John, ed. *The War Diaries of Oliver Harvey*. London: Collins, 1978.

Hastings, Max. *All Hell Let Loose: The World at War 1939–45*. London: Harper Press, 2011.

Hastings, Max. *Finest Years: Churchill as Warlord 1940–45*. London: Harper Press, 2010.

Hermiston, Roger. *All behind You, Winston: Churchill's Great Coalition 1940–45*. London: Aurum Press, 2016.

Horne, Alistair. *Macmillan 1894–1956: Volume I of the Official Biography*. London: Macmillan, 1988.

Jones, William. *Twelve Months with Tito's Partisans*, 1st ed. London: Bedford Books Limited, 1946.

Kimball, Warren F., ed. *Churchill & Roosevelt: The Complete Correspondence, Vol. 1: Alliance Emerging: Oct 1933–Nov 1943*. Princeton, NJ: Princeton University Press, 1984.

Kurapovna, Marcia Christoff. *Shadows on the Mountain: The Allies, the Resistance, and the Rivalries That Doomed WWII Yugoslavia*. Hoboken, NJ, USA: John Wiley & Sons, Inc., 2010.

Lees, Michael. *The Rape of Serbia: The British Role in Tito's Grab for Power*. New York: Harcourt Brace Jovanovich, Publishers, 1990.

Lehrman, Lewis E. *Churchill, Roosevelt & Company: Studies in Character and Statecraft*. Guilford, CT: Stackpole Books, 2017.

Mackenzie, W. J. M. *The Secret History of SOE: The Special Operations Executive 1940–1945*. London: St. Ermin's Press, 2000.

Maclean, Fitzroy. *Eastern Approaches*. London, UK: Penguin Books, 1991. First Published by Jonathan Cape 1949.

Maclean, Fitzroy. *The Heretic: The Life and Times of Josip Broz-Tito*. New York: Harper & Brothers, Publishers, 1957.

Martin, David. *The Web of Disinformation: Churchill's Yugoslav Blunder*. New York: Harcourt Brace Jovanovich, Publishers, 1990.

McConville, Michael. *A Small War in the Balkans: British Military Involvement in Wartime Yugoslavia 1941–1945*. Uckfield, East Sussex, UK: The Naval & Military Press Ltd., 2007.

Milazzo, Matteo J. *The Chetni Movement and the Yugoslav Resistance*. Baltimore: John Hopkins University Press, 1976.

*The National Archives of the UK.* "The Cabinet Papers: Records of the Cabinet Office." *CAB*, London, 2018. http://discovery.nationalarchives.gov.uk/SearchUI/browse/C44?v=h.

*The National Archives of the UK.* "Records Created or Inherited by the Foreign Office." *FO*, London, 2018. http://discovery.nationalarchives.gov.uk/SearchUI/details?Uri=C130.

*The National Archives of the UK.* "Records Created or Inherited by the War Office, Armed Forces, Judge Advocate General, and Related Bodies." *WO*, London, 2018. http://discovery.nationalarchives.gov.uk/browse/r/h/C259.

*The National Archives of the UK.* "Records of the Prime Minister's Office." *PREM*, London, 2018. http://discovery.nationalarchives.gov.uk/SearchUI/details?Uri=C233.

The Office, U. S. Secretary, Office of the Combined Chiefs of Staff 1943, ed. *SEXTANT Conference November-December 1943: Papers and Minutes of Meetings SEXTANT and EUREKA Conferences*. Washington, DC: Joint History Office, 2003.

Pavlowitch, Stevan K. *Hitler's New Disorder: The Second World War in Yugoslavia*. New York: Columbia University Press, 2008.

Reynolds, David. *In Command of History: Churchill Fighting and Writing the Second World War*. New York: Random House, 2005.

Roberts, Walter R. *Tito, Mihailović and the Allies, 1941–1945*. New Brunswick, NJ: Rutgers University Press, 1973.

Rootham, Jasper. *Miss Fire: The Chronicle of a British Mission to Mihailovich*. London: Chatto & Windus, 1946.

Rothwell, Victor. *Anthony Eden: A Political Biography, 1931–1957*. Oxford, UK: Manchester University Press, 1992.

Sand, G. W., ed. *Defending the West: The Truman-Churchill Correspondence, 1945–1960*. Westport, CT: Praeger, 2004.

Shepherd, Ben. *Terror in the Balkans: German Armies and Partisan Warfare*. Cambridge, MA: Harvard University Press, 2012.

Snyder, Timothy. *Bloodlands: Europe between Hitler and Stalin*. New York: Basic Books, 2010.

Stafford, David. *Camp X*. Toronto: Lester & Orpen Dennys, 1986.

Tomasevich, Jozo. *War and Revolution in Yugoslavia, 1941–1945: The Chetniks*. Stanford: Stanford University Press, 1975.

Trew, Simon. *Britain, Mihailović, and the Chetniks, 1941–42*. London: St. Martin's Press, 1997.

Trifković, Gaj. "'Damned Good Amateurs': Yugoslav Partisans in the Belgrade Operation 1944." *The Journal of Slavic Military Studies* 29, no. 2 (April 2016): 253–78.

*United States' Library of Congress, Federal Research Division of*. "Yugoslavia: The Resistance Movement." Last Accessed 29 May, 2018. www.loc.gov/item/91040323/.

*USSR Foreign Ministry, Commission for the Publication of Diplomatic Documents*. "Correspondence between the Chairman of the Council of Ministers of the USSR and the Presidents of the USA and the Prime Ministers of Great Britain during the Great Patriotic War of 1941–1945. Volume 1: Correspondence with Winston S. Churchill and Clement R. Attlee (July 1941–November 1945)." Moscow: Progress Publishers, 1957.

*USSR Foreign Ministry, Commission for the Publication of Diplomatic Documents*. "Correspondence between the Chairman of the Council of Ministers of the USSR and the Presidents of the USA and the Prime Ministers of Great Britain during the Great Patriotic War of 1941–1945. Volume 2: Correspondence with Franklin D. Roosevelt and Harry S. Truman (August 1941–December 1945)." Moscow, USSR: Progress Publishers, 1957.

Wheeler, Mark C. *Britain and the War for Yugoslavia 1940–1943*. New York: Columbia University Press, 1980.

Wheeler-Bennett, Sir John, ed. *Action This Day: Working with Churchill*. London: Macmillan Press, 1968.

Williams, Heather. *Parachutes, Patriots and Partisans: The Special Operations Executive and Yugoslavia, 1941–1945*. Madison: University of Wisconsin Press, 2003.

Woodward, Sir Llewellyn. *History of the Second World War: British Foreign Policy in the Second World War*, Vol. 1. London: Her Majesty's Stationery Office by McCorquodale & Co., 1970.

Woodward, Sir Llewellyn. *History of the Second World War: British Foreign Policy in the Second World War*, Vol. 3. London: Her Majesty's Stationery Office by McCorquodale & Co., 1971.

Woodward, Sir Llewellyn. *History of the Second World War: British Foreign Policy in the Second World War*, Vol. 5. London: Her Majesty's Stationery Office by McCorquodale & Co., 1976.

Yapou, Eliezer. "Yugoslavia: Between Četniks and Partisans." *Governments in Exile, 1939–1945*, 2006. http://governmentsinexile.com/yapoucontents.html.

# 10 Wartime collaborations in rural North China

*Lu Xun*

In China, the Second World War has been remembered as the Chinese Resistance War against Japan, dating from 1931 to 1945, according to a recent textbook change.[1] The long war opened a Pandora's box and let loose all curses on the Chinese people's suffering and surviving. Drawing on archival documents and oral history interviews, this chapter aims to tell the strategy of peasant survival in North China.

The concept of collaboration carries strong negative connotations as it is closely associated with the term *jian* or *hanjian*, suggesting disloyalty and betrayal. Since the 1960s, however, scholars like Stanley Hoffmann and Bertram Gordon have redefined this concept to interpret the complex relationship in trans-cultural conflicts. In principle and practice, collaborationists were distinguished from collaborators. According to Hoffmann and Gordon, the collaborator is a deliberate service to the enemy, whereas the collaborationist is a deliberate advocacy of cooperation with the foreign force which is seen as a champion of some desirable domestic transformation.[2] Scholars have stripped the word of its moral connotation when referring to engagements with foreign occupiers. Philippe Burrin has suggested *accommodation* replace the notorious term of collaboration.[3] Excluding "an extreme and evil few," Timothy Brook narrows the meaning of collaboration back to *hezuo*, a neutral expression in Chinese.[4] More recently, Konrad Lawson distinguished the military, police and other security collaborationist forces from other collaborators.[5] The term collaboration is employed in this chapter, referring to the act of cooperation between different racial or ideological groups under the state of war without the imposed moral implication. Collaborationists are usually referred to as collective collaborators, underlining their identity as government employees.

Furthermore, the study of wartime collaboration in China is not as rich as its European counterpart. The existing scholarship on the Chinese collaboration concentrates on several case studies in the Yangtze River Delta.[6] Some scholars have studied the collaborationist troops in Shandong and nationwide.[7] Some paid attention to the postwar treason trials in court and outside the court.[8]

Another body of scholarship, including the rich historiography on the rise of the Chinese Communist Party in North China, considers the experience of Japanese occupation as a catalyst for revolution and resistance. North China remains a revolutionary terrain as portrayed by a series of outstanding works.[9] Voices of collaborators in North China, especially in rural areas, have largely been ignored by historians.

This chapter attempts to reevaluate the military, social and economic circumstances before and after local residents chose to resist or collaborate. Thanks to the newly available Chinese sources, it is now possible to focus on the rural political ecosystems and conflicts in northern China during World War II.[10]

## The ruling troika

The terrain is flat in the vast Yellow River plain. It links the fertile land of Manchuria on the north with the commercialized belt of the Yangtze River on the south. Mines of ore and coal are scattered in the surrounding hilly areas from the Taihang Mountains of Shanxi on the west to the Jiaodong Peninsula of Shandong on the east. In William Skinner's macroregion of North China, it was second only to the Lower Yangtze in population density but lowest in the level of rural commercialization.[11] The political ecosystem remained more complicated in North China than in the Yangtze Delta.

The two major political parties were fighting heatedly against each other in the south when the Japanese tanks rolled down from Manchuria to the Great Wall in early 1933. From then on to 1935, the Kwantung Army continued to weaken Chinese sovereignty in northern China through a policy of supporting autonomous breakaway administrations. In 1936, the Japanese forces in North China were enlarged to twice their original size. Their major targets of collaboration included provincial militarists namely Yan Xishan in Shanxi, Song Zheyuan in Chahar, Shang Zheng in Hebei and Han Fuqu in Shandong. Meanwhile, the Communists were also eager to win over these former warlords in the North to lash out at the Nationalist policy of "Non-Resistance." However, the anti-Japanese sentiment remained highbrowed and out of touch for most rural residents until 1937.

After the unexpected military clash in July 1937 in Beiping (Beijing), the Japanese sent a large number of troops to seize the railways and trade centers, bringing great social disruption to northern China. In the face of the menacing Japanese invasion, the Nationalist government in the northern provinces was evacuated southward. The troops fought tremendously against the Japanese in two major blocking campaigns commanded respectively by Yan Xishan in Shanxi and Li Zongren in Shandong, but they failed. Lu Zhonglin led a limited number of Nationalist resistant guerrillas in the southern Hebei province. The Communist Eighth Route Army, now under the anti-Japanese united front, also took a small share of resistance with Yan and later marched into mountainous areas ignored by the Japanese vanguard. Together with a few Nationalist guerrillas, they harassed Japanese supply lines by sabotaging railways. After a short-term symbolic coalition, both party troops fell again into chronic hostility and continual frictions. As Mao Zedong reiterated in one of his public speeches in November 1937 in Yan'an, the class struggle remained a priority for the Chinese Communist Party and the Nationalist resistance because its basis of the landlords and bourgeoisie was "partial," "incomplete" and "doomed to failure."[12]

In the months of anarchy that followed in the lost territories, local administrative organizations sprang up, led by the social elite to fill the power vacuum. They maintained the social order. These organizations had to answer the claims on supplies usually from Japanese, Communist and Nationalist troops.

The county of Zhengding was near the northern suburb of Shimen (Shijiazhuang), the regional hub on the Beiping-Hankou Railway. On October 8, 1937, Zhengding fell after two days of ferocious resistance, carried by Nationalist 32nd Army Commander Shang Zheng and the Japanese 1st Army led by General Kiyoshi Katsuki. To avenge the dead, Japanese troops slaughtered civilians and raped women in villages around the county seat. A later headcount by the Japanese indicated the disappearance of 1,560 former county residents shortly after the takeover.[13] Against this backdrop, Wu Zanzhou, a 52-year-old county native, was found with other refugees by the local gentry in a Catholic chapel to negotiate with the Japanese. An early graduate of the Baoding Military Academy, Wu had studied at the Imperial Japanese Army Academy since the 1900s. Katsuki was his schoolmate. The Japanese commander agreed to restrain his troops, should Wu come forward to organize the county maintenance association. Wu finally agreed to collaborate. He adopted effective measures to stop Japanese looting and atrocities and restored the order in the county seat.[14]

The situation deteriorated in impoverished rural areas and in occupied towns and cities. A Communist report commented on chaos brought about by the emergence of different kinds of Chinese armed forces in the middle Hebei area:

> There is no common way to solve the problem of military supply for the colorful newly established anti-Japanese forces. They commandeer grains and money wherever station [. . .] with no limits or standards. Most of those bandits, warlord and conservative troops set up checkpoints to levy taxes on almost everything . . . Crowed a village usually a large number of cadres from twenty to sixty, fed by the village and responsible only for pressing for taxes and corvée labor.[15]

As the war lingered on, collaboration became part of the occupation. On December 14, 1937, one day after the fall of the Nanjing capital, the Japanese sponsored the first collaborationist government in the former Beiping and now Beijing headed by Wang Kemin, controlling provinces of Hebei, Shanxi and Shandong. On March 10, 1938, the Beijing government issued collaborationist currency *lianyinquan*. In a sense, the Japanese replaced former local warlords to establish a new government, whose responsibility included protecting subjects from bandits.

Meanwhile, the Communist Shanxi-Chahar-Hebei (SCH) border area government was founded in Fuping in January 1938, ruling a populace of 10 million in 36 counties. In mid-1939, the government expanded its branches to 67 counties of 12 million people. In the fall of 1940, the Communists claimed actual control over 90% of the villages in the area. Its population reached up to 20 million within 110 counties in September 1944. To support the regime, the Communists increased incomes by radical fiscal policies, although in the name of reasonably distributed burdens (see Table 10.1).

They imposed direct taxation from the village instead of the county, which had formerly been responsible for collecting taxes under the Nationalist rule. The so-called reasonable distribution was actually a poll tax, levied on every individual in the household (excluding long-term hired hands) and even on any child under five years old, who was counted as half a person. Both family properties and incomes were quantified in taxation counts, which actually added extra burdens to relatively rich and middle peasants. Communist statistics showed that after reform, the number of taxpayers increased by 50–80%. In addition to taxes in money, peasants had to hand in grain taxes and took the responsibility of preserving them. By the fall of 1939, villages in middle Hebei alone had paid 25 million kilograms of millets, which could feed thirty thousand troops and cadres for three years. The border government also staged a bond campaign to cover its deficit. The Country Salvation Bonds had maturities that extended out as far as 34 years with the interest rate of 4%. The forceful sale, however, did not produce disappointing sales figures. The first bond issue in July 1938 quickly met its goal of two million yuan, and the second issue actually raised 1.54 million, exceeding its goal of one million by 50%.[16]

Like many other counties in North China, Zhengding was divided by three power spheres. The Japanese 110 Division was stationed to the south of the county seat. In February 1938, Wu became head of the collaborationist county government, which replaced the provisional maintenance association. There were nominally 94 out of 290 villages under Japanese control. To earn

*Table 10.1* Communist taxing indexes in the Shanxi-Chahar-Hebei border area (1938–1941)

| Year | 1938 | 1939 | 1940 | 1941 |
|---|---|---|---|---|
| Money | 100 | 300.54 | 532.34 | 2747.15 |
| Grains | 100 | 67.11 (after floods) | 195.07 | 231.94 |

(Source: Chinese Ministry of Finance ed., *Geming genjudi de caizheng jingji* [Finance and Economy in Revolutionary Bases], Chengdu: Zhongguo caizheng jingji chubanshe, 1985, 135.)

a living, most village heads were two-faced, pro-Japanese in the daytime and pro-resistance at night. Communist underground county government functioned in the northwest of the county as a branch of the SCH border area, controlling 147 villages.[17] Interestingly enough, its Nationalist counterpart seized the southeast part of the county. From late 1938 to mid-1939, a dozen currencies circulated here. Apart from Nationalist *fabi* and collaborationist's *lianyinquan*, the Communists in different areas issued their own notes such as *bianbi, jinanbi* and *beihaibi* to exert control.[18] Communist guerrillas even shot passers-by who had with them the collaborationist currency after body searches.[19] During Japanese mopping-ups from 1941 to 1943, it was the most difficult time for residents in Zhengding. Peasants had to supply the Japanese and collaborationists, as well as the Nationalist and Communist government as usual.[20]

The situation was similar in Shandong. After Japanese mopping-ups in 1942, 65% of the rural populace were in the occupied areas. (See Table 10.2.) The costs for accommodation were heavy. One village of seven hundred residents lay in the center of Jiaodong peninsula under direct Japanese occupation. In the two months from December 1941 to January 1942, these peasants paid to the Japanese a dozen taxes, including flour, meat, firewood, vegetables, soy sauce, chicken, eggs, quilts, mattings, tofu and bean sprouts, equaling 5,466.5 silver yuan. They also had to hand in taxes to the Communists, equaling 12,773 silver yuan per annum. In contrast, the five hundred residents in another village near the city of Rizhao in the southeastern coastal area were the people who really lived in limbo. They became the prey of Japanese, collaborationists, Nationalists and Communists. During the summer harvest of 1942 (approximately from May to August), they paid dozens of taxes, all together equal to 19,251.44 silver yuan. A breakdown shows Nationalist guerrillas claimed 9473.55 silver yuan, the biggest share at 49.2%; the collaborationists next, 21.6%; Japanese demands of 3164.9 accounted for 16.4%; the Communists also shared 1060.65, accounting for 5.5%; the rest, 7.3%, was for the village's own administration.[21]

## Family encounters

Kouzi was a small hamlet that lay tucked on the northern foot of Mount South in the Jiaodong Peninsula. The county seat of Huang was two miles to the north. If one continued northward, you would find the seaport of Longkou, literally "the dragon's mouth," a traditional springboard to Manchuria and Korea. With a relatively mobile population of thirty households, Kouzi was not a single-surname village but one with a clearly dominant lineage – the Lu families. In the 1930s, most residents here were poor peasants except Lu Guozhong. The big family of Guozhong was the only prosperous one in the village and included his four sons, Dianyang, Dianbang, Diangang and Dianke. The eldest brother, Dianyang, ran a small livestock business and earned some money. He owned fifteen *mu* of farmland and hired one

Table 10.2 Rural population in Japanese, Communist and pending areas in Shandong (December 1942–August 1945)

| Year | | 1942 | 1943 | 1944 | 1945 |
|---|---|---|---|---|---|
| Japanese controlled | Population | 19,988,540 (65%) | 14,295,255 (46%) | 8,818,966 (28%) | 6,402,658 (20%) |
| | Villages | 43,932 (62%) | 25,400 (36%) | 20,713 (30%) | 12,204 (17%) |
| | Land | 373,309 (63%) | 239,688 (40%) | 154,304 (26%) | 112,938 (19%) |
| Communist controlled | Population | 3,997,708 (13%) | 8,476,959 (27%) | 16,007,075 (52%) | 20,828,588 (66%) |
| | Villages | 10,128 (15%) | 25,027 (36%) | 33,526 (48%) | 47,168 (68%) |
| | Land | 82,958 (14%) | 184,697 (31%) | 329,010 (56%) | 402,624 (68%) |
| Pending | Population | 6,765,352 (22%) | 8,113,736 (27%) | 6,225,665 (20%) | 4,454,283 (14%) |
| | Villages | 15,730 (23%) | 19,364 (28%) | 15,553 (22%) | 10,421 (15%) |
| | Land | 136,287 (23%) | 168,165 (29%) | 109,233 (18%) | 76,999 (13%) |
| Total | Population | 30,751,600 (100%) | 30,885,950 (100%) | 31,051,706 (100%) | 31,685,529 (100%) |

(Source: Shandong Provincial Archives and Shandong Social Sciences Academy eds., *Shandong geming lishi dang'an ziliao xuanbian* [A Selection of Archives Materials on the History of the Revolution in Shandong], Jinan: Shandong remin chubanshe, 16 (1982): 405–411. The population under Nationalist control should presumably be included in the category of pending areas.)

long-term hand and several casual laborers, which was unusual in the eyes of other peasants. All three of his brothers had a similar amount of farmland, and the youngest, Dianke, was head of the village in 1938.[22] Thus, Guozhong's family represented the village authority.

Among the adequate was Lu Mingdao's family, which owned four *mu* of farmland. Mingdao had a personal grudge against Dianyang. They belonged to contending family branches. So Mingdao became the most desirable activist of the Communists. In January 1938, a Communist night school was open in the neighboring village of Dalu, asking Kouzi to send their residents. There Mingdao was instigated by a school teacher, Lu Song, and was supported in the rift against Dianyang.[23]

The war was coming. Nationalist Provincial Governor Han Fuqu had withdrawn his troops from the county on November 17, 1937. On February 6–10, 1938, the Japanese 5th Division swept across the county seat without leaving a garrison. Du Lexian was nominated as head of the county maintenance association. According to Lu Mingdao, the Communist regular forces passed through later on February 14, and some 1,500 stopped at Kouzi for refreshment and left.[24] Due to the internal strife, the maintenance association could no longer be maintained and welcomed Wang Jingsong, the former county director of the educational settlement, back to resume the Nationalist reign. Wang secured an agreement with local Communist forces who would submit to government rules under the terms of sharing arms from the maintenance defense forces. In late April, however, the Communists assembled guerrilla forces from the south to overthrow the short-lived resistance government under Wang Jingsong.[25] Then the Communists called themselves "The Third Army" instead of "The Eighth Route," who veiled their partisanship and mobilized villagers under the flag of resistance. All men above 18 must join "The Third Army" in order to "improve people's lives, especially for the poor." In May, the Communists fathered a united front government headed by Yuan Yiting of the local gentry. Yuan never showed up. That nominal government lasted for only a couple of months and then was replaced by a real Communist government.[26]

The Communist leadership saw the bases in Shandong as crucial. As early as two weeks after the Japanese takeover of city Tai'an in January 1938, Yan'an provided principal guidelines. Among them, one of the most important read: "It is imperative to stick to the principle of building up and maintaining forces in all party networks, mass mobilizations, and the guerrilla warfare. In short, it is 'to come if makes money and to ward off any loss.'"[27] In the summer of 1938, Mao transferred four hundred to eight hundred veterans to Shandong as base cadres. As a result, 12 counties, including Huang, were under Communist control. From May 1939 to December 1940, the Communists expanded to another 79 counties before the Japanese mop-up operations.[28] During the interval of successive Japanese invasions, the Communists confiscated machines and materials from all eight ironworks in Huang under the name of borrowing and the gold ore from the neighboring county of Zhaoyuan for its own munitions factory in the mountainous south.[29] Most of the party grassroots stipulated their missions as four: to recruit members, to enlarge the army, to buy bullets and to drive a wedge between Japanese and collaborationist troops.[30] The Communists in Shandong rarely sought out offensives with the Japanese occupation forces, and their figure took a steady and significant upward trend.

As in the southern coastal area, the Communist government in Huang also levied taxes in money and grains. At Kouzi, taxes (*juan*) were as heavy as five or six times a year. Villagers who were at odds with their chief sometimes had to provide additional meals for a couple hundred of come-and-go guerrillas; otherwise, they would be beaten by troops or receive later punishments from the district Communist authority. The troops generally paid them with unrefundable tickets.[31] From 1938 to 1939, there also existed a Nationalist guerrilla group led by Xu Shuming, the former director of the county bureau of education. They had shootouts with the Communists to seize taxes from villagers, too.[32] The grains were the most fabulous and important war trophies of Communist militias.[33] The clashes between Mingdao and Dianyang indeed focused on rates and standards of reasonable distribution of burdens.[34]

Dianyang maintained a personal relationship with Communist guerrilla leader Li Peimao, deputy commander of the 2nd Battalion, 14th Regiment, stationed four miles southward. Li reportedly took a bribe from Dianyang and acted beyond his authority to beat Mingdao. In late 1938, 40-year-old Mingdao joined the Communist Party. From then on, he received directions from Lu Song and acted as a branch head.[35] Mingdao told his district superior about Li. Li was later purged in 1940.[36]

Having lost his backer in the Communists, Dianyang asked his younger brother Dianke to report to collaborationist troops. *Guanxi*, personal relationships in China, were stronger than any racial or ideological hurdles. Dianke brought a false charge against Mingdao's followers, but the collaborationists failed to catch them. In retaliation, Mingdao meant to kill Dianke but gave up his plan for the reason that Dianke had many children. Later, Dianyang's son Mingxing joined the Communist troops but deserted for an unknown reason.[37]

On March 2, 1939, the county seat returned to Japanese hands. The Communists set fires to it before they fled one day earlier to the northeast coast.[38] Its real leader, Jiao Feng, and his underground government remained active in the southern mountainous areas and conscripted the locals into a militia group.[39] Poorly equipped as they were, the militias functioned as the rural arbiter and saboteur to the occupation state, especially as the assassinator of collaborationists.

Lu Mingyu was then the village head, following the common two-faced strategy: "[I] was a village leader by the *Balu* [Communist Eighth Route Army]," he identified himself decades later, "but also had to pay the grain and tax to the Japanese when they came. How dare [we] not pay the Japanese grains?" He furthered, "Sometimes the *huzi* [bandits] came, [and you] cannot tell them from the *Balu*."[40] No matter what position Mingyu held during wartime, his leadership was based on the satisfaction of overlapped demands from the Communists, the Japanese and the bandits. From the fall of 1941 to 1942, the village paid taxes to the Japanese. Cui, a village one mile away, had paid taxes for seven years.[41] Meanwhile, the Communists had its own taxation offices and mobile posts on private exports.[42]

Communist guerrillas also dispersed their food and cloth storages, hid in the eastward mountain caves and left a dozen homemade grenades as the responsibility of the local militia. However, guerrilla warfare required not only tedious sentry duties. Zhan Deben recalled the chilling experience of a false alarm. Once, shortly before the Chinese Lunar New Year festival, the Communists ordered a surprise inspection of one wheat stock of three thousand to five thousand kilograms. The villagers shouldered the sacks from one cave to the school playground to check them off. Suddenly, intelligence reported that a Japanese detachment had been called out from the county seat. The village was mobilized. Zhan led the militia to guard the north entrance with the only rifles bought by themselves and the dozen grenades. The rest cadres, on the one hand, made the residents ready to flee and, on the other, sent out for the nearest Communist liaison. Fortunately, the Japanese did not arrive.[43]

In the spring of 1942, Mingdao was promoted to the rank of township head. Unfortunately, he was captured on his way back home by collaborationist soldiers from the Dayuan village near the gold ore. Mingdao recalled he was beaten and asked for money. It was said that he had also agreed to work for the collaborationist government. After he was released, Mingdao pretended to be sick but collected 30 yuan in *lianyinquan* from villagers and sent it to Dayuan. That sum of money might not satisfy those collaborationists. In 1943 or 1944, they rushed Kouzi and robbed only Mingdao's house.[44]

However, local resistance failed to win popular support as formerly imagined. Lu Heyuan, of adjacent Dalu, had led a local militia group of more than 20 men until he was captured and tortured to death by the Japanese. While he was in custody, fellow villagers revealed their hatred for his forced conscriptions so much that they handed petitions to the foreign occupier for the extreme penalty.[45] We can get a glimpse of country aversions from one piece of a report in a local Communist paper in mid-1944:

> The acquaintance from other villages uttered when met [the militia leader], "you don't need to appear severe, and you have got the [Japanese] devils' attention for long." Even relatives persuaded, "you ought to learn to be smart. Can the Eight Route [Communist Army] always take care of you here?" "What're you doing? Are we [peasants] able to fight the Japanese? Is [the rifle] a tool easy for us to carry?" Some neighbors once moaned, "our village will turn sooner or later ashes for the sake of you." Others groaned, "[we]'d better pay more or less [the Japanese taxes]; or, how much will it cost if they [the devils] come and burn a house?!"[46]

It shows the timidity and rationality of countrymen under occupation state without necessary protection from any Chinese government.

Communist rhetoric turned out to be lip service, and their provocative sabotages only invited violent Japanese reprisals. In September 1939 alone, the Japanese were engaged in 1,265 fights in northern China with 462 killed and 1,061 injured, bringing heavier losses to Chinese troops: 13,887 corpses and 1,704 captives.[47] During the most difficult time in 1941–1942, the Japanese looted villages east of the Tianjin-Pukou Railroad and burned houses to ashes, especially those which had accommodated Communist troops. To partly ease local tensions, Communist authorities made cautious policies prohibiting villages located more than 1.6 miles off the Japanese or collaborationist stronghold from reporting their whereabouts but allowing villages within the distance circle to report their censored information.[48]

It was the local residents who paid for guerrilla sabotages. When the Communists cut electrical wires and dug large holes in the road, the Japanese took nearby villagers instead, torturing them, oftentimes to death. In the winter of 1940, a Japanese motorized unit was rumbling along the highway between the cities of Linyi and Mengyin when three tanks abruptly fell into a deep pit and killed more than 10 soldiers. The villagers ran away before the searching troops arrived, but their homes were burned to the ground.[49] Out of 29,591,100 civilians under the Communist reign in Shandong, 3,766,597, or 13%, were disposed of by the Japanese during the eight years, which does not take into account those in the guerrilla or occupied areas. Among the 13%, 895,714 were executed, 1,610,883 disabled and the rest were captured or disappeared.[50]

During late 1944 to early 1946 in the Shandong bases, the Communists started staging a string of political campaigns – "Voice Grievances" – against the rural rich and collaborators at the same time. It made the classes struggle to put on the rosy clothes of nationalism. The "Voice Grievances" campaign, as an appetizer, was immediately followed by or coincidently supplied with the main course – "Reduce Rent and Interest" – which aimed at wooing poor and middle peasants, especially in the newly occupied areas, to support the Communist government in the ongoing civil war.[51]

By 1944, the Communists had strengthened their control over Kouzi and planned to hold a struggle session against Dianyang's family. Dianyang ran away with his son Mingxing to nearby Qixia County. On August 29, 1945, the Communists took over the Longkou port by force from the defeated Japanese waiting to surrender to Chinese Nationalists. Two years later, Zhan and his followers went to Qixia, kidnapped Mingxing and brought him back to the village. They eventually held a struggle session against Mingxing and beat him to death. Dianyang's wife, who came to rescue her son, was also beaten to death. Additionally killed were two collaborationists from other villages who had served the Japanese at Dayuan.[52] Dianyang fled to Yantai and came back with Nationalist troops to Huang, where he sought revenge. However, the county seat was soon taken over by the Communists. Dianyang was spared and taken back to the village, where he lived on his remaining 4.6 *mu* of land until his death.[53]

## Secret societies

Flood, drought, banditry and poverty made rural North China a cradle of heterodoxy and rebellion.[54] Just like rebellion, collaboration was one strategy of peasant survival in chaos. Elizabeth Perry argued, "there is little evidence that the Japanese were successful in converting many Red Spears [secret society] to their side."[55] If we take the other revolutionary force into account, however, that was rarely the case, at least in Shandong.

Some secret societies collaborated with the Japanese because of Communist oppression. The Red Spears are a perfect example of traditional xenophobia. In the spring of 1940 in Changqing County, a west suburb of Jinan, the Red Spears, headed by Zhu Cunzhen, were cooperating with the Communists to resist Japanese occupation. The food shortage in the base area west of Mount Tai resulted into a Communist policy of "borrowing" grains from surrounding counties, which strained local relations. Then in June, the Communists staged an enthusiastic round of purges against dissents to "down with the collaborators" and "quasi-collaborators." They executed collaboration suspects before the summer wheat harvest.[56] The slaughter pushed Zhu to the Japanese.[57]

The Communists often "borrowed" grains from villagers. During ten months of 1942 in three counties along the southeastern Shandong coast, the Communists borrowed 109,661 kilograms of grains from 1,355 households, but the grain was seldom returned. Even its provincial leader admitted in public that "we are basically wrong in the problem of grain debts, for instance [we] do not repay it. Strictly speaking, it is in a tyrannical manner. . . . We take it for granted and thus force [villagers] to lend us grains."[58]

As a victim of Communist policy, Zhu was definitely not alone. Qi Xiangde led another group of the Red Spears, also known as Hard Fist Way *Yingquan dao*, in Laiwu County, which was twenty miles east of Mount Tai. Like Zhu, Qi was won over by the Communists at the beginning of Japanese occupation and fought vigorously against the Nationalist guerrillas in 1938. The next year witnessed the same tide of Communist purging sweep across Laiwu. Two of the immediate followers of Qi got also killed, as well as many ordinary citizens. They fought back but were expelled from the county. In 1940, Qi made a decision to go over the Japanese and to return to Laiwu.[59]

It was difficult for any sect of military nature to earn a living under the Communist, Nationalist and Japanese forces. Like the Red Spears, Zhang Wenzheng, the leader of Middle Way *Zhongyang dao* in Laiwu, at first cooperated with the Communists after the Japanese takeover of the county seat. The Middle Way was a declining descendent of once the most popular society *Shengxian dao* in the late Qing Dynasty in Shandong and Zhili and now had around one thousand troops. They soon clashed with the Communists and fled south. In 1938, Zhang led his followers to serve under a local Nationalist commissioner. Three years later, in order to return to their hometown, the group surrendered themselves to the Japanese but kept secret contacts with the Nationalists. In 1942, Zhang's forces were besieged by the informed Japanese. Zhang escaped with a few hundred others and joined a collaborationist army. After V-J Day, Zhang switched his allegiance again to the Nationalists. He ended by fighting a battle against the Communists in 1946.[60]

The Great Purge of the Soviets shadowed Communist lives in Shandong bases. It is a traditional Communist practice to eliminate "traitors" specifically as Trotskyists, collaborators or another heterodoxy from within. In the vocabulary of Chinese Communists, *hanjian* collaborators had been originally associated with the determinative Trotskyite.[61] In Shandong, the relatively concrete Communists controlled a universal witch hunt; one best-known case was the "Huxi Incident," which killed over three hundred people.[62] Suspected collaborators in bases had been executed without question. In Huang, more than sixty people, accounting for one-fifth of the County militia group, were purged under the name of collaboration during the winter of 1941.[63] The Communist county head, Sun Zhizhong, admitted that the collaborator elimination had been so "mystified and intensified" that it had "harmful effects."[64] However, the mystification and intensification lay not simply in the nature of collaborator punishment but in the authoritarian system of the party itself, functioning only by means of top-down heavy-handedness.

In 1942, the Communists officially gave up a coalition with secret societies and changed to a policy of wiping out any dissent. Riding the recent tide of the Rectification Movement from Yan'an, the Communists poured their energy in a new round of discipline and punishment. In the excuse of anti-*hanjian*, the recently established Shanxi-Hebei-Shandong-Henan border area government announced a prohibition on secret societies within its power limits:

> Banned are all the organizations, societies and brotherhoods utilized by the enemy to spread rumors and to hoodwink the masses. Those who conspire against the state, or violate the order of anti-Japanese war and refuse to realize their mistake, if discovered and seized, must be treated as collaborators.[65]

In other areas, however, the Green Gang collaborated with the Japanese openly. The latter found the two-century-old society still energetic in North China and willing to cooperate. They made good use of each other. The sect of former Grand Canal boatmen and salt smugglers used to perform organized violence under different jurisdictions and administrations. Featured by a powerful network of human resources, the Green Gang induced politicians, military and businessmen of the Chinese, and even some of the Japanese, to become members. Many collaborationists in Huang also joined the Green or *Sanfanzi* or *An Qing daoyi hui*. Sponsored by the Japanese, the society had enrolled 22,650 members by June 1942 in Shandong alone.[66] Its prominent members in Huang were Du Lexian, head of the county maintenance association, and Lin Xiangpu, the deputy commander of the county collaborationist army.[67]

## Collaborationists and families

*Er Guizi* – "the second-hand devil" – was the name given to military collaborationists, which was more popular than the ideological one, the puppet army *Weijun*. Most Kouzi villagers had sour experiences with them, depicted as blackmail experts. They were stationed five miles away at Dayuan. They were not "the puppet" but active evil producers.

Neither did collaborationist generals admit they were puppets. They justified their position as anti-Communist and loyal to the Chinese nation. Their top generals in Shandong vindicated their surrender to the Japanese occupier in October 1942:

> To our Chinese state, we are not the traitors, but the Communists really are. We collaborate with the Japanese army just to eliminate them. Till now, we still accept provisions and funds from Chongqing. If your army of honor will fight with the Central government, we cannot collaborate [on that point] which we hope to gain your forgiveness.[68]

If true, racial confrontation submitted to the ideological one. Highbrow as that account of collaboration was, it carefully curbed itself in line with the traditional Confucius ideology.

In China, the ongoing ideological conflicts between Communists and Nationalists made military collaborationists useful cannon fodder for both parties. Konrad Lawson argued that most military and police collaborationists had been spared in Shandong due to the Communist Party's "tactical and military rather than political goals."[69] But the policy of leniency aimed at neither civilian collaborationists nor those suspected collaborators, including collaborationist families.

During the war, the Communists kept testing whether a collaborationist was worthy of leniency. To force rural collaborationists into submission, the Communists sometimes made clandestine demonstrations. In 1942 in Huang County, one parade was made of four hundred men equipped with a scant three steeds and four or five machine guns. Then two-faced village chiefs were summoned and demanded to continue supplying their load of taxes in grains and money. If the demonstration happened in vain, militias also sneaked into houses of dissenting village chiefs at night and abducted them, sometimes demanding their families pay a ransom.[70] The collaborationists would be indoctrinated, persuaded and released or executed, according to their responses.[71] If those two-faced chiefs could not be captured, the Communists took the neighborhood patrols instead and required petitions from families of the hostages to the Japanese for the removal of pro-Japanese village headmen. By doing so, they successfully forced at least one suburban village close to the Huang county seat to pay Communist taxation.[72] The Communists admitted, "it is common that [we] demanded unlimited or more supplies from occupied areas [than the base area]."[73]

Considering the banditry tradition, it is easy to understand that some villagers rarely distinguished collaborationist families from those of the Communists' until the wedging campaign in 1942. To exercise its influence upon collaborationist troops and to "make friends with the enemy," the Communist government tightened their control over their family members with discriminative dossier registration, shame offensives and regular summoned meetings.[74] As a curse and humiliation, the Communists hung up "black coffin" lanterns during the Chinese lantern festival on the house gate of those families.[75] They also produced dossiers for collaborationists by dotting a red point for previous pro-Communist performance or a black one for the opposite.[76] It was haphazard to determine how many black points meant a death sentence, but this practice was made known to collaborationist families as a deterrent.[77]

The Communists were the ones with whom the collaborationists collaborated. It was common that the latter acquainted themselves with the former's existence for mutual survival, and the former was eager to maintain the cooperation relationship due to lack of ammunition. One of the Communist principles provided:

> [We] should actively begin to win over a relationship with puppet armies once a watchtower is built. If he ignores or keeps hostile, [we] just ambush when he is relieved and continue to make [the newcomer] to collaborate. If he does not destroy the course of resistance and offers our activities some convenience, we can give them some means to answer the coercion of the enemy.[78]

Among them, a collaborationist soldier, nicknamed *Xiaodaoshi* by the Communists for his early experience as a Taoist disciple, sent a message to the Communists to defect. Xiaodaoshi had been reportedly bullied so much by the Japanese and his collaborationist superiors that he pledged to open the fort in front of any prospective Communist attack. His wife, child(ren), and a comrade Ai would be with him. Although the Communists preferred him acting as a long-term infiltrator, they arrived at a hurried decision to blitz the collaborationist stronghold on the eve of Xiaodaoshi's sudden transfer. At 10:00 on the night of April 26, 1943, about 40 county militias signaled under the fence. Xiaodaoshi ushered them in but shortly got shot by an ignorant militia member. The blitz turned out to be a flop, and Xiaodaoshi died in vain.[79] Without benefits, the Communists rarely considered these military collaborationists anything different from other collaborators they had executed in base areas.

Under the direction of the party, two bureaus dealt with anti-collaboration affairs: on the one hand, it was the "Traitor Elimination" who did the dirty job; on the other, it was "Enemy and Puppet Work" for those who actually took the responsibility of cooperating with those military collaborationists. It was required that the two bureaus not target the same person.[80]

Enemy and Puppet Work was conducted with considerable skills. After the withdrawal of Nationalist General Yu Xuezhong in September 1943, Mao instructed another five thousand troops be sent from Jiangsu to Shandong.[81] During late 1943 through early 1945, the Communists maintained a relationship of tacit coexistence with collaborationist troops. They did not rashly offend the precinct of each other and even traded munitions.[82]

Nevertheless, punishing collaboration was a universal indication of governance legitimacy. From the viewpoint of Traitor Elimination, collaborationist families fell to the worst ragtag, or the lowest caste, whose lives and possessions became anyone's property. Peng Dehuai was supposed to be a general of nationalism in the Communist Party. Shortly after the major Communist initiated offensive, he proposed to make a distinction between landlords and collaborators. In other words, these two groups of people had been treated almost the same in the Communist practice. "Confirmed collaborators' land should be confiscated by the [Communist] government," General Peng insisted, "and distributed to peasants with land insufficient or none, especially to the family member of anti-Japanese soldiers who own no land."[83]

After V-J Day in Yantai, the Communist police also took 26 collaborationist family members into custody, along with other 249 collaboration suspects. All of them were instructed to make public confessions to pass the vetting, and some never passed. Other 217 collaborationist families without local estates were forcedly repatriated to their birthplace. Unlike the treatment of Japanese prisoners and civilians, however, they were given only a passport, probably with the title "puppet" on it, and ordered to leave in five days.[84]

## Conclusion

Peasants in North China had long been prepared for outside threats with a developed strategy of survival. As natural disasters and poverty raged on in the last century, local peasants held a tradition of banditry as well as organized resistance. However, they also had to choose to collaborate with the occupation state in most cases when there had been few alternatives.

In hindsight, however, resistance is justified by its ends rather than its means, and collaboration is often judged harshly for its subservience to a despised alien rather than the costs of the action. In the face of the great threat of violence, resistance was not necessarily a reasonable choice for peasants.

Under occupation, the peasants had to endure unbearable life burdens imposed by the foreign occupier and Chinese resistance forces as well. Usually, most peasants in limbo had to satisfy Communist, Nationalist, Collaborationist and Japanese requirements with seemingly endless taxes and corvée labor. Overlooked was the violence performed by the resistance and victorious regimes. Political allegiance could not guarantee protection for one's life or body, and one had to rely on his or her own personal relations for self-salvation. In contrast to ideological conflicts, the racial confrontation was seldom recalled in the daily life of lost territories. It was surely not easy to have survived a world war, and to live was not shameful.

Moreover, existing studies indicate secret societies in northern China rarely collaborated with the Japanese. Yet, archival evidence often shows just the contrary: at least the Green Gang (*Sanfanzi* and *An Qing daoyi hui*) and the Red Spears (including Hard Fist Way) collaborated with the Japanese in Shandong.

Collaborationists were political pariahs of the war. They were human beings rather than puppets. Regardless of the wartime circumstance of violence, almost every judgment made from the top down is inclined to be a rejection of human dignity rather than a salute to it.

## Notes

1 In January 2017, the Chinese Ministry of Education mandated the phrase "14-year Chinese People's War of Resistance Against Japanese Aggression" in primary and secondary teaching materials. See "China to revise textbook language on anti-Japanese war," *China Daily*, 11 January 2017. Last Accessed 30 June 2018. www.chinadaily.com.cn/culture/2017-01/11/content_27924549.htm

2 Stanley Hoffmann, "Collaborationism in France during World War II," *The Journal of Modern History* 40, no. 3 (September 1968): 375–95; Bertram M. Gordon, *Collaborationism in France during the Second World War* (Ithaca, NY: Cornell University Press, 1980), 2–3.

3 Philippe Burrin, *France under the Germans: Collaboration and Compromise* (New York: New Press, 1996), 460.

4 Timothy Brook, *Collaboration: Japanese Agents and Local Elites in Wartime China* (Cambridge: Harvard University Press, 2005), 9–10.

5 Konrad Mitchell Lawson, "Wartime Atrocities and the Politics of Treason in the Ruins of the Japanese Empire, 1937–1953" (PhD, Cambridge, MA: Harvard University, 2012), 271.

6 Poshek Fu, *Passivity, Resistance, and Collaboration: Intellectual Choices in Occupied Shanghai, 1937–1945* (Stanford: Stanford University Press, 1993); Frederic Wakeman, Jr., "Hanjian (Traitor)! Collaboration and Retribution in Wartime Shanghai," in *Becoming Chinese: Passages to Modernity and Beyond*, ed. Wen-hsin Yeh (Berkeley, CA: University of California Press, 2000), 298–341; Parks Coble, *Chinese Capitalists in Japan's New Order: The Occupied Lower Yangzi, 1937–1945* (Berkeley, CA: University of California Press, 2003); Zhang Sheng et al., *Riwei guanxi yanjiu: yi Huadong diqu wei zhongxin [A History of Relations Between Japan and the Puppets: Focusing on the Northeast Area]* (Nanjing: Chubanshe, 2003); Timothy Brook, *Collaboration: Japanese Agents and Local Elites in Wartime China* (Cambridge: Harvard University Press, 2005).

7 Takeshi Baba, "Santo shou no kairaigun ni tsu i te [On the Puppet Armies of Shandong Province]," *Shakai Kagaku Token* 39, no. 3 (March 1994): 843–72; Ximing Liu, *Weijun: qiangquan jinzhu xia de zuzi (1937–1949) [Puppet Armies: Pawns in a Power Struggle]* (Taipei: Daixian Chubanshe, 2002).

8 Dongyoun Hwang, "Wartime Collaboration in Question: An Examination of the Postwar Trials of the Chinese Collaborators," *Inter-Asia Cultural Studies* 1(2005): 75–97; Charles D. Musgrove, "Cheering the Traitor: The Post-War Trial of Chen Bijun, April 1946," *Twentieth-Century China* 30 (2005): 3–27; Margherita Zanasi, "Globalizing hanjian: The

Suzhou Trials and the Post-World War II Discourse on Collaboration," *The American Historical Review* 3 (2008): 731–51; Koichi Masui, *Kankan saiban shi 1946–1948 [A History of Trials of Hanjian: 1946–1948]* (Tokyo: Misuzu Shobo, 1977); Yun Xia, *Down with Traitors: Justice and Nationalism in Wartime China* (Seattle: University of Washington Press, 2017); Jiu-jung Lo, "Juntong tegong zuzhi yu zhanhou hanjian shenpan [Juntong and the Post-War Trial of Hanjian]," *Zhongyang yanjiuyuan jindaishi yanjiusuo jikan* 6 (1994): 267–91.

9  Chalmers A. Johnson, *Peasant Nationalism and Communist Power* (Stanford: Stanford University Press, 1962); Elizabeth J. Perry, *Rebels and Revolutionaries in North China, 1845–1945* (Stanford: Stanford University Press, 1980); Yung-fa Chen, *Making Revolution: The Communist Movement in Eastern and Central China, 1937–1945* (Berkeley, CA: University of California Press, 1986); Joseph W. Esherick, *The Origins of the Boxer Uprising* (Berkeley: University of California Press, 1987); David S. Goodman, *Social and Political Change in Revolutionary China: The Taihang Base Area in the War of Resistance to Japan, 1937–1945* (Lanham, MD: Rowman & Littlefield, 2000).

10  The oral history interviews were conducted and recorded by Misters Zhang Zhengkun, Sheng Yuan and Shu Lin of the Institute of Modern History in 1965, just before the Cultural Revolution. I would like to thank Dr. Zhao Qingyun for sharing with me seven volumes of the interview records.

11  G. William Skinner, "Regional Urbanization in Nineteenth Century China," in *The City in Late Imperial China*, ed. G. William Skinner (Stanford: Stanford University Press, 1977), 213.

12  Mao Zedong, "The Situation and Tasks of Anti-Japanese War after the Fall of Shanghai and Taiyuan," 12 November 1937; *Mao Zedong xuanji* [Selected Works of Mao Zedong], Vol. 2 (Beijing: Renmin chubanshe, 1991), 388, 391.

13  Japanese Defense Agency, *Hokushi no chiansen* [The War of Pacification in North China], Vol. 1 (Tokyo: Asagumo Shinbunsha, 1968), 180.

14  Wu Zanzhou papers, n. d., Zhengding County Archives, see on line materials at the website: Last Accessed 30 June 2018. http://danganju.zd.gov.cn/mingren.asp?method=list&id=17

15  Chinese Ministry of Finance, ed., *Geming genjudi de caizheng jingji* [Finance and Economy in Revolutionary Bases] (Chengdu: Zhongguo caizheng jingji chubanshe, 1985), 127.

16  Ibid., 118, 129–33.

17  CCP Zhengding County Committee, *Zhongguo gongchandang hebei sheng zhengding xian zuzhi shi ziliao* [CCP Organization History of Zhengding County, Hebei Province] (Shijiazhuang: Hebei renmin chubanshe, 1991), 46–7.

18  Interview with Lu Wenhui, n.d., 1965, conducted by Shu Lin, *Kouzi cunshi caifang jilu* [Interview Records of History of Kouzi Village] (hereafter cited KZCS), vol. 3, 8; see also interview with Liu Zifang, Oct. 12, 1965, conducted by Zhang Zhengkun and Sheng Yuan, *KZCS*, vol. 6, 5.

19  Interview with Zhang Jin, conducted by Liu Shida, *Longkou shi dangshi ziliao* [Communist Historical Materials of Longkou] (hereafter cited as LKDS), vol. 2, 1988, 59.

20  Chinese Ministry of Finance, ed., *Geming genjudi de caizheng jingji*, 390.

21  Shandong Provincial Archives and Shandong Social Sciences Academy eds., *Shandong gemin lishi dang'an ziliao xuanbian* [A Selection of Archival Documents on the History of the Revolution in Shandong Province] (hereafter cited as SDGLD), Vol. 9 (Jinan: Shandong renmin chubanshe, 1983), 175–7.

22  Interview with Lu Wenxue, Sept. 9, 1965, conducted by Zhang Zhengkun, *KZCS*, vol. 2, 18.

23  Ibid., 24.

24  Interview with Lu Mingdao, Sept. 12, 1965, conducted by Zhang Zhengkun, *KZCS*, vol. 3, 7; see also interview with Lu Wenxue, Sept. 21, 1965, *KZCS*, vol. 4, 19.

25  Li Xiujie, "The advent and developments of anti-Japanese troops in the Huang County," *LKDS*, vol. 1, 1987, 92–5; see also Sun Zhizhong's memoir, "The base construction and developments in the Huang County during the anti-Japanese war period," *LKDS*, vol. 1, 1.

26  Interview with Liu Zifang, Oct. 12, 1965, conducted by Zhang Zhengkun and Sheng Yuan, *KZCS*, vol. 5, 26; vol. 6, 1.

27  Telegram, CCP Central Committee to Shandong Provincial Committee, Jan. 15, 1938, in ed. CCP Shandong Provincial Committee, *Shandong kangRi genjudi* [Anti-Japanese Bases in Shandong] (Beijing: Zhonggong dangshi ziliao chubanshe, 1989), 27.

28  Ibid., 8–10.

29  Li Jitao, "The advent and developments of the munitions factory at Quanyangjia in the Huang County during the early anti-Japanese war period," *LKDS*, vol. 1, 98–9.

30  Sun Zhizhong's memoir, "The base construction and developments in the Huang County during the anti-Japanese war period," *LKDS*, vol. 1, 20.

31  Interview with Lu Wenxue, Sept. 9, 1965, conducted by Zhang Zhengkun and Sheng Yuan, *KZCS*, vol. 2, 18, 20; see also interview with Lu Wenxue and Lu Mingjin, Sept. 21, 1965, *KZCS*, vol. 4, 22.

32  Wang Ziyi, "Memories of works in the third district of Huang County during the anti-Japanese war period," *LKDS*, vol. 1, 42.

33  SDGLD, vol. 16, 68–9.

34  Interview with Lu Mingdao, Sept. 14, 1965, conducted by Zhang Zhengkun, *KZCS*, vol. 3, 21–4.

35  Interview with Lu Mingdao, Sept. 14, 1965, conducted by Zhang Zhengkun, *KZCS*, vol. 3, 20.

36  Interview with Zhan Deben, Sept. 13, 1965, conducted by Zhang Zhengkun, *KZCS*, vol. 3, 14.

37  Interview with Lu Mingdao, Sept. 14, 1965, conducted by Zhang Zhengkun, *KZCS*, vol. 3, 24.

38  Interview with Liu Zifang, Oct. 12, 1965, conducted by Zhang Zhengkun and Sheng Yuan, *KZCS*, vol. 6, 2.

39  Interview with Jiao Feng, conducted by Liu Shida, *LKDS*, vol. 2, 62.

40  Interview with Lu Mingyu, Sept. 11, 1965, conducted by Sheng Yuan and Shu Lin, *KZCS*, vol. 3, 4.

41  Interview with Zhan Deben, Sept. 11, 1965, conducted by Zhang Zhengkun, *KZCS*, vol. 3, 2.

42  Sun Zhizhong's memoir, "The base construction and developments in the Huang County during the anti-Japanese war period,"*LKDS*, vol. 1, 14.

43  Interview with Zhan Deben, Sept. 11, 1965, conducted by Zhang Zhengkun, *KZCS*, vol. 3, 2–3.

44  Interview with Lu Mingdao, Sept. 12, 1965, conducted by Zhang Zhengkun, *KZCS*, vol. 3, 20; see also interview with Lu Wenxue and Lu Mingjin, Sept. 21, 1965, *KZCS*, vol. 4, 22.

45  Interview with Chen Tiankui and Lu Lanying, Sept. 16, 1965, conducted by Zhang Zhengkun, *KZCS*, vol. 4, 2–3.

46  "Militia instructor Jiang Renhou," *Dazhong ribao* [The Masses Daily], 1 July 1944, 1.

47  Japanese Defense Agency, *Hokushi no chiansen* [The War of Pacification in North China], Vol. 1 (Tokyo: Asagumo Shinbunsha, 1968), 144.

48  The Communist 115 Division, "Experience Sum-ups of guerrilla warfare on the plains around Hebei-Shandong borders," Oct. 1942, in SDGLD, vol. 9, 109.

49  Wen Damin, "The Crimes Committed by the Japanese and the Puppet Troops in the Southwestern Shandong Province," in *Wenshi ziliao xuanji* [Compilation of Historical Resources] (Jinan: Shandong renmin chubanshe, 1985), 202.

50  CCP Shandong, *Shangdong kangri genjudi* [Anti-Japanese Bases in Shandong], 17–18; see also SDGLD, vol. 16, 394.

51  CCP Shandong Bureau, "Directives on the all-out campaigns of Reduce Rent and Interest, and Oppose Treason Voice Grieves," May 2, 1946, SDGLD, vol. 16, 421–3.

52  Interview with Lu Wenxue, Sept. 9, 1965, conducted by Zhang Zhengkun and Sheng Yuan, *KZCS*, vol. 2, 20.

53 Interview with Lu Mingjin, Aug. 11, 1965, conducted by Zhang Zhengkun, *KZCS*, vol. 1, 4; see also interview with Lu Wenxue, Sept. 9, 1965, conducted by Zhang Zhengkun and Sheng Yuan, *KZCS*, vol. 2, 22.

54 Joseph W. Esherick, *The Origins of the Boxer Uprising* (Berkeley: University of California Press, 1987), 39.

55 Elizabeth J. Perry, *Rebels and Revolutionaries in North China, 1845–1945* (Stanford: Stanford University Press, 1980), 185.

56 Military order, Luo Ronghuan and Li Yu to the military districts, April 24, 1943, SDGLD, vol. 9, 451.

57 Lu Yao, *Shandong minjian mimi jiaomen* [Secret Societies in Shandong] (Beijing: Dangdai zhongguo shubanshe, 2000), 528.

58 Zhu Rui, "A conclusion of ten months mass works in the Coastal Area," 1943, SDGLD, vol. 9, 351, 358.

59 Liu Zhengce, "Shandong sheng laiwu xian weijun shiliao" [History of Puppet Troops in Laiwu County, Shandong Province], June 7, 1947, J108–01–0090–002, Shandong Provincial Archives (hereafter cited as SDPA). See also Lawson, "Wartime Atrocities and the Politics of Treason," 299.

60 Liu Zhengce, "Shandong sheng laiwu xian weijun shiliao," J108–01–0090–002, SDPA.

61 Interview with Zhang Jin, conducted by Liu Shida, *LKDS*, vol. 2, 60.

62 Guo Yingqiu, *Wangshi manyi* [Memories] (Beijing: Zhongguo renmin daxue chubanshe, 1986), 99–109.

63 Interview with Lu Wenxue and Lu Mingjin, Sept. 21, 1965, conducted by Zhang Zhengkun and Sheng Yuan, *KZCS*, vol. 4, 23.

64 Sun Zhizhong's memoir, "The base construction and developments in the Huang County during the anti-Japanese war period," *LKDS*, vol. 1, 22.

65 "Jin Ji Lu Yu bianqu zhengfu qudi feifa mimi jiaomen fangzhi dijian liyong huodong" [Shanxi-Hebei-Shandong-Henan Border Area Government Prohibition on Illegal Secret Societies to Avoid Being Employed by the Enemy and Collaborators], *Jie Fang Ri Bao* (March 30, 1942): 1.

66 Zhongguo di'er lishi dang'anguan, ed., *Mingguo Banghui Yaolu* [Important Records of Secret Societies in the Republic] (Beijing: Dangan chubanshe, 1993), 121.

67 Liu Shida, "The history of peaceful liberation of the Huang County," *LKDS*, vol. 1, 155.

68 Inaba Masao, ed., *Okamura Yasuji taisho shiryo, senjo kaisohen* [Materials on General Okamura Yasuji: Wartime Memoirs], Vol. 1 (Tokyo: Harashobo, 1970), 327.

69 Lawson, "Wartime Atrocities and the Politics of Treason," 280.

70 Interview with Chen Yaoting, conducted by Liu Shida, *LKDS*, vol. 2, 66.

71 Interview with Sun Zhizhong, conducted by Liu Shida, *LKDS*, vol. 2, 13–14, 17.

72 Wang Ziyi, "Memories of works in the third district of Huang County during the anti-Japanese war period," *LKDS*, vol. 1, 41–2, 44.

73 SDGLD, vol. 9, 130.

74 CCP County committee decision on making dossiers for family members of puppet soldiers, June 22, 1942, G052–01–0045–001, SDPA.

75 Interview with Sun Zhizhong, conducted by Liu Shida, *LKDS*, vol. 2, 1988, 14.

76 Wang Ziyi, "Memories of works in the third district of Huang County during the anti-Japanese war period," *LKDS*, vol. 1, 45.

77 See also Lawson, "Wartime Atrocities and the Politics of Treason," 319–20.

78 The Communist 115 Division, "Experience Sum-ups of guerrilla warfare on the plains around Hebei-Shandong borders," SDGLD, vol. 9, 114.

79 Li Jitao, "The history of Independent Battalion of the Huang County," *LKDS*, vol. 1, 131–2.

80 The CCP Shandong Sub-Bureau, "Decisions on Organizational Leadership over the Enemy and Puppet Work," July 1, 1943, SDGLD, vol. 9, 29.

81 Mao's chronicle entries on Sept. 3, 1943, Party Literature Research Office of CCP Central Committee, ed., *Mao Zedong nianpu, 1893–1949* [A Chronicle of Mao Zedong], Vol. 2 (Beijing: Zhongyang wenxian chubanshe, 1993), 528.

82  Wang Ziyi, "Memories of works in the third district of Huang County during the anti-Japanese war period," *LKDS*, vol. 1, 46; see also interview with Sun Zhizhong, conducted by Liu Shida, *LKDS*, vol. 2, 15.
83  Peng Dehuai, "Lecture to the assembly of high ranking cadres of the Northern Bureau," Sept. 25, 1940, *Jinchaji kangri genjudi shiliao xuanbian* [Compilation of historical documents of anti-Japanese bases in the provinces of Shanxi, Chahar, and Hebei], Vol. 1 (Shijiazhuang: Hebei renmin chubanshe, 1983), 418.
84  Weihai Public Security Bureau, "PSB Work Summery of 1945," G042–01–0014–010, *SDPA*.

## Selected bibliography

Baba, Takeshi 馬場毅. "山東省の傀儡軍について [On the Puppet Armies of Shandong Province]." *Shakai Kagaku Token* 39, no. 3 (March 1994): 843–72.

Barrett, David P., and Lawrence N. Shyu, eds. *Chinese Collaboration with Japan, 1932–1945: The Limits of Accommodation*. Stanford: Stanford University Press, 2000.

Boyle, John Hunter. *China and Japan at War, 1937–1945: The Politics of Collaboration*. Stanford: Stanford University Press, 1972.

Brook, Timothy. *Collaboration: Japanese Agents and Local Elites in Wartime China*. Cambridge: Harvard University Press, 2005.

Brook, Timothy. "Hesitating before the Judgment of History." *The Journal of Asian Studies* 71, no. 1 (February 16, 2012): 103–14.

Burrin, Philippe. *France under the Germans: Collaboration and Compromise*. New York: New Press, 1996.

Chen, Yung-fa. *Making Revolution: The Communist Movement in Eastern and Central China, 1937–1945*. Berkeley: University of California Press, 1986.

Coble, Parks. *Chinese Capitalists in Japan's New Order: The Occupied Lower Yangzi, 1937–1945*. Berkeley: University of California Press, 2003.

Conroy, Hilary. "Thoughts on Collaboration." *Peace and Change* 1, no. 1 (1972): 43–6.

Deák, István, Jan Tomasz Gross, and Tony Judt, eds. *The Politics of Retribution in Europe: World War II and Its Aftermath*. Princeton, NJ: Princeton University Press, 2000.

Dikötter, Frank. "The Emergence of Labour Camps in Shandong Province, 1942–1950." *The China Quarterly*, no. 175 (September 1, 2003): 803–17.

Duara, Prasenjit. *Culture, Power, and the State: Rural North China, 1900–1942*. Stanford: Stanford University Press, 1988.

Esherick, Joseph W. *The Origins of the Boxer Uprising*. Berkeley: University of California Press, 1987.

Fu, Poshek. *Passivity, Resistance, and Collaboration: Intellectual Choices in Occupied Shanghai, 1937–1945*. Stanford: Stanford University Press, 1993.

Goodman, David S. G. *Social and Political Change in Revolutionary China: The Taihang Base Area in the War of Resistance to Japan, 1937–1945*. Lanham, MD: Rowman & Littlefield, 2000.

Gordon, Bertram N. *Collaborationism in France during the Second World War*. Ithaca, NY: Cornell University Press, 1980.

Graefe, Nils. *Liu Guitang (1892–1943): Einer Der Grössten Banditen Der Chinesischen Republikzeit*. Abhandlungen Für Die Kunde Des Morgenlandes Band 64. Wiesbaden: Harrassowitz Verlag, 2008.

Hoffmann, Stanley. "Collaborationism in France during World War II." *The Journal of Modern History* 40, no. 3 (September 1968): 375–95.

Huang, Philip. *The Peasant Economy and Social Change in North China*. Stanford: Stanford University Press, 1985.

Hwang, Dongyoun. "Wartime Collaboration in Question: An Examination of the Postwar Trials of the Chinese Collaborators." *Inter-Asia Cultural Studies* 1(2005): 75–97.

Inoue, Hisashi 井上久士, ed. 華中宣撫工作資料 [*Materials on Pacification Work in Central China*]. Tokyo: Fuji shuppan, 1989.

Japanese Defense Agency 日本防衛研修所. 北支の治安戦 [*The War of Pacification in North China*], 2 vols. Tokyo: Asagumo Shinbunsha, 1968.

Johnson, Chalmers A. *Peasant Nationalism and Communist Power*. Stanford: Stanford University Press, 1962.

John Whittier Treat. "Choosing to Collaborate: Yi Kwang-su and the Moral Subject in Colonial Korea." *Journal of Asian Studies* 71, no. 1 (2012): 81–102.

Kuwajima, Setsuro 桑島節郎. 華北戦記：中国にあったほんとうの戦争 [*A Record of the War in North China: The Real War in China*]. Tokyo: Asahi Shinbunsha, 1997.

Lai, Sherman Xiaogang. *A Springboard to Victory: Shandong Province and Chinese Communist Military and Financial Strength, 1937–1945*. Leiden and Boston: Brill, 2011.

Lawson, Konrad Mitchell. "Wartime Atrocities and the Politics of Treason in the Ruins of the Japanese Empire, 1937–1953." Ph.D., Harvard University, 2012.

Li, Lincoln. *The Japanese Army in North China, 1937–1941: Problems of Political and Economic Control*. New York: Oxford University Press, 1975.

Liu, Ximing 劉熙明. 偽軍：強權競逐下的卒子 (1937–1949) [*Puppet Armies: Pawns in a Power Struggle*]. Taipei: Daixian Chubanshe, 2002.

Lo, Jiu-jung 羅久蓉. 她的審判：近代中國國族與性別意義下的忠奸之辨 [*Her Trials: Contextualizing Loyalty and Disloyalty in Modern China from the Gendered Nationalist Perspective*]. Taipei: Institute of Modern History, Academia Sinica, 2013.

Lo, Jiu-jung 羅久蓉. "軍統特工組織與戰後漢奸審判 [Juntong and the Post-War Trial of Hanjian]." *Zhongyang yanjiuyuan jindaishi yanjiusuo jikan* 6 (1994): 267–91.

Lo, Jiu-jung. "Trials of Taiwanese as Hanjians/War Criminals and Post-War Search for Taiwan Identity." In *Imagining National Identity in Modern East Asia*, ed. Kai-sing Chow, Kevin M. Doak, and Poshek Fu, 279–316. Ann Arbor: University of Michigan Press, 2001.

MacMinnon, Stephen, and Diana Lary, eds. *China at War: Regions of China, 1937–1945*. Stanford University Press, 2007.

Masui, Koichi 益井康一. 漢奸裁判史 1946–1948 [*A History of Trials of Hanjian: 1946–1948*]. Tokyo: Misuzu Shobo, 1977.

Mitter, Rana. *The Manchurian Myth: Nationalism, Resistance, and Collaboration in Modern China*. Berkeley: University of California Press, 2000.

Musgrove, Charles D. "Cheering the Traitor: The Post-War Trial of Chen Bijun, April 1946." *Twentieth-Century China* 30 (2005): 3–27.

Nemoto, Kei 根本敬. 抵抗と協力のはざま：近代ビルマ史のなかのイギリスと日本 [*Between Resistance and Collaboration: England and Japan in Modern Burma*]. Tokyo: Iwanami Shoten, 2010.

Novick, Peter. *The Resistance Versus Vichy: The Purge of Collaborators in Liberated France*. London: Chatto & Windus, 1968.

Paulson, David Mark. "War and Revolution in North China: The Shandong Base Area, 1937–1945." Ph.D., Stanford University, 1982.

Perry, Elizabeth J. *Rebels and Revolutionaries in North China, 1845–1945*. Stanford: Stanford University Press, 1980.

Sartre, Jean-Paul. "What Is a Collaborator?" In *The Aftermath of War* (Situations III), trans. Jean-Paul Sartre and Chris Turner, 41–62. Oxford: Seagull Books, 2008.

Skinner, G. William, ed. *The City in Late Imperial China*. Stanford: Stanford University Press, 1977.

Treat, John Whittier. "Choosing to Collaborate: Yi Kwang-su and the Moral Subject in Colonial Korea." *The Journal of Asian Studies* 71, no. 1 (February 16, 2012): 81–102.

Uchida, Tomoyuki 內田知行. 抗日戦争と民衆運動 *[Mass Movements and the War of Resistance against Japan]*. Tokyo: Sodosha, 2002.

Wakeman, Frederic, Jr. *The Shanghai Badlands: Wartime Terrorism and Urban Crime, 1937–1941*. New York: Cambridge University Press, 1996.

Wakeman, Frederic, Jr. "*Hanjian(Traitor)!* Collaboration and Retribution in Wartime Shanghai." In *Becoming Chinese: Passages to Modernity and Beyond*, ed. Wen-hsin Yeh, 298–341. Berkeley: University of California Press, 2000.

Xia, Yun. *Down with Traitors: Justice and Nationalism in Wartime China*. Seattle, WA: University of Washington Press, 2017.

Yeh, Wen-Hsin, ed. *Wartime Shanghai*. New York: Routledge, 1998.

Yoshimi, Yoshiaki. *Comfort Women: Sexual Slavery in the Japanese Military during World War II*. Trans. Suzanne O'Brien. New York: Columbia University Press, 2000.

Zanasi, Margherita. "Globalizing *hanjian*: The Suzhou Trials and the Post-World War II Discourse on Collaboration." *The American Historical Review* 3 (2008): 731–51.

Zhang, Sheng 張生 et al. 日偽關係研究：以華東地區為中心 *[A History of Relations Between Japan and the Puppets: Focusing on the Northeast Area]*. Nanjing: Chubanshe, 2003.

# 11 "For a New European Order"

## Total war and irregular warfare of the Italian Social Republic abroad 1943–45

*Federico Ciavattone*

### The signing of the armistice

On 8 September 1943, the Italian government publicly declared it had signed an armistice with the Allies;[1] after having fought alongside the Germans on all fronts with varying degrees of success, Italy was retiring from the conflict. In actuality, however, the war wasn't over for Italy and the Italian people; a few days after the armistice, the Germans freed the Duce, who, on 23 September, announced the foundation of a new Fascist state, the *Repubblica Sociale Italiana* (*RSI*)/Italian Social Republic, led by Mussolini, once again allied with the German Reich.[2] This move was countered by the creation of the Regno del Sud/Southern Kingdom in Italy's South under the leadership of Pietro Badoglio and Vittorio Emanuele III:[3] two political choices (the Italian Social Republic and the Southern Kingdom) that caused Italy to plunge into civil war. In particular, the *RSI* showed a strong desire for revenge, both inside and outside of Italy. Mussolini intended to continue playing a major role in the Fascist project of the "New European Order" and wanted to prove that Hitler's Germany could still rely on Fascist Italy both militarily and in international diplomacy.[4]

### The choice of Fascist soldiers abroad

8 September 1943 was a dramatic moment for Italy and its armed forces. For the units that found themselves abroad, the situation became even more difficult because they were deployed in operational territory, far from the homeland. On 8 September, there were 42 Divisions outside Italy's borders, plus some non-divisional units, totalling 14 Army corps.[5] When the news of the armistice was received, the units reacted in different ways: central commands broke up; some Divisions melted away like "snow under the sun"; individuals and even entire units tried to make their way home or joined the partisan groups they had been fighting until a few hours earlier. The great majority surrendered to the Germans and were deported to the Reich's lagers, while a few others fought against the German troops (Cephalonia being the

most emblematic of such cases). Finally, some decided to carry on fighting alongside the German units.

What were the reasons that determined the Fascist choice of continuing to fight alongside Germany?

The choice of the *RSI* was the result of circumstances, personal relationships, environmental influences and moods that converged into a determination to "rebel" against 8 September.

Starting from an analysis of the climate of those days, and considering the emotional state of many Italians, we can say that the causes of the choice of Fascism had both remote and contemporary origins. The remote causes include all those "institutions" that, in Italian society at the time, played a role in the education and training both of individuals and of collectivities. During the *Ventennio*, these "institutions" were the family, the Fascist Party, and the schools.[6]

The contemporary causes are instead to be sought in the betrayal and shame that, if considered as a single element, form a platform on which all the various choices of militancy in the *RSI* were built. It was precisely on account of the elaboration of betrayal and shame that both young and not-so-young chose the Social Republic, identifying the sole path to follow in "honor" and "fidelity" to the homeland and to the word given to the Germans.

For what regards betrayal, this was perceived on several levels.

> What I felt was anger and dejection. I felt betrayed, I felt that the Germans had been betrayed. Now we had an ally who was to become an enemy and on top of everything was in our country. Our betrayal was a dirty business, it's always an ugly thing, but when it's dirty like that it's always worse. All those events impressed me to the point of crushing me. I thought that if one day I met a German and he said to me, "Italians are traitors and cowards!" I wouldn't have an answer for him.[7]

First and foremost, it was a political betrayal. Badoglio and the King were considered the two most responsible for what happened in Italy in 1943. In the eyes of the Fascists, their way of acting was so "foul" that numerous fighting units, once they had taken their place alongside the Germans again, eliminated all Savoy emblems.

Secondly, the betrayal was military: the government and the top echelons of the Royal Armed Forces had abandoned soldiers to themselves.

The elements of betrayal also included not having kept faith with the Germans. Italy and German had been linked by a formal alliance pact cemented by three years of war fought together in France, Africa, the Balkans and Russia. A pact based on mutual "loyalty" and sense of "honor", beyond any sentimentality or practical interest, strengthened by "faith", friendship and the fallen in the hundreds of combat operations carried out together. All this, however, Italy had failed to respect.[8]

Beyond the political and military aspects, betrayal was also felt with regard to the past constituted by the battles of Curtatone and Montanara (Italian

Independence Wars), the battles of the Carso (World War One) and the Fascist "revolution", which, from the Fascist point of view, had helped to make Italy become a great country.[9]

> Everything I felt boiled down to the family I grew up in. Our family was very tightly knit, united around that ideology. On 8 September I was just a boy and didn't feel the responsibility for it as much. You feel something you aren't even able to describe. You start to ask: "What happened? Why did it happen? What was the reason?" But the person who suffered from it the most was my father, who had been a military man since 1915, without interruption. He felt very humiliated and was the one who conveyed this feeling of gloom, this sense of betrayal, to the whole family: to my grandfather, to my uncle, to me and my brother. When the time came to embrace the cause in which we all firmly believed, from the youngest to the oldest, we went and enlisted. My grandfather was 74 years old, I was 14 and a half.[10]

A sense of betrayal and shame that, in the case of the Fascist choice, combined to produce a "rebellion" that consisted of continuing to fight, initially alongside the Germans and later in the ranks of the *RSI*. The Fascists of the *RSI* considered themselves to be the "paladins" and authentic defenders of the honor of the betrayed homeland, the defenders of fidelity.[11]

> I joined the *RSI* on 13 or 14 September 1943. I volunteered because I wanted no part of the destiny of the world's youth who, with a cowardly act, failed to keep a commitment and accepted a secondary role, one of subjection.[12]

Among those who joined the Italian Social Republic, the defence of honor and loyalty was perceived also towards Mussolini. It was a transversal perception, ranging from the youngest to the old Fascists.

> I enlisted as a volunteer in the Militia because of our leader Benito Mussolini and after 8 September I didn't shirk my duty and headed north with the Germans. My choice was dictated by loyalty, loyalty to being a good Italian, and I always say that if necessary I would do it again, more than willingly.[13]

Even now, the surviving Fascists who joined the *RSI* claim the rightness of their choice, considering themselves the "best youth" because, in a moment as dramatic as 8 September 1943, they put love of country and loyalty to one's word above their own personal interests.[14] In the weeks and months to come, this choice of militancy would contribute to Italy's fall into the maelstrom of civil war.[15]

These elements – shared by all *RSI* combatants – are joined by additional ones, specific to the units located abroad. The individuals, groups or units who immediately opted to continue to fight alongside the Germans made a clearly militant, ideological choice. Indeed, Mussolini had not yet been freed and the Italian Social Republic would not be constituted until 23 September.

> Here at the front I'm in a German battery that shoots very well. Our German comrades are very good to us, they call us MUSSOLINI's soldiers and like us a lot. Our faith is very high here also because we are helped by your German comrades . . . but the German comrades make sure we get a lot of instruction so we won't die like fools.[16]

Thus, the combat units that chose to continue the war alongside the Germans did so because they shared and believed in the ideals of the Nazi war effort and because they wanted to realize – through fighting – the project for a "New European Order". This was a genuine trait leap compared to the past: after 8 September 1943, both in Italy and abroad, a gradual process of Nazification of the Italian armed forces and of the Fascist war was seen, a Nazification that clearly emerged in the *RSI*'s increasingly regarding the Nazi totalitarian model as a point of reference, in the ever more central role assumed by the terror "apparatuses", in the leading role played by anti-Semitism.[17]

Together with the "inspired", "idealist" and "combatant" elements, there were also sceptics and undecideds who avoided deportation by choosing the "lesser evil" of opting to stick with the Germans and increasing the numbers of the Auxiliary Battalions in the hope of quicker repatriation.

This choice, lived either as a last attempt to achieve the "New European Order" or a chance for an earlier return home, led these soldiers to fully experience the events of the Tripartite Pact until the end of the conflict.

> Consider that here there are entire CCNN (Blackshirt) battalions who have been doing the impossible for 8 months to be sent to the Italian front, without success. We Italians scattered in the Balkans are a mass of forgotten, not to say abandoned by our government . . . The spirit certainly isn't strengthened in these conditions.[18]

When the founding of the Italian Social Republic was proclaimed on 23 September 1943, the Fascists who found themselves fighting abroad, deployed alongside the Germans, felt their choice was further legitimized: if, on the one hand, they were fighting under the operational control of the Reich to create a "New European Order", on the other, with the proclamation of the *RSI*, they felt part also of a Fascist state that was making its contribution to build a "new" Europe.

The phenomenon of former units of the Royal Armed Forces siding with those of the Reich occurred on all fronts where Italian units were present:

from France to Germany, from Russia to Romania, from Hungary to the Balkans, from Greece and the islands of the Aegean. Some units deployed in the Far East also decided to continue fighting alongside the old ally. The estimated numbers range from the tens of thousands to the hundreds of thousands.[19] This support involved both individuals and organic units of all sections of the Italian Armed Forces: Army, Navy, Air Force, Militia and Auxiliary units.

The fact that these soldiers were operating outside of Italy should give a further element of insight into how the war was actually perceived. These units had the opportunity to fight against the Allied troops – living the experience of total war in all its fundamental elements (land, air and sea) – and the partisan groups in irregular warfare. Their role was therefore not at all marginal: from a tactical and strategic point of view, taking the German side following 8 September 1943 could hardly have brought about a different outcome of the war, but if analysed in terms of active and ideological participation, these men experienced the progressive process of Nazification of the war in Europe first hand. The decision to carry on fighting alongside the former ally should be seen – in regards to a large portion of these soldiers – as a last-ditch attempt to pursue the values of Fascism and the project for a new model of European civilization on the Old Continent. A "New European Order" that could only be created by fighting to the finish their historic enemies: French, British and American "demo-plutocracies"; international communism; and the world-wide Jewish-Masonic "conspiracy".

## The diplomatic apparatus of the *RSI*

In order to play some role in international politics again and thus to be able to lay claim later to a prominent position in the new European order, it was necessary for the Italian Social Republic to reconstitute a diplomatic apparatus.

In diplomacy, Mussolini personally took on the role of Foreign Affairs Minister (Serafino Mazzolini was appointed Undersecretary).[20] Filippo Anfuso was the only top-ranking diplomat to stay at Mussolini's side.[21] It was Anfuso who succeeded in swiftly setting up an efficient network of diplomatic missions in Europe as well as on other continents. The diplomat managed to surround himself with highly qualified personnel, later sent to the foreign missions (in allied countries of Fascist Italy, in those occupied by the Third Reich and in neutral countries), thereby creating a Fascist Republican diplomatic network. In Europe, embassies were re-opened in Germany and France.[22] Diplomatic legations were set up in Bulgaria, Croatia, Romania, Slovakia and Hungary.[23] Consular offices were created in Albania, Belgium, Bohemia-Moravia, Denmark, Greece, Luxembourg, the Principality of Monaco, the Netherlands and Serbia.[24] In addition, the *RSI* was able to set up semi-official diplomatic missions in the neutral European countries of Ireland, Portugal, San Marino, Spain, Sweden, Switzerland and the Vatican.[25]

In practice, the diplomatic activity was one-way, aimed exclusively at Germany and its allied or satellite states. In the autumn of 1944, following the Allied advance on all fronts, the diplomatic representations of the *RSI* were limited to Germany, the states of the Far East and a few neutral states. The diplomatic activity and international relations were therefore practically null.

## Total war and irregular warfare of the *RSI* abroad

Let's start with the details of the operational activities of the Fascist units that, deployed abroad and operationally dependent on the Germans, had the occasion to engage in total war against the Allies and counter-insurgency against the partisans. As said, immediately following 8 September 1943, Italian Forces worked hand in hand with the German units on all fronts. This occurred in all operational sectors in which the former Royal Armed Forces were present: the Western front; the Eastern front; the Balkan front; and the territory of the Reich. These units which, starting on 9 September 1943, opted to continue to fight with the Germans constituted the first units of the future Republican Armed Forces.

Precise, definitive data on the presence of the Republican Armed Forces abroad do not exist, unfortunately. The most plausible estimate is a maximum figure of about 350,000 soldiers. The most precise data are those regarding the units of the future National Republican Army. Between September and October 1943, the *RSI* recorded 130,000 soldiers in the National Republican Army abroad, equal to 185 battalions, identified mainly in the Balkans and on the Western front. Between November and December 1943, the number rose to around 145 units: 45% on the Balkan front; 42% on the Western front; 10% on German territory; and 2% on the Eastern front.[26] From February to August 1944, their strength increased by around 10,000 units per month, reaching the maximum level of 220,000 men in August 1944.[27] This steady increase was due to military contingents sent from Italy to form four Divisions in Germany as reinforcements for the German Flak units and to sign-ups by Italian soldiers held as prisoners in German concentration camps. After August 1944, the presence of Army personnel abroad began to decline, reaching 131,000 men in December 1944.[28] This drastic drop-off was the consequence of the losses suffered as a result of the Allied offensives and to the return to Italy of soldiers in training in Germany.

With such a large presence of soldiers abroad, the National Republican Army was able, between 1943 and 1945, to fight both the regular war against the Allied armies and to conduct counter-insurgency against European partisans.[29] The irregular warfare, without a doubt the greatest effort was in the Balkans, included 14,700 soldiers between combat and auxiliary unit in November 1944.[30]

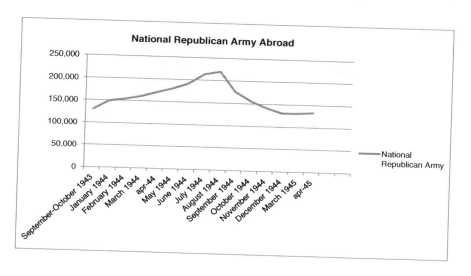

National Republican Army Abroad

Among the Fascist units that sided with the Germans after 8 September 1943, there was, for example, the 49th *San Marco* Blackshirts Assault Legion.

> At about 12 am, the commander of the Legion is presented to the Colonel commanding the Ragusa stronghold, Schimituber, stating that the Legion supports all the German comrades and never thought of betraying. The statement is received with sympathy and satisfaction.[31]

This unit, in Croatia and Herzegovina starting in April 1941, was expert in counter-insurgency.[32] On 12 September 1943, the Legion – deployed at Dubrovnik and with a strength of around 1,400 men – came under the *Prinz Eugen* SS Division.[33]

> The Battalions do not take part in the fights that take place in the areas where they are displaced, they just wait for the reason has the upper hand, and that the fire, useless and harmful, cease to mitigate the decision, now matured in the heart of all: continue the fight alongside Allied Germany.[34]

In the following days and weeks, it thus had occasion to carry out a series of anti-partisan operations in the zones of Bileća, Zavala and Ravno.[35]

> In one of these last fights the combat unit had three deaths, including a Company Commander, and about thirty wounded. But the action succeeded so well that the area was cleaned up by the partisans and the German Command granted eight decorations to the Value, while others are in progress.[36]

The Legion was then placed under the 118th Jäger Division and the 369th Infantry Division of the Wehrmacht, stationed in the zone of Mostar. Here, surveillance of the Mostar-Dubrovnik railway line was added to the counter-insurgency activity.[37] The reports of the Republican Army General Staff show that the legionnaires still had high morale and a strong combat capability.

This situation, however, was in danger of falling apart at any time because the soldiers wanted to return to Italy and fight against the British and Americans.

> The legionaries of the 49th Legion today have only one desire: "To revise their families and return to the orders of the DUCE to fight in their homeland the hated invader".[38]

The German Commands never granted this request, of course: the German Armed Forces had no intention of depriving themselves of such a precious and expert unit in the struggle against the insurgents. In December 1944, the San Marco Legion returned to the dependency of the 118th German Jäger Division, following its fate until the end of the war. In fact, the blackshirts surrendered to the Allies in May 1945, when they were at the gates of Trieste.[39]

For what regards the National Republican Army units engaged in the total war against the Allies, the largest Fascist presence was on the Eastern front and the French front. In November 1944 there were 3,000 Republican Army soldiers present on the Eastern front. The units deployed there included the *IX Settembre* Battalion under the *Brandenburg* Division. At the end of a long cycle of anti-partisan fighting in Italy, the unit was transferred to Prussia and used in defending the stronghold of Angerburg from late November 1944 to January 1945.[40] In addition to the *IX Settembre* Battalion, we should cite the *Gruppo Arditi Camionettisti Italiani*/Italian Light Lorry Group made up of the survivors of the *Reggimento Giovani Fascisti*/Young Fascists Regiment.[41] Inserted in the 2nd *Fallschirmjäger* Division,[42] it received German uniforms and weaponry and had Italian SPA 42 light lorries equipped with Breda 35 and 20/65 machine guns. In November 1943, the Young Fascists arrived on the Russian front, in the zone of Zhytomyr. Their baptism by fire came at the end of the month, 40 kilometres from Kiev.[43] From December 1943 to February 1944, the Light Lorry Group took part in regular combat, defensive operations and counterattacks in the Pervomaisk area against Mongol and Tatar units.[44]

> Every day, the company of which we were part narrowed more and more, because we were counterattacked by the Tartar and Mongol patrols equipped with light rifles and fast horses.[45]

The fighting continued at Olshanka, Yuzefpol and Chausovo. The 2nd Fallschirmjäger Division and the Young Fascists then fell back into the bend of the Dniester River. The clashes continued also in the localities of Duschka and Onizkan. The retreat ended only when the Light Lorry Group arrived in Romania.[46]

The Russians were able to enter Romania and had already expanded a bridgehead on this side of the river Prut. My combat unit, with the help of aviation and an Armored Division, counterattacked the Russian's bridgehead. It was a tough battle, with five assaults to get the bridgehead over the river and destroy the bridges with explosive.[47]

Soon after the Normandy landing, the 2nd Fallschirmjäger Division and the Young Fascists were sent to France. The first combat against the Allies took place at Carhaix, Landerneau and on the Monts d'Arrée. As a result of the Allied pressure, the paratroops and the Young Fascists retreated to the fortress city of Brest, participating in clashes in the localities in the vicinity of the stronghold (Gouesnou, Guipavas and Plouzané-Bohars).[48]

With the Anglo-American invasion, Brest remained cut off from the German retreating to Paris. Therefore, we had to defend this place like strategic stronghold. At Brest, the combat unit of which I was part of, was reinforced by young volunteers from the Hitler-Jugen, which was named *"Ganze" Companie*. Our task was to work in the night behind the American lines. In late September, as usual, we went out for our night raids. On that occasion, we had a tremendous hand to hand combat against Americans. We suffered losses but managed to disengage and return to our base.[49]

The fighting later continued inside Brest itself: the Young Fascists fought the Allied advance in the quarters of Saint-Pierre, Recouvrance, Borgueu, Bellevue and Quéliverzan. On 20 September 1944, the stronghold of Brest surrendered and with it also the Republican Army Unit.

There was a greater number of National Republican Army units that waged total war against the British and Americans in France. In November 1944, approximately 60,000 soldiers were present: 20,000 combatants and 40,000 auxiliaries.[50] Part of these men, on 6 June 1944, faced the Allied troops in Normandy. Light Lorry Units were present in the Wehrmacht's 716th Infantry Division. Light Infantry Machine Gunners units were added to the 716th Division as well. Army Artillerymen were also included in the German's 1261st Artillery Regiment and in the 4th Battery of the Fort du Marcouf, near Utah Beach.[51] Other Italian soldiers were included in the German 1261st, 1262nd and 1707th Artillery Regiments which, between 19 and 27 June 1944, were almost totally annihilated in their attempt to block the advance of the American tanks at Montebourg.[52]

Republic Army Units – specifically of the Republican National Guard – were also present in the South of France and found themselves opposing the advance of the Allies and the French partisans following the landing in Provence. This was the case of the Republican National Guard's *Nizza* Battalion. Under the German command of the Nice Sicherheitsdienst and of the local Feldkommandantur, on 18 August 1944 it came under the 8th Reserve

Grenadier Regiment and, starting on 23 August, participated first in the clashes around Nice and later fought in the city centre. The most significant battles took place between 24 and 27 August 1944 at the Hermitage, the Avenue Notre Dame, Place Masséna, the Casino Municipal, the Vieille Ville, Place Gambetta, the Lycée Musical, the Esplanade of the Gare du Sud and between the Avenue de la Victoire and the Avenue Thiers. Only on 28 August, at 8:30 p.m., did the survivors of the Fascist Battalion and of the 8th Grenadier Regiment abandon Nice, reaching Menton.[53]

Combat units of the Republican Navy and Air Force were also present abroad. In the case of the National Republican Navy,[54] the largest units were located in France and Germany. After 8 September 1943, the point of reference was *Betasom*, the Italian Atlantic submarine base at Bordeaux.[55] Admiral Enzo Grossi[56] tried to rally around himself all the naval personnel possible: the detached Navy units in Danzig and Gdynia, the Smokescreen Battalions in the Baltic, the Autonomous Companies of Zeitz and Pillau.[57] Part of *Betasom*'s sailors constituted the *Volontari di Francia*/Volunteers of France Company[58] – later inserted in the *Fulmine* Marine Battalion of the *Decima MAS* – while the majority were included in the 1st Marine Atlantic Division whose task was to defend Bordeaux and other German strongholds.[59] The seagoing personnel instead became part of the 4th Vorposten-Flottille/Exploration and Surveillance Flotilla of the Kriegsmarine, operating in the section of the French coast between Arcachon and Brest.[60] In August 1944, following the landing in Normandy, the Republican Navy units of the *Betasom* base found themselves surrounded. Together with the German units, however, they succeeded in forcing their way through the Anglo-American lines, retreating first to Germany and later to Italy. The gunners of the Republican Navy were instead included in the coastal batteries, both along the English Channel and in other French strongholds. At Bordeaux, for example, the Italians were responsible for six of the batteries at the mouth of the Gironde.[61] Other German strongholds where Italian Artillerymen were present were Brest, La Rochelle, Saint-Nazaire, Lorient, Ouessant, Guernsey, Jersey and Toulon. A special case is that of the Italian sailors detached to the batteries on Cézembre. This fortified island, located just off Saint-Malo, is 500 metres long and a little over 250 metres wide. On this "rock", bunkers were built and artillery pieces positioned. The Allied siege began on the first days of August 1944 with heavy shelling. On 17 August, Saint-Malo surrendered, but the installations on the island continued to resist. The Allies responded by bombing the Italo-German positions with napalm. On 28 August, however, the guns on the island opened fire on the Anglo-American positions again. Two days later, 265 bombers dropped thousands of armour-piercing bombs and barrels of napalm on Cézembre. Overall, in a month of bombardments, over 120,000 tonnes of bombs fell on the island. The German admiral, commander of the installation, did not issue the surrender order until 1 September 1944. The soldiers coming out of the bunkers included 69 Italian Republican sailors.[62]

It should also be mentioned that the fighting units of the National Republican Navy included the personnel of a squadron of five CB midget submarines that continued to operate in the waters of the Black Sea against Russian shipping. The CB Squadron only abandoned the port of Constanța on 25 August 1944, when the Russians were on the outskirts of the city.[63]

The National Republican Air Force also had units deployed abroad in 1944. The biggest two were the *Terracciano* Air Transport Group and the *Trabucchi* Air Transport Group.[64] The *Terracciano* Group, under the command of Major Egidio Pellizzari, was composed of three squadrons and equipped with SM 79 and Junker 52 planes. The *Trabucchi* Air Transport Group, commanded by Major Alfredo Zanardi, was comprised of only two squadrons and was equipped with SM 82s. In 1944, both groups had occasion to operate in Germany, Finland, Karelia, Czechoslovakia, Prussia, Lithuania, Latvia, Estonia, White Russia, Pomerania and Silesia.

Duce, from the sky of the eastern front and Finland, returning at home the airmen of the "Terracciano" Group, always ready to execute all your orders, now more than ever, certain of victory that will give our Italy peace and greatness.[65]

The task entrusted to the Italians was to resupply the German units and transfer reinforcement troops to the zones of the front where particularly critical situations had been created. Numerous Italian crews, for their activity, received decorations and promotions both from the Italian and the German Military Authorities.

A crew member of a multi-engine aircraft, a volunteer on the Eastern front in the first Aerotrasport Group, he always carried out long and numerous War actions under the overwhelming enemy offense, always demonstrating expertise, courage and firmness of mind. In particularly critical circumstances, with aircraft struck in several parts, he saved flying material and cargo, a constant example in the perfection of discipline and obedience to duty and sacrifice, for the ideal of a reborn homeland.[66]

In the autumn of 1944, the units were demobilized on account of the wear on the planes, and the personnel, upon returning to Italy, formed the Anti-Paratroop Battalions to operate against the partisans.[67]

## The last months of war of the *RSI* units abroad

In 1945, notwithstanding the gradual retreat of the Germany Army on all fronts, hundreds of thousands of Italian soldiers were still operating abroad. Most of the available information regards the units of the National Republican Army. In March 1945, there were 131,000 soldiers outside the national borders: 85,000 in Germany, 45,000 in the Balkans and 600 on the Western front.[68] In April 1945, the number of Army personnel increased slightly (133,000) after sending to Germany a contingent for the German anti-aircraft artillery and the "discovery" of an Italian combat unit of 450 men that had been operating on the Russian front since 8 September 1943.[69]

In 1945, however, units belonging to other components of the *RSI*'s Armed Forces were also present abroad. In January, for example, a contingent of airmen of the National Republican Air Force was located in Hungary.[70] Parts of the Republican Navy operated in support of the German 20th Flak Division, while various specialized units of the Armed Forces carried out convey escort activities in the territories of the Reich.[71] In Bulgaria, airmen of the Air Force fought with the 4th Luftwaffe Regiment.[72] Finally, there were the smokescreen units which, on the one hand, used their chemical equipment to defend the Reich's industries from Allied air incursions and on the other fought as infantry against the Russian advance.

> Republican Army soldiers on the Baltic front: during a violent action in a stronghold of East Prussia, a combat unit of the *Mussolini* Smokescreen Battalion, after having performed the task in its own specialties, participated, with weapons in hand, to the furious fighting that inflicted heavy losses to the Bolshevik formations.[73]

In 1945, the Smokescreen Battalions were deployed in Wilhelmshaven (North Sea), Swinemünde (islands of Usedom and Wollin), Heydebreck and Zeitz (in the vicinity of Leipzig).[74]

> I didn't know either that I would spend the night of the Epiphany of 1945 at Wilhelmshaven, on the North Sea. Not that – in the night between 16 and 17 January 1945 – I would be able to see in action – in a sea of flames – the Republican smokescreen troops deployed in Zeitz while they defended the vital installations located there for the production of synthetic petrol – so essential for the new fighter planes – from a devastating attack by English bombers.[75]

The combat units of the *RSI* abroad continued to fight on all fronts against the Allies and the partisans until April–May 1945. In large part, they failed in returning to Italy, so their surrender took place abroad. The units present in Germany surrendered to the Russians or the Anglo-Americans. The battalions of Blackshirts retreating from the Balkans – which fought the Russian advance to the end and suffered partisan attacks – surrendered to Soviet troops in Austria, Slovenia and Croatia. On 3 May 1945, the 1st Smokescreen Battalion of Swinemünde surrendered "amid the red glare of the fires and the blasts of the explosions, after having held its positions for months against the tide of Bolshevik hordes and helped save tens of thousands of refugees".[76] Among the last *RSI* combat units to surrender to the Allies on the European front were the soldiers who still occupied the islands of the English Channel, the French fortress towns[77] and the islands of the Dodecanese and the eastern Mediterranean.[78] Between 11 and 12 May 1945, for example, the *Italienisches* Regiment of Rhodes surrendered,[79] followed by the *Italienische Freiwillige* Legion of Crete.[80]

In 1945, the Italian Social Republic's Units abroad were not limited only to Europe, however; combat units of the Navy were still operating in the Far East. After 8 September 1943 and the proclamation of the armistice, 90% of Italian military personnel in the Fast East chose to swear allegiance to the Italian Social Republic. The Italian units present in Shanghai, Singapore, Malaysia and Japan joined.[81] On 8 September 1943, a contingent of 300 marines of the *San Marco* Marine Regiment found themselves at the historic Italian colony of Tien-Tsin (Tianjin). The marines, initially captured and imprisoned by the Japanese, later adhered in large part to the *RSI* and were freed and freshly armed.[82] The units in the Far East followed the military events of Japan and participated in the hostilities until September 1945. When Japan, too, surrendered to the Allies, the Italians were captured by the Americans and held in a concentration camp until January 1947.[83]

One very peculiar situation is that of the Italian submarines which found themselves operating or in port in the Far East.[84] There were three vessels overall, the *Torelli*, the *Cappellini* and the *Giuliani*.

After no less than four years of service at *Betasom*, on 25 June 1943 I embarked for a particular mission on the submarine *Torelli*. The *Torelli* arrived in Sumatra on 26 August 1943. A few days later the crew was surrounded by the Japanese, who carried rifles with fixed bayonets! In Italy, the King had accepted unconditional surrender. In the confusion caused by this shameful betrayal, the officers decided to obey the King and to sink their vessels. The crews rose up, however, and prevented the order from being carried out.[85]

The submarines passed under the control of the Far East U-Boat Command and received new names. They were manned by mixed Italian and German crews. When Germany capitulated, the submarines and the military personnel joined the Japanese Navy and continued to operate in the Far East until September 1945.[86]

## The Battle of Berlin and the Twilight of the Gods

This narration of the events of the project for a "New European Order" of the *RSI* and of the total and irregular warfare fought by the Fascists abroad can only conclude with the role played by the Italians before and during the Battle of Berlin. The Reich's capital wasn't simply a city: in 1945, Berlin incarnated all the "ideals" of the project for a New European Order.[87] Thus, when it appeared clear that all had now been lost, thousands – especially among the European volunteers of the Waffen-SS – rushed to the defence of the German capital to fight that last battle, an appointment that those who had believed in the project for a New European Order could not miss.[88] It was the *Götterdäm-merung*, the "Twilight of the Gods," where the sun would set on the project for a Europe united under Nazism and Fascism.[89]

The thousands of soldiers who found themselves in Berlin in 1945 also included Italians. For these soldiers, the Fascist governmental apparatus of reference was constituted by the Italian Military Mission in Germany.[90] First under the command of General Emilio Canevari and later of General Umberto Morera, the Military Mission was active in Berlin starting on 18 October 1943. Morera and his subordinates left Berlin on 10 April 1945 and headed towards Graz, where they surrendered to French colonial troops on 7 May 1945.[91] The Mission's main responsibilities were:

1  Repatriating sick Italian soldiers;
2  Recruiting reserves;
3  Attending to soldiers and units incorporated into the Wehrmacht;
4  Following the training of the Italian troop formations;
5  Attending to combat units of the *RSI* that were operating abroad; and
6  Attending to military internees, workers and the fallen.[92]

The Italian military personnel in Berlin were impacted both directly and indirectly by the advancing Russian front, on the one hand, and the Allied air offensive on the other. On one side, the Italians were witnesses to the steady flow of refugees arriving from the east who described the unstoppable Russian advance:

> We learn about the climate and the news brought by the refugees coming from the east.
> Streams of heavily swaddled women, waiting immobile in the snow and mud for the distribution of water from hydrants and fountains. They told of hordes of Kazakhs and Kyrgyz that, led by Chuikov, were literally engulfing all resistance.[93]

Between January and April 1945, the *RSI* combatants present in Berlin were subject to the full force of the Allied air offensive. The bombardments of 3 and 26 February 1945 left an indelible mark in the Italians' memories:

> On 26 February there was a repeat of 3 February. The US bombers unleashed an even more devastating attack but we couldn't have cared less! We were happy as clams because for the moment the Bolshevik offensive had been stopped. It was a rather strange happiness, to tell the truth, because we knew very well that – despite the fiery incitements to resist by the German authorities – the flood tide of the Red Army, combined with the rain of fire of the US bombers, would soon overwhelm us.[94]

The Italian soldiers present in Berlin had occasion to watch as defence systems were slowly readied in the streets and squares to block the Russian offensive. Every day in the German capital, new anti-tank ditches, new artillery positions and new machine-gun nests could be seen.

> The city was preparing for defence against the last assault of the Red Army: anti-tank trenches, mines, barricades, barbed wire entanglements and machine-guns appeared in ever greater numbers, but without succeeding in giving the people confidence.[95]

In those weeks in Berlin, as the members of the Military Mission recall, is was mainly the middle-aged members of the Volksturm militia and the youths of the Hitlerjugend who were hard at work on completing the defensive system.

> Middle-aged Volksturm members, equipped with anti-tank weapons and shovels, toiled away at raising barricades and obstacles: there was no lack of material among the ruins, scrap metal, and shattered buses and trams. The 14-year-olds of the Hitlerjugend pitched in with determination and maturity, while the engineers of the Wehrmacht buried heavy tanks at the most important intersections in craters dug out by the bombs, leaving only their turrets and cannons showing.[96]

As stated earlier, in the month of January in Berlin, in addition to the Italian Mission, thousands of Italian soldiers of the Italian Social Republic were present and continued to fight under the German Armed Forces:

> Now I was there, in Berlin, with my red insignia with the lions of San Marco and the Republican gladii, not far from Stalin's armies and with very slim odds of returning home.[97]

A large part of the soldiers who found themselves in Berlin in April 1945 came from either the Russian front or the Western front. These were small Combat Units or individuals who, since 8 September 1943, had chosen to continue to fight under the command of the German Army. Between the autumn and winter of 1944, these soldiers consisted in large part of a training brigade. In February 1945, still deployed in Germany, the unit had an overall strength of 1,569 men.[98]

> The personnel come from a variety of places and it happens in the Brigade that a legionary who has fought in the Balkans until a short time before finds himself rubbing shoulders with a soldier from Greece who had passed over to the rebels after 8 September and then to the Germans and finally to work in Germany.[99]

Thus, on the eve of the Battle of Berlin, there were thousands of Italians in the Reich's capital. If, on the one hand, there were many doing everything possible to try to return to Italy, on the other there were still many "believers" who pursued the chimera of the New European Order and wanted to fight the last battle alongside the old ally.

Officially, the last convoy of Italian soldiers left Berlin on 10 April 1945.

> We stayed at our post until 10 April 1945, when the order arrived from Italy to retreat, just when the Red Army was beginning its preparations to totally surround the stronghold.[100]

Not all the soldiers returned to Italy, however; a number which is hard to quantify chose to join the German combat units, in particular the European volunteers of the Waffen-SS, and elicited great admiration among the Italians present in Berlin, increasing the desire to participate in the defence of the Reich's capital:

> The soldiers of the *RSI* look on perplexed at the magnificent vanguards of the SS units of the foreign volunteers that begin to flow into the city to prepare its defence. Some of the *RSI* soldiers would like to be among them and participate in the imminent defence of the last European bastion against Bolshevism. It would have been glorious and exciting indeed for the young soldiers to tear off their insignia and join up with one of the many foreign units, for example with the SS of the French Charlemagne Division, who begin to stream in and make ready for combat.[101]

Today, in fact, through a number of memoires of survivors of the Battle of Berlin, we know that there were also Italian soldiers of the *RSI* defending the smoking ruins, streets and metropolitan of the Reich's capital.

### Conclusion

After 8 September 1943, there were always thousands of Italians soldiers who still believed in the values of Fascism, of Nazism and in the creation of a "New European Order". Italian soldiers to realize this project also chose to stay to fight abroad and to participate, finally, in the Battle of Berlin.

At the end of the Second World War, Fascism and Nazism were defeated. For the "believers" and "fighters" who chose to follow the Italian Social Republic, this has led to not recognizing the new Italian Republic and the new Europe based on values opposed to Fascism. Even today, in fact, the survivors of the Italian Social Republic consider themselves as "exiles in the homeland".

From a military point of view, the participation of the *RSI* Combat Units in the war abroad could not have changed the course of the conflict. Some significant results were achieved, but none of them definitive. The limits of the action, on one hand, must be sought in the supervision of the German commands and, on the other, in the material and human limits of the Social Republic.

A substantial part of these soldiers continued to fight with the illusion of a final victory and hoped to build the "New European Order". Without a shadow of a doubt, the most tangible result of the participation of the Italian Social Republic in the regular and irregular war abroad is the exponential increase in the level of violence. This "globalization" of violence allows us to affirm that *RSI* wanted to try to play a leading role in the final phase of the Second World War and that, for the Italian Social Republic, the Second World War, under the ideological profile, was perceived and had all the characteristics of a European civil war.

## Notes

1 Elena Aga Rossi, *Una nazione allo sbando. L'armistizio italiano del settembre 1943 e le sue consequenze* (Bologna: Il Mulino, 2003); Melton Davis, *Chi difende Roma? I quarantacinque giorni: 25 luglio-8 settembre 1943* (Milan: Rizzoli, 1973).

2 For more information: Giorgio Bocca, *La repubblica di Mussolini* (Milan: Mondadori, 2004); Roberto Chiarini, *L'ultimo fascismo. Storia e memoria della repubblica di Salò* (Venice: Marsilio, 2000); Fredrick Willian Deakin, *La brutale amicizia. Mussolini, Hitler e la caduta del fascismo italiano* (Turin: Einaudi, 1990); Renzo De Felice, *Mussolini l'alleato. La guerra civile 1943–1945* (Turin: Einaudi, 1997); Luigi Ganapini, *La repubblica delle camicie nere* (Milan: Garzanti, 1999); Francesco Germinario, *L'altra memoria. L'estrema destra, Salò e la Resistenza* (Turin: Bollati Boringhieri, 1999); Frank Joseph, *Mussolini's War: Fascist Italy's Military Struggles from Africa and Western Europe to the Mediterranean and Soviet Union 1935–1945* (England: Helion & Company, 2009); Aurelio Lepre, *La storia della Repubblica di Mussolini. Salò, il tempo dell'odio e della violenza* (Milan: Mondadori, 1999); Gianni Oliva, *La Repubblica di Salò* (Florence: Giunti, 1997); Gianni Oliva, *Le tre Italie del 1943. Chi ha veramente combattuto la guerra civile* (Milan: Mondadori, 2004); Gianni Oliva, *L'Italia del silenzio. 8 settembre 1943: storia del paese che non ha fatto i conti con il proprio passato* (Milan: Mondadori, 2013); Amedeo Osti Guerrazzi, *La Repubblica sociale italiana* (Milan: Unicopli, 2008); Claudio Pavone, *Una guerra civile. Saggio storico sulla moralità della Resistenza* (Turin: Bollati Boringhieri, 1994); Wolfgang Schivelbush, *La cultura dei vinti* (Bologna: Il Mulino, 2014); Marco Tarchi, *Esuli in patria* (Parma: U. Guanda, 1995).

3 For more information: Silvio Bertoldi, *Il regno del Sud* (Milan: BUR, 2003); Agostino Degli Espinosa, *Il Regno del Sud* (Rome: Editori Riuniti, 1973).

4 For more information: Jonathan Adelman, ed., *Hitler and his allies in World War II* (Oxon: Routledge, 2007); Enzo Collotti, *L'Europa nazista. Il progetto di un nuovo ordine europeo (1939–1945)* (Florence: Giunti, 2002), 407–41; Gustavo Corni, *Il sogno del 'grande spazio'. Le politiche d'occupazione nell'Europa nazista* (Bari: Laterza, 2005); Salvatore De Carlo, *Europa Inquieta* (Rome: XX Secolo, 1942); Mario Luciolli, *Mussolini e l'Europa. La politica estera fascista* (Florence: Le Lettere, 2010); Matteo Pretelli, *Il fascismo e gli italiani all'estero* (Bologna: Clueb, 2010); Davide Rodogno, *Il nuovo ordine mediterraneo. Le politiche di occupazione dell'Italia fascista in Europa (1940–1943)* (Turin: Bollati Boringhieri, 2003); Renzo Santinon, *I fasci italiani all'estero* (Rome: Settimo Sigillo, 1991).

5 Gerhard Schreiber, *I militari italiani nei campi di concentramento del Terzo Reich* (Rome: Ufficio Storico Stato Maggiore Esercito, 1992).

6 For more information: Jürgen Charnitzky, *Fascismo e scuola. La politica scolastica del regime 1922–1943* (Roma: La Nuova Italia, 1999); Renzo De Felice, *Mussolini il duce. Lo stato*

*totalitario 1936–1940* (Turin: Einaudi, 1981); Ganapini, *La repubblica delle camicie nere*; Antonio Gibelli, *Il popolo bambino. Infanzia e nazione dalla grande guerra a Salò* (Torino: Einaudi, 2005); Oliva, *Le tre Italie del 1943. Chi ha veramente combattuto la guerra civile*; Ivan Tognarini, *Il vecchio libro. La scuola del ventennio fascista: Balilla e piccole italiane, soldati e massaie* (Torino: Polistampa, 2009); George L.Williams, *Fascist Thought and Totalitarianism in Italy's Secondary Schools: Theory and Practise, 1922–1943* (New York: Peter Lang, 1994).

7    C., interview.

8    Pavone, *Una guerra civile.*

9    Federico Ciavattone, "La memoria della guerra civile nei reduci della R.S.I." (M.A. diss., Pisa: University of Pisa, 2005).

10    B., interview.

11    Ciavattone, "La memoria della guerra civile nei reduci della R.S.I."

12    F., interview.

13    B., interview.

14    Ganapini, *La Repubblica delle camicie nere.*

15    Federico Ciavattone, *The Italian Social Republic, the Second World War and the Memory of the "Vanquished"*; Pavone, *Una guerra civile.*

16    B., interview.

17    Ciavattone, "La memoria della guerra civile nei reduci della R.S.I."

18    Ciavattone, "La memoria della guerra civile nei reduci della R.S.I.," 110.

19    Archivio Ufficio Storico Stato Maggiore Esercito (hereafter, AUSSME), Fondo Repubblica Sociale Italiana (RSI) I-1, Busta (B) 44, "Reparti autonomi dislocati fuori del teatro operativo nazionale" (June-July-August-September-October-November-December 1944, January-February-March-April 1945).

20    Serafino Mazzolini was a volunteer in the First World War; he participated in the March on Rome and was a member of the XXVII Italian legislature. In 1928, he joined the Ministry of Foreign Affairs. He holds diplomatic assignments in Brazil, Montevideo (here he was appointed Minister) and Jerusalem. At the outbreak of World War II, he was appointed, first, Plenipotentiary of Egypt and, later, Governor of Montenegro. After 8 September 1943, he joined the Italian Social Republic and then on 31 July in 1944, he was elevated to the rank of Ambassador. He died of natural causes on 23 February 1945. For more information: Gianni Scipione Rossi, *Mussolini e il diplomatico. La vita ed i diari di Serafino Mazzolini, un diplomatico a Salò* (Catanzaro: Rubbettino, 2007).

21    Filippo Anfuso began his diplomatic career in 1925. He held diplomatic positions in Munich, Budapest, Berlin and China, and in 1937 he was appointed Chief of Staff of the Ministry of Foreign Affairs and received his appointment as Plenipotentiary. After the armistice, on 13 November 1943, he became Ambassador to Berlin. On 15 March 1945, following the death of Mazzolini, he was appointed Undersegretary Ministry of Foreign Affairs of the Italian Social Republic. For more information: Filippo Anfuso, *Roma, Berlino, Salò (1936–1945)* (Milan: Garzanti, 1950).

22    Marino Viganò, *Il Ministero degli Affari Esteri e le relazioni internazionali della Repubblica Sociale italiana 1943–1945* (Milan: Edizioni Universitarie Jaca, 1991), 82–206.

23    Ibid., 207–72.

24    Ibid., 297–329.

25    Ibid., 341–430.

26    Nino Arena, *Forze Armate della Repubblica Sociale. La Guerra in Italia 1943* (Parma: Albertelli, 1999), 181–293.

27    AUSSME, Fondo RSI I-1, B. 44, "Reparti autonomi dislocati fuori del teatro operativo nazionale" (June-July-August 1944).

28    AUSSME, Fondo RSI I-1, B. 44, "Reparti autonomi dislocati fuori del teatro operativo nazionale" (December 1944).

29    Elena Aga Rossi and Maria Teresa Giusti, *Una guerra a parte. I militari italiani nei Balcani 1940–1945* (Bologna: Il Mulino, 2011), 89–128.

30  AUSSME, Fondo RSI I-1, B. 44, "Reparti autonomi dislocati fuori del teatro operativo nazionale" (November 1944).

31  Archivio Centrale dello Stato (hereafter ACS), Fondo Repubblica Sociale Italiana (RSI), Guardia Nazionale Repubblicana (GNR), Diari Storici (DS), "Legione d'Assalto San Marco" (September 1943).

32  Ettore Lucas and Giorgio De Vecchi, *Storia delle unità combattenti della Milizia sicurezza nazionale 1923–1943* (Rome: Volpe, 1976); Stato Maggiore Esercito, ed., *Le operazioni delle unità italiane in Jugoslavia 1941–1943* (Roma: Ufficio Storico Stato Maggiore Esercito, 1978).

33  ACS, Fondo RSI, GNR, DS, "Legione d'Assalto San Marco" (September 1943).

34  Ibid.

35  ACS, Fondo RSI, GNR, DS, "Legione d'Assalto San Marco" (October 1943–February 1944).

36  AUSSME, Fondo RSI I-1, B. 13, "Promemoria del Centurione Toscani Domenico, Legione CC.NN. d'assalto San Marco" (23rd February 1944), 1.

37  ACS, Fondo RSI, GNR, DS, "Legione d'Assalto San Marco" (December 1944).

38  AUSSME, Fondo RSI I-1, B. 13, "Promemoria del Centurione Toscani Domenico, Legione CC.NN. d'assalto San Marco" (23rd February 1944), 3.

39  Gianni Scipione Rossi, *Mussolini e il diplomatico. La vita ed i diari di Serafino Mazzolini, un diplomatico a Salò* (Catanzaro: Rubbettino, 2007), 167–82.

40  Andrea Di Nicola, *Da Tolone a Vittorio Veneto. Storia del I Battaglione M "IX Settembre"* (Chieti: Marino Solfanelli Editore, 1995), 163–9.

41  Antonio Cioci, *Il Reggimento giovani fascisti nella Campagna dell'Africa Settentrionale 1941–1943* (Parma: Albertelli, 1998).

42  Willi Kammann, *Der Weg der 2. Fallschirmjägerdivision* (München: Schild Verlag GmbH, 1998).

43  Antonio Cioci and Daniele Guglielmi, "I volontari italiani nella 2. Fallschirmjäger Division," *Storia & Battaglie*, no. 9 (September 2002): 21–5.

44  Arena, *Forze Armate della Repubblica Sociale*, 220.

45  Author's private archive, "Memoriale P. E.," undated, 2.

46  Arena, *Forze Armate della Repubblica Sociale*, 225.

47  Author's private archive, "Memoriale P. E.," 3.

48  Cioci and Guglielmi, "I volontari italiani nella 2. Fallschirmjäger Division," 25.

49  Author's private archive, "Memoriale P. E.," 5.

50  AUSSME, Fondo RSI I-1, B. 44, "Reparti autonomi dislocati fuori del teatro operativo italiano" (November 1944).

51  "Contro lo Shaef in Normandia," *Acta*, no. 1 (January–March 2008): 6–7.

52  Flavio Russo and Roberto Di Rosa, *Festung Europa. 6 giugno 1944* (Rome: Ufficio Storico Stato Maggiore Esercito, 1994); "1943–45: anche reparti della RSI presidiano la Francia," *Acta*, no. 1 (January–March 1992): 14–15.

53  Federico Ciavattone, "La Guardia nazionale repubblicana nella difesa di Nizza," *Storia & Battaglie*, no. 11 (November 2012): 25–30.

54  Enrico Cernuschi, "La Marina Repubblicana 1943–1945," *Storia Militare*, no. 188–189 (June 2009): 41–61.

55  For More information: Erminio Bagnasco, *In guerra sul mare. Navi e marinai italiani nel secondo conflitto mondiale* (Genova: Storia Militare, 2012); Erminio Bagnasco and Maurizio Brescia, *I sommergibili italiani 1940–1943* (Genova: Storia Militare, 2013); Athos Fraternale, *Il "moschettiere" dell'Atlantico* (Massa: Edizioni Sarasota, 2009); Mario Leoni, *Il sommergibile Malaspina è rientrato a Betasom. Le avventure del Comandante Leoni sul smg. Malaspina e il c.t. Malocello* (Marina di Carrara: Tipografia CRD, 2007); Francesco Mattesini, *La Marina e l'8 settembre* (Rome: Ufficio Storico Marina Militare, 2002); Ubaldino Mori Ubaldini, *I sommergibili negli oceani* (Roma: Ufficio Storico Marina Militare, 2002).

56  Enzo Grossi, *Dal "Barbarigo" a Dongo* (Pavia: Aurora Edizioni, 2001).

57   AUSSME, Fondo RSI I-1, B. 11, DS, "Comando II Battaglione Nebbiogeni" (1st September 1943–31st January 1944).

58   Bruna Pompei and Piero Delbello, eds., *Volontari di Francia. Da Bordeaux alla Venezia Giulia nella Xᵃ Mas per l'onore d'Italia 1943–1945* (Milan: Ritter, 2008); Andrea Vezzà, *I ragazzi di quai de bacalan. I "volontari di Francia" della Xᵃ MAS* (Milan: Ritter, 2012).

59   "Quegli irriducibili nell'isola-bunker che non volevano cedere agli Alleati." *Corriere della Sera*, 30 May 2004.

60   "1943–1945: anche reparti RSI presidiano la Francia," 14–15; "Marinai repubblicani all'estero," *Nuovo Fronte*, no. 1 (January 1992): 4.

61   "Quegli irriducibili nell'isola-bunker che non volevano cedere agli Alleati."

62   Francesco Maria Puddi, "L'isola che non voleva arrendersi," *Storia Militare*, no. 9 (September 2007): 25–8.

63   Form more information: René Greger, "I CB nel Mar Nero," *Storia Militare*, no. 21 (June 1995): 45–51; Pier Francesco Lupinacci, *Attività in Mar Nero e Lago Ladoga* (Rome: Ufficio Storico Marina Militare, 2003); Remo Paulon, "L'epopea dei sommergibili CB," *Nuovo Fronte*, no. 3 (March 2000): 12–16; Giorgio Pitacco, "MAS italiani in Mar Nero," *Storia Militare*, no. 41 (February 1997): 13–18.

64   Nino Arena, *L'Aeronautica Nazionale Repubblicana* (Parma: Albertelli, 1998), 130–8. For more information: Giancarlo Garello, *L'Aeronatica Nazionale Repubblica* (Genova: Storia Militare, 2015).

65   ACS, Ministero Forze Armate (MFFAA) RSI, Gabinetto, B. 1, "Lettera del Comandante del Gruppo Terracciano" (October 1944).

66   ACS, MFFAA RSI, Gabinetto, B. 1, "Concessione Medaglia di Bronzo al Valore al Tenente Pilota Foresti Romeo" (undated).

67   Grande, "Il Gruppo Terracciano," 25–31.

68   AUSSME, Fondo RSI I-1, B. 44, "Reparti Autonomi dislocati fuori dal teatro operativo italiano" (March 1945).

69   AUSSME, Fondo RSI I-1, B. 44, "Reparti Autonomi dislocati fuori dal teatro operativo italiano" (April 1945).

70   AUSSME, Fondo RSI I-1, B. 53, "Rimpatrio 1ᵃ Compagnia Aviazione Italiana" (2nd February 1945).

71   AUSSME, Fondo RSI I-1, B. 53, "Militari Italiani provenienti dalla Balcania in forza ad Unità Germaniche" (5th March 1945).

72   AUSSME, Fondo RSI I-1, B. 53, "Reparti composti da militari italiani in servizio nelle forze armate germaniche segnalati a questo ufficio dal 1 gennaio al 15 gennaio 1945" (23rd February 1945).

73   *La Domenica del Corriere* (18 April 1945).

74   AUSSME, Fondo RSI I-1, B. 44, "Reparti Autonomi dislocati fuori dal teatro operativo italiano" (April 1945).

75   Remo Zora, "Soldati della RSI Oltralpe," *Acta*, no. 6 (September–November 1991): 13.

76   "Battaglioni nebbiogeni della RSI," *Acta*, no. 3 (May–June 1993): 15.

77   Andrea Rossi, *Le guerre delle camicie nere. La milizia fascista dalla guerra mondiale alla guerra civile* (Pisa: BFS, 2004), 183–90; "I soldati italiani sui fronti esteri," *Acta*, no. 4 (July 1990): 14.

78   Peter Schenk, "Dodecaneso 1943–1945," *Storia Militare*, no. 90 (March 2001): 14–18; "I soldati italiani sui fronti esteri," 14.

79   ACS, Fondo RSI, Carteggio Ordinario (CO), B. 114, "Reggimento Rodi" (January 1945); "L'Italia a Rodi fino al maggio 1945," *Acta*, no. 5 (July–September 1993): 1–9.

80   ACS, Fondo RSI, CO, B. 114, "Reggimento Rodi" (January 1945); Rossi, *La guerra delle camicie nere*, 183–96; "La missione militare in germania," *Acta*, no. 1 (January–March 1990): 8; "L'Italia a Rodi fino al maggio 1945," 1–9.

81   Achille Rastelli, *Italiani a Shanghai. La Regia Marina in Estremo Oriente* (Milan: Mursia, 2011).

82 Luigi Fulvi, Tullio Marcon and Ottorino Miozzi, *Le fanterie di marina italiane* (Rome: Ufficio Storico Marina Militare, 1988); Luigi Fulvi, *Sotto le insegne del leone alato. I marinai dei Battaglioni "San Marco" nella guerra 1940–43* (Parma: Albertelli, 1990); F.F., "I trecento di Tien Tsin," *Nuovo Fronte*, no. 6 (June 1993): 4.

83 Yoshikawa Kazunori, "Dall'Italia al Giappone," *Nuovo Fronte*, no. 12 (December 2001): 13.

84 Achille Rastelli, *Sommergibili a Singapore. 1943: l'odissea di un marinaio friuliano* (Milan: Mursia, 2006).

85 "Il Giappone, e la RSI," *Acta*, no. 6 (September–November 2002): 7.

86 Ibid., 6–7.

87 For more information: Antony Beevor, *Berlino 1945. La caduta* (Milan: Rizzoli, 2003); Yves Durand, *Il nuovo ordine europeo. La collaborazione nell'Europa tedesca (1938–1945)* (Bologna: Il Mulino, 2002); Maria Luisa Gennaro, *La battaglia di Berlino* (Milan: De Vecchi Editore, 1974); MacGregor Knox, *Destino comune. Dittatura, politica estera e guerra nell'Italia fascista e nella Germania nazista* (Turin: Einaudi, 2000); Mark Mazower, *L'impero di Hitler. Come i nazisti governavano l'Europa occupata* (Milano: Mondadori, 2010); Wilhelm Willemer, *La difesa di berlino. Aprile-Maggio 1945* (Genova: Italia Storica, 2014).

88 For more information: Robert Forbes, *For Europe: The French Volunteers of the Waffen-SS* (Mechanicsburg, PA: Stackpole Books, 2010); Nicola Guerra, *I volontari italiani nelle Waffen-SS. Pensiero politico, formazione culturale e motivazioni al volotariato* (Chieti: Solfanelli, 2014); Eric Lefèvre, *Sturmbataillon "Charlemagne" a Berlino. I volontari francesi delle Waffen SS impegnati nell'ultima difesa del Reich* (Pavia: CDL Edizioni, 1997); Tony Le Tissier, *Charlemagne: The 33rd Waffen-Grenadier Division of the SS* (South Yorkshire: Pen & Sword, 2010).

89 Ulrich Völklein, *Bunker. Tra incubo e follia dagli archivi segreti del KGB le ultime ore di Hitler ed Eva Braun* (Alessandria: PIEMME, 1999).

90 ACS, Fondo RSI, Segreteria Particolare del Duce (SPD), Carteggio Riservato (CR), B. 22, "Missione Militare Italiana in Germania" (undated), 1–39.

91 Viganò, *Il ministero degli affari esteri e le relazioni internazionali della Repubblica Sociale Italiana 1943–1945.*

92 ACS, Fondo RSI, SPD, CR, B. 22, "Missione Militare Italiana in Germania," 1–39.

93 Remo Zora, "Berlino assediata e soldati della RSI," *Acta*, no. 6 (September–November 1997): 11.

94 Zora, "Soldati della RSI oltralpe," 15.

95 Ibid., 14.

96 Ibid.

97 Ibid., 15.

98 ACS, Fondo RSI, SPD, B. 22, "Brigata di riserva" (November 1944): 6.

99 ACS, Fondo RSI, SPD, B. 22, "Brigata complementi" (February 1945): 7.

100 Zora, "Soldati della RSI Oltralpe," 15.

101 Zora, "Berlino assediata e soldati della RSI," 13.

## Bibliography

"1943–45: anche reparti della RSI presidiano la Francia." *Acta*, no. 1 (January–March 1992): 14–15.

Adelman, Jonathan, ed. *Hitler and His Allies in World War II.* Oxon: Routledge, 2007.

Aga Rossi, Elena, and Giusti, Maria Teresa. *Una guerra a parte. I militari italiani nei Balcani 1940–1945.* Bologna: Il Mulino, 2011.

Aga Rossi, Elena. *Una nazione allo sbando. L'armistizio italiano del settembre 1943 e le sue conseguenze.* Bologna: Il Mulino, 2003.

Anfuso, Filippo. *Roma, Berlino, Salò (1936–1945).* Milan: Garzanti, 1950.

Arena, Nino. *L'Aeronautica Nazionale Repubblicana*. Parma: Albertelli, 1998.

Arena, Nino. *Forze Armate della Repubblica Sociale. La Guerra in Italia 1943*. Parma: Albertelli, 1999.

B. G. "*Mantova* Combat Group." Interview by the Author. May 2004. Audio.

B. R. "Wehrmacht Special Services." Interview by the Author. February 2002. Audio.

B. T. "1st Waffen-SS Division." Interview by the Author. June 2005. Audio.

Bagnasco, Erminio. *In guerra sul mare. Navi e marinai italiani nel secondo conflitto mondiale*. Genova: Storia Militare, 2012.

Bagnasco, Erminio, and Brescia, Maurizio. *I sommergibili italiani 1940–1943*. Genova: Storia Militare, 2013.

"Battaglioni nebbiogeni della RSI." *Acta*, no. 3 (May–June 1993): 15.

Beevor, Antony. *Berlino 1945. La caduta*. Milan: Rizzoli, 2003.

Benanti, Franco. *La guerra più lunga. Albania 1943–1948*. Milan: Mursia, 2003.

Bertoldi, Silvio. *Il Regno del Sud*. Milan: BUR, 2003.

Bocca, Giorgio. *La repubblica di Mussolini*. Milan: Mondadori, 2004.

C. P. "Italian Waffen-SS." Interview by the Author. May 2001. Audio.

Cernuschi, Enrico. "La Marina Repubblicana 1943–1945." *Storia Militare*, no. 188–189 (June 2009): 41–61.

Charnitzky, Jürgen. *Fascismo e scuola. La politica scolastica del regime 1922–1943*. Roma: La Nuova Italia, 1999.

Chiarini, Roberto. *L'ultimo fascismo. Storia e memoria della repubblica di Salò*. Venice: Marsilio, 2000.

Ciavattone, Federico. "La Guardia nazionale repubblicana nella difesa di Nizza." *Storia & Battaglie*, no. 11 (November 2012): 25–30.

Ciavattone, Federico. "La memoria della guerra civile nei reduci della R.S.I." M.A. diss., Pisa: University of Pisa, 2005.

Cioci, Antonio. *Il Reggimento giovani fascisti nella Campagna dell'Africa Settentrionale 1941–1943*. Parma: Albertelli, 1998.

Cioci, Antonio, and Daniele Guglielmi. "I volontari italiani nella 2. Fallschirmjäger Division." *Storia & Battaglie*, no. 9 (September 2002): 21–5.

Collotti, Enzo. *L'Europa nazista. Il progetto di un nuovo ordine europeo (1939–1945)*. Florence: Giunti, 2002.

"Contro lo Shaef in Normandia." *Acta*, no. 1 (January–March 2008): 6–7.

Corni, Gustavo. *Il sogno del "grande spazio". Le politiche d'occupazione nell'Europa nazista*. Bari: Laterza, 2005.

D'Auria, Francesco Paolo. *Einer von millionen. Ferdinand, la mascotte della Leibstandarte*. Milan: Mursia, 2011.

Davis, Melton. *Chi difende Roma? I quarantacinque giorni: 25 luglio–8 settembre 1943*. Milan: Rizzoli, 1973.

Deakin, Fredrick Willian. *La brutale amicizia. Mussolini, Hitler e la caduta del fascismo italiano*. Turin: Einaudi, 1990.

De Carlo, Salvatore. *Europa Inquieta*. Rome: XX Secolo, 1942.

De Felice, Renzo. *Mussolini l'alleato. La guerra civile 1943–1945*. Turin: Einaudi, 1997.

De Felice, Renzo. *Mussolini il duce. Lo stato totalitario 1936–1940*. Turin: Einaudi, 1981.

Degli Espinosa, Agostino. *Il Regno del Sud*. Rome: Editori Riuniti, 1973.

Di Nicola, Andrea. *Da Tolone a Vittorio Veneto. Storia del I Battaglione M "IX Settembre"*. Chieti: Marino Solfanelli Editore, 1995.

Durand, Yves. *Il nuovo ordine europeo. La collaborazione nell'Europa tedesca (1938–1945)*. Bologna: Il Mulino, 2002.

F. T. *"Benito Mussolini Bersaglieri* Battalion." Interview by the Author. March 2002. Audio.

Forbes, Robert. *For Europe: The French Volunteers of the Waffen-SS.* Mechanicsburg, PA: Stackpole Books, 2010.

Fraternale, Athos. *Il "moschettiere" dell'Atlantico.* Massa: Edizioni Sarasota, 2009.

Fulvi, Luigi. *Sotto le insegne del leone alato. I marinai dei Battaglioni "San Marco" nella guerra 1940–43.* Parma: Albertelli, 1990.

Fulvi, Luigi, Tullio Marcon, and Ottorino Miozzi. *Le fanterie di marina italiane.* Rome: Ufficio Storico Marina Militare, 1988.

Ganapini, Luigi. *La repubblica delle camicie nere.* Milan: Garzanti, 1999.

Garello, Giancarlo. *L'Aeronautica Nazionale Repubblicana.* Genova: Storia Militare, 2015.

Gennaro, Maria Luisa. *La Battaglia di Berlino.* Milan: De Vecchi Editore, 1974.

Germinario, Francesco. *L'altra memoria. L'estrema destra, Salò e la Resistenza.* Turin: Bollati Boringhieri, 1999.

"Il Giappone, e la RSI." *Acta,* no. 6 (September–November 2002): 7.

Gibelli, Antonio. *Il popolo bambino. Infanzia e nazione dalla grande guerra a Salò.* Torino: Einaudi, 2005.

Grande, Giuseppe. "Il Gruppo Terracciano." *Storia Militare,* no. 72 (September 1999): 25–31.

Greger, René. "I CB nel Mar Nero." *Storia Militare,* no. 21 (June 1995): 45–51.

Grossi, Enzo. *Dal "Barbarigo" a Dongo.* Pavia: Aurora Edizioni, 2001.

Guerra, Nicola. *I volontari italiani nelle Waffen-SS. Pensiero politico, formazione culturale e motivazioni al volotariato.* Chieti: Solfanelli, 2014.

"L'Italia a Rodi fino al maggio 1945." *Acta,* no. 5 (July–September 1993): 1–9.

Joseph, Frank. *Mussolini's war. Fascist Italy's Military Struggles from Africa and Western Europe to the Mediterranean and Soviet Union 1935–1945.* UK: Helion & Company, 2009.

Kammann, Willi. *Der Weg der 2. Fallschirmjägerdivision.* München: Schild Verlag GmbH, 1998.

Kazunori, Yoshikawa. "Dall'Italia al Giappone." *Nuovo Fronte,* no. 12 (December 2001): 13.

Knox, MacGregor. *Destino comune. Dittatura, politica estera e guerra nell'Italia fascista e nella Germania nazista.* Turin: Einaudi, 2000.

"La Missione Militare in Germania." *Acta,* no. 1 (January–March 1990): 8.

Lefèvre, Eric. *Sturmbataillon "Charlemagne" a Berlino. I volontari francesi delle Waffen SS impegnati nell'ultima difesa del Reich.* Pavia: CDL Edizioni, 1997.

Leoni, Mario. *Il sommergibile Malaspina è rientrato a Betasom. Le avventure del Comandante Leoni sul smg. Malaspina e il c.t. Malocello.* Marina di Carrara: Tipografia CRD, 2007.

Lepre, Aurelio. *La storia della Repubblica di Mussolini. Salò, il tempo dell'odio e della violenza.* Milan: Mondadori, 1999.

Le Tissier, Tony. *Charlemagne: The 33rd Waffen-Grenadier Division of the SS.* South Yorkshire: Pen & Sword, 2010.

Lucas, Ettore, and De Vecchi, Giorgio. *Storia delle unità combattenti della Milizia sicurezza nazionale 1923–1943.* Rome: Volpe, 1976.

Luciolli, Mario. *Mussolini e l'Europa. La politica estera fascista.* Florence: Le Lettere, 2010.

Lupinacci, Pier Francesco. *Attività in Mar Nero e Lago Ladoga.* Rome: Ufficio Storico Marina Militare, 2003.

"Marinai repubblicani all'estero." *Nuovo Fronte,* no. 1 (January 1992): 4.

Mattesini, Francesco. *La Marina e l'8 settembre.* Rome: Ufficio Storico Marina Militare, 2002.

Mazower, Mark. *L'impero di Hitler. Come i nazisti governavano l'Europa occupata.* Milano: Mondadori, 2010.

Mezzasoma, Anna. *Budapest Roma Salò. Emozio e ricordi 1933–1945.* Rome: Settimo Sigillo, 2003.

Mori Ubaldini, Ubaldino. *I sommergibili negli oceani.* Roma: Ufficio Storico Marina Militare, 2002.

Oliva, Gianni. *L'Italia del silenzio. 8 settembre 1943: storia del paese che non ha fatto i conti con il proprio passato.* Milan: Mondadori, 2013.

Oliva, Gianni. *La Repubblica di Salò.* Florence: Giunti, 1997.

Oliva, Gianni. *Le tre Italie del 1943. Chi ha veramente combattuto la guerra civile.* Milan: Mondadori, 2004.

Osti Guerrazzi, Amedeo. *La Repubblica sociale italiana.* Milan: Unicopli, 2008.

Paulon, Remo. "L'epopea dei sommergibili CB." *Nuovo Fronte,* no. 3 (March 2000): 12–16.

Pavone, Claudio. *Una guerra civile. Saggio storico sulla moralità della Resistenza.* Turin: Bollati Boringhieri, 1994.

Pitacco, Giorgio. "MAS italiani in Mar Nero." *Storia Militare,* no. 41 (February 1997): 13–18.

Pompei, Bruna, and Piero Delbello, eds. *Volontari di Francia. Da Bordeaux alla Venezia Giulia nella Xª Mas per l'onore d'Italia 1943–1945.* Milan: Ritter, 2008.

Pretelli, Matteo. *Il fascismo e gli italiani all'estero.* Bologna: Clueb, 2010.

Puddi, Francesco Maria. "L'isola che non voleva arrendersi." *Storia Militare,* no. 9 (September 2007): 25–8.

"Quegli irriducibili nell'isola-bunker che non volevano cedere agli Alleati." *Corriere della Sera,* May 30, 2004.

Quigley, Paul, and Hawdon James, eds. *Reconciliation after Civil Wars: Global Perspectives.* Oxon: Routledge, in press.

Rastelli, Achille. *Italiani a Shanghai. La Regia Marina in Estremo Oriente.* Milan: Mursia, 2011.

Rastelli, Achille. *Sommergibili a Singapore. 1943: l'odissea di un marinaio friulano.* Milan: Mursia, 2006.

Rodogno, Davide. *Il nuovo ordine mediterraneo. Le politiche di occupazione dell'Italia fascista in Europa (1940–1943).* Turin: Bollati Boringhieri, 2003.

Rossi, Andrea. *Le guerre delle camicie nere. La milizia fascista dalla guerra mondiale alla guerra civile.* Pisa: BFS, 2004.

Rossi, Gianni Scipione. *Mussolini e il diplomatico. La vita ed i diari di Serafino Mazzolini, un diplomatico a Salò.* Catanzaro: Rubbettino, 2007.

Russo, Flavio, and Roberto Di Rosa. *Festung Europa. 6 giugno 1944.* Rome: Ufficio Storico Stato Maggiore Esercito, 1994.

Santinon, Renzo. *I fasci italiani all'estero.* Rome: Settimo Sigillo, 1991.

Schenk, Peter. "Dodecaneso 1943–1945." *Storia Militare,* no. 90 (March 2001): 14–18.

Schivelbush, Wolfgang. *La cultura dei vinti.* Bologna: Il Mulino, 2014.

Schreiber, Gerhard. *I militari italiani nei campi di concentramento del Terzo Reich.* Rome: Ufficio Storico Stato Maggiore Esercito, 1992.

"I soldati italiani sui fronti esteri." *Acta,* no. 4 (July 1990): 14.

Stato Maggiore Esercito, ed. *Le operazioni delle unità italiane in Jugoslavia 1941–1943.* Roma: Ufficio Storico Stato Maggiore Esercito, 1978.

Tarchi, Marco. *Esuli in patria.* Parma: U. Guanda, 1995.

Tognarini, Ivan. *Il vecchio libro. La scuola del ventennio fascista: Balilla e piccole italiane, soldati e massaie.* Torino: Polistampa, 2009.

"I trecento di Tien Tsin." *Nuovo Fronte,* no. 6 (June 1993): 4.

Vezzà, Andrea. *I ragazzi di quai de bacalan. I "volontari di Francia" della Xª MAS.* Milan: Ritter, 2012.

Viganò, Marino. *Il Ministero degli Affari Esteri e le relazioni internazionali della Repubblica Sociale Italiana 1943–1945.* Milan: Edizioni Universitarie Jaca, 1991.

Völklein, Ulrich. *Bunker. Tra incubo e follia dagli archivi segreti del KGB le ultime ore di Hitler ed Eva Braun*. Alessandria: PIEMME, 1999.

Willemer, Wilhelm. *La difesa di Berlino. Aprile-Maggio 1945*. Genova: Italia Storica, 2014.

Williams, George L. *Fascist Thought and Totalitarianism in Italy's Secondary Schools: Theory and Practise, 1922–1943*. New York: Peter Lang, 1994.

Zora, Remo. "Berlino assediata e soldati della RSI." *Acta*, no. 6 (September–November 1997): 9–13.

Zora, Remo. "Soldati della RSI oltralpe." *Acta*, no. 6 (September–November 1991): 14–15.

# 12 The UN search for stolen and hidden Polish children (1944–47)

*Katherine Rossy*

Reporting from the Nuremberg trials in 1948, Polish Child Search Officer Roman Hrabar sat in disbelief. He was attending Case 8, also known as the infamous Race and Settlement Main Office, *Rasse und Siedlungshauptamt* (RuSHA) Trial, where he learned how various German organisations and ministries had kidnapped and Germanised children.[1] Reporting in the Polish Workers' Party newspaper *Zycie Warszawy*, Hrabar revealed the tremendous difficulties he faced in trying to locate stolen and hidden Polish children in Germany after the war.

> "Do the Germans report of their own free will the fact of possessing a child taken away from Poland?" "Do they report?" Dr. Hrabar smiled ironically. "In Hesse only 77 children were reported and later on 33.000 were found." [. . .] "Is it not certain then that our children will be recovered in Germany and returned to Poland and their families?" "No, it is not certain, the more so as the germanization process has unfortunately progressed very far. There were cases of complete germanization, as for instance the case of a 15-year old girl, taken to Germany 7 years ago, whose mother was in Poland. The girl did not want to return. The interview was very painful as the girl spoke German – she could not speak Polish any more. But they're cases that remind one of fairy tales and the stealing of children by witches."[2]

The girl in question was one of the estimated 50,000 children who were forcibly seized and uprooted from their homes in East-Central Europe by the Nazis during the Second World War, a number that German historian Isabel Heinemann has determined to be around 20,000 in the case of stolen Polish children.[3] Recent scholarship has revealed that Heinrich Himmler implemented a fanatical plan to kidnap and Germanise as many 'racially valuable' children from German-occupied and annexed territories as possible. Such work is instrumental to efforts to piece together otherwise marginalised accounts of children and childhood under the Nazis. Scholars like Nicholas Stargardt and Tara Zahra have blazed the trail for histories of children both during and in the immediate aftermath of the Second World War.[4] Others, like Georg Lilienthal and Dorothee Shmitz-Köster, have investigated the role of various Nazi organisations in perpetrating crimes against children and have greatly complicated scholarly understanding of Nazi racial attitudes toward children as a result.[5]

What the scholarship lacks, however, is sufficient consideration of the role that the United Nations played in uncovering Nazi kidnapping crimes toward the end of the war. As the extent of Nazi crimes and atrocities came to light during the mid-1940s, evidence emerged that the Germans had kidnapped and Germanised 'racially valuable' children from German-occupied territories during the war. These 'stolen' and 'hidden' children, as they came to be called during the post-military period, were hiding in plain sight. Some lived with Germans or in camps and institutions, oblivious of their origins, while others roamed the streets and sought refuge in bombed-out attics or dank cellars. Most children had no papers and could barely recall their parents or where they had come from. Others, moreover, could remember nothing at all. Uncovering such a crime was not a fortuitous discovery, however – it involved the painstaking detective work of dozens of United Nations (UN) child search officers and representatives of national governments, like Hrabar, who attempted to retrace the trajectories of children as they were forcibly seized and ripped away from families and loved ones. This chapter will shed light on this often-forgotten aspect of the Second World War. It will build on previous scholarship as well as new archival documents from the International Tracing Service to reveal how the United Nations came to discover and, ultimately, crack one of the greatest detective stories of our time.[6]

## Seizing children

In a decree of March 12, 1942, Adolf Hitler authorised Heinrich Himmler to assume total responsibility over all nationality matters, providing him with the powers necessary to plot the creation of "a numerous and healthy progeny of the SS."[7] By then, the kidnapping and Germanisation of children was already underway. Post-war investigations revealed that numerous Nazi agencies and ministries were implicated in the plot, from the KFDV [The Reich Commissioner for the Consolidation of German Nationhood, *Reichskommissar für die Festigung deutschen Volkstums*] Main Staff Office who on Himmler's instructions had ordered the registration and forced removal of the 'racially valuable' children to the "race experts from the RuSHA responsible for the selection of the children," and finally to the "staff of the Ethnic German Central Office (VoMi) who had brought the children into the camps and oversaw them there."[8] But most welfare reports, such as those written by Blackey as well as French International Refugee Organisation (IRO) worker Denise Grunewald, who conducted a major investigation into the Lebensborn in the French occupation zone, suggest that it was the Lebensborn that was implicated in the final placement of Germanised children. As one IRO report states, the organisation bore "sole responsibility for questions on the

Germanization of foreign orphans" through its "placing of kidnapped alien children into 'proper' German families."[9] While this is partly true, as the Lebensborn did decide where to place children, the Lebensborn by no means acted alone. It would not have been able to operate if the National Socialist People's Welfare, *Nationalsozialistische Volkswohlfahrt* (NSV), had not played a part in forcibly removing and temporarily caring for children, had RuSHA not authorised it to act as the legal guardian of kidnapped children, or had the Ministry of the Interior not given it the authority to change children's names and birth certificates.[10]

Founded in Berlin on December 12, 1935, and later transferred to Herzog-Max Strasse in Munich, the very location where a synagogue had been destroyed during *Kristallnacht*, the Lebensborn was initially used as a maternity ward for women and children, and its patients were the wives, fiancées, girlfriends, and relatives of SS men.[11] Most of the children who were born in Lebensborn homes were illegitimate, and "doctors were bound to secrecy" and were obligated to "stand up for the honour of expectant mothers" and to "protect [them] from social ostracism."[12] As then-United Nations Relief and Rehabilitation Administration (UNRRA) Child Search Officer Gitta Sereny later recalled in her memoirs, most Germans viewed the Lebensborn as "the most progressive of the Nazis' many social organizations," in that it provided "periods of respite for overburdened mothers, and care for pregnant single girls and illegitimate children."[13] Initially, only German women were admitted, but heavy casualties eventually led to the acceptance of foreign women of 'Germanic race' provided that they could prove that their children fulfilled Nazi racial criteria.[14] Much of the controversy surrounding the Lebensborn concerns claims that it may have served as a breeding ground for 'racially pure' babies. This belief is unfounded and has never been proven. Nevertheless, there is no scholarly consensus on what happened behind closed doors. Lilienthal insists that there is no proof that the Lebensborn acted as a 'human breeding ground' since couples were not matched together by Lebensborn officials.[15] Hillel and Henry flirt with the idea that these centres were either "maternity wards or human breeding grounds" but cannot provide a definitive answer, arguing that it depends on the perspectives of Lebensborn personnel, patients, and public opinion.[16] Shmitz-Köster's interviews with forty-seven Lebensborn children finds no conclusive evidence to suggest that Lebensborn homes were 'stud farms.'[17] That the Lebensborn was such a secretive organisation does not help matters, in that the public only really learned about the extent of its activities during the RuSHA Trial at Nuremberg from October 1947 to March 1948.[18] In fact, it was probably the organisation's 'sterling reputation' that kept the German public's suspicions at bay, Sereny suggests, especially when Himmler decided to make it the "executant of the Germanization project" during the winter of 1941.[19]

There were thirteen Lebensborn homes in existence by 1945, six to eight centres in the Wartheland in Nazi-occupied Poland, such as Puschkau and

Posen, and at least three outposts in Cracow, Norway, and Copenhagen. The clustering of homes around Warthegau is very telling, as these were the sites of the most ruthless kidnapping and Germanisation schemes in all of Nazi-occupied Europe. These kidnappings occurred simultaneous to the "violent large-scale population changes" carried out by the Nazis, Polish sociologist Kiryl Sosnowski argues, such as "deportation operations throughout the 'incorporated' and occupied territories: Alsace and Lorraine, Luxembourg, the Eupen and Malmedy district of Belgium, Slovenia and also Poland (Pomerania, Silesia, Poznan province and Zamosc region)."[20] Efforts to kidnap and Germanise 'racially valuable' children must therefore be understood as one part of the Nazi's broader population transfer and settlement policies that were designed to bring about "the biological-physical destruction of the peoples under German occupation."[21] This also explains why certain places that did not exist before the war, like Posen, Puschkau, and Litzmannstadt, which were Germanised from Poznań, Pastuchów, and Łódź, are often interchangeably cited in archival documents and search records.

Polish children were Himmler's favourite targets, as he considered many to be of 'ethnic German' origin who had "obviously descended from Nordic parents" and would "as bearers of valuable German blood and characteristics be returned to German nationality and Germanized."[22] In June 1941, he expressed his aspirations for Polish children: "I would consider it right if small children, of Polish families, who show especially good racial characteristics were apprehended and educated by us in special children's institutions and children's homes which must not be too large."[23] "After half a year," he continued, "the genealogical tree and documents of descent of those children who prove to be acceptable should be procured. After altogether one year it should be considered to give such children as foster children to childless families of good race." There was to be no "contact between the children and their relatives or old acquaintances" while they awaited transfer to Germany, and a special registry was established to make it difficult for frantic parents to trace their children.[24] After the war, UN search officers and even the governments themselves did not know how many children had been stolen and Germanised. It seemed, however, to depend on the territory from which they were seized.

"In the occupied city of Lodz," Zahra argues,

> practices of Germanization were more violent and in keeping with the harsher Nazi occupation regimes in Poland and the Soviet Union. Children were selected for Germanization by racial scientist Dr. Herbert Grohmann, who focused exclusively on the children's genealogy and physical appearance.[25]

Over the course of one week in January 1941, she continues, Grohmann "examined 448 Polish foster children and orphans for Germanization, and declared 32 to be 'racially valuable.' Another 54 were deemed 'racially useable' while the rest ruled unworthy of Germanization and returned to Polish foster parents or orphanages." Once in Germany, children's origins were hidden. "The expression 'Polish children suitable for Germanization' may not reach the public to the detriment of the children," as stolen children were "rather to be designated as German orphans from the regained Eastern Territories."[26] Six-year-old Anna Bagroszewska was one of the children who was kidnapped from a Polish home. She was "physically well developed" and showed "no signs of skin diseases or infectious diseases" and was "a case of mixed race with distinct east-Baltic characteristics, with whom the Nordic characteristics [were] predominant."[27] After being racially examined in a German institution, she was determined to be "a desirable increase of the population" and was approved for 're-germanization.'[28]

Children were kidnapped both individually and in groups and were brought to 'collection points' where their "physical and mental desirability" was assessed before they were either brought to Germany or deported to camps.[29] Children who were "pretty, healthy and well built, and had blonde or light-brown hair and blue eyes" were "abducted off streets, from playgrounds, schools and homes" by the SS and the Brown Sisters who, "in an odious attempt at reassurance, played the 'good' cops when they accompanied the SS men."[30] Together, they made the "first rough selection of children suitable for Germanization" and forced them to undergo a 'special examination' at the German Racial and Settlement Headquarters in Łódź, Poland.[31] After being subjected to extensive IQ and racial examinations, x-rays, delousing, and TB and syphilis testing, 'racially valuable' children were separated from 'racially inferior' children and were sent for additional x-rays before undergoing extensive physical and psychological assessment in "special institutions by top scientific professionals brought into the Germanization machinery by Nazis from many different Universities in the Reich and Austria." Once approved for re-Germanisation, a term used to "justify this scavenger hunt for German blood" in a "longstanding battle for the souls of children in multilingual regions of Eastern Europe," children between the ages of two and six were sent to Lebensborn homes where they underwent a further six weeks of testing before they were placed with German foster families.[32] Those old enough, primarily children who were between six and twelve years of age, were sent to *Heimschule* (boarding schools) to learn the German language and be indoctrinated with Nazi ideology before they were placed with families.[33] As Nicholas Stargardt points out, kidnapped and Germanised children had been "sent through the mill of German institutions, SS *Lebensborn* homes and camps until they came out the other end as 'Ethnic German orphans' from the Wartheland, ready for adoption."[34] Himmler instructed Max Sollmann, director of the Lebensborn, to give 'orphan foreign children' Christian German names as well as the surnames of their new adoptive parents.[35] Fake birth certificates with new birthdates were chosen by Gregor Ebner, the chief Lebensborn physician.

## The search begins

It was certainly no secret that children had been kidnapped en masse from territories that had fallen prey to Nazi atrocities. The problem, however, lay in the difficult task of locating these children. As the full extent of Nazi crimes and atrocities came to light, UN search officers and representatives of national governments, like Roman Hrabar, worked around the clock to retrace stolen children's trajectories in an effort to bring them home. The other problem was that nobody truly knew how many children were seized. During the war, governments sent their missing children estimates to British Red Cross headquarters in London even though "there was no possibility of determining who or how many were missing," UNRRA Child Search Officer Eileen Blackey noted in her June 1947 closure report, especially since "communications were destroyed" and "populations were milling back and forth across Europe" well after hostilities ended.[36] The Supreme Headquarters Allied Expeditionary Force (SHAEF) resumed tracing operations in February 1944 before transferring this responsibility to the military authorities in Germany in late 1945, who then delegated it to the UNRRA.[37] Starting in early 1946, UNRRA carried out child recovery processes under its Central Tracing Bureau (CTB) in Bad Arolsen, Germany, where it continues to operate today under the International Tracing Service (ITS).

The majority of missing children from the Netherlands, Belgium, and Denmark were recovered by the time UNRRA closed its doors in mid-1947; however, the French government claimed that France was missing anywhere between 4,000 and 300,000 children who had either been born in Germany to French civilian labourers or had been brought there through the SS-Lebensborn, one of the main Nazi organisations involved in the plot.[38] Norway had not sent any estimates of its missing children, nor had Yugoslavia or the Soviet Union, both harsh critics of the UN's legitimacy to mediate refugee and Displaced Persons (DP) affairs.[39] The Czechoslovakian government received 1,449 missing children's reports from anxious relatives, including 100 after the Lidice massacre. This figure was likely higher, Blackey assumed, since "there may be additional Czech children in Germany who have no one alive to ask for them." But the largest outcry came from Poland, whose repatriation officers claimed that 150,000 to 200,000 Polish children had been kidnapped.[40] While we now know that the number of Polish plot children hovered around 20,000 and that a total of 50,000 children were kidnapped across Europe, according to Isabel Heinemann's study of German records, UNRRA workers believed that the number of stolen Polish children was likely 'many times that number.'[41] Even though evidence suggested that hundreds, if not thousands, of children were abducted and brought to Germany, there was simply no way of accurately determining the extent of the problem:

The size of the problem and the actual number of children missing from each country is still an unknown quantity and makes future planning with regard to the problem extremely difficult. Nor do we have an estimate of the children born in Germany. We are convinced, however, that even with the limited forecasts available, we are by no means nearing the end of the problem.[42]

These 'stolen' and 'hidden' children, as they came to be called during the post-military period, were hiding in plain sight – some lived with Germans or in camps and institutions, oblivious of their origins, while others took to the streets in search of family, food, and shelter. Most had no papers and could barely recall their parents or where they had come from, while others could remember nothing at all. Hungry, barefoot, and disoriented, these young people were the unsuspecting targets of one of Heinrich Himmler's most fanatical schemes.

Unravelling the plot required serious detective work by the Allied military authorities and United Nations organisations that operated in former conflict zones after the war. Post-war Europe, and especially ex-enemy countries like Germany, Austria, and Italy, were now political and humanitarian problems; there was a desperate need to supply emergency assistance to the displaced and civilian populations who were affected by wartime atrocities. But the Allied authorities had limited powers. While they could deliver aid during Liberation, they were not equipped to provide long-term relief to the millions of refugees and DPs who fell under their control.[43] UNRRA emerged in the wake of this humanitarian crisis. Created by SHAEF in October 1944, it served as the principle humanitarian organisation of the post-military period by coordinating the health, welfare, registration, administration, and repatriation of all United Nations refugees and DPs found in enemy or ex-enemy territory.[44] A UN specialised agency, UNRRA was the world's first truly international effort to prevent famine, destitution, and disease after a major conflict. Between its creation in 1943 by forty-four UN member states and its closure in 1947, UNRRA provided emergency relief and long-term rehabilitation to millions of refugees and displaced persons (DPs).[45] By the end of its mandate, the agency had provided nearly 4.5 billion dollars in aid to war-torn Europe and Asia and had a staff of over 50,000 people.[46]

UNRRA's opening session was held in Atlantic City in November 1943 and predated the formal creation of the United Nations on October 24, 1945. In many ways, Jessica Reinisch argues, UNRRA was an 'agent of internationalism,' which she defines as a "broad umbrella term for the complex social, cultural, political and economic connections between individuals from different states, regions and locales" that can be applied to "the domain of international relations, as formal diplomatic contacts between nations, as much as the movement (both linear and circular) of people and their ideas, networks and imaginations across borders."[47] As a specialised United Nations agency, UNRRA's work on the international stage radically altered the humanitarian blueprint for decades to come. But the agency faced a colossal task. As UNRRA's first Director General Herbert H. Lehman pointed out in 1944,

One of the most serious and difficult problems developing out of the war is the problem of displaced persons . . . Germany, in the pursuit of her military, political, economic and racial objectives, has shifted the populations of Europe at will.[48]

In light of such unprecedented displacement, it was clear that a new kind of professionalised humanitarianism was needed. UNRRA's mission was debated during its second meeting in Montreal in September 1944, where it was decided "to avoid the now acknowledged errors committed in 1919":

Then, assistance was confined to relief; now relief is to be extended to include rehabilitation. Then, relief consisted in the main of foodstuffs drawn from the United States and distributed chiefly in France and Belgium, which were more accessible than Eastern Europe, whose distress was in fact greater; now the range of relief is to be wider, clothing in particular being included.[49]

This shift from 'relief' to 'relief and rehabilitation' had a profound impact on millions of displaced men, women, and children. It was, as Ira Hirschmann wrote in his memoirs, "the greatest relief operation in history."[50]

International protection was not a luxury afforded to all who fell under UNRRA's sphere in Germany, however. UNRRA was mandated to help 'United Nations Nationals' who had been internally or externally displaced by war from September 1, 1939, onward, including stateless persons and displaced Italian nationals.[51] Excluded from assistance were those who did not belong to a United Nations member state, including 'enemy or ex-enemy nationals' from Austria, Bulgaria, Germany, Hungary, Japan, Romania, and Siam; nationals of neutral countries; ex-Wehrmacht personnel; "war criminals, collaborators, quislings or traitors of whatever race, nationality or religion"; and, finally, 'Volksdeutsche' (ethnic Germans) and 'German Balts' from Latvia, Estonia, and Lithuania.[52] SHAEF authorised UNRRA to create and run 450 assembly centres in Germany that would be controlled by the military authorities, and personnel was recruited from UN member states who trained in Granville, France, before transferring to Germany.[53]

Such strict eligibility criteria determined who was eligible for aid and who was not. This would have particular consequences on displaced children. By February 1947, there were 1,352 unaccompanied children receiving UNRRA care and maintenance in the British zone, 4,917 in the U.S. zone, and 123 in the French zone.[54] IRO, UNRRA's successor agency, took 4,090 unaccompanied children under its wing in July 1947, including 1,417 Polish children, 400 stateless children, 123 children of undetermined nationality, and 2,550 children from over thirty nationalities.[55] This included 728 children in the U.S. zone, 633 in the British zone, and 82 in the French zone.[56] These children were determined to belong to a UN member state, and any child who belonged to an 'enemy' or 'ex-enemy' country like Austria or Germany was excluded from aid. Curiously enough, this meant that German Jews were also ineligible for aid. As Israeli politician and later Minister of Religions Rabbi Zerach Warhaftig notes in his 1944 study on UNRRA and Jews, the specific needs of Jews are "not specifically mentioned in the official documents," but "their existence is implied."[57] Another category of children who were excluded from UN care was *Volksdeutsche* (ethnically German) children. This included at least 3.5 million expellee children who were forcibly transferred from Poland, Czechoslovakia, and Hungary under the Potsdam Agreement and were ineligible for international protection.[58] As R.M. Douglas points out, ethnic German children were excluded from international protection even though the Allies were technically signatories of the League of Nations' 1924 Declaration of the Rights of the Child, which promised that children in war would "be the first to receive relief in times of distress" regardless of "race, nationality or creed."[59] Child 'infiltrees' and 'neo-refugees' who fled East-Central Europe for the western zones were also excluded from international assistance. The exclusion of 'ethnic German' and Jewish German children from UN care and maintenance reveals much about the nature of international humanitarian practice during the immediate post-war situation. It was precisely this lack of total inclusion in relief practices that made stolen and hidden children difficult to spot and caused them to remain undetected for much of the post-war period.

## Concluding thoughts

The exclusion of 'ethnic German' children from UN aid reveals much about post-World War II humanitarian practice and culture. It complicated many aspects of UN recovery operations since UNRRA search officers were trying to locate Germanised Polish children who could have also passed for ethnically German children. This meant that the UNRRA was searching for children that it had technically excluded from its humanitarian mandate, children who were cast aside from international protection. That stolen children were often hiding in plain sight added dimension to the confusion. Kidnapped and Germanised children blended in with the 'racially pure' German population and were therefore not always located in refugee camps. In many instances, they were scattered throughout the civilian population and could be found living with German foster families and in institutions. From a humanitarian perspective, this meant that stolen Allied children could have easily been mistaken for ex-enemy and non-United Nations children, like German or Austrian children, and that they would have fallen through the cracks and remained undetected. Stolen children could have also been caught up in the chaos of the twelve to fourteen million German expellees who were forcibly transferred from Poland, Hungary, and Czechoslovakia under Article 13 of the Potsdam Agreement (August 1945), a number that included 3.5 million children under the age of seventeen.[60] Or perhaps they were camouflaged amongst the thousands of neo-refugees who fled the new communist regimes of Central and Eastern Europe and could be found begging or bartering for food and warm clothing alongside the rest of the benighted civilian and DP population. Whatever the case, nobody knew for certain how many stolen children were wandering around post-war Europe. That they were hiding in plain sight and out of the public eye made them forgotten targets on a forgotten front, with no guarantee that they would ever find their way home.

## Notes

1 "Polish Children Astray among Germans," *Zycie Warszawy*, February 27, 1948, Archives nationales, Pierrefitte-sur-Seine, AJ/598–599.
2 Ibid.
3 Isabel Heinemann, *"Rasse, Siedlung, deutsches Blut": Die Rasse und Siedlungshauptamt der SS und die rassenpolitische Neuordnung Europas* (Göttingen: Wallstein, 2003), 508–9. See also Heineman, "'Until the Last Drop of Good Blood': The Kidnapping of 'Racially Valuable' Children and Nazi Racial Policy in Occupied Eastern Europe," in *Genocide and Settler Society: Frontier Violence and Stolen Indigenous Children in Australian History*, ed. A. Dirk Moses (Oxford: Berghahn Books, 2012), 260.
4 Nicholas Stargardt, *Witnesses of War: Children's Lives Under the Nazis* (New York: Alfred A. Knopf, 2006); Tara Zahra, *The Lost Children: Reconstructing Europe's Families after World War II* (Cambridge: Harvard University Press, 2011).
5 Georg Lilienthal, *Der "Lebensborn e. V." Ein Instrument nationalsozialistischer Rassenpolitik* (Frankfurt: Fischer Taschenbuch Verlag, 2003); Dorothee Shmitz-Köster, *"Deutsche Mutter, bist du bereit . . ." der Lebensborn und seine Kinder* (Berlin: Aufbau Taschenbuch, 2010).
6 "Statement for BBC," undated, Archives nationales, Pierrefitte-sur-Seine, AJ/43/302.
7 Adolf Hitler, "Verfügung des Führers," March 12, 1942, Archives nationales, Pierrefitte-sur-Seine, AJ/43/596–597; War Crimes report on 'Lebensborn', October 24, 1947, Archives nationales, Pierrefitte-sur-Seine, AJ/43/596–597.
8 Heinemann, "Until the Last Drop of Good Blood," 247.
9 Basic Information Regarding Heimschule Participation in the Germanization of Allied Children, August 13, 1947, The International Tracing Service, Bad Arolsen, 6.1.2 / 82486370.
10 Gitta Sereny, *The German Trauma: Experiences and Reflections, 1938–2001* (London: Penguin Books, 2001), 44–5.
11 Boris Thiolay, *Lebensborn – la fabrique des enfants parfaits: Enquête sur ces Français nés dans des maternités SS* (Paris: Flammarion, 2012), 17–18.
12 War Crimes report on 'Lebensborn'.
13 Sereny, *The German Trauma*, 40.
14 Note de Renseignements les enfants français en Allemagne, January 3, 1948, Centre des Archives Diplomatiques du ministère des Affaires étrangères, La Courneuve, PDR 5/213.
15 Lilienthal, *Der "Lebensborn e. V."*, 151.
16 Marc Hillel and Clarissa Henry, *Au nom de la race* (Paris: Fayard, 1975), 85–6.
17 Dorothee Shmitz-Köster, "A Topic for Life: Children of German Lebensborn Homes," in *Children of World War II: The Hidden Enemy Legacy*, ed. Kjersti Ericsson and Eva Simonsen (Oxford: Berg, 2005), 213, 215.
18 Lilienthal, *Der "Lebensborn e. V."*, 1.
19 Sereny, *The German Trauma*, 40–1.
20 Kiryl Sosnowski, *The Tragedy of Children Under Nazi Rule* (New York: Howard Fertig, 1983), 46–7.
21 Heinemann, "Until the Last Drop of Good Blood," 247.
22 Germanization of Children from former Polish Orphanages and Polish Foster Families, February 19, 1942, AJ/43/596–597.

23  Official Transcript of American Military Tribunal I in the matter of the United States of America against Ulrich Greifelt, et al, defendants, March 10, 1948, AJ/43/604.

24  Establishment of Special Registration Office in the Children's Home Kalisch/Warthegau, December 10, 1942, Archives nationales, Pierrefitte-sur-Seine, AJ/43/596–597.

25  Tara Zahra, *Kidnapped Souls: National Indifference and the Battle for Children in the Bohemian Lands, 1900–1948* (Ithaca: Cornell University Press, 2008), 199.

26  Official Transcript of American Military Tribunal I in the matter of the United States of America against Ulrich Greifelt, et al, defendants, March 10, 1948, AJ/43/604.

27  Municipal Health Office (Litzmannstadt) to RuSHA, November 27, 1941, ITS, 4.1.0 / 82476379.

28  RuSHA to Youth Office (Litzmannstadt), April 7, 1943, ITS, 4.1.0 / 82476380.

29  Closure Report of United Nations' Unaccompanied Children in Germany, June 1947, AJ/43/596–597.

30  Sereny, *The German Trauma*, 41.

31  Basic Information Regarding Heimschule Participation in the Germanization of Allied Children, August 13, 1947, ITS, 6.1.2 / 82486370.

32  Zahra, *The Lost Children*, 126.

33  Germanization of Children from former Polish Orphanages and Polish Foster Families, February 19, 1942, Archives nationales, Pierrefitte-sur-Seine, AJ/43/596–597.

34  Stargardt, *Witnesses of War*, 358.

35  Orphan Foreign Children: Subsequent Authentication of Birth and Change of Christian Names and Surnames, June 4, 1943, Archives nationales, Pierrefitte-sur-Seine, AJ/43/596–597.

36  Suzanne Brown-Fleming, *Nazi Persecution and Postwar Repercussions: The International Tracing Service Archive and Holocaust Research* (Lanham: Rowman & Littlefield, 2016), 3; Closure Report of United Nations' Unaccompanied Children in Germany.

37  Brown-Fleming, *Nazi Persecution and Postwar Repercussions*, 3.

38  Henri Fesquet, "Les Enfants Nés en Allemagne Pendant la Guerre," *Le Monde*, August 6, 1946, Centre des Archives Diplomatiques du ministère des Affaires étrangères, PDR 5/238.

39  Closure Report of United Nations' Unaccompanied Children in Germany.

40  There is no consensus on the number of stolen Polish children. IRO historian Louise Holborn writes that Minister Wladyslaw Wolski of the Polish government's newly created Ministry of Public Affairs believed that the number of stolen Polish children hovered around 150,000 (Louise Holborn, *L'Organisation international pour les refugiés: agent specialisée des Nations Unies (1946–1952)* (Paris: Presses Universitaires de France, 1955), 314–15). The Polish government's Operation for the Revindication of Children, created in 1947 and run by Dr Roman Hrabar to recover and repatriate missing Polish children, claimed that 200,000 Polish children had been stolen. On Hrabar's search efforts and findings in Germany, see Roman Hrabar, Zofia Tokarz, and Jacek Wilczur, *The Fate of Polish Children during the Last War* (Hamburg: Verlag Interpress, 1981).

41  Isabel Heinemann, *"Rasse, Siedlung, deutsches Blut": Die Rasse und Siedlungshauptamt der SS und die rassenpolitische Neuordnung Europas* (Göttingen: Wallstein, 2003), 508–9.

42  Summary Statement on Unaccompanied Children in Germany, March 24, 1947, AJ/43/596–597.

43  UNRRA Welfare Guide, February 15, 1945, Archives nationales, Pierrefitte-sur-Seine, AJ/43/16.

44  Agreement between UNRRA and SHAEF, October 14, 1944, Archives nationales, Pierrefitte-sur-Seine, AJ/43/14.

45  Corinne Lewis, *UNHCR and International Refugee Law: From Treaties to Innovation* (London: Routledge, 2012), 8.

46  Richard Jolly, *UNICEF: Global Governance That Works* (London: Routledge, 2014), 10.

47  Jessica Reinisch, "Introduction: Agents of Internationalism," *Contemporary European History* 25, no. 2 (May 2016): 200.

48 Herbert H. Lehman, "Half a Billion Hungry People," *New York Times Magazine*, 30 January 1944.

49 "UNRRA and its Tasks," *The Times*, 9 September 1944.

50 Ira A. Hirschmann, *The Embers Still Burn: An Eye-Witness View of the Postwar Ferment in Europe and the Middle East and Our Disastrous Get-Soft-with-Germany Policy* (New York: Simon and Schuster, 1949), 6.

51 Statement on Displaced Persons, January 24, 1946, Archives nationales, Pierrefitte-sur-Seine, AJ/43/16.

52 Order No. 52: Eligibility for UNRRA Assistance, June 24, 1946, Archives nationales, Pierrefitte-sur-Seine, AJ/43/18;

53 Statement on Displaced Persons, April 6, 1945, Archives nationales, Pierrefitte-sur-Seine, AJ/43/16.

54 Table VIII, UNRRA Statistics, February 28, 1947, Archives nationales, Pierrefitte-sur-Seine, AJ/43/169.

55 Holborn, *L'Organisation international pour les refugiés*, 316.

56 Ibid.

57 Zorach Warhaftig, *Relief and Rehabilitation: Implications of the UNRRA Program for Jewish Needs* (New York: Institute of Jewish Affairs of the American Jewish Congress and World Jewish Congress, 1944), 3.

58 Refugee Children, Summary Report; Report of the Executive Secretary on the Question of the Volksdeutsche in Austria, January 27, 1948, Archives nationales, Pierrefitte-sur-Seine, AJ/43/169.

59 Raymond M. Douglas, *Orderly and Humane: The Expulsion of the Germans after the Second World War* (New Haven: Yale University Press, 2012), 240.

60 Refugee Children, Summary Report, August 10–16, 1948, AJ/43/598–599.

# Glossary

| | |
|---|---|
| **ACF** | African Colonial Forces, Britain |
| **AMG** | Allied Military Government |
| **AOI** | Italian East Africa (*Africa Orientale Italiana*) |
| **AVNOJ** | Anti-Fascist Council for the National Liberation of Yugoslavia |
| **BCS** | Burma Country Section (SOE – British) |
| **BLO** | British Liaison Officer |
| **BUF** | British Union of Fascists |
| **CBI** | China-Burma-India Theatre |
| **CCNN** | *Camicie Nere*, Italy |
| **CFS** | French Somaliland (*Côte Française de Somalis*) |
| **CIGS** | Chief of the Imperial General Staff, Britain |
| **CPMH** | The Central Partisan Movement Headquarters, Soviet Union |
| **CTB** | Central Tracing Bureau (of the UNRRA) |
| **DP** | Displaced Persons |
| **GRU** | Main Intelligence Directorate (*Glavnoye razvedyvatel'noye upravleniye*), Soviet Union |
| **HMS** | His/Her Majesty's Ship, Britain |
| **HQ** | Headquarters |
| **IJN** | The Imperial Japanese Navy |
| **IRA** | Irish Republican Army |
| **IRO** | The International Refugee Organisation (IRO) |
| **MI5** | The Security Service (United Kingdom's domestic security agency) |
| **MP** | Member of Parliament |
| **NDH** | Independent State of Croatia (*Ustaša – Hrvatski revolucionarni pokret*) |
| **NKGB** | People's Commissariat for State Security (*Narodny komissariat gosudarstvennoi bezopasnosti*), Soviet Union |
| **NKL** | Northern Kachin Levies, Allied Burma |
| **NKVD** | People's Commissariat for Internal Affairs (*Narodnyy Komissariat Vnutrennikh Del*), Soviet Union |
| **NSV** | National Socialist People's Welfare (*Nationalsozialistische Volkswohlfahrt*), Nazi Germany |

| | |
|---|---|
| **OSS** | Office of Strategic Services, United States |
| **PMH** | Partisan Movement Headquarters, Lithuania and Estonia |
| **RAF** | Royal Air Force, Britain |
| **RKFDV** | The Reich Commissioner for the Consolidation of German Nationhood (*Reichskommissar für die Festigung deutschen Volkstums*), Nazi Germany |
| **RSI** | Italian Social Republic (*Repubblica Sociale Italiana*) |
| **RuSHA** | Race and Settlement Main Office (*Rasse und Siedlungshauptamt*), Nazi Germany |
| **SCH** | Communist Shanxi-Chahar-Hebei, China |
| **SD** | German Security Service |
| **SEAC** | South East Asia Command, Allied |
| **SHAEF** | The Supreme Headquarters Allied Expeditionary Force |
| **SMERSh** | Main Directorate of Counter-Intelligence, Soviet Union |
| **SOE** | Special Operations Executive, Britain |
| **UK** | United Kingdom |
| **UNRRA** | United Nations Relief and Rehabilitation Administration |
| **US** | United States |
| **USAAF** | United States Army Air Forces |
| **USSR** | Union of Soviet Socialist Republics |
| **VoMi** | Ethnic German Central Office |
| **WVS** | Women's Volunteer Service, Britain |

# Index